The Evolution of EC Consumer Protection in the Field of Consumer Credit

European University Studies
Europäische Hochschulschriften
Publications Universitaires Européennes

Series II
Law

Reihe II Série II
Rechtswissenschaft
Law

Vol./Bd. 5339

PETER LANG
Frankfurt am Main · Berlin · Bern · Bruxelles · New York · Oxford · Wien

Inga Łobocka-Poguntke

The Evolution of EC Consumer Protection in the Field of Consumer Credit

PETER LANG
Internationaler Verlag der Wissenschaften

Bibliographic Information published by the Deutsche Nationalbibliothek
The Deutsche Nationalbibliothek lists this publication in the Deutsche Nationalbibliografie; detailed bibliographic data is available in the internet at http://dnb.d-nb.de.

ISSN 0531-7312
ISBN 978-3-631-62348-0

www.peterlang.de

To my parents for their abundant love and support during the long-lasting writing process and to my husband Thomas without whom the book would have never been finished

Preface

Consumer protection is a contested battle ground within the EU. This is where competing, and at times conflicting visions clash and sometimes lead to incoherent or even contradictory legislation. By focusing on the example of consumer credit legislation this book analyses how such underlying concepts related to the major streams of economic philosophy can explain the specific nature of legislation in this field. More precisely, I use the analysis of the evolution of European consumer credit legislation in order to demonstrate, first, how the EU consumer protection legislation has evolved in general; and second, how the EU legislator's approach towards consumer protection has changed; and finally, who are the addressees of the recent EU consumer legislation, and by the same token, what consumers nowadays are needed for. The EU consumer credit regulations seem to be a perfect example of illustrating the changes which take place on the European level as far as consumer law is concerned. The undisputedly ambiguous character of consumer credit regulations as such (disregarding temporarily the EU level) - since they belong to many categories and as a whole cannot be pigeonholed entirely into anyone specific category – provokes a debate about a kaleidoscope of issues which alternate with each other in the field of consumer credit and which I shall address in my work. First and foremost, the general problem of consumer protection in the field of consumer credit is characterized by the fact that on the one hand, consumer credit is an important economic activity and as such could be assigned exclusively to the sphere of economic law. Nevertheless, on the other hand, consumer credit entails a significant number of social problems, which implies that consumer credit legislation belongs also to the area of social private law. Thus, the question arises as to whether one can consider merely an economic dimension of such legislation or in addition to this, a social dimension as well. This entails certain considerations concerning the remedies to the problems caused by consumer credit, namely whether the economy itself should/is capable of solving these problems or whether certain doses of public intervention are advisable or even necessary (and if so, how big). At the same time, one must also consider the potential side effects of such interference in the market, and also the likely consequences of a lack of such an intervention. On the European level, the issue of the character of law which regulates consumer credit translates into the question of the legislative competences shared by the EU and member states legislators in this respect, thus whether the whole consumer protection legislation should stem from the EU legislative institutions or whether it should be left entirely, or at least in part to the national ones. This, in turn, is inseparable from the choice between the minimum or maximum harmonisation approaches. Furthermore, any solution eventually considered must also take into account the level of homogeneity of the societies of the respective member states. This issue is tightly linked to the problem of the premises of and the reasons for the recent shift from the minimum to maximum harmonisation.

My core argument shall be that all above-mentioned issues converge into a common focal point. Therefore, first and foremost, I would like to demonstrate the tension between two fundamental goals of the European Community, namely, on the one hand economic efficiency (understood as a competitive market society) i.e. the realization of the idea of the internal market, and on the other hand, consumer protection (and broadly speaking a social justice society with its distributive role).

Thus, it follows, and this will be shown by this study, that much of the apparent indecisiveness or even incoherence that we often find in EU law-making is not primarily the result of poor policy-making, but flows from exactly these inherent contradictions. This tension cannot easily be reconciled (if at all), and this work aims at reconstructing this tension as it is reflected within scholarly debate using the example of consumer credit. Arguably, this is an almost ideal case study to exemplify these inherent contradictions as it is an ideal representation of where both principles collide, that is, the idea that actors should be allowed to act freely in the market place, and the idea that consumers need protection, as they would otherwise fall victim to the actions of unconstrained market actors. In the field of consumer law, this tension translates into two opposing concepts: the neoliberal and the social market approach. Adopting one of the above-mentioned approaches determines the way in which one defines the meaning of the notion 'consumer' and consequently, the way one perceives the consumer-oriented intervention in the market coming from public authorities with regard to its scope as well as its intensity. These aspects are discussed in Chapter 4 which is preceded by a discussion on the concept of the internal market (Chapter 2) and an analysis of the evolution of the EU consumer credit legislation in Chapter 3.

I believe that in the field of consumer credit regulation, this tension is identifiable in almost all crucial facets of such issue, thus the general question of my work is at the end of the day which of these two goals of the European Union prevails? In order to conduct this analysis, I take into consideration four aspects of consumer credit law which represent a suitable case study to illustrate my main argument. These aspects are the following: 1) the choice between the minimum and maximum harmonisation approach (Chapter 5); 2) the issue of information duties and the right to withdrawal (Chapter 6); 3) the principles of responsible lending (Chapter 7) and finally, 4) the problem of consumer bankruptcy and financial exclusion (Chapter 8).

My thesis is that the EU legislator adopted the neoliberal approach in the 2008 Directive on credit agreements[1] and consistently subordinated these four aspects, in an instrumental way, to the execution of the overriding goal of the EU, that is, the realization of the idea of the European internal market. Thus consumer protection not only lost in the competition with the market efficiency idea, it actually became a tool in the realization of the prevailing goal. The EU legislator – by downplaying national diversities, and passing over the crucial

1 Directive 2008/48/EC of the European Parliament and of the Council of 23 April 2008 on credit agreements for consumers and repealing Council Directive 87/102/EEC.

problems like consumer insolvency, financial exclusion, responsible lending - only took into account the economic dimension of the consumer credit issue. Arguably, economic efficiency cannot be accomplished under conditions ignoring the well-being of the majority of consumers. In other words, considering the entire issue from a purely economic, pragmatic perspective, ignoring the well-being of the majority of consumers may undermine the viability of the neoliberal approach in the long run.

The language correction of the manuscript was financially supported by the Law Department of the European University Institute.

Table of Contents

Introduction

As we have already learned and in principle accepted, one cannot hold back the process of globalisation or successfully oppose the fundamental mechanics of capitalism. This neoliberal approach assumes that the poor, as weaker members of a society, should find a solution to defeat financial hardships by themselves, but at the same time the poor are deprived of the means for this self-help in the name of market efficiency. If one assumes that 'market' means a rivalry, in the sense of a pretty ruthless economic competition, and that the 'market' creates a perfect environment where players merely seek to maximise their profits or to minimise their costs, then it has to be kept in mind that the EU internal market is still a 'market' in this economic sense. Nevertheless, the neoliberal approach tends to disregard the existence of actors who do not necessarily strive for maximizing their profits. Consumers also act on this market, however their principal aim is to satisfy their needs. These non-commercial market players in their market decisions assume quite different rationales than the commercial entities.

In the European Union most of the credit providers belong to private sector enterprises. Hence, it is totally understandable and natural that they act like every ordinary market player, thus they focus mainly on making profits, maximising gains and minimising the losses, thus in their credit decisions they favour the rich, and discriminate against the poor, and do not take into consideration any other values. And if one assumes that the major driving force in the society, or at least in its economic activity, is the urge to, or as some prefer, the greed for maximizing profits (at all costs), then the society/state/Community should find some remedy to oppose and counterweight this driving force, because the market itself i.e. the "invisible hand", will never provide any limits to it.

That is why in organised societies there is necessarily a place for morality, social considerations and, above all, effective law. Certainly, it does not mean that legal provisions should or can replace consumer responsibility or consumer awareness of obligation. Nevertheless, it implies that such protective provisions should act as a lifebelt providing social solutions in the situations in which a consumer is at a disadvantage on the marketplace.[2] One of the manifestations of the Community/state's activity interfering in the mechanics of the market is consumer protection legislation, which is not a neutral tool; on the contrary, its role is to restore equilibrium between powerful businesses and vulnerable consumers.[3] The public authorities are a factor which can mitigate market forces and at the same time restore equi-

---

2 From 'Round Table on Credit Directives an EU Action Plan', Responsible Credit, Brussels 2006, 6th International Conference on Financial Service, conference materials.

3 Bourgoignie, 'Elements pour une theorie du droit de la consommation (Universite Catholique de Louvain, E. Story-Scientia, Centre de droit de la Consommation, No. 16, 1988) after J. Stuyck, 'European Consumer Law after the Treaty of Amsterdam : Consumer Policy in or beyond the Internal Market ?', CMLR 37 : 367-400, 2000.

librium between the market players, the equilibrium which is upset by the contrast between powers of the opposing sides. The dual task of the public intervention is to improve market transparency and to regulate market behaviour.

In their preface to 'EC Consumer Law', Howells and Wilhelmsson determine that the development of consumer protection law is (besides the general growth of EC law) the most important legal development in Western Europe in the second half of the twentieth century.[4] The comprehensive scrutiny of these legal regulations allowed the authors to build the notion of a 'consumer protection ideology', which contains two basic features. First, it is a recognition of the importance of the role that a consumer has in the market and, generally, the role of private consumption, and as a result the assumption that a consumer deserves additional protective provisions in addition to those offered by the legal system to a professional. The second feature refers to the issue of consumer protection, which is seen to arise out of the consumer relationship with the professional.[5]

For centuries now, consumers have experienced protection and have been treated in a special way, long before the "Molony Report" was published[6] or President Kennedy made his famous Message to the Congress of 15 March 1962, spelling out fundamental consumer rights. When looking into historical studies on legal regulations, one can easily find some mention of protection measures as early as in the Roman law,[7] however, the concept of contemporary consumer law (in the form that it is used nowadays) poses a rather new issue. Only in modern times has the protection of employees, tenants, patients and, finally consumers changed the paradigm of civil law: before this, the freedom of contract was perceived as the only prevailing value of contract law. Today the same importance has been attributed to the protection of the weaker party.[8] Within the framework of the European Community, the history of modern consumer protection law starts in an official way with the first[9] and the second consumer programme,[10] both adopted by the Council of Ministers in 1975 and in 1981, thereby following the line of the Kennedy Declaration and still posing the starting point of the European Consumer Policy.

At present, in the modern reality, it is rather commonly accepted that one of the major roles which legal order plays in the society is to protect the weaker party in the contractual relationship. At the same time, whereas the freedom of contract, as the basic principle of

---

4 G. Howells, T. Wilhelmsson, 'EC Consumer Law', Ashgate Dartmouth, 1997, preface.

5 Ibid., p. 1.

6 Final Report of the Committee on Consumer Protection, 1962.

7 See G. Hadfield, R. Howee, M. Trebilcock, 'Information-Based Principles for Rethinking Consumer Protection Policy', 1998, 22 JCP 131.

8 E. Hondius, 'Consumer Law and Private Law: the Case for Integration' in 'Neues Europäisches Vertragsrecht und Verbraucherschutz: Regelungskonzepte der Europaeichen Union und ihre Auswirkungen auf die nationalen Zivilrechtsordnungen', edited by W. Heusel, 1999 Bundesanzeiger Verlagsges., Köln.

9 OJ C 92, 25.4.1975.

10 OJ C 133, 3.06.1981.

legal order, cannot be challenged, and the protective provisions by their very nature violate the broadly understood economic freedoms, as well as the principle of the binding force of contractual obligation, such an intervention by states requires legitimisation. One of the justifications of these protective regulations is market failure as interventionist provisions step in the market in order to improve a consumer's position in contractual relationship. However, there is always a vivid debate as to just how much intervention is really required and what is the extent to which a legislator is entitled to intervene in the free market, and in private law relationships. In other words, the question arises as to how to strike a balance between providing effective consumer protection and maintaining the principles of contract law, and also a balance between an effective consumer protection and the costs that society must pay as a result. Obviously, overregulation is one of these costs.

Consumer credit legislation is a perfect field for analysing all the aspects of consumer protection. It is indisputably a very complex issue and there are several reasons for that. First, consumer protection regulations - as such (i.e. as a separate quasi-branch of law in general) - pose a very fragile, particularly sore area. This statement results from a certain paradox: on the one hand consumer protection law refers to economic relationships which are initially based on the market exchange of goods and services, and which are regulated by pure civil law provisions where the bargaining position of the parties is originally (assumed to be) equal and where freedom of contract plays a protagonist role and as such consumer protection law is classified as a quasi-branch within the private law sector. On the other hand, at the same time, these inner original civil law rules have been violated by introducing a vulnerable actor who has a much weaker bargaining power, and whose market decisions are not necessarily always rational. Most importantly, however, it is maintained that economic profits and economic considerations play only a marginal role in the universe of consumer interests (if they are taken into consideration at all). After all, most economic activities of consumers are not commercial but simply seek to satisfy personal needs. This brings us directly to the question of whether consumer law, and here particularly consumer credit law, belongs to the category of economic or social law, as on the one hand it relates to the typical economic aspects and on the other hand, at this point, a whole range of social aspects cannot be ignored.

Second, the 'paradox' of consumer credit itself is sketched by its very ambivalent facets. Consumer credit is a tool adapting the form of monthly income to the investment needs of modern private households, and banking institutions play the role of social intermediaries able to lend consumers their future income.[11] The main purpose of credit is – from the borrowers' perspective – to enable them to participate in economic life and in the development and progress thereof, as credit provides them with the opportunities to use all the achievements of present times, with opportunities unknown to people existing in the cash society.

11 U. Reifner, 'Credit in Europe. Responsible Lending?', Responsible Credit, Brussels 2006, 6th International Conference on Financial Service, conference materials.

There is a great number of advantages provided by access to credit, both for consumers-borrowers, as well as for the whole society. What cannot be downplayed is that credit also makes an undeniably relevant contribution to the well-being of the overall economy, as it propels demand and thus stimulates supply, and indirectly also technological development and innovations. Nevertheless, on the other hand, credit represents a risk for money-lenders and, for a growing number of consumers also a threat of overindebtedness, insolvency and even social exclusion. In the discussion on consumer credit, one should necessarily also take into account the problems that are inseparable from such phenomenon: that is, the general issue of consumer protection, the issues of interest charges (especially usurious interest), the activity of predatory lenders; the problems of exploitation of the consumers' vulnerable position, consumers' naivety; and the threat of insolvency etc., as all this can contribute in the long-run to such socially undesirable side effects as permanent impoverishment, and finally social exclusion of bankrupt borrowers and of whole families. Thus, consumer credit being on the one hand a condition for the well-being of consumers and for the development of the overall economy, at the same time poses a huge risk to consumers and entails serious negative consequences. In other words, on the one hand, credit is an essential element of an economic activity, and on the other hand it entails a range of social problems.

The other factor which adds additional complications to the picture is that the discussed topic *nomen omen* refers to credit which is a crucial economic instrument in present society. One can risk a statement that credit as such is one of the very few services which - although not being (as yet) legally recognized as the services of general economic interest *per se* - in practice actually already belong to that category, since it is in fact inconceivable to fully participate in contemporary society and at the same time be deprived of the possibility of borrowing money.

The peculiarity of the consumer credit contract refers also to the temporal length of its binding legal force. When it comes to credit contracts, contrary to the majority of the other consumer contracts, one deals with the problem of long-lasting obligations, which burden (mainly) borrowers often for many years. The long-lasting character of this obligation involves also uncertainty, and the risk of insecurity, since borrowers enter the credit contract in certain financial circumstances in which they find themselves on the day of the conclusion of agreement, and in addition their creditworthiness is being checked to that date, whereas the predictability of various life circumstances especially in the case of borrowers-individuals, is very limited. Hence the characteristic feature of the credit contract is the permanent risk it entails.

The last feature which demonstrates the peculiarity of the credit agreement is its technical complexity. On the one hand, the credit contract – as was stated above – could be rated among the services of general economic interest, being a tool commonly used in a modern society, nevertheless, on the other hand, this contract belongs unquestionably to the most technically complex category of consumer contracts which - in order to be properly comprehended - require not only a meticulous scrutiny, but also an extensive background knowledge of the legal and economic aspects of banking. Therefore, the information asymmetry between a professional creditor and a consumer-borrower is particularly serious in the case of the credit contract. Hence, due to all these reasons consumer credit legislation poses a special case where the necessity for protection of consumers-borrowers is particularly clear.

The Idea of a European Integrated Market

T. Bourgoignie and D. Trubek state that in order to understand the most central issue of European market integration, in the first place one needs to understand the problematic of consumer protection in the common market context. The reason for such thinking is the fact that consumer protection is connected to the core issue of European economic integration, 'for it brings into very sharp relief the dialectics of open borders, protectionism, and bona fide intervention of the member state to protect legitimate societal values and goals even if at the expense of interrupting the free flow of goods on which the idea of a common marketplace is postulated'.[12]

Historical Review

The idea of the single market became the core objective and, finally, the main achievement of the European Community, as well as the binding joint of the whole European Union. It is considered to be the key factor in Europe's economic prosperity and its ability to compete in the global economy.[13] Moreover, until now, economic integration has been considered as the tool serving the improvement of the position of consumers via the stimulation of a more competitive market.[14]

The legal bases for the harmonisation of laws which lead to EC market integration are placed in two EEC Articles – in Article 100 (Article 94 after the Amsterdam Treaty entered into force in 1999 and Article 115 after the Treaty of Lisbon) which speaks about the creation of a 'common' market and after the entry into force of the Single Market Act in Article 100a (Article 95 TEC and today - Article 114) referring to the creation of an 'internal' market. The distinction between these two notions - 'common' and 'internal' market - are being belittled by some authors[15] or, on the contrary, emphasised by the others.[16]

---

12 T. Bourgoignie, D. Trubek, "Consumer Law, Common Market and Federalism", Berlin 1987, De Gruyter, p. vi.

13 J.Van Oudenaren, "Uniting Europe. An Introduction to the European Union", Lanham 2005, Rowman & Littlefield Publishers, Inc., p. 143.

14 S. Weatherill, "EU Consumer Law and Policy", Cheltenham, UK/Northampton, MA, USA 2005, Edward Elgar, p. 63.

15 Ibid. at p. 62.

16 According to P. VerLoren van Themaat the notion 'internal market' in the Single European Act does not cover all aspects of the notion of 'common market' in many Articles of the EEC Treaty. As evidence to this end, Themaat points out that considering Articles 2 and 3 of the EEC Treaty the concept of 'the internal market' does not cover e.g. the harmonization or coordination of legislation for reasons other than the elimination of barriers between the national markets. – P. VerLoren van Themaat, „The Contributions to the Establishment of the Internal Market by the Case-Law of the Court of Justice of the

There were two distinct concentrated phases in the development and evolution of this 'economic core of EU': from 1958 to 1968, with the completion of the Common Market and the customs union, and from 1986 to 1992, with the single market programme.[17] The history begins from when - in order to coordinate Marshall aid - the Organisation for the European Economic Cooperation (OEEC) was established in 1948; then after four years, the European Coal and Steel Community (ECSC) was created. However, most scholars indicate the year 1958 – the year in which the European Community (EC) was founded and the customs union and the common external tariff in the Treaty of Rome were established - as the starting point of the development of the European market. It soon turned out to be a huge success, with the European economy experiencing a high post-war boom, although this period of prosperity did not throw any light on how to level the still remaining barriers to trade. Later, the recession of 1970 and that of 1980 stand out as turning points and as a first initial factor, that is, the recession reminded the chief executives of Europe's largest companies of the possibilities of a further evolution of the European market (the European Roundtable of Industrialists – ERT).

Starting from 1985, among the European Communities' institutions:[18] the idea - embodied in the Commission's White Paper 'Completing the Internal Market'[19] - emerged to finalise the EC internal market by a deadline of December 1992. The White Paper indicated 300 measures (including a detailed timetable) that would be necessary in order to achieve the objective of creating the single market. This initiative triggered the amendment of the EC Treaty: at the beginning of 1986, the Single European Act[20] was signed. According to Article 8A of the EC Treaty supplemented by Article 13 of the Single European Act, 'the internal market shall comprise an area without internal frontiers in which the free movement of goods, persons, services and capital is ensured in accordance with the provision of this Treaty'.

Indeed the European Community institutions succeeded in achieving this goal: most of the measures were adopted within the deadlines, however, much remained to be done with regard to implementing the measures adopted at a national level.[21] Lord Cockfield, the European Commissioner responsible for the single market in 1986, described the story of the single market, his brainchild, 'as a story of success achieved'. [22]

European Communities" in R. Bieber, R. Dehousse, J. Pinder, J.H.H. Weiler (eds.), "1992: One European Market?", Baden-Baden 1988, Nomos Verlagsgesellschaft, p. 110.

17 J.Van Oudenaren, "Uniting Europe...", p. 19.

18 'Programme of the Commission for 1985'.

19 'Completing the Internal Market' White Paper from the Commission to the European Council COM (85) 310 final, June 1985.

20 OJ 1987 L 169/1.

21 P. Eeckhout, "The European Internal Market and International Trade. A legal Analysis", Oxford 1994, Clarendon Press.

22 L. Cockfield, "The European Union. Creating the Single Market", Wiley Chancery Law, 1994p. 147.

According to the Communication "EU Consumer Policy strategy 2007 – 2013, Empowering consumers, enhancing their welfare, effectively protecting them,"[23] although the beneficial role of the internal market is not questionable, still the consumer dimension of the internal market needs to be further reinforced in order to tackle the fragmentation of the internal market and to improve the functioning of consumer markets. According to the above mentioned document, at present, as the result of the enlargement that took place in 2007, almost 500 million EU consumers are the lifeblood of the economy: a yearly gross national product (GNP) exceeds $8 trillion,[24] and their consumption represents nearly 60 % of EU GDP - which clearly demonstrates the dimension of the initiative to introduce a new consumer credit legislation. The Communication[25] highlights the role which this significant group plays in the modern economy, however in order to fulfil that role, consumers have to be confident, well-informed and empowered, that is, they have to be equipped with effective protection from the circumstances they cannot tackle as individuals.

Commission's View Point

In the Communication "EU Consumer Policy strategy 2007 – 2013, Empowering consumers, enhancing their welfare, effectively protecting them," the Commission stresses that while technological means are increasing, business and consumer behaviour lags far behind, restrained respectively by internal market obstacles and a lack of confidence in cross-border shopping. According to the Communication, the EU consumer policy can do much to shift the focus of regulation towards citizen-focused outcomes, and in addition it can address market failure harmful for consumer welfare and social and economic inclusion by guaranteeing access to essential services at affordable prices. According to the Communication, opening up cross-border shopping retail markets is the key to unlocking the benefits from the retail internal market, which has a potential to be the biggest retail market in the world (in economic terms). In its Green Paper on Financial Services,[26] the Commission admits that constant attention is needed to ensure that citizens reap the benefits of the single market. Furthermore, it notices that in general, retail financial services are still not properly integrated, nor is competition in retail banking markets sufficient. The consequence of such a situation is the consumers' inability to take full advantage of the benefits of the single market.

Unquestionably, the European Union policies have made a significant contribution towards the establishment of the internal market. However, while this has created a flourishing business-to-business internal market, with regard to the business-to-consumer market it

23 Communication from the Commission to the Council, the European Parliament and the European Economic and Social Committee, "EU Consumer Policy strategy 2007 – 2013, Empowering consumers, enhancing their welfare, effectively protecting them", COM (2007) 99 final.

24 J.Van Oudenaren, "Uniting Europe...", p. 119.

25 COM (2007) 99 final.

26 COM (2007) 226 final.

does not seem to be a story of success. The B2C market remains largely fragmented along national lines.[27] In consequence, both: a lack of consumer confidence, but also companies' reluctance to make cross–border offers to consumers, restricts the extent to which EU citizens could benefit from the internal market.

The recent data[28] demonstrate clearly, however, that only the minority of the European consumers actually take advantage of the internal market. Overall, in the year 2007, 25% of all Europeans made a cross-border purchase in the European Union. There is even a minimal drop in comparison with the year 2006, explained though at least partially by the low levels of cross-border transactions in Romania and Bulgaria who joined the EU in January 2007. The reason for such a result can stem partly from the fact that only half of Europeans believe that their consumer rights are actually protected and respected by existing consumer protection measures, and additionally Europeans in general have doubts about the functioning of dispute-resolution bodies, whereas public authorities that can protect the rights of consumers are trusted by 54% of European citizens. Moreover, less than one-third of European consumers believes that it is easy to resolve disputes with sellers/providers through the courts. As a result, close to two-thirds (57%) still remained not interested in making cross-border purchases in the following year (after the poll was carried out - i.e. 2008).

From the business perspective, the situation does not look so different either. Three-quarters of the EU business entities only sell domestically.[29] Overall, one in five EU retailers (21%) sell cross-border to at least one other EU country. However, the majority of these cross-border professionals limit themselves only to few member states: only 4% of those retailers trade to 10 or more member states. As the main obstacle to cross-border trade they mostly indicate the cost of the insecurity of transactions (potential fraud or non-payment). However, if harmonised consumer regulations were put in place across the EU, only (or as much as) 41% of retailers would choose not to sell cross-border.[30]

---

27 Business attitudes towards cross-border sales and consumer protection. Fieldwork: February 2008. Publication: August 2008. Available at: http://ec.europa.eu/consumers/strategy/docs/fl224%20_eurobar_cbs_summary.pdf.

28 Consumer protection in the internal market. Fieldwork February – March 2008. Publication October 2008. Available at: http://ec.europa.eu/consumers/strategy/docs/eurobar_298_summary_en.pdf .

29 Business attitudes towards cross-border sales and consumer protection Fieldwork: February 2008. Publication: August 2008. Available at: http://ec.europa.eu/consumers/strategy/docs/fl224%20_eurobar_cbs_summary.pdf.

30 Synthesis report on consumer and business attitudes to cross-border sales and consumer protection in the internal market. Publication: October 2008. Available at: http://ec.europa.eu/consumers/strategy/docs/eurobar_298_synthrep_oct2008_en.pdf. In the EU 27, language is a key barrier to increasing the level of cross-border sales and purchases. 59% of retailers say they are able to use more than one language with consumers, while 33% of consumers say they are willing to purchase goods and services in another EU language. Thus many consumers may be prevented from gaining access to the wider choice and lower prices that cross-border shopping potentially offers.

In financial services, cross-border trade is limited and activity through cross-border establishment or mergers is lower than in most other sectors. According to "Eurobarometer 230: Public Opinion in Europe on Financial Services", August 2005, only 1 % of EU consumers currently buy financial services cross-border at a distance, while 26 % of consumers do so domestically (e.g. via phone, internet etc.).

The Commission states that due to differing regulatory and consumer protection frameworks, taxation policies and fragmented infrastructures which create legal and economic barriers to market entry - without further efforts – EU financial markets are likely to remain fragmented. The consequences of those barriers are restriction of consumer choice as well as increase of prices for consumers. According to Meglena Kuneva, the European Consumer Affairs Commissioner,[31] the goal of the EU authorities is to ensure that "the consumers are able to benefit from buying the best quality at the cheapest price – no matter where in the internal market these goods or services might be on sale. And it should be easy for the retailers to sell their products or services wherever the demand is within the internal market. The potential for further internal market integration in this field is considerable – so it is clearly a priority to ensure that legal and practical barriers do not prevent consumers and businesses from trading cross-border – whilst ensuring a consistently high level of consumer protection."

The Commission claims that the development of the internal market is an essential element in meeting Europe's economic challenges and delivering tangible benefits for EU citizens.[32] Its Consumer Policy Strategy 2007-2013 calls for the consumer dimension of the internal market, as well as the integration of retail markets to be further developed. The advantages of the internal market for consumers should be a wider choice of products and the best possible prices, however, at the same time a consistent high level of consumer protection. The fulfilment of the potential for cross-border shopping should help the development of a better functioning internal market.

The Commission adopted three main objectives for the period 2007-2013 for consumer policy to empower EU consumers, i.e. putting consumers in the driver's seat benefits not only them, but at the same time it also boosts competition. The aim of the policy is to provide consumers with effective protection and solid rights through the tools of real choice, accurate information, market transparency as well as confidence. The second objective is to enhance EU consumers' welfare – described as being at the heart of well-functioning mar-

---

In the majority of member states, less than a half of consumers are willing to make purchases in a foreign language.

31 M. Kuneva, Speech available at: http://ec.europa.eu/consumers/strategy/docs/ip_crossbordershopping.pdf.

32 Synthesis report on consumer and business attitudes to cross-border sales and consumer protection in the internal market. Publication: October 2008. Available at: http://ec.europa.eu/consumers/strategy/docs/eurobar_298_synthrep_oct2008_en.pdf.

kets – in terms of price, choice, quality, diversity, affordability and safety. The third goal is ensuring consumers a high level of protection.

Unquestionably general financial services pose a very attractive category from the EU point of view, because financial services can easily be offered across borders as no transportation or similar costs arise. This is why the EU regards them as a welcome component of the internal market.[33] There can be no doubt that the internal consumer credit market is still an ongoing objective of the EU. The single EU market will improve efficiency and economies of scale for bank institutions, but it also will increase the competition among banks, especially in markets where nowadays only few creditors dominate. Consequently, this will ensure better conditions for consumers. Again this improvement will be the result of a better allocation of resources, better response to the needs of a very heterogeneous market in terms of size and structure,[34] and the possibility of designing pan-European consumer credit products. Consumers will also benefit from a reduction of costs as competition and the opening of national markets to foreign creditors will lead to lower interest rates and a cheaper and wider selection of products. The main consequence of this – the extension of consumers' choice – all means a more fair and competitive credit market. This becomes even more important nowadays, in the age of Internet loans, but also with regard to Internet sale contracts.

It is a well-known fact that the diversity of law between member states means an increase of costs to enter foreign markets for financial institutions. In addition, for consumers, this variety stands for a significant reduction in consumers' confidence in foreign banks and creates an enormous level of uncertainty about the law governing each contract. Differences between the national legal systems prevent a complete market integration, and this causes the need for harmonisation at the EC level – 'common rules for a common market', a market which constitutes an area without any internal frontiers, in which the free movement of goods, persons, services and capital is ensured in accordance with the provisions of the Treaty.

Since the internal market has almost been completed, business has become easier, and more consumer transactions are also being conducted cross-borders. Consequently, the Commission is expected to strengthen consumer trust in international transactions by providing consumers with rights against businesses. The uncertainty concerning which law is applicable when a transaction is conducted across borders is lessened (due to the harmonisation of civil law rules posing a sort of guarantee to consumers that there is some common minimum protection level of their rights all over the EC), but not eradicated, since the har-

33 P. Rott in H.-W. Micklitz, N. Reich, P. Rott, "Understanding EU Consumer Law", Kluwer, 2008.

34 F. Heinemann, M. Jopp, "The Benefits of a Working European Retail Market for Financial Services", Report to European Financial Services Round Table, Institut für Europäische Politik (IEP), 2002 Berlin.

monisation adopted is in general a minimum[35] one.[36] Thus, as a result, the current rules governing the contracts are still provided by the member states.

The recent steps the Commission took in the sphere of European consumer law demonstrate however that for the sake of fully realising the idea of the internal market, more and more issues are being removed from the member states' competence due to the introduction of the maximum harmonisation approach in the new consumer directives. The last activity of the Commission concerning consumer credit reveals in a sense that the main goal of the European Union is not only to establish an internal market, but also to enable all lenders to operate freely on that market. However, consumer protectionists perceive this opening of the market to the influential and often also unscrupulous creditors who do not respect national traditions and culture in credit regulations, as a threat to the idea of a unified Europe.[37] They claim that an efficient internal credit market cannot exist without the sufficient protection of consumers' interests.

35 Under present law - the rule of minimum harmonization – EU member states are entitled to provide a stricter national legislation (than that established in the Directive), as long as the minimums set in it are respected in the transposed law.

36 H.-W. Micklitz, S. Weatherill, 'European Economic Law', Ashgate Dartmouth, 1997, p. 371.

37 From 'Round Table on Credit Directives an EU Action Plan', Responsible Credit, Brussels 2006, 6th International Conference on Financial Service, conference materials.

EC Consumer Credit Legislation

Credit is an integral part of our daily lives, remaining a driving force for economic growth and the well-being of consumers. Nowadays, the statistics show that between 50 and 65 % of consumers use consumer credits to fund the purchase of goods or services[38] and 30% of consumers enjoy an overdraft facility on their current account, whereas in the 1960s and '70s Europeans lived in a "cash society" with credit playing a very small part and involving essentially two products, namely the "hire-purchase" agreement or "instalment plan" to fund the purchase of moveable property, and the traditional form of credit i.e. the personal loan.

Moreover, what cannot be forgotten, as Reich notices "[t]he internationalisation of consumption has led to an 'internationalisation of consumer transactions',"[39] thus nowadays one can consider consumer credit an issue in the cross-border categories - being it either a credit provider offering his services in a country other than that of his premise place (more often), or an active consumer dealing with a creditor in another country.

Today, credit is made available to consumers via a wide range of financial instruments and it has become the lubricant of economic life. Credit has three fundamental roles according to which different kinds of credit products have been designed.[40] Firstly credit in the form of overdrafts, credit cards etc. smoothes short-term fluctuations in income and expenditure of households over time. Next, instalment credit enables individuals to purchase 'big ticket items', and lastly mortgage credit, students loans etc. take part in consumers investments by providing capital required for increasing future income or wealth and reducing future expenditure.

The historical overview, which is so important for a wide understanding of the miscellaneous models of credit regulations, demonstrates that, the evolution of consumer credit has not been identical in the European arena. Hence, it should be stressed, consumer credit remained for a long time a purely domestic activity.[41]

However, many factors which strongly influence the expansion of consumer credit are now coming into play: the laws governing credit, the level of social and economic develop-

---

38 In 2006: 56% of consumer credit loans were granted for personal consumption, 31% were granted for vehicle finance and 13% - mortgage. More details available at: www.eurofinas.org.

39 N. Reich, Chapter: "Cross-border Consumer Protection" in H.-W. Micklitz, N. Reich, P. Rott, "Understanding EU Consumer Law", Antwerp-Oxford-Portland, intersentia.

40 D. Gibbons, The European Coalition for Responsible Credit and Debt on our Doorstep, the response to UK Government's consultation on the implementation of the Consumer Credit Directive. Available at: http://www.responsible-credit.net/index.php?id=1980&viewid=43056.

41 To give the idea of these differences: Great Britain passed its first laws on loans to individuals in the nineteenth century, whereas Italy – in 1992 on a EU Directive, concerning advertising of credit operations - R.M. Gelpi, F. Julien-Labruyère, "The History of Consumer Credit: Doctrines and Practices", Macmillan Press LTD 2000, La Fondation Cetelem.

ment, household income and the availability of consumer goods, government monetary and financial policies, as well as consumer habits, their social and extended family relationship and the cultural context all play a role in such expansion.[42] Due to these influences, it is possible to create a simplified map of the expansion of consumer credit among the European states: Northern European societies are more favourable to money–lending while Southern Europe is generally biased-minded towards credit.[43] Furthermore, some contemporary historical repercussions also exist, resulting in zoning Europe into Western and Eastern parts.

Initially, the idea of federate European markets occurred on a large scale in the early 1960s, after the Treaty of Rome. The main objective of this Treaty was to stimulate economic integration among member states through the creation of the Common Market and a level playing-field whereby enterprises could operate under equal competitive conditions and across which goods, persons and services could be exchanged unhindered.[44] The Treaty, among other achievements, opened up the frontiers for car manufacturers, to sell their goods beyond their national territories. Virtually simultaneously in the middle of the 1960s, due to the introduction to European consumers of new products such as the credit card and generally new banking achievements by American banks, the need for cross-boarder personal lending regulations became apparent. Most of these initiatives came from European companies themselves, and indicated an eventual unification of the European market, both in terms of actors and its products and services.

It is also useful to mention here the activities initiated before 1985 by two associations Eurofinas and the Amstel Club (among others the German Kunden Kredit Bank <KKB>); however, only Eurofinas managed to activate and bracket together national associations into a European federation in order to confer the law regulations, but also political orientations of the profession. Finally, the EC took over the initiative in this respect by deciding to establish the single European market, and to include the service sector in such market.[45]

The EC Treaty provides the legal bases for the European Institutions to approximate the laws of member states to the extent required for the functioning of the common market (Art. 3 paragraph 1 <h>). According to Art. 95 of the EC Treaty, for the achievement of the objectives set out in Article 14 (establishing the internal market), the Council must adopt measures for the approximation of the provisions laid down by law, regulation or administrative action in member states which have as their object the establishment and functioning of the internal market. Moreover, Art. 95 is a legal base for all (with only one exception) con-

42 M.E. Leitão Marques, C. Frade, "Searching for an Over-indebtedness Regulatory System for Portugal and the European Union" in J. Niemi-Kiesiläinen, I. Ramsay and W. C. Whitford (eds), "Consumer Bankruptcy in Global Perspective", p. 122.

43 R.M. Gelpi, F. Julien-Labruyère, "The History of Consumer Credit...", p. 145.

44 M. Dougan, "Minimum Harmonization and the Internal Market", Common Market Law Review 37, 2000 Kluwer Law International, p. 853.

45 R.M. Gelpi, F. Julien-Labruyère, "The History...", p. 150.

sumer directives. It is considered[46] that financial services pose a special category of consumer law that reflects most accurately the current philosophy of the Commission in the field of consumer law.

The main measure in the issue of consumer credit on the European Union level is based primarily on the Consumer Protection and Advertising of Conditions of Credit Directive 87/102.[47] This regulation was an aftermath of the first consumer protection programme of 1975. The Directive 87/102 was adopted with a view to promoting the setting-up of a common market for credit and establishing minimum Community rules to protect consumers. The Directive was amended twice: first, by the Directive 90/88[48] relating to the calculation of annual global effective rates and then by the Directive 98/7[49] (dealing with banking coordination). What is quite an exception among EC directives in general, CCD was very seldom the subject of European Court of Justice case-law. The reason for this – according to Rott[50] – is the low level of consumer protection the Directive was offering. The legal base for the Directive 87/102 on consumer credit is derived from the EC Treaty: Article 100 (Article 94 after the Treaty of Amsterdam, and now Article 115 after the Treaty of Lisbon), and for both amending Directives this is Article 100a (Article 95 after the Treaty of Amsterdam, at present Article 114) today).

The UE directives were aimed at establishing the minimum Community rules to protect consumers, harmonizing national measures in this field and as a consequence setting-up a common market for consumer credit. These two goals of the Directives – the protection of consumers/debtors and the creation of an integrated market for consumer credit – possess a 'dual aim'.[51] The core assumption of the Directives is that the harmonisation of consumer credit rules is the most suitable tool to facilitate competition on the supply side between grantors of credit, and, as a result, it enables consumers to incur credit in other member states. It is also stressed that harmonisation is necessary in order to integrate the market for goods and services obtainable on credit.[52]

The great achievement of the CCD was the scope of application determined by the definition, according to which credit agreements are agreements whereby a creditor grants or promises to grant to a consumer credit in the form of a deferred payment, a loan or other similar financial accommodation. Rott[53] considers this definition to be "revolutionary", since it looked at the economic purpose rather than doctrinal categories such as sale, loan, or leas-

---

46 P. Rott in H.-W. Micklitz, N. Reich, P. Rott, "Understanding EU...

47 OJ 1987 L42/48.

48 OJ 1990 L61/14.

49 OJ 1998 L101/17.

50 P. Rott in H.-W. Micklitz, N. Reich, P. Rott, "Understanding...

51 Case C-208/98 Berliner Kindl Brauerei AG v. Andreas Siepert [2000] ECR I-1741, para.20; Case C-264/02 Cofinoga Meringnan SA judgment of 4.03.2004, para. 25.

52 S. Weatherill, "EU Consumer Law...", p. 86.

53 P. Rott in H.-W. Micklitz, N. Reich, P. Rott, "Understanding...

ing. The Directives did not regulate however many problematic issues such as inter alia protection from usury or protection from overindebtedness. The provisions of the Directive were focused mainly on two protectionist instruments: regulation of advertisement of credit products and regulation of required information which had to be placed in the agreement – both instruments containing the requirement of indicating the percentage rate of charge index (APR). The APR was highly criticised – also after two amendments by the Directives 90/88/EEC and 98/7/EC - for not including all the relevant costs of the credit and not fulfiling its major function, namely due to differences in its calculation formulas in every member state it was not comparable Europe-wide. Moreover, the Directive 87/102/EEC contained a few other protectionist instruments: the mandatory writing form of the credit agreement, as well as provisions on linked credit agreements and a right to early repayment.

Proposals for a Directive on Consumer Credit

The initiative to amend the Directive came up in the 1990s with the Commission's new efforts to create an internal market for financial services encompassing the regulation of financial markets and the relationship between consumers and service providers. In the aftermath of that trend the Directive 97/5/EC on cross-border credit transfers was adopted,[54] which laid down rules governing transparency and the performance of cross-border payments, which also covers the legal issue of consumer credit followed by Regulation (EC) No. 1103/97 on certain provisions relating to the introduction of the euro,[55] and consequently by Regulation (EC) No. 2560/2001 on cross-border payments in Euro.[56] As a result, the Directive 97/5/EC had to be replaced by the new one (Directive 2007/64/EC) on payment services in the internal market,[57] whose goal was to create a whole intuitional and substantive legal framework for cross-border payment. In the meantime, the Distance Marketing of Financial Services Directive 2002/65/EC was adopted which embodies the whole category of banking and investment contracts as well as insurance services.[58] The Directive 2004/39/EC on Markets in Financial Instruments[59] is also part of the trend.

In accordance with the above mentioned general tendency concerning financial services and as a result of the strong criticism of the Directive 87/102, particularly under fire on account of the fact that the regulation was enacted a long time ago and as a regulation which concerned a fast changing field, needed to be updated, in 1995 the Commission presented a

54 O.J. 1997 L 43/25.

55 O.J. 1997 L 162/1/.

56 O.J. 2001 L 344/13.

57 O.J. 2007 L 319/1.

58 O.J. 2002 L 271/16.

59 O.J. 2004 L 145/1. The Directive replaced the earlier one 93/22/EC on investment services in the securities field, O.J. 1993 L 141/27.

report on the operation of the 1987 Directive.[60] The result of the report was a very broad consultation of the parties involved undertaken by the Commission in respect of implementation of the Directive in the member states. Next, in 1996 the Commission presented a report on the operation of Directive 90/88/EEC amending Directive 87/102/EEC, concerning the annual percentage rate of charge (APR).[61] In 1997 the Commission presented a summary report of reactions and comments.[62]

According to the reports and the consultations, there are enormous differences between the laws of the various member states in relation to credit for natural persons in general and consumer credit in particular: some member states went much further than the minimum required by the Directive, whereas only a few had settled for that minimum. Consequently Directive 87/102/EEC no longer reflects the current situation on the consumer credit market and is therefore in need of revision.[63]

To this end, the Commission ordered a series of studies on various specific issues[64] and carried out a detailed and comparative study of all the member states' national transpose legislation. Moreover, an additional incentive for the Commission to foster the new Proposal in this field posed the national intentions expressed in many member states to revise their national legislation.

Consequently, in 2000 the Commission started consultations to revise the Directive. According to the Commission, the Directive - as an out of date act, suiting the 'cash society' of the 1970s and badly adapted to the functioning of the single market (since minimal harmonization allowed member states to go beyond the Directive's provisions) - could not rule the European consumer credit market anymore.

The Commission departments involved in the activity presented a discussion paper on 8 June 2001 which set out six guidelines for a revision of Directive 87/102/EEC, and which was followed by consultations with parties representing member states as well as the lend-

---

60 European Commission, report on the operation of Directive 87/102/EEC, COM(95)117 final.

61 European Commission, report on the operation of Directive 90/88/EEC, COM(96) 79 final of 12.04.96.

62 COM(97) 465 final of 24.09.97.

63 Communication from the Commission – Financial services: enhancing consumer confidence – follow-up to the Green Paper on "Financial services: meeting consumers' expectations", COM(97)309 final.

64 M.J. Lea, R. Welter, A. Dübel, , « Study on the mortgage credit in the European Economic Area. Structure of the sector and application of the rules in the directives 87/102 and 90/88. Final report on tender n° XXIV/96/U6/21 Seckelmann, R., « Methods of calculation, in the European Economic Area, of the annual percentage rate of charge, Final Report 31 October 1995, Contract n° AO 2600/94/00101, Reifner, U., 'Harmonisation of cost elements of the annual percentage rate of charge, APR', Hamburg 1998, Project n° AO-2600/97/000169. Domont-Naert, F., et Lacoste, A.-C., « Etude sur le problème de l'usure dans certains états membres de l'espace économique européen, Louvain-la-Neuve 1997, Contrat n° AO-2600/96/000260 ; Domont-Naert, F., et Dejemeppe, P, 'Etude sur le rôle et les activités des intermédiaires de crédit aux consommateurs', contrat n° AO-2600/95/000254, 1996, Balate, E., et Dejemeppe, P., "Conséquences de l'inexécution des contrats de crédit à la consommation." Etude AO-2600/95/000270 Commission européenne, rapport final.

ers' sector and consumers. The result of these activities was presented by the Commission Proposal for a Directive of the European Parliament and of the Council on the harmonisation of the laws, regulations and administrative provisions of the member states concerning credit for consumers,[65] with which the Commission intended to achieve two purposes: a high degree of consumer protection, as well as maximum harmonisation of consumer credit laws in Europe.

The Proposal was much more extensive and complex in comparison to the hitherto Directive. It redefined the scope of the directive in such a way that almost all kinds of consumer credit were included. The Proposal covered basically all consumer credits no matter what the form was (loan, hire-purchase, overdraft facilities, rolling credit, financial lease, etc.), with no floor or ceiling with regard to the amount, and any surety (a guarantor or a mortgage) or insurance. However, loans that met two conditions were excluded from the scope of the Proposal: loans which were mortgages or loans used for acquiring or improving real estate. Mortgages used for other purposes, i.e. mortgage-backed consumer credit ("equity release") were included in the Proposal.

The main issue of the Proposal was to adopt maximum harmonisation with a purpose to improve the quality of lending and to promote cross border competition. The new credit provisions were providing an improved harmonisation of the calculation of the annual percentage rate (APR) by streamlining its content and further refining the standard EU formula for calculating the APR that was adopted in 1998; APR representing the classical concept of the "total cost of credit to the consumer" from the perspective of a consumer (i.e. no matter whether he pays a lender, an intermediary, a treasury or other third party) and serving for comparative reasons.

In the Proposal the two new notions were introduced, namely - first a "total lending rate" (TLR) which originally was supposed to help to indicate what a consumer had to pay to a lender and secondly - the “sums levied by the creditor" (SLC) expressing what a consumer pays to a lender. All those means were designed in order to provide a comparison of creditor's offers on national and cross-border basis.

The new Proposal also introduced a concept of 'responsible lending' according to which, a creditor's task would be to advise a consumer on the most appropriate product in his product range and to conscientiously assess a borrower's ability to repay before granting him a new credit, as well as to provide a consumer with a right of withdrawal within 14 days. In addition to this, the Proposal stipulated that in case a consumer uses his right to withdraw from a credit agreement, he would only have to pay interest for the days in which the money was actually available to them.

The Proposal provided professionals with an improved freedom of circulation of quality solvency data across-borders, thus the creditor's right of access to solvency data was strengthened, therefore facilitating execution by a lender of the 'responsible lending' re-

65 COM/2002/0443 final - COD 2002/0222.

quirements. Moreover, the proposed act covered the provisions on the registration of lenders and credit intermediaries as well as the basic rules for the operation of intermediaries.

The Proposal extended the protection provisions on personal guarantors, which was also a novelty with respect to the Directive 87/102/EEC. The Proposal also stipulated the joint liability of lenders and suppliers in certain circumstances. In particular, joint liability would arise when retailers offer financing to fund the purchase of their goods.

In general this initial Proposal by the Commission, issued in September 2002, was considered to be very ambitious in terms of the level of integration in legislation that it proposed. However, it triggered a wide, very critical discussion from almost all interested parties: the banking associations criticised it as too comprehensive and strict, whereas the consumers associations found it too lax and reproached it for its total harmonisation approach. Finally, the economists wondered whether it would have any discernible impact on market integration.[66] So as a result, the Commission later decided to replace the initial Proposal with a new version which was narrower in scope and at the same time the Commission removed its most controversial elements. However, even the new version met decisive criticism. The European Parliament adopted its amendments in the first reading in April 2004.

In October 2004, following the European Parliament 1st reading opinion – the conservative-liberal majority of the European Parliament, supporting the banking industry's voice, adopted a substantial number of amendments and provided only for minimum harmonisation. In consequence, the Commission adopted its modified Proposal, and after a year it issued a second amended Proposal of an entirely different character in comparison with the original one from 2002.

The Proposal from October 2005 was significantly limited as compared to the previous ones: the Commission completely removed some provisions such as a requirement for the member states to ensure the operation of central databases in their territories (this was rejected initially by the Parliament). Moreover, the Commission removed the provisions on unfair credit terms and performance of credit agreements and narrowed down other provisions (e.g. the concept of responsible lending). However, it was not possible to fully maintain the idea of the full harmonisation approach – due to political reasons, as it was one of the most criticized elements by the European Parliament and by member states. Consequently, the Commission's reply was an attempt to introduce the idea of "mutual recognition" to the consumer credit directive. According to Art. 21 (2) of the Proposal, member states were not supposed to restrict the activities of creditors established in another member state and operating within their territory, either through freedom of establishment or free provision of services. The concept of "mutual recognition" was limited mainly to consumer protection in private international law, so more precisely - a targeted harmonisation approach, i.e. full harmonisation though some provisions and national leeway in others, was proposed.

66 N. Jentzsch, K. Lannoo, "Much Ado about Little? Agreement on the Consumer Credit Directive Reached.", ECRI Commentary No. 2 (23. May 2007).

The new Proposal opted merely for a selective harmonisation of certain fundamental issues such as: pre-contractual information, contractual information, right of withdrawal, early repayment and annual percentage rate of charge. The scope of the Proposal was limited to loans from €200 to €100.000. All mortgage credits, credit agreements granted in the form of an overdraft facility and repaid within one month, and hiring and leasing agreements where an obligation to purchase the object is not foreseen, were exempted from the Proposal. Still several controversial provisions were preserved such as a right of withdrawal, an early repayment and linked agreements, as well as the rules for database access (i.e. duty for the member states to ensure access to such databases on non-discriminatory terms).

In its Explanatory Memorandum,[67] the Commission stated that the main objective in the area of consumer credit was to establish the conditions for a genuine internal market, as well as to ensure a high level of consumer protection – establishing a set of modern rules that would guarantee consumers a good level of protection no matter which member state they would enter into credit contract in, and finally, improving the clarity of EC regulation by recasting the three existing Directives on consumer credit. The Commission also stressed that these "objectives are in line with the Lisbon Strategy, as the development of an internal market in credit will increase the competitiveness of EU creditors by enhancing competition and promoting product innovation".

Since the Commission believed that the parallel development of an internal market in credit would cause an increase in the competitiveness of creditors acting in the EU arena, it focused in the Proposal on the harmonisation of consumer protection laws in credit (a key aspect of the Commission strategy for developing the retail financial services market) as well as on targeted mutual recognition ("a natural follow-up to the introduction of a single currency, which removes the exchange rate risk between euro-zone countries and renders price comparisons more transparent").[68] This problem raised the question of the harmonisation method in the new future directive, especially since credit relations seemed to be deeply ingrained into national habits and practices, and, even more significant were these relations that were based on trust, no matter how advanced the credit instrument was.[69] As it was evident that the minimum harmonisation approach, simultaneously with a tendency prevalent among the member states' legislators to guarantee the highest level of consumer protection to their citizens, were the main cause of the diversity of national laws on consumer credit, the Commission suggested a fully harmonised approach, that should include, however, a degree of flexibility for national legislators in the specified areas. The Commission substantiated that choice by explaining that full harmonisation was the optimal way to establish

---

67 Explanatory Memorandum, Modified Proposal for a Directive of the European Parliament and of the Council on credit agreements for consumers amending Council Directive 93/13/ec Com(2005) 483 final2002/0222(cod).

68 Ibid.

69 K. Lannoo, A. de la Mata Muñoz, „Integration of the EU Consumer Credit Market...

a genuine single market in consumer credit, a single market which not would only allow moneylenders to operate across borders, but also would simultaneously ensure a high level of consumer protection regardless of the state entering into the credit contract.

Opinions about Proposals

In the opinion of the authors of the "Economic analysis..." - Kösters, Paul and Stein,[70] the first CCD Proposal introduced many gaps and ambiguities which would contradict its projected goal and would obstruct the creation of a single European market for financial services. As such the new regulation would also block the increase in competition and the harmonisation of consumer protection rules EU-wide.

The Proposal was reproached by the authors of the analysis contending that unrealistic requirements were put on the creditors. The proposed consumer credit regulation assumed that banks should take account of all the cost components of a loan in advance. Kösters et al. argued that it was not feasible, because the costs for appointed collateral vary greatly, and furthermore, because there are many uncertain charges in the event of non-fulfilment of a credit agreement which are uncertain at the moment of signing a contract. In addition, certain insurance premiums depend on the precise life and contractual circumstances and above all, in general it is not possible to quote reliable costs for all components of a credit at the moment of concluding a contract.

The second argument against the proposed regulation was that the provision of Art 14 (3) – stating that a "variable borrowing rate may not vary until the end of agreed periods provided for in the credit agreement and may do so only in line with the agreed index or reference rate" - interfered with the bank's price autonomy and deprived creditors of the opportunity to respond appropriately to qualitative changes in their risk position.

The Proposal also contradicted the central regulation of the binding for all European Community's banks – the New Basel Capital Accord. The Accord requires creditors to assess a borrower's credit rating as accurately as possible i.e. to carefully consider the value of collateral and the risk of loss and how these factors change throughout the lifetime of the credit. According to the Accord, in case of changes to the risk parameters during the term of the loan or to the collateral, assuming that the credit rating gets worst, then the creditor has to adjust the rate of interest. According to the Proposal, such adjustment was illegal. Furthermore on top of that, such pricing control would entail excessive bureaucratic expenses.

Also the right to withdrawal met with the experts' disapproval since in consequence – according to the authors of the analysis – it would prompt consumers to make hasty and careless decisions without previously considering the legal effects of their activity.

70 W. Kösters, S. Paul, S. Stein, "An economic analysis of the EU Commission's proposal for a new Consumer Credit Directive. Offering consumers more protection or restricting their options?", RWI: Materialien, Heft 9, Essen 2004.

However, the strongest criticism of Kösters, Paul and Stein related to the responsible lending provisions. The three Articles of the first Proposal which created together the title "Responsible lending" i.e. Art. 6 (exchange of information and duty to provide advice), Art. 8 (central database) and Art. 9 (assessment of creditworthiness), were reproached as being a superfluous regulation (as the credit rating system is already in use), and furthermore, as being vague and not feasible in fact to become applied in practice.[71]

Kösters, Paul and Stein also raised their objection towards the introduction of the advice duty by the future consumer credit directive which they saw as an additional burden for all money lenders.[72] They criticised mainly the banks' obligation to point to the most "suitable" loan for a consumer, since such a provision would in consequence very likely cause court disputes which would be very difficult to solve.

The authors of the analysis believed that the Proposal, instead of improving consumers' position on the European credit market, would threaten a reduction of the volume of credit agreements and would increase their price due to the increased liability risks for banks. In complying with the Art. 9, money lenders would not be able to determine the risk of lending, and in consequence they would have to change the way in which they offered loans - i.e. creditors would offer fewer loans or raise the interest rates and exclude certain groups of consumers from the possibility of obtaining a loan. The excluded consumers would lose any state protection, since - no longer being able to obtain credit - they would turn to other money lenders which fall outside the scope of the future directive, which at the end of the day would result in a substantial increase in the number of overindebtedness cases. In the long-term, such a regulation might lead to the reduction of the gross domestic product growth rates and to the increase of the unemployment rate.

Consumer advocates were very sceptical about the new Proposal and generally about the tendency prevailing in the Commission's recent activity. The reason for that was that – according the consumers' circles - the Proposal did not create any added value from the point of view of a consumer and even the existing consumer credit Directive granted consumers better protection. But first and foremost, consumer supporters asked the basic question, i.e. why did the European Union need a new or just 'improved' consumer credit act. In response they provided the answer that the new Proposal fulfils merely the demand from the business side, namely bank institutions, while at the same time not taking into account the special consumer needs.

U. Reifner[73] accepted certain arguments expressed by the Commission: he agreed that the enlargement of the credit market and the abolition of legal protectionism combined with

71 See also: the chapter "Responsible Lending".

72 Ibid.

73 Prof. Dr. U. Reifner, Director of iff institute for financial services, registered association, in Round Table on Credit Directives and EU Action Regulation, Responsible Credit, Brussels 2006, 6th International Conference on Financial Service, conference materials.

an increased competition and innovation could improve the supply of credit; however, the EC legislator could not pass over the other crucial, and in fact equally relevant aim, namely, the legal guarantee for an affordable, accessible credit which moreover would come with the sufficient precautions against overindebtedness. In Reifner's opinion, in the Commission's as well as in the Parliament's activity, a strong commitment to supporting the enlargement of the credit market prevailed, and the problem of core consumer protection was being purposefully omitted.

Generally speaking, in the eyes of consumer advocates the new Proposal was a very short–term solution. While focusing on ensuring conditions for the further development of the internal 'free' credit market, it passed over its first goal – i.e. consumer protection. This became evident when reading the new provisions which attempted to create cheap business opportunities for creditors, to improve efficiencies and economies of scale for them, and at the same time the new Proposal hardly introduced any improvements worth mentioning in relation to consumer protection issues compared with the old Directive - where national legislation had a leeway to introduce in any case much more protective provisions. In its current form, the Proposal represented the retreat from the national legal position.[74] The Proposal fell far behind existing consumer protection in Germany, France, the Benelux countries, Scandinavia and even Mediterranean countries with their short history in credit legislation.

Furthermore, the Proposal created an uncertainty because of its wide set of exceptions, in which it subordinated consumer protection to contracts which were in most cases drafted by creditors. Moreover, it created the new rights for lenders over consumers, and damaged the efforts made in member states also to combat overindebtedness through preventive measures and to make lenders accept joint responsibility. It seemed thus that the Commission intended to create bureaucratic barriers and unnecessary legal disputes, and it opened the door to the continental European consumer credit market for providers who, without consultation, made a profit from vulnerable consumers using cleverly devised systems.

According to the consumer supporters, in its new Proposal the Commission stood by its objective of using its authority to restrict consumer protection in the member states, making "a mockery of the principle of responsible lending." In some areas, the Commission sought to extend the principle of home country control i.e. control by the member state of origin in contract law, which meant the application of foreign law to consumers. Such a solution might be considered as being in breach of the Treaty of Rome, which established the right of consumers to recourse to the law of their country of habitual residence.

74 Institute for financial services (iff) (Hamburg), Draft Consumer Credit Directive 2005 Critical Introduction and Selected Reading from the Modified proposal for a Directive of the European Parliament and of the Council on credit agreements for consumers amending Council Directive 93/13/EC Brussels, 7.10.2005 COM(2005) 483 final 2002/0222(COD).

In the opinion consumers' circles, the Proposal – if adopted - would open up all kinds of freedoms for banks and for other moneylenders with a particular interest in high-cost. It would open up freedoms for: combined loans incorporating serial rescheduling and harsh penalties for delayed payments, for loans arranged over the internet or through brokers and involving guarantees from family members (suretyship), as well as preference for a sequence of small, cumulative loans.

Whereas the consumer organisations had a rather hostile attitude towards the whole legislation initiative regarding a new consumer credit directive, and even when involving in the discussion on the following Proposals, in general were not concealing doubts and kept asking what the initiative was launched for at all, the banking industry – on the other hand – was looking forward to the new act.

According to the European Banking Federation[75] - introducing itself as the voice of the European banking sector, and representing some five thousands European banks - consumer credit is one of the core businesses in the retail banking market. The FBE foresees that in the future decades such credit will be of major importance for boosting the economic growth of the Community.

Unquestionably, the creditors strive for further integration in the financial retail markets since their purpose is to sell their products on a much larger market than merely their domestic one. They strive for achieving economies of scale, e.g. by applying the same IT support or the same procedures to be respected in order to comply with rules relevant for a respective consumer.[76]

The banking sector representatives gathered in the European Banking Industry Committee[77] advocated the right balance between demand and supply side and hence stressed the necessity of an adequate consumer protection, however at the same time stated also that the Commission should recognize the costs associated with ensuring consumer protection which ultimately have to be borne by the end users of financial services i.e. by the consumers. Similarly, the counterproductive role of protectionists regulation might mean a decrease in the range of products and services on offer or information overload.

The representatives of the European Banking Industry Committee[78] expressed their opposition to the introduction of the banking products or services for consumers which would

75 European Banking Federation Observations on the Modified Proposal for a Directive on Credit to Consumers, 31.08.2006.

76 European Financial Services Round Table "Consumer Protection – Consumer Choice. Deepening EFR's Concept on Consumer Protection in Retail Financial Services", January 2006.

77 EBIC response to the Green Paper on Retail Financial Services in the Single Market, 19 July 2007. EBIC was established by the main european banking industry federations : Banking Federation of the European Union, European Savings Banks Group, European Association of Cooperative Banks, European Mortgage Federation, European Federation of Building Societies, European Association of Public Banks and Eurofinas.

78 Ibid.

be standardized through legislative measures EU-wide. They claimed that such a solution is likely to lead not only to market distortions, but also to a decrease in product innovation. The flexibility of banks in designing their offers allows them to react to the market changes as well as to response to customer needs.

The European Financial Services Round Table (EFR),[79] an assembly of the chairmen and chief executives of leading European banks and insurers, analysing the situation of consumer loans in the European Community and the European legislation in the field, came to the conclusion that consumer protection provisions for retail financial services products which differ from one member state to the other, and which are being described as "a patchwork" of diverse regimes, pose the real barriers not only for providers of services to efficiently organize their operations and distribution activities, but also for consumers themselves to choose the right products corresponding in reality to their needs. In other words, according to the banking sector, such a diversity is one of the main obstacles to an integrated retail financial services market. It has been stressed that also from a consumers' perspective the diverse national regulations are very disadvantageous, since in those circumstances consumers cannot benefit from the competition between service providers of various European countries as consumers are exposed to e.g. different terminologies, different calculation methods, different information for similar products, uncertainty regarding the relevant legal regimes etc. Thus, the EFR found a solution to overcome that situation, namely full harmonisation of some essential issues and leaving others, not essential for mutual acceptance among member states.

As a starting point of the discussion on projected consumer protection issues in retail financial services, the members of the European Financial Services Round Table criticised the approach of the EU legislator: such approach was based on the principle of minimum harmonisation. That approach caused a situation where instead of having the convergence or harmonised provisions as was initially intended, one dealt with the very diverse rules which were felt to be red tape impeding services providers across the EU from fully benefiting from the integrated European market.

The representatives of the financial services providers opted for an opening up of markets, an increase in cross-border business which would automatically lead to more variety in product design and product availability, as well as lower costs for the EU consumers.

A superlative option - from the point of view of services providers and from the point of view of the efficiently functioning internal market - would be, according to the EFR, harmonisation of all areas of civil, commercial and procedural law, which would, as a result, successfully eliminate any kind of divergence and would lead to one single EU-wide legal regime. However, such an option, being in general very dubious, was unquestionably politically unrealistic, and as such should be a priori rejected from further considerations.

---

79 European Financial Services Round Table "Consumer Protection – Consumer Choice...

Instead, the EFR representatives proposed a compromise, i.e. firstly to look closer at the field and determine, after such an in-depth scrutiny, the principles for a distinction between essential and non-essential rules, which should be the guiding principles for a further harmonisation. Next, having done so, the EU legislator should fully harmonize the key rules at the EU level, and build the 'common core standards' in order to facilitate further integration. In other words the EU legislator should apply targeted full harmonisation to essential rules and with regard to the remaining non-key provisions, the mutual recognition approach (home country principle) should be adopted. Moreover, in order to make it possible for consumers to compare similar financial services products being offered by different providers, the EFR proposed to introduce a compulsory Pan-European Info Box (PEIB) which would contain only the basics, the most relevant information free of superfluous overburdening. According to the EFR, if consumers were able to compare offers via PEIB and at the same time were provided with the same protection regarding the key issues EU-wide, a step setting towards further integration would have been made.

Furthermore, the EFR proposed to adopt five principles which should form a solid basis for both national and EC legislators to agree upon. Moreover, the principles should form part of recitals of each EC legislative measure and as such should help to provide guidance to further integrate retail financial services and establish common rules for the appropriate protection of consumers on the European level. These principles were as follows: the guarantee of the appropriate information and advice, the guarantee of the right of withdrawal, the possibility to obtain redress and the flexibility in product design which in other words meant the guarantee that products and services should not be standardized by the legislator.

The members of the EFR – in order to prevent the excessive indebtedness of the consumers - opted for the authorities' long-term strategy based on developing the financial capability of consumers, providing the latter with a financial education, and on fostering positive databases in the entire EU. The financial services providers recommended the development of the positive databases. Such databases were regarded by consumers and banks as an adequate and reliable response to their common concern with excessive borrowing, in that it would safeguard the economic stability and soundness of both parties. In support of such recommendation, the EFR stated that already the pure negative databases of credit information offices nowadays tended to become more risk sensitive and more predictive than the mere bank accounts.[80] They cited the study by the Italian consultant Nomisma[81] - according to which - a lack of positive databases has a detrimental influence on GDP to an extent of more than one percentage point.

80 See Schufa's Schuldenkompass 2003 and 2004, available at: http://www.schuldenkompass.de/downloads/index.php.

81 Available at: http://www.nomisma.it, quoted e.g. by Avanti 17.11.2003 "Trend positivo per il credito al consumo" at http://www.avanti.it.

The EFR advocated a true flexibility in product design which meant that the creditors should not be bound by legal constraints. The banking industry warned that too strict consumer protection rules would make it difficult for financial services providers to design products and in consequence limit innovations. As a result, the EFR was not in favour of product standardization or simplification, hence it recommended to allow creditors to design their products as they wished as long as consumers were provided with the complete information before entering the contract.

Regarding the proposed changes of regulation of an annual percentage rate of charge, the EFR's representatives opted for a narrow definition of the APRC which would encompass only the cost of credit in a strict sense, since only such an APRC would allow an adequate comparison of rates. Furthermore, the EFR proposed that voluntary insurances should not be included in the index if the insurance would not change the bargaining situation of the prospective borrower, for example allow him to obtain a better rate,

As to the so called "non-key issues," the members of the European Financial Services Round Table warned against ignoring or neglecting these, since although on the one hand, from a consumer protection perspective they might seem not to be very important, on the other, they might create an obstacle to further integration, thus the EFR stressed the necessity of addressing such issues. That is why the EFR's proposition was to apply the principle of origin in relation to these non-essential issues, namely, member states of destination of a product would have to mutually accept diverging rules. However, at the same time the EFR's representatives hesitated a bit, since in the area of financial services the experience of applying mutual recognition was quite scarce. It has also been highlighted that such an approach would bring the threat of a reverse discrimination, that is, creditors might face stricter regulations in their home markets than their credit provider competitors from outside the European Community.

The members of the EFR admitted that since financial products would need to comply with those host country rules which possibly did not fall under the mutual recognition principle, in exceptional cases legal uncertainties might remain. The natural consequence of not harmonizing non-key issues EU-wide would be the realization of differences in national legal orders. These differences might be so substantial and so significant that member states might find it difficult to mutually accept the provisions of other countries. Thus the question has been raised as to how to converge the national provisions in order to make it possible for member states to mutually accept them. The EFR suggested that in such cases member states should examine whether national exceptions are justified by real needs. There were two possible solutions to the problem: the first solution assumed that member states could adopt minimum standards in these non-key issues, in other words minimum harmonisation would be reintroduced combined with mutual recognition principle. The second solution foresaw the 'comply and explain' principle. However, according to the EFR both solutions would have to evaluated by a group of experts.

The representatives of financial services providers were aware of the fact that certain issues which from the creditors' perspective were not that essential, might be perceived by consumers as key, so as a consequence it would raise the dispute as to whether to totally harmonize or not. A good example of this were rules on fairness in competition among financial institutions and on the impressions created by advertising. These provisions - according to EFR - could be subject to mutual recognition of the respective law of the creditors, because otherwise efficient enforcement would appear difficult.

In the end, the EFR took into consideration two other feasible, however quite revolutionary solutions: namely the 'opt into other legal regime' option, and the 'optional pan-European regime' option. These two options have been presented to the Commission to study the possibility to apply them in the future.

The first idea meant giving the consumer the possibility of choosing national legal regimes other than his domestic one, and simultaneously to opt out of the mandatory rules of the country of his residence. The EFR stressed that presently when consumers were concluding contracts, more often via internet, they should have the same opportunities regardless of whether they were travelling in person to another member state, using the postal system, or using the internet. However, there were presently two obstacles making it impossible or difficult to put that option into practice: the Rome Convention from 1980,[82] and Regulation relating to Jurisdiction, Recognition and Execution of Judgments in Civil and Commercial Matters (Brussels I).[83] The legal acts foresaw that actions by a customer might be brought either before the court of his residence or before the court of a provider's premises, and actions by a provider might only be brought before a customer's court what – the EFR feared – might constitute an obstacle for a provider to offer the 'opting-in' option.

Regarding the second proposed option, the 'optional pan-European regime', this was described by the EFR as an optimum solution, valid uniformly across the whole Community, and was considered to be a solution that would open a completely new perspective and a new quality in the common market. Such an optional regime would be applicable to a situation when a consumer wanted to take a cross-border loan from a creditor based in another member state than that of the consumer (active consumer) or in a reverse situation, when a provider was active and approached a consumer and offering him credit products from abroad (passive consumer). Moreover, the members of the EFR suggested that such a pan-European regime should also be in force between two contracting parties from the same member state, since otherwise there was a risk of confusing consumers as well as a risk of creating some disadvantages for purely national or purely nationally active providers. The EFR believed also that the pan-European regime would have a very positive influence on national legislations which might turn out to be insufficient or excessive when "clashing" with the pan-European order's standards. Furthermore, the parallel existence of both re-

82 See below: p. 144.

83 Art. 9 seq. of Community Regulation No. 44/2001 of December 22, 2000.

gimes in a single member state would bring an added value in the sense that the European regime would also face a constant need to be improved as it would be competing on regular bases with the national provisions. This would mean a competition between the legal regimes within every single country and not among the countries. The EFR was convinced that this would be an optimal solution of compromise which would even offer a "safety relief valve" for the advocates of a slower European integration, and of the conservation of the integrity of national legal orders.

The first Proposal for a new consumer credit regulation from October 2002[84] was strongly reproached by banking industry representatives for being an over-protective act which would had created an unacceptable burden on the creditors. The element which was criticised the most was the principle of responsible lending as a provision totally violating the traditional rules referring to the classic contractual relationship.

In reaction to the first Proposal, the banking industry also called for the exclusion of mortgage credits as well as sureties and guarantor agreements from the scope of the future directive.

The issue of linked credit agreements, hardly mentioned by the Directive 87/102/EEC, was of big interest for the Commission and in its first Proposal the Commission foresaw the far-reaching model of joint and several liability of the creditor and the trader of the linked contract, however due to the strong criticism of banks, that idea failed. At the end of the day, the Commission also had to eliminate the limited regulation on liked agreements from the Directive 87/102/EEC, since the principle of total harmonisation otherwise would have meant a mandatory ban on any national protective regulations.[85]

The reaction of the European Banking Federation (EBF) to the modified Proposal of October 2005 of the directive was more positive than the response to the previously proposed act.[86] According to the FBE, many of the banking industry's concerns with regard to consumer credit regulation were taken into account in the modified Proposal.

From the FBE's perspective, the idea of excluding all mortgage credit, sureties and guarantor agreements from the scope of the future directive and in general from the consumer credit regime, as well as to establish the threshold above which credit is not considered for consumption purposes (in the modified Proposal the threshold was halved down to € 50.000) was a milestone.

In the process of modification of the Proposal, the Commission also acceded to the creditors' concern regarding the concept of a duty to advise; hence the Commission left it to the member states to decide whether to introduce such duty in their national legislation.

84 COM (2002) 443 final.

85 P. Rott in H.-W. Micklitz, N. Reich, P. Rott, "Understanding EU...

86 Press Release "Banks welcome the release of the new consumer credit proposals", available at: http://www.ebf-fbe.eu/DocShareNoFrame/Docs/7/KOJBHCNADJPFEGMDAMKFCNEISHAP87QLBOQHUYBD2YBY/EBF/docs/DLS/communication20051010-2005-02210-01-E.pdf.

The bank sector especially appreciated that the Commission made it clear in the modified Proposal that the consumer is always to be considered responsible for his final decision regarding the conclusion of a certain contract agreement.

The Federation also praised the new approach offered by the modified Proposal namely the combination of harmonisation and mutual recognition concepts which – according to the EBF - would allow such an act to overcome the main fault lines of the first Directive of 1987, which as a minimum harmonisation directive resulted in a fragmented regime for the cross-border offer of consumer credit. The FBE had been advocating that innovation and applauded its introduction in the important area of retail banking.

However, the modified Proposal was not free from criticism by the money lenders. The European Banking Federation[87] reproached the EU legislator for introducing the modified Proposal, with a lack of impact assessment of the envisaged set of rules. Without such rigorous assessment, it would be impossible to assess whether the Proposal's provisions indeed facilitated a proportionate outcome against its projected goals.

The EBF warned against the mutual recognition as a mechanism which would risk jeopardizing the achievement of the goals of the Proposal, since it would appear inconsistent with the targeted full harmonisation approach.

Moreover the EBF enumerated several elements of the Proposal which according to the banking industry should be changed. Those amendments concerned inter alia overdrafts which should be left out of the scope of the future directive; the definition of the liked credit agreements which should be amended; the right of withdrawal which, as the key element of consumer credit regulation, should be covered by the maximum harmonisation regime and which period should be shortened up to seven days with an optional possibility for a consumer to waive such right by way of written request in case of credits concluded at the point of sale and consumers willing to receive the product immediately.

The EBF called for excluding small credit agreements (below € 500) and overdrafts from the scope of the future directive, since putting them even under a "light" regime would make them disproportionately expensive and potentially unprofitable for creditors, and consequently – the EBF predicted – many lenders would quit granting small loans.

As to the early repayment provisions, which foresaw a right for a consumer to repay the loan at any time irrespective of what was agreed in the contract and without any justification, the EBF's representatives objected such provisions, since this would interfere in the civil law principle 'pacta sunt servanta'. The early repayment right which means allowing consumers to repay their credits, would also interfere – from the creditors' perspective - in the prudential liquidity and interest rate management mechanisms. The EBF claimed that in reality the early repayment right would become an extended over 14 days right of withdrawal. As such it might be particularly harmful for the fixed-interest loans that, thanks to

87 European Banking Federation Observations on the Modified Proposal for a Directive on Credit to Consumers, 31.08.2006.

their funding mechanism relying on primary market investment products requiring long-term repayment commitments, can be offered to consumers at low interest rates. The EBF's representatives suggested to introduce the early repayment right however only with a stipulation that the creditor would be fully compensated for the loss incurred.

The reaction of the European Banking Federation to the Proposal on April 2007[88] was in general a positive one, although banking industry criticized the calculation method for the early repayment as not economically justifiable. The EBF suggested that such a solution would force creditors to re-coup costs not recovered by the prescribed flat rate in the overall interest rate charged. In consequence – according to the view of the EBF – that could lead to the more expensive credit and would impact not only those customers who settled early, but also those not in a position to do so. The EBF were also advocating excluding overdrafts from the scope of the new directive, since overdrafts are "flexible multiple-purpose credit products that have developed to suit the needs of the local markets in which they operate and including them in the scope of the Directive would make them less user-friendly for consumers." The banking sector was also criticizing the proposed way of calculating the Annual Percentage Rate of Charge. It was suggested – in order to make this index more handy for consumers to compare offers from the different service providers – to exclude from the APRC other costs except for those which a creditor receives for his own benefit. Remaining costs should have been solely highlighted by the creditor outside the APRC figure.

This brief juxtaposition of the opinions concerning the Proposals of the future consumer credit directive coming from the different circles of interests demonstrates that whereas the banking industry makes sure that their voice is forcibly expressed and clearly audible in the discussion on the shape of the new consumer credit legislation and furthermore, banking organisations offer the EU legislator constructive solutions, the voice of consumers, and more specifically the voice of the organisations which represent consumer interests is very poorly audible, especially when one takes into account hugely significant differences between consumers in different member states. This is easily understandable and explicable. First, consumer organisations will always have scarce financial resources as typical non-profit organisations, especially in comparison to banks for which spending money on lobbyists is a pragmatic long-term investment. Moreover, in the more affluent countries the activity of consumer organisations will be always more noticeable than in the less wealthy member states, thus in public debate the opinions of the former will be better audible than the opinions of the latter, and since one cannot deny the big differences between individual member states, and therefore between their citizens, consequently there is a huge potential risk that the voice of consumers from some EU countries will never reach the ears of the European legislator. Therefore, if the aim of Brussels is to represent all the members of the Community

88 "European Banks hopeful of Solution for Consumer Credit Directive", Brussels, 30.04.07, available at: http://www.ebf-fbe.eu/DocShareNoFrame/Docs/5/KOJBHCNADJPFEGMDAMKFCNEI5T16BDG3PDB39 DBWT19D /EBF/docs/DLS/CCD3004-2007-00875-01-E.pdf.

i.e. (for the sake of simplicity) natural persons as well as legal entities, then the EU legislator should pay more attention to consumers needs, trying to scrutinise them deeper, also from the perspective of differences between them instead of playing a role of an impartial arbiter who judges exclusively on the basis of arguments presented to him by both, considering them to be equally competent and strong parties.

Neither diminishing nor belittling the above mentioned problem, the EU legislator should probably also dedicate more attention to the differences between money-lenders. The frequently repeated mistake is that credit providers are treated as a homogeneous group. A lot has been said about the complex structure of consumer-borrower side homogeneity, whereas a lot less attention is paid to the real stratification of the financial industry. And when one discusses certain issues from the lenders' perspective, one should not forget that this group is significantly diverse. The line of distinction is determined firstly by the size or in other words the market power of the individual lenders, and secondly, by the sphere of their market activity - i.e. whether they act only in a specific region, in one country or whether one deals with international companies having branch networks in many member states. The next distinguishing feature is described by the hitherto existence on the market, namely whether one considers a lender who is a well-established provider, having many regular customers or whether he is at the stage of expanding his business into another market or even entering the market and trying to conquer only the very first customers. Lastly, the national dimension – so often emphasized when consumers come into question – requires deeper consideration also when the money lenders are at stake, as the present European Community consists of 27 distinct states, with economies on various levels which entails in turn different preferences, different needs that the money-lenders from these respective states may have. The fact that credit providers cannot be treated as a homogeneous group leads to the conclusion that individual lenders may have simply different views on certain issues related to consumer credit. Furthermore, in spite of efficiently functioning banking organisations on the European level, there are still providers whose voice does not reach the EU legislator. Those include small entities or money-lenders active merely in one member state, which fit to the specificities of their individual markets.

In other words, the EU legislator should reject the fiction that firstly, the interests of both parties (consumers and banking industry) are equally present in the debate on the shape of the future consumer credit directive and secondly, all credit providers speak with the same, unanimous voice which is expressed by the banking organisations.

The New Directive

Under the co-decision procedure, the Parliament and the Council negotiated the final version of a text for a new directive. In May 2007 finally the compromise was reached with the political agreement at the EU Competitiveness Council in Brussels - a so-called "common position." Notwithstanding, that compromise was very fragile, as it relied on finding a middle ground among the member states' positions, so that they would all accept the clauses even though none of the States were entirely satisfied with them.[89]

The agreement concerned most of the controversial issues such as the pre-contractual and contractual information, the rights of withdrawal and early repayment, the potential right for a creditor to compensation for the loss in interest in such cases and the calculation of the Annual Percentage Rate of Charge (APR). For the pre-contractual and contractual information, it was decided to introduce a standardized format 'Standard European Consumer Credit Information Form' in order to enable comparisons of credit products for consumers and thereby increase market transparency. The Council adopted a 14-day withdrawal period. As to the early repayment provision, the Council decided to include a right of compensation for the creditor in some circumstances (in cases where the early repayment falls within a period for which the borrowing rate is fixed). In addition, the creditors can indicate the interest rate and the charges and/or display the APR according to the national law. The Council put an obligation on the member states to inform the Commission about national measures if they would make use of the regulatory choices provided for in the Directive. The Commission shall then make the information public. Next, the Directive obliges member states to take appropriate measures to diffuse that information amongst national creditors and consumers. That measure aims to improve national transparency.

The European Parliament adopted these amendments to the text of the Consumer Credit Directive (CCD) in January 2008. The European Council adopted the Directive 2008/48/EC on credit agreements for consumers and repealed the Council Directive 87/102/EEC[90] on April the 7th, 2008 – after more than a decade of discussions and almost six years after issuing the first Proposal. The decision was reached by approving the amendment voted by the European Parliament with almost unanimous support – three countries Belgium, Greece, and Luxembourg decided to abstain and only the Netherlands voted against the Directive. The Directive enters into force after its publication in the Official Journal of the EU, and member states have two years to incorporate the new rules in their national legislation. The new Act will thus be applicable from 2010 on, and it must be transposed by June 2010.[91]

---

89 F. Figueira, "The Consumer Credit Directive: Lost in the labyrinth of EU policy-making?", ECRI Commentary No. 3, 25 January 2008.

90 Directive 2008/48/EC of the European Parliament and of the Council of 23 April 2008 on credit agreements for consumers and repealing Council Directive 87/102/EEC Official Journal L 133 , 22/05/2008 P. 0066 – 0092.

91 Germany, Portugal and France taking the advantage of the process of transposition of the new Directive introduced a few social elements: Portugal a usury ceiling, Germany a ban on separate credit life insurance and France a ban on revolving credit card from department store cards.

In many respects the new Directive continues the concept of consumer protection present in the previous 87/102/EEC Act, however, naturally the EU legislator had to take into consideration the latest (30-year-long) developments in the consumer credit market, as well as the fact that in most of the member states the hitherto protectionist legislation was more consumer-oriented than the minimum provided by the old Directive, not forgetting about the Directive 2002/65/EC on the distance marketing of consumer financial services which is also reflected in the 2008 Act.[92]

As the final compromise between the European Institutions, the Directive will deal with contracts between creditors and consumers, so the personal scope of application of the Directive remained unchanged. The Directive will cover credit agreements in their economic sense (similarly like the old Directive) i.e. personal loans of between EUR 200 and 75,000 repayable after more than a month. However, it will apply only to loan contracts on which interest is paid. The Directive will not apply to mortgages or to deferred debit cards nor to credit agreements which are secured by another comparable security commonly used in a member state on immovable property or secured by a right related to immovable property. Hiring and leasing agreements where an obligation to purchase the object of the agreement is not laid down either by the agreement itself nor by any separate agreement – are excluded from the scope of the Directive. The Directive will only cover credit contracts; it will not cover guarantors nor other aspects of credit agreement law. The new Act also foresees optional exemptions in specified cases. In general the list of exemptions is much longer than the one in the preceding Proposals.

The issue of exemptions immediately gives rise to the question of whether the scope of application of the new Directive prohibits more extensive national legislation in the fields excluded from the interest of the Directive (i.e. the issues which are left outside the scope of the Act). In the recitals of the Directive one can find a partial answer to that question, namely, as to the personal scope (e.g. agreements with natural persons who request credit in order to set up a business[93]) and concerning the agreements involving amounts of less then 200 and more than 75,000 Euros, member states keep their competence to rule these issues. However, where partial exemptions are concerned (e.g. overdraft facilities), member states lose their freedom to legislate in such field. Nevertheless, in the areas that fall completely out of the scope of the Directive, member states are entitled to introduce (or maintain the already existing) national provisions.

In the new Directive the key points are fully harmonised: a 14-day right of withdrawal from the contract and the right to repay the credit early at any time, as well as the protection measures by pre-contractual and contractual information requirements including the annual percentage rate of charge.

92 P. Rott, Chapter 5 'Consumer Credit' in H.-W. Micklitz, N. Reich, P. Rott, "Understanding EU...

93 Ibid.

According to the new Directive, the consumer will have a period of 14 calendar days in which he will be entitled to withdraw from a recently concluded credit agreement without giving any reason. The Directive stipulates an exception to the rule, namely this 14-day period may be reduced "at the explicit request of the consumer" to correspond to the specific period provided for in the member states' legislation.

The next, contentious issue was the right granted to consumers for early repayment. According to the new Directive, a consumer will have the right to pay off the credit before the due date stipulated in a credit contract, however the new provisions lay down rules for the calculation of the compensation. In such a case, a creditor will be entitled to claim compensation, provided the repayment falls within a period for which the borrowing rate is fixed, and additionally, where the reference interest rate at the date of the early repayment is less than that in force at the date of the conclusion of the credit contract. The compensation is designed for the possible costs borne by a lender in connection to exercising by a borrower of the right to early repayment. It is stressed that these costs have to be fair and objectively justified and directly linked to early repayment of credit. Furthermore, the Directive reserves a limit for the compensation due to a creditor, which may not exceed 1 % of the amount of credit repaid early (0,5 % if the repayment is made within 12 months of the end of the credit agreement). The amount of compensation may not exceed the amount of interest the customer would have paid if the duration of the loan had not been reduced. However, in this respect, the Directive leaves a leeway to member states: the domestic legislators are entitled to stipulate that a creditor may exceptionally claim a higher compensation (for example where the credit institution can prove that the loss suffered from early repayment exceeds the basic maximum amount laid down in the Directive), but on the other hand, the Directive enumerates situations in which no compensation can be claimed.

The following key issue during the long-lasting legislation process was the requirement for delivering the adequate precontractual and contractual information, including the indication of the annual percentage rate of charge (APR) which will be an EU-wide standardised index. The new Directive obliges the lenders to display the standard information in advertising relating to loans, as well as to provide consumers with the exhaustive precontractual and contractual information, as the aim of these regulations is to enable consumers to make fully-informed decisions. As to precontractual information, a Standard European Consumer Credit Information form must be given to the consumer before signing the contract, whereas contractual information must be included in the contract. With this end in view, lenders will be expected to provide a consumer with information on the borrowing rate and on any charges included in the total cost of the credit. As far as the harmonisation level is concerned, it will go further as regards the contractual information as opposed to precontractual information. The new Directive also foresees the standardisation of definitions.

The provision which derives from the previously mentioned 'responsible lending' concept, present in the Directive, is the creditor's obligation to verify a consumer's creditworthiness on the basis of information obtained from the consumer and, where necessary, on the basis of a consultation of the appropriate databases accessible in all the member states, before the conclusion of the credit contract. Moreover, if a lender refuses a loan on these grounds, the consumer will have the right to get acquainted, without a charge, with the information in that database and where needed, will be entitled to correct any errors. The Directive however stipulates that where a law laying down similar measures already exists in a member state, that mechanism will be retained; otherwise it must be put in place. A creditor's duty to inform a consumer of the result of the database consultation carried out for the purpose of assessing the consumer's creditworthiness – designed for the sake of ensuring transparency in this respect – fails to do so, since consumer still will not get acquainted with the grounds of the refusal.[94]

Reich[95] draws attention to another aspect of the new Directive, that is, conflict of law. Whereas the previous consumer credit regulation (87/102/EEC) did not contain conflict of law provisions, thus the provisions of the Rome Convention prevailed, the present Act already contains conflict of law provisions (i.e. it does not contain its own concrete conflict of law provisions, but leaves it to the member states to take the "appropriate measures" in this respect), whereby the consumer is provided with protection against opt-out clauses with regard to third countries. Reich stresses that implementation of these provisions "must be fulfilled without any infringement of the Rome Convention."

The European Parliament[96] praises its legislative solution, stating inter alia, that the new Directive ensures all EU consumers the right to the same information for choosing the best offer in their country or another EU member state. Thank to this, consumers will also be able to benefit from bank products that are not available in their own country. The EP also finds the new act advantageous for the banking sector, since the Directive will facilitate money lenders offering their products on the Europe-wide scale. Further, the EP predicts that the new Directive should enable the European economy to take advantage of the potential of the consumer loans market which is worth some EUR 800 billion annually due to the development of the cross-border trade in the field of consumer credit. According to the Parliament's report, by removing obstacles the new Act will cause competition to boost, and will prompt credit institutions to improve their performance by diversifying and enhancing their products for consumers around Europe. Moreover, the Parliament in its report stresses that the Directive will be a proper tool for avoiding consumers' insolvency, since a well informed consumer will take a responsible decision whereas the creditor provided with the right and duty to inspect consumers' databases, will be in a position to assess the solvency of the consumer before concluding a contract.

---

94 P. Rott in H.-W. Micklitz, N. Reich, P. Rott, "Understanding EU...

95 N. Reich, Chapter: "Cross-border Consumer Protection" in H.-W. Micklitz, N. Reich, P. Rott, "Understanding EU Consumer Law", Antwerp-Oxford-Portland, intersentia, 2009.

96 European Parliament, "MEPs adopt consumer credit directive, cross-border credit easier and simpler", available at: http://www.europarl.europa.eu/news/expert/infopress_page/063-18342-014-01-03-911-20080111IPR18242-14-01-2008-2008-true/default_en.htm.

The critical voices concerning the new Directive come from the member states which abstained during the Council voting on April the 7th. The Greek representatives[97] stated that they cannot approve the Directive which contains the Article concerning compensation in case of early repayment as this provision is not justifiable in the light of the aim of the Directive.

A very disapproving statement comes from the Belgian representatives[98] who also abstained during the voting in the Council: in their opinion the Directive does not meet the objectives which were initially put before it, since it foresees a low level of harmonisation and as such, poses a useless tool. Moreover, Belgium reproached the Directive with ignoring the "cornerstone of quality credit", i.e. the principle of responsible lending.

Luxembourg[99] criticised the Directive for the lack of far-reaching harmonisation and mutual recognition. The Luxembourg representatives complained that the Directive gives rise to serious legal uncertainty for the parties concerned since it contains a large number of derogations combined with a wide margin of maneuver accorded to member states, and as such – in Luxembourg's opinion – the Directive is contrary to the European Council's objectives. The Directive, instead of eliminating frontiers and barriers in the European market, reintroduces them, losing the potential opportunities of the EU-wide credit market. Moreover Luxembourg considered the text of the Directive to be materially very complex which will force member states to change the rules without offering any benefits in return.

The new Directive instantly met a firm criticism from consumer organizations too. U. Reifner[100] commented on the new Directive: "We were not successful in getting adequate regulations from Brussels on good credit in a time when the lessons from deregulated markets are apparent."

The new Act was reproached with disregarding the most urgent problems in the field of consumer credit, namely: usury, refinancing in a difficult situation (where banks use their power either to cancel or to adapt the credit for imposing very disadvantageous conditions) and variable rate credits. Reifner[101] claims that still, according to the new Directive, credit providers will be able to charge usurious fees under the guise of insurance products - without disclosure in the Interest Rate of the Credit. Consumer advocates also criticize early repayment which the EU legislator describes paradoxically as a significant achievement of the Directive, since – due to full harmonisation of these provisions – as a result, in many member states consumers will have to pay more than they were paying previously to date.

Consumer advocates also provide some very detailed and specific examples in order to reveal the real (i.e. anti-consumerist) approach of the Commission. The Directive rejects no-

---

97 7633/08 ADD 1.

98 7633/08 ADD 2.

99 7633/08 ADD 2.

100 U. Reifner, Newsletter of ECRC 12, May 2008.

101 U. Reifner, http://www.responsible-credit.net/index.php?id=1980&viewid=41182.

tice to guarantors in the matter of family guarantees, which signifies a step backwards in comparison to many member states' legislation. Loans secured by mortgage are exempted from the scope of the Directive, which is an especially problematic form of the misuse of the home as security for credit for durables, and which is one of the measures being promoted.

U. Reifner[102] enumerates the key points of defeat of the new Act: he criticizes inter alia the regulation of the disclosed Interest Rate (APRC), which according to him, will remain highly misleading, being incomplete, wrong and on the top of this will pose an invitation to cheat consumers. A further big disadvantage of the Directive is, that it excludes from its scope or places into "light" regime all the small loans, credit card credit and payday loans, whereas these forms of credit are actually mostly involved in predatory lending practices.

Furthermore, the prevention of overindebtedness is not regulated in the Directive, even though it is initially indicated as an objective; there is no requirement for warnings against overindebtedness in credit transactions. In addition, the requirements of the written form in concluding credit contracts will be abolished. The Commission also intends to allow loan agreements to be made via Internet, which creates a serious risk for consumers: the Commission simply has not taken into account the socially harmful experiences of the UK and the USA. Moreover, it is stressed that admitting unregulated credit cards to be available over the Internet "at the click of a mouse", is only justified with low costs and predicted economies of scale. No less risky is the approval of uncontrolled credit card lending with excessive interest charges - exempted from numerous regulations - which is a hallmark of overindebtedness in the USA and the UK.

In passing, in the consumer advocates' view, the Commission seems to be very consistent in its anti-consumerist approach, because also in its Directive 97/5/EC of 27 January 1997 on cross-border credit transfers, it intends to remove the privilege of banks in consumer credit to the advantage of all credit card companies.

The consumer advocates believe that many problems have been simply ignored by the EC legislator in the Directive. These include: the extension of unified pricing to cross-selling; monitoring and transparency where consumers are over-burdened with risk (interest rate changes); protection of the family in guarantee situations and where there is real estate security; restriction of the exploitation of poverty through risk-based pricing and protection from pressure to take out useless additional services; the restriction of serial debt rescheduling and the mis-use of mortgages for consumer credit, together with ensuring provision of appropriate advice and consideration. Moreover, several other components are missing e.g. provisions on: alternative dispute resolution, licensing of money lenders, minimum and maximum levels of applicable loans, and finally, on common arrangements for data sharing.[103] The Directive does not include any provisions concerning the most significant problems in

102 ECRC Newsletter 12.0, May 2008.

103 U. Reifner, "The Lost Penny, Social Contract Law and Market Economy, p. 164 in T. Wilhelmsson, S. Hurri (eds) From Dissonance to Sense, Ashgate 1998.

the consumer credit market, such as defective competition, inadequate clarity in pricing and long-term commitments. According to consumer protectionists, the free market takes precedence, and is the main objective of the Proposal.

Consumer supporters even argue – opposing the frequently used argument of the other side - that as a result of the new provisions, the cost of credit will not fall, since in reality most borrowers pay more in the free market. The proof of this assumption is easy to see on the UK and the US markets. And as a result, in its current form, the Directive will give rise only to additional cross-border consumer credit where especially vulnerable consumers have no other choices and are relegated in some countries to Internet loans from abroad. Another point that is stressed is that the Directive lacks any impact studies, and there has not been enough consultation with the consumer side.

According to Reifner,[104] the complexity of the Directive and the impossibility to harmonise its economic structure with the legal culture of general civil law on the continent has created a body of strange law within national law which is difficult to digest. The Commission, as the example with the new consumer credit Directive demonstrates, reserves the general right to define which areas will be regulated at the European level and which at the national level. It refers particularly to the total harmonisation principle which turned over competence from the member states to the Community[105] without a change in the European Treaty and as such, is impossible to implement. Such an approach is strongly criticized by consumer advocates, since it negates the principles on which the European Treaty is based.[106] Moreover, the combination of the maximum harmonisation approach on one hand and on the other hand leaving certain issues to the realm of member states creates great confusion as it is not in fact clear what areas of law are truly covered by the Directive and hence no longer belong to the member states' legislative realm. It is also not clear how general civil law especially the duty to advise relates to the new advice in the Directive, and whether or not the APRC legislation is binding for usury ceilings.[107]

---

104 U. Reifner, ECRC Newsletter 2009 H1, July 2009, available at: http://www.responsible-credit.net/media.php?id=3525.

105 The German Constitutional Court holds that such cold transfer of powers needed the consensus of the national parliament. Judgment of 30 June 2009 – 2 BvE 2/08, 2 BvE 5/08, 2 BvR 1010/08, 2 BvR 1022/08, 2 BvR 1259/08 and 2 BvR 182/09 Press release available at: http://www.bundesverfassungsgericht.de/en/press/bvg09-072en.html.

106 Some countries are characterised by a greater informal consensus on solidarity than others, some use administrations and others have an abundance of courts and judges, while others again have strong NGOs or central commissions in which all market players participate.

107 U. Reifner, ECRC Newsletter 2009 H1, July 2009, available at: http://www.responsible-credit.net/media.php?id=3525.

L'Union Luxembourgeoise des Consommateurs[108] expresses the complaints that the directive does not impose more harmonization on the member states, and in particular, that it should concern a lender's obligation of individual advice for consumers, as well as the control of the solvency of the consumers in order to prevent overindebtedness, by imposing obligations on the intermediaries or civil and criminal sanctions. The ULC claims that by leaving the leeway to the member states to fix their own level of protection regarding all these aspects, the fundamental disparities will remain between the member states. As a result the ULC fears that the Luxembourg legislator – while transposing the Directive to the legal order - will limit himself to the bare minimum by not ensuring a level of protection equivalent to that which has been already reached elsewhere in Europe. The following reproaches concern the provisions which overwhelm the consumers with an abundance of the very complex technical and legal-wise information which consumers will never be able to digest and which at the same time create superfluous burden for money lenders.

According to the BEUC European Consumers' Organisation[109], contrary to what the ULC states, the complex information duty is a significant advantage of the Directive. However, the BEUC also reproaches the EU legislator with ignoring the problem of overindebtedness by passing over the core of the responsible lending concept. The BEUC praises the cap for compensation in case of early repayment as a proper tool which will ensure that these charges will be subject to control. Even before the Directive was adopted, the BEUC[110] altered and highlighted some undesirable tendencies in the progress of the CCD amendments for instance - the too narrow scope of the Directive (in particular, excluding overdrafts and equity releases) - which was introduced later on to the adopted version.

The Polish Office for Consumer and Competition Protection points out that as a result of adopting the new Directive, Polish consumers will lose in some respects, for example, among other things, at present money lenders are not allowed to charge any fees for early repay-

---

108 Communiqué de presse de l'Union Luxembourgeoise des Consommateurs, Nouvelles règles européennes décevantes sur le crédit aux consommateurs, available at : http://www.responsible-credit.net/media.php?t=media&f=file&id=3006.

109 The consumers-borrowers' organization which represents their interests on European level is the BEUC - European Consumer's Organization. However, there are also many national consumer organizations which represents consumers not only on domestic level, but also on European one i.e. firstly the domestic members of BEUC, secondly public or semi-public institutions that advise and assist consumers in debt, thirdly, the organizations which fight against predatory practices in lending and lastly the European Coalition for Responsible Credit promoting discussion on responsible lending between all the stakeholders.
"BEUC Statement on Consumer Credit", available at:
http://docshare.beuc.org/docs/1/PNHPCMMBNGLFDMAICKCIGNCHPDBW9DBDTD9DW3571KM/BEUC/docs/DLS/2008-00070-01-E.pdf.

110 "Consumer Credit : Consumers at risk", available at:
http://docshare.beuc.org/docs/6/PNHPCMMBNGLFDMAICKCIGNCHPDBW9DBDGN9DW3571KM/BEUC/docs/DLS/2008-00046-01-E.pdf.

ment of the credit. However, there are also advantages introduced by the Directive such as a longer withdrawal period (at present – 10 days), and a wider scope (at present a consumer credit is only until the limit of PLN 80.000, ca. EUR 20.000). On the other hand, there is a risk that the adoption of the new Directive in the Polish legal order may repeal the landmark of Polish protectionist legislation in the field, namely the anti-usury act.[111] J. Bańka[112] even calls it "a natural consequence" of the Directive coming into force, since the Polish consumer will soon be able to make their choices among foreign credit offers, and the anti-usury restrictions will become unnecessary.

The issue tightly related to consumer protection in the financial services is the new Payment Services Directive of December 2005. This document – in the view of the consumers' organizations – is burdensome for some consumers and ignores existing consumer protection by demolishing national consumer protection in the name of unrestricted access to the market for providers. It abolishes the banks' monopoly over payment transactions and consumer credit in the interest of market liberalization, which may result in the long-term in overindebtedness. The Directive also largely consolidates existing European regulations governing transfers abroad without offering much that is new for the consumers. Consumer supporters claim that this Directive furthers the interests of credit card providers, finance companies and the foreign transactions of the banks' corporate clients. Consumer advocates foresee that as a consequence, the floodgate to unrestricted money dealings – predatory lending and extortion - will be opened.

The first voices from the banking sector also do not portend a wide acceptance of the new act, as the Directive – according to the sector's representatives – burdens money lenders with a series of unnecessary information duties.

The reaction from the European Banking Federation[113] on the newly adopted Act was the expression of hope combined with a certain fear. On the one hand, the EBF claimed that the banking industry is a keen supporter of the efficiencies and opportunities that further integration in retail financial markets would bring for both the industry and consumers through economies of scale, and consequently more intense competition.

However, on the other hand, the EBF raised several objections. Those reservations, related to the doubts generated by the new Directive, concern the real effect of the Act in

---

111 Ustawa z dnia 7 lipca 2005 r. o zmianie ustawy - Kodeks cywilny oraz o zmianie niektórych innych ustaw, Dz.U. z 2005 r. Nr 157, poz. 1316 – The Act prohibited charging consumers with the interest higher than the limit indicated by Polish National Bank.

112 The opinion of J. Bańka (Związek Banków Polskich – Polish Banks' Association), available at: http://www.twoja-firma.pl/wiadomosc/16777718,dyrektywa-o-kredycie-konsumenckim-moze-uchylic-ustawe-antylichwiarska.html.

113 "Adoption of the Consumer Credit Directive: A First Step but Reservations remain", Brussels, 16 January 2008, available at: http://www.ebf-fbe.eu/DocShareNoFrame/Docs/3/KOJBHCNADJPFEGMDAMKFCNEI1DB3GT9CKTHN6CYDYDBN/EBF/docs/DLS/D0074C-_Press_release__final__on_CCD_vote_16_Jan-2008-00063-01-E.pdf.

building a more integrated and competitive consumer credit market in Europe. More specifically, the banking industry was in favour of full targeted harmonisation on some key points and yet criticized too much national discretion which still remain. Furthermore, it stressed the necessity of a maximally consistent national implementation. The EBF reproached the EU legislator with desisting from conducting a thorough impact assessment in order to clearly identify the benefits of any regulatory initiative which would have helped to make prudent, better informed decisions concerning the scope of the Directive or the level of information requirements it imposes.

The early repayment possibility which allows for repayment of any amount of credit and at any time during the credit contract is very criticised by the banking industry, since for creditors it creates the necessity to convert electronic systems. From the point of view of hire purchase, the creditors also reproached the new Directive with a prolonging withdrawal period, which might in the future cause confusion in the systems, which very soon will be found very unattractive for financial institutions and sellers, whereas customers will prefer credit cards instead.

According to the data collected in the Oxera report concerning the future probable costs caused by the new Directive, in Great Britain the increase of GDP would be 0,09 % lower, and the consumption expenditures would drop by over € 2 billon. The other adverse effect of the new regulation is an amount of consumers excluded (again in Britain – one and a half million), devoid of access to legal sources of credit to finance their needs.

The Polish banking industry expresses many reservations towards the European legislation initiative in the field. In general, the black scenario assumes that the main effects of the New Directive will be: a more difficult access to credit for consumers, higher credit costs and the collapse of hire purchase systems.[114] The representatives of the Polish Conference of Financial Enterprises[115] stress that the information duties are excessively complex and thus they will have an adverse effect on consumers' financial consciousness. The KPF also has serious doubts as to the projected improvement of the cross-border credit activity. Above all, Polish creditors complain about the costs required in order to adjust their credit activity to the new provisions.

The Polish Bank Association[116] also stresses another problem, that is, the problem of overregulation raised by the new Directive, i.e. the extension of the credit granting procedure which turns out to be very bureaucratic instead of easy and cheap, and consequently it will only discourage the consumer instead of attracting him. The ZBP also criticised the idea of including insurance premiums in the total cost of credit and of fixing a maximal amount of consumer credit, since already 50,000 (from the Proposal) was claimed to be overstated considering the consumers' income differences. The Polish banking industry proposed that

114 M.A. Dudek, „Zagłaskać na śmierć", Gazeta Bankowa, available at: http://www.gb.pl.

115 Konferencja Przedsiębiorstw Finansowych, KPF.

116 Związku Banków Polskich, ZBP.

this amount should be flexible, in that it should depend on a multiply of the average salary in a respective member state.

On the other hand the Polish banking sector sees a great opportunity in the new Directive, as it is supposed to manage – thanks to the new regulation – to expand its offer to the customers from the other EU countries, especially from the new member states. Along the same lines, the Polish Office for Credit Information[117] praised the New Directive for its innovative approach towards the use of data bases by money lenders in the process of creditworthiness examination, not only in the countries of their premises, but also in the other member states.

What seems to be ignored by experts from the "old" EC member states are the crucial differences between western European well-developed financial markets and the still developing economy of eastern and south-eastern European member states. In these cases, apart from legal and linguistic barriers, and in general, cultural differences between 27 countries, here additionally one has to face a very diverse level of development of financial markets and their infrastructure, as well as a very different level of consumers' incomes, as compared with that of western Europe.

The general opinion about the newly adopted Act from the academics is rather negative. N. Jentzsch and K. Lannoo[118] from the European Credit Research Institute challenge whether the new Directive will really have a major impact on a further integration of cross-border consumer credit markets in Europe. They observe an unquestionable advantage for the banking sector as the Directive might decrease the costs of business for the banking industry, however they doubt whether common standards for consumer protection will manage to immediately convince consumers to accept banking services from the foreign money lender. Jentzsch and Lannoo base their estimations on historical experiences: the first Directive of 1986 did not manage to change the picture of Europe's integration of consumer credit markets leaving most retail banking still national. The authors accused the EU legislator of ignoring the investigation of the demand-side of the consumer market i.e. common and strong protectionists provisions will not reach the assumed goals if consumers are not interested in dealing with a foreign service provider, if language, distance or information costs pose enough discouragement from the consumers' perspective.

In a similar vein, Rott[119] questions the alleged crown achievement of the goals of the new Directive i.e. "the establishment of an internal consumer credit market, in which cross-border consumer credit actually happens." According to the author,[120] although the aim and at the same time the justification of the whole legislation initiative launched already in 2002

117 Biuro Informacji Kredytowej, available at: http://www.bik.pl/NR/rdonlyres/D7BBF125-8527-4B26-8EB6-D7947114CC34/0/DyrektywaoKredycieKonsumenckimasystwyminf.pdf.

118 N. Jentzsch, K. Lannoo, "Much Ado about Little?...

119 P. Rott, Chapter 5 'Consumer Credit' in H.-W. Micklitz, N. Reich, P. Rott, "Understanding EU...

120 Ibid.

was to harmonise completely consumer credit regulations EU-wide, and at the end of the day to establish an internal consumer credit market with cross-border consumer credit as a protagonist, nevertheless, it does not seem plausible that the new Act reaches that goal. One reason for such a prediction is that the remaining differences between national legal orders in many spheres of consumer credit fields are still too substantial. In other words, the new Directive does not encompass many problems, leaving them in the member states' competence to be handled nationally. According to the author, still the idea of realization of the single market in the field will encounter difficulties in the form of the still remaining legal differences between legal orders concerning consumer credit in the individual member states, since the Directive either does not regulate certain aspects of consumer credit at all, or it sometimes leaves national legislators the leeway to maintain some legal instruments. Rott also points out the existence of other barriers to the creation of the internal credit market. Language barriers and local credit cultures, which remain and which will definitely not foster the development of the internal market, have not been or could not have been removed. In conclusion, Rott - having in mind these arguments - finds it unlikely that an internal credit market will develop in the near future. For him, the result of the newly adopted Act is ambiguous. On the one hand, from the perspective of less protective member states total harmonisation of protectionist provisions means a significant improvement, that is, upgrading of consumer protection provisions in member states who applied only minimum required rules from the 87/102/EEC Directive. On the other hand, the new Directive will cause the deterioration of the position of consumers in countries with a strong protective attitude - i.e. it will result in the reduction of consumer protection provisions in the member states who took advantage of the minimum harmonisation clause under the previous act and thus created a more protective system.

Franken assesses the new Directive very similarly, stating that the new Act "is unlikely to meet the ambitious goal of the Commission, of fostering a vibrant EU-wide consumer credit market while, at the same time, guaranteeing a high level of consumer protection."[121]

Also, the technical layer of the newly adopted Act was criticised for being unclear in its wording. Micklitz further claims that the Directive[122] contains "long, intransparent and sometimes even contradictory recitals".

Reich[123] sees the downsides of the new EU document differently. He stresses and actually supports the fact that the new Directive left not harmonised and therefore, left leeway to

121 S.M. Franken, "The Political Economy of the EC Consumer Credit Directive" in J. Niemi, I. Ramsay, W.C. Whitford (eds.), "Consumer Credit, Debt and Bankruptcy. Comparative and International Perspectives.", 2009, Hard Publishing, Oxford and Portland, Oregon, p. 129-152.

122 H.-W. Micklitz, "The Targeted Full Harmonisation Approach: Looking Behind the Curtain" in G. Howells, R. Schulze (eds.) "Modernising and Harmonising Consumer Contract Law", sellier european law publishers.

123 R. Reich, "Crisis or Future of European Consumer Law?" in "The Yearbook of Consumer Law 2009", D. Parry, A. Nordhausen, G. Howells, Ch. Twigg-Flesner (eds.), ASHGATE 2008.

the member states legislators, the issues of 'social protection' of the consumer-debtor (e.g. the problem of usury, the problem of unfair/harsh collection clauses, insolvency issue), although the obvious consequence of such an approach is the limitation of the cross-border effect of the act despite its rhetoric in Recital (9).[124]

At present, we already know roughly (as the new Directive does not totally harmonise all the issues of a consumer credit contract) what will be the future character of the EC consumer credit legislation. The crucial question as to whether the Common Market idea is really going to prevail over the consumer protection goal already gained its answer, however the assessments differ significantly depending on the views of the diverse authors executing such assessments. The heated discussion concerning, in particular, the question as to whether the EC legislator was going to adopt a maximum harmonisation approach and thereby deprive the member states from a possibility to give the legal regulation a more protective shape, is closed. Although the Directive has already been adopted, there is still no common agreement on whether it handles the urgent and continuously growing problem of consumer overindebtedness. Consumer advocates reject such a statement, since the Directive literally does not contain any provisions concerning the issue, whereas the European Parliament in its press release claims that this Directive is indeed designed to prevent overindebtedness.

Actually, none of the stakeholders – neither the banking industry nor consumers' circles - are fully satisfied with the new Act. The representatives of banks as well as consumer advocates and academics – all reproach the EU legislator for not conducting any impact assessment of the future provisions. Such a study, with regard to both demand and supply side, could have allowed to design the legal tools adequately, according to the intended aims of the Directive, and at the same time could have allowed for avoidance of some potential adverse side effects. An apt example concerns the information duties imposed on creditors: whereas in the opinion of the bank representatives, the Directive requires too many information duties and consequently satisfying these requirements is too burdensome for creditors, and, at the end of the day, would be naturally translated into a higher cost of credit. On the other hand, for consumers this information is too complex and hence not really helpful in making a credit decision, and as a result, the consumers who will not be taking the advantage of this information, will still be facing the higher credit costs.

The prevailing opinion is that the Directive does not meet two major objectives that it is faced with. First, it does not create an adequate environment for the realization of the idea of the internal consumer credit market, since it leaves certain issues to the discretion of the national legislators, and does not take at all into consideration a number of objective obstacles to the realization of the internal consumer credit market idea (for example - national credit cultures, language barriers etc).

---

124 'Full harmonisation is necessary in order to ensure that all the consumers in the Community a high and equivalent level of protection of their interests and in order to create a genuine internal market.'

Second, the Directive fails also as a consumer protection act: it is reproached with its 'anti-consumerist' attitude as it undermines the legal position of consumers initially reached (under the minimum harmonisation approach of the previous act) in many countries. Moreover, by excluding from the scope of consumer credit many of the most menacing sources of credit (like mortgage, Internet loans, credit cards etc.) and abandoning the 'responsible lending' idea as well as ignoring the problem of overindebtedness, the Directive provides proof that the EU legislator eliminated the consumer-oriented direction for good.

At present, after adoption of the new Act, all the attention is focused on the way member states handle the implementation of the EU provisions into their legal orders. The issues that are fully harmonised do not raise any questions, but all the problems that have been left to member states will very soon arouse very emotional debates this is especially true with regard to the fact that the Directive left certain elements of consumer credit completely untouched, by the same token giving freedom to the national legislators to either provide some comprehensive regulations in this respect, or to ignore these issues entirely. There will be room to display different views from different interested groups, so the heated debate is not yet over - the battle field has only moved to the national arena.

Internal Market and Consumer Protection

The Commissioner for Consumer Protection M. Kuneva, in her speech at the end of the year 2007 made a statement according to which "a small loss in respect of certain aspects of national consumer law could be more than compensated by an increase in cross-border offers and in the overall EU level of protection".[125]

According to the Commission of the European Communities,[126] A new Citizens' Agenda for Europe must deliver peace, prosperity and solidarity in a new context, globalisation. Furthermore, the Commission declares that the Agenda should deliver an open and fully functioning single market and effectively turn the four freedoms into reality; promote solidarity, opportunity, access and sustainability; and increase security. It stresses that this is an agenda for the benefit of all Europe's citizens, building on achievements to date, and following the course set already. In the opinion of the Commission the single market, alongside effective competition policy, has brought huge benefits to Europe's citizens, securing choice and opportunity for the Europeans. Next, one can read in the Agenda about the success of the creation of the euro, which has in turn reinforced the dynamism of the single market and strengthened financial and economic integration, making the EU stronger globally. Finally, the revised Lisbon strategy has set the base for the modernisation of EU economies in order to deliver growth and jobs for all citizens.

The Commission also draws up projects for the future. In order to meet the challenges of the globalisation process, it states that EU economic policy has to boost the integration and convergence of European economies by promoting the completion and smooth functioning of Economic and Monetary Union and completing dynamically the strong, open, competitive single market which can be a major part of Europe's response to the challenge of globalisation. Finally, the Commission declares that it commits itself to removing the remaining barriers to a single market, to enable European citizens and entrepreneurs to enjoy the full benefits of the EU.

Apparently – on the basis of what is quoted above - the Commission does not perceive any tension between the line of completion of the single market on the one hand, and the realization of the citizen's/consumer's interests on the other hand.

Notwithstanding, in the literature on consumer protection legal regulations much has been said about the antagonism between two major objectives of the European Community: to achieve an efficiently functioning single market and to protect consumers. The threat of a "race to the bottom" – which in this case means the danger of establishing a lower level of

---

125 M. Kuneva, "Stakeholders' Conference on the „Review of the Consumer Acquis"", Brussels, 14 November 2007, the speech - text available at: http://ec.europa.eu/commission_barroso/kuneva/speeches/speech_14112007-2_en.pdf p. 3.

126 Commission of the European Communities, Communication from the Commission to the European Council a Citizens' Agenda Delivering Results for Europe, Brussels, 10.5.2006 COM (2006) 211 final.

protection entailed by applying the principles of the common market to national consumer laws - is still present in many studies in the field.

Reich[127] characterises EC consumer law and policy as Janus-faced, as it aims at creating a common internal market, but at the same time strives for the protectionist goals - both faces, however, are looking in the opposite directions. Initially, the reason for this was a constitutional one: since in the Treaty there was no legal basis for the protective measures (until the Treaty of Maastricht which recognised promotion of consumer protection as one of the EU objectives - now Art. 3, Art. 153), the secondary consumer legislation was justified with reference to the internal market and to existing disparities of laws which create barriers to trade within the internal market and distort competition between actors from the different member states (ex Article 100). However, in fact, this has been perceived only from the business point of view. As Stuyck[128] states, consumer protection was originally seen as a by product of the common market programme.

The evolution of the EC consumer protection policy went through different stages. The first stage was "an initial indirect recognition of consumer interests as a regulatory element of community law." Afterwards came the 'golden era' of the policy sealed by expressing certain consumer rights. The third stage appeared with the idea of "internal market" and consumer protection being an element of it.[129] An attempt to create an autonomous consumer protection policy by expressing "consumer rights" including, inter alia, the right to protection of economic interests, and the right of information and education – took place in two programmes: first in 1975[130] and then in 1981.[131] Overall, the situation of the emancipation of consumer protection law was improved also by the Cassis de Dijon[132] where the ECJ developed the broader 'principle of consumer protection as an independent ground of justification' against member states' restrictions to free movement (provided restrictions' proportionality and that they were non-discriminatory from EC law perspective).

At the end of 1980s through the Single European Act with its new Article 100a EEC (Article 95 EC, at present Article 114),[133] consumer policy obtained its place in the law of the in-

---

127 N. Reich, 'Europäisches Verbraucherrecht.', Baden-Baden 1996: Nomos, p. 56.

128 J. Stuyck, 'European Consumer Law after the Treaty of Amsterdam...

129 N. Reich, Chapter: "Economic Law, Consumer Interests and EU Integration" in H.-W. Micklitz, N. Reich, P. Rott, "Understanding EU...

130 O.J. 1975, C 92/1.

131 O.J. 1981, C 133/1.

132 120/78 Rewe-Zentral AG v Bundesmonopolyverwaltung für Branntwein [1978] ECR 649, [1979] 3 CMLR 494.

133 After the Treaty of Lisbon, in consolidated versions of the Treaty on European Union and the Treaty on the Functioning of the European Union (2008/C 115/01) Official Journal C 115 , 09/05/2008, the content of the Article 95 TEC was moved to Article 114 "1. Save where otherwise provided in the Treaties, the following provisions shall apply for the achievement of the objectives set out in Article 26. The European Parliament and the Council shall, acting in accordance with the ordinary legislative procedure and after consulting the Economic and Social Committee, adopt the measures for the approximation of the

ternal market. However, at the same time, the concept of a 'single European/internal market' changed the role of the EU consumer protection policy. In essence it reduced the role of EC protective policy to increasing the freedom of choice of individual consumers as equivalent participants of free trade. Hence the idea of a social state protective policy almost vanished. Nevertheless, one should keep in mind that the "internal market" as such, was assumed to be the means to an increase in quality of life including an increase in consumer welfare (Article 2 of the EEC Treaty). The concept of 'communicating vessels' assumed the following chain: more market freedoms (open competitive, non-discriminatory market); more focus on production and distribution; increase of quality of life, and automatically of consumer welfare. In other words the increase in consumer welfare was a simple consequence of the increase of individual freedom of choice which in turn was guaranteed by the "four freedoms" of the internal market.

And finally the Maastricht Treaty expressed that consumer protection is an independent principle under the EC law (Articles 129a and 3(s) EEC), and a new chapter XI on Consumer Protection was introduced. According to Article 129a (later Article 153, at present Articles 169 and 12), the Community should contribute to the accomplishment of a high level of consumer protection through measures adopted pursuant to Article 100a in the context of the completion of the internal market, as well as through specific action which supports and supplements the policy pursued by the member states to protect the health, safety and economic interests of consumers and to provide adequate information to consumers. This Article had, however, a marginal impact on the development of consumer law. It was followed by the Treaty of Amsterdam amending the Article 129a into Article 153 EC and establishing the autonomous consumer rights like the right to information, to organise themselves in order to safeguard their interests. The list of consumer rights and interests applied to both internal market and non-internal market measures. It was also expressed that consumer protection requirements should be taken into account in defining and implementing other Community policies and activities.

At the same time, the ECJ in its deliberations over Directive 94/19/EC of 30th May, 1994 on deposit-guarantee schemes stated that "although consumer protection is one of the objectives of the Community, it is clearly not the sole objective", and further "no provision of the Treaty obliges the Community legislature to adopt the highest level of protection which can be found in a particular member state."

---

provisions laid down by law, regulation or administrative action in Member States which have as their object the establishment and functioning of the internal market. (...) 3. The Commission, in its proposals envisaged in paragraph 1 concerning health, safety, environmental protection and consumer protection, will take as a base a high level of protection, taking account in particular of any new development based on scientific facts. Within their respective powers, the European Parliament and the Council will also seek to achieve this objective."

Now, both objectives – consumer protection and internal market – are already present on the level of the Treaty. According to the changes introduced to the EU law by the Treaty of Lisbon,[134] Article 12 (ex Article 153(2) TEC)[135] proclaims that consumer protection requirements shall be taken into account in defining and implementing other Union policies and activities, whereas Article 3 (ex Article 2 TEU)[136] describes the various EU tasks. Such tasks are, for instance: establishing an internal market characterised e.g. by "a highly competitive social market economy" with "a high level of protection; and in addition, combating social exclusion and promoting social justice (point 3). One can draw a conclusion on the basis of these two Articles, that the economic efficiency (the competitive internal market) and consumer protection are both valid commitments of the European Union.

Nevertheless, the secondary consumer legislation is still usually primarily justified with the same reference to the promotion of the internal market; thereby the Commission prefers to relate consumer protection legislation to the aim of creating an efficient internal market, although at present consumer protection measures could have been directly justified with the protective arguments.[137] One cannot resist the impression that, whenever introducing any consumer protection provision to the Community's legal order, the EU legislator is trying to find a counterbalance or, in other words, is trying to somehow compensate the business side for its proconsumer attitude. This may indicate not only an inner dispute which is carried on by the EC legislator, dispute which is based on the question of which of the two goals of the EC - consumer protection or establishing an internal market - should prevail. Recognising the internal market goal as an only adequate justification also for introducing new consumer protection provisions, proves that actually the Community's legislator has already in a way managed to answer this sensitive question.

Nowadays though, in Reich's[138] opinion, according to the provisions of Article 3(t) and 153 EC,[139] the European economic law is still the law of the internal market and it protects

---

134 2007/C 306/01 Treaty of Lisbon amending the Treaty on European Union and the Treaty establishing the European Community, signed at Lisbon, 13 December 2007.

135 Consolidated Version Of The Treaty On The Functioning Of The European Union, Official Journal of the European Union C 115 Volume 51.

136 Consolidated Version Of The Treaty On European Union, Official Journal of the European Union C 115 Volume 51.

137 T. Wilhelmsson, 'The Abuse of "Confident Consumer" as a Justification for EC Consumer Law', Journal of Consumer Policy 27 (2004), p. 317.

138 N. Reich, Chapter: "Economic Law...

139 The Treaty Establishing the European Community (consolidated version) 29.12.2006 Official Journal of the European Union C 321 E/37: Article 3 (t) "For the purposes set out in Article 2, the activities of the Community shall include, as provided in this Treaty and in accordance with the timetable set out therein: (...) (t) a contribution to the strengthening of consumer protection" and Article 153 "1. In order to promote the interests of consumers and to ensure a high level of consumer protection, the Community shall contribute to protecting the health, safety and economic interests of consumers, as well as to promoting their right to information, education and to organise themselves in order to safeguard their

consumer interests only 'indirectly', i.e. 'interests' which are identified with enhancing the 'quality of life' defined in turn as the right to information, freedom of choice on the market, legal protection, access to justice etc.

The European Commission assumes that consumer welfare can be guaranteed by proper functioning of the internal market and competition, hence one can add to the catalogue of the EU citizens' rights, the right to free choice i.e. "the individual rights of the citizens to participate in cross-border transactions in accordance with Community law." Reich stresses that the EU legislator's strong focus on information, being in accordance with a market economy and ignoring to a certain extent the socio-political, distributive dimension of the market reality. The question arises as to whether a deeper unification (via inter alia full harmonisation) could not deprive consumers of any remaining social values in contract law, since so far there are almost exclusively only member states who are active in this sphere.

Since the 1980s the Commission has striven to link two objectives of the European Community, namely to establish the Common Market and to guarantee consumer protection. Commission policy documents show these attempts clearly: the first of its three-year action plan for 1990-92 focused on the necessity of building the 'confident consumer' in order to support the creation of the internal market,[140] while one of the issues of the second one for 1993-95 was "Placing the single market at the service of European consumers"[141] and again the plan stressed the need for a confident consumer within the EC integrated market. Generally, all of the subsequent consumer policy documents issued by the Commission, the current Consumer Policy Strategy for 2002-2006[142] and the Internal Market Strategy – Priorities 2003-2006[143] inclusive, focus not only on the close interaction between the objectives of establishing the single market and protecting consumers in their activities with-

---

interests. 2. Consumer protection requirements shall be taken into account in defining and implementing other Community policies and activities. 3. The Community shall contribute to the attainment of the objectives referred to in paragraph 1 through: (a) measures adopted pursuant to Article 95 in the context of the completion of the internal market; (b) measures which support, supplement and monitor the policy pursued by the Member States. 4. The Council, acting in accordance with the procedure referred to in Article 251 and after consulting the Economic and Social Committee, shall adopt the measures referred to in paragraph 3(b). 5. Measures adopted pursuant to paragraph 4 shall not prevent any Member State from maintaining or introducing more stringent protective measures. Such measures must be compatible with this Treaty. The Commission shall be notified of them."

After the Treaty of Lisbon, in consolidated versions of the Treaty on European Union and the Treaty on the Functioning of the European Union (2008/C 115/01) Official Journal C 115 , 09/05/2008, the content of the Article 153 TEC was moved to the Article 169 and Article 12.

140 COM (90) 98.

141 COM (93) 378.

142 OJ 2002 C137/2.

143 Commission Communication of May 2003. COM (2003) 238 final.

in the market, but also on the array of benefits that consumers should expect from the completion of the common market.

The new view on consumer protection legislation has been grasped and demonstrated in the DTI consultation report,[144] namely the authors of the work stress the existence of the explicit link between consumer empowerment and a healthy economy and give an example of consumer policy used as a tool in order to make competition more effective. That pattern proceeds as follows: empowered consumers who have the capacity not only to make informed choices, but also to assert their rights and to complain about defective services and products, put pressure on the professionals giving the latter a significant incentive to improve the quality of their offers.[145] Such a perspective adds a new (or alters the so far prevailing) rational to consumer protection legislation, i.e. next to (or instead of) protecting the weaker party to the contract, the well-being of the economy appears.

The representatives of the banking sector also perceive and react to the problem of balancing two competitive goals of the European policy. Notwithstanding, their point of view understandably differs from the one expressed by consumer advocates or by the majority of academics. Therefore, the bank representatives[146] claim that with the development of online banking and the enhanced mobility of European citizens, there is a growing need to take the necessary legislative measures allowing providers to offer their retail financial services uniformly across Europe. Hence, the representatives of business gathered in the European Financial Services Round Table (EFR) raised the issue of the consequences resulting from rules of consumer protection which were too strict i.e. a too protective consumer law. From the point of view of service providers, who act in the consumer protective environment, it becomes very difficult to design products, since lenders are bound by legal constraints which in fact limit innovation. However, a concern - over the tension between consumer protection and the opening of the single market - has also aroused in bank environments. The EFR notices that every time retail financial services are discussed, the EC legislator needs to strike the right balance between these two aims ‘of equal importance’ - consumer protection and the opening of the single market, the balance which – again according to the representatives of the industry - can be reached only by creating a level playing field. In other words, in order to ensure the right balance between consumer protection and a single market, a common standard must be found which will at first sight make the traditional differences more apparent.

The authors of “An economic analysis of the EU Commission’s proposal for a new Consumer Credit Directive”[147] reflect, to a large extent, the view of the EC legislator, as they as-

144 DTI, “Extending Competitive Markets: Empowered Consumer, Successful Business”, 2004.

145 G. Howells, „The Potential and Limits of Consumer Empowerment by Information”, Journal of Law and Society, Vol. 32, Nr. 3, Sept 2005, pp. 349 – 370.

146 Consumer Protection – Consumer Choice, European Financial Services Round Table, January 2006.

147 W. Kösters, S. Paul, S. Stein, “An economic analysis...

sume that consumers are protected most effectively when the credit market is functioning competitively within member states and throughout the Community as a whole. In other words, when the idea of the single market for financial services is put into effect, then consumers have a free choice between different service providers. Under such circumstances the market power of the money lenders would become reduced, and as a result the market mechanism would force them to adjust their credit offer to consumers' preferences. As a result, a consumer would get a well-tailored, innovative product at a lower price. To this end, the legislator should ensure diverse credit providers an open market with a free access for the new creditors and a free way out for existing ones. Also the demand side should meet certain requirements: the responsible and sovereign consumers should be capable of distinguishing 'good' products (i.e. those which meet their needs) from 'bad' ones. For a complete single market picture one needs the transparency of markets which requires government regulations over the creditors as well as over the quality information, consulting etc.

EU Consumer

The whole discussion about consumer protection being one of the two major goals of the European Union and the possible (alleged) tension between consumer protection and the internal market goal should actually begin with certain clarifications as to what one in fact understands under the notion of 'consumer'. The realization of the meaning of the notion of 'consumer' allows to comprehend the approach a legislator adopts in his attempts to design a piece of the consumer protection regulation. In other words, without making a stipulation as to the meaning of the word 'consumer', one cannot judge the steps taken by the EU legislator as far as the consumer protection issue is concerned. The point here is not to create another formal definition, since there are already enough of them in all the pieces of the EU legislation. We know that a consumer is a natural person, an individual who concludes a contract for a personal use, i.e. for the purposes being outside his trade or professional activity; however a picture which emerges from this description is not unambiguous. First, it is, to some extent, nationally determined in that there is a significant difference between the way a consumer is perceived in the US and in Europe, and in Europe itself again some distinctions can be traced, and second, it is pretty clear that different stakeholders (the EU institutions, the consumer organizations, the representatives of the business) have a very different picture before them as far as a consumer is concerned.

In broad outline, simplifying, nowadays the main distinction can be drawn between two actually non-overlapping meanings of the notion 'consumer', namely a 'consumer-citizen' and a 'consumer-shopper'.

A 'consumer-citizen' is an initial beneficiary of consumer protection legislation in the sense that the primary EU consumer protection legislation was designed for the sake of such an actor. A 'consumer-citizen' is a 'market player *sui generis'*, as he enters the market not with a purpose to reap the profits (like any other market player, particularly commercial entities), but with an aim to satisfy (to a large extent) his basic needs (like housing, transport, food, clothing, travelling etc.). The other feature that gives a 'consumer-citizen' a status of a market player *sui generis*, is that he is not necessarily rational in his market decisions and often not because of the lack of information or the lack of alternatives, but just because of some very simple, human "weaknesses", unfamiliar to the rational commercial market players. Hence, he requires very special treatment when entering a market and dealing with the market professional actors i.e. he requires protection in the sense of a certain handicap. This protection should be ensured to him by an apt consumer protection legislation.

In the literature, there is a significant number of authors who strongly support the 'consumer-citizen' meaning of the notion of 'consumer'. First and foremost, it is backed by the representatives of consumer organizations, but not exclusively by them. Reifner[148] emphasises that while the main goal and advantage for all the 'commercial' players on the market is to reach a certain, preferably maximum level of profits or to minimise their costs, consumers present a different set of characteristics, since they are human beings who only seek to satisfy their personal needs. He even states that these 'personal needs' are "in fact the core element of consumer protection" since they "form the basis of consumption" which "again underlies individual demand."[149] In consequence, the EC legislator should also adopt a different approach to different groups in the society, because while the 'commercial' users may require information and support, consumers require even more than this - they require laws to protect them.

Offer[150] contends that the 'rational consumer' is a fiction, and that choice is often fallible, since the choices consumers make do not always accord with what, from a different temporal viewpoint, they would judge as being good for themselves. And similarly, Schwartz[151] invokes behavioural economics which assumes that people are not perfectly rational, not entirely self-interested and have limited willpower.

148 U. Reifner, 'Proposal for a Directive of the European Parliament and of the Council on the harmonisation of the laws, regulations and administrative provisions of the Member States concerning credit for consumers Expertise and Alternatives developed for the Verbraucherzentrale Bundesverband e. V. (vzbv), the Federation of German. Consumer Organisations, available at: www.ecri.be/media/documents/Reifner-consumer_credit_directive.pdf .

149 Ibid.

150 Offer in I. Ramsay, "Consumer Law and Policy..., p. 76.

151 P. Schwartz, "Personal Bankruptcy Law: A Behavioural Perspective" p. 61 in J. Niemi-Kiesilainem, I. Ramsay, W.C. Whitford (eds.), "Consumer Bankruptcy in Global Perspective", 2003, Hard Publishing, Oxford and Portland, Oregon.

Trumbull[152] mentions a 'consumer-political actor', characteristic of the French model which perceives consumers primarily as political actors with a distinct social status from producers. In general, the idea that the general interest is best guarded by the state prevails in French consumer law.[153] Thus there is a strong case for insulating consumers from market risk altogether, i.e. not exposing them to market risk on a par with the professional actors.

Next to the 'old', initial idea of the 'consumer-citizen', 'consumer-political actor', nowadays emerges an idea of a 'consumer-shopper' which changes the paradigms of the recent consumer protection legislation. A 'consumer-shopper' is a confident individual who wants to maximize his profits on the internal market and to this end is willing to deal cross-border. As such, he is a rational market actor aware of legal provisions, set free from all the national habits, prejudices etc. Such constructed definition, prevailing in Germany, grants consumers the status similar to that of producers,[154] thereby consumers – here treated as economic market actors - should bear their share of market risk.

Close to the idea of the 'consumer-shopper', the 'consumer-economic actor', is Pearson's[155] notion of a *"financial citizen"* i.e. an active, informed, and responsible market participant, ready to bear his share of market risk. Between the rational consumer-shopper and the vulnerable consumer-citizen is inter alia Drexl's[156] consumer who does not make choices on the basis of purely economic considerations, however at the same time whose right of self-determination, and freedom to choose should not be ignored.

One cannot help noticing that the idea of the confident 'consumer-shopper' clearly prevails in the recent documents issued by the Commission, and poses the main assumption of the new consumer credit Directive as well. Such a perception of the meaning of the notion 'consumer' is, moreover, very much in line with the interests expressed by the business.

According to the judgements of the European Court of Justice[157] it follows that the ECJ sees consumer as an active and critical information-seeker, or "an average consumer who is reasonably well informed and reasonably observant and circumspect." The Court rejected

---

152 G. Trumbull, "Consumer Capitalism. Politics, Product Markets, and Firm Strategy in France and Germany", p.22.

153 J. Stuyck, 'European Consumer Law after the Treaty of Amsterdam...

154 G. Trumbull, "Consumer Capitalism...

155 G. Pearson, , "Financial literacy and the creation of financial citizens", pp.3-27 in: M. Kelly-Louw, P. J. Nechf and P. Rott, "The future of Consumer Credit Regulation. Creative Approaches to Emerging Problems." Ashgate, 238 pp. (2008).

156 J. Drexl, Habilitationschrift, Publisher with the title Die wirtschaftliche Selbstbestimmung des Verbrauchers., Tuebingen, J.C.B. Mohr, 1998. In J. Stuyck, 'European Consumer Law after the Treaty of Amsterdam...

157 Case C-238/89, [1990] ECR I-4827, Pall Corp; Case C-315/92, Verband Sozialer Wettbewerb eV v. Clinique Laboratories SNC, [1994] ECR I-317, Case C-470/93, Verein Genge Unwesen In Handel und Gewerbe Köln V v. Mars GmbH, [1995] ECR I-1923, Case C-373/90, Procureur de la République v. X, [1992] ECR I-131, Case C-210/96, [1998] Gut Springenheide and Tusky, ECR I-4657.

the measures aimed at protecting the consumer who was more vulnerable, and weaker than average.[158]

Whitman[159] draws a distinction between two meanings of the notion of 'consumer' from a perspective of two kinds of interests consumers have in the market. The author distinguishes two different meanings of the expression "protecting the interest of consumer." Namely, one can consider consumer economic interest as an opportunity to purchase goods and services at the lowest possible price, with a wide access to goods and services, also with easy access to credit etc. On the other hand, however, under this expression "protecting the interest of the consumer", one can also understand consumer safety legislation, the legislation which protects consumers against the risk of dangerous or low-quality goods and services. Whitman claims that these two interests are definitely not identical: whereas the consumer safety legislation paternalistically limits consumer choice, the goal of the "economic interests" approach is to maximize consumer choice. So consequently, in extreme cases they can even exclude each other. Whitman[160] opposes W. Weyl and R. Nader, who treat two groups of consumer interest - namely consumer safety interest and consumer economic interest - as identical. Whitman, on the other hand, states that these two interests are quite different. While consumer safety provisions, paternalistic, and "bureaucratic" by nature, limit consumer choice, consumer economic legislation, emphasizing consumer's sovereignty and being immune to bureaucratic interference, heads towards maximizing consumer choice. However, Whitman, observing the issue of consumer protection from the wider, transatlantic perspective, states that generally lawyers in Europe – as opposed to their American colleagues – prefers the second meaning, choosing consumer safety interest and the protective legislation, whereas in the US, the economic interests approach prevails. 'Freedom' in the consumer legislation context for Americans means "the freedom of a fully sovereign consumer, who is deemed to be the best judge of his own interests." In continental Europe however the same notion has a completely different significance, that is, it denotes "supervised freedom", in other words "self-determination under the watchful eye of a caring, supportive government." The question emerges as to whether even, after the recent changes made to the EU consumer law, one could confirm this.

Garcia Porras and van Boom,[161] in respect of two different meanings of the notion 'consumer', distinguish two main strands of regulatory strategies as far as consumer credit is concerned: the social market approach to consumer credit which is described as interventionist and paternalistic, and a neoliberal approach.

158 J. Stuyck, 'European Consumer Law..., p. 299.

159 James Q. Whitman, „Consumerism versus Producerism: On the Global Threat of <Consumerism> and the Mission of Comparative Law." Yale Law School, Yale Law School Faculty Scholarship Series, Year 2006 Paper 6.

160 James Q. Whitman, "Consumerism versus Producerism...

161 C.I. Garcia Porras, W. H. van Boom, "Information disclosure in the EU Consumer Credit Directive: Opportunities and limitations", electronic copy available at: http://ssrn.com/abstract=1538111.

The social market approach is oriented on protecting a 'consumer-citizen' and as such is primarily focused on non-economic concerns, social values, such as distributive justice and 'access to credit'. The advocates of such an approach, in their strive for inter alia redistribution of wealth, invoke human rights and constitutional principles. In the field of consumer credit, this approach assumes regulations on compulsory interest rate ceilings, lender liability for irresponsible lending, controls on termination and default penalties, and restrictions on debt recovery from consumers.

On the other hand, a neoliberal approach is based on the perception of a consumer as a shopper - as an economic actor. The approach assumes that a consumer, as a "rational maximizer of his own utility," makes "optimal resource allocation decisions." In the field of consumer credit, the way of protecting such a consumer, or speaking more precisely - *empowering* him, is to provide him with sufficient information, thus information disclosure duties together with some controls on contractual unfair terms are the means of consumer protection which corresponds with this approach.

New Concept of EU Consumer Protection

It is frequently observed that the philosophy represented by the European Union approach towards consumer protection issues evolves over time. Whereas in the first phases of the EU consumer legislation in the foreground was a 'consumer – citizen' with his 'consumer rights' clearly highlighted, in a nutshell, a weaker actor who needed a special legal protection while entering the market, already in 1992 the EU legislator adopted a more 'internal market approach'.[162] The contemporary consumer had evolved into an active market player on the cross-border market. Such a consumer needs his choice opportunities to be protected by confidence building measures, including legal protection in 'business to consumer' contracts.

To illustrate the attitude of the Commission towards consumer protection, one can also quote the DG Internal Market statement included in its Green Book on Financial Services "Protecting Consumer Interests":[163] "The Commission does not see consumer protection as a secondary or subordinated goal to the realisation of the internal market. Both goals are of equal importance, its implementation has to go hand in hand." However, it continues, "If there were no advantages for the consumer – [...] - the internal market would benefit only the suppliers of goods and services."

According to another document – a 1997 paper on Financial Services: "Strengthening Consumer Confidence",[164] it is stressed that a consumer must have the full benefit of the advantages of the internal market. However, the Commission mentions a very peculiar and

162 N. Reich, "Protection of Consumers' Economic Interests by EC Contract Law - Some Follow-up Remarks", 28 Sydney L. Rev. 37, March, 2006.

163 COM (96)209.

164 COM(97) 309 final version 26.6.1997.

odd way of achieving the goal of strengthening the role of a consumer - the "true consumer interest" - namely, through the further abolition of trade barriers. According to the Commission, reaching this goal would help to overcome the distinction made between consumer protection and consumer access to the benefit of the market.

The next Commission document – "The Green Paper on Consumer Protection in the European Union from 2 October 2001" - states that neither group of the society is currently taking full advantage of the potential of the internal market; and as a solution it envisages a simplification of the national rules and a more effective guarantee of consumer protection. However, the simplification of the rules may also involve the harmonisation of the European Community legislation in the consumer protection field. The Green Paper also plans to identify the main areas for this harmonisation. According to the Paper, such a "simplification of existing rules and deregulation, where possible, could help both consumers and businesses. Reducing the burdens on businesses would increase their competitiveness, and consumers would have access to a greater choice of products at better prices."

However, according to J. Stuyck,[165] in the judgements of the ECJ (where national measures were shown to serve consumer protection, the Court has found this to be very often in conformity with the free movement provisions of the Treaty) as well as the history of changes of the EC legislation (most of the consumer law directives were adopted on the bases of those Treaty Articles which aimed at establishing the Common Market or stressed the necessity of a "confident consumer" for the proper functioning of the common market) prove that the tension between the two goals of the EU was exaggerated. The author admits though that the "vast majority" of consumer directives actually are based on the Treaty provisions which aim at realisation of the internal market idea.

Finally, the different understanding of the specificity of the notion of consumer in the EU legislation is glaringly demonstrated in: the previously mentioned Communication from the Commission to the Council, the European Parliament and the European Economic and Social Committee EU Consumer Policy Strategy 2007-2013 Empowering consumers, enhancing their welfare, effectively protecting them from 2007.[166] In this document the Commission actually indirectly admits a firm shift of its perception of consumers, since for the long-term strategy for the *consumer protection legislation* the Commission places "empowering consumers" as its first objective, and emphasizes that the major needs of such "empowered consumers" are: real choices, accurate information, market transparency and confidence, being an intended result of effective protection and solid rights. The second objective still oscillates towards a consumer-shopper i.e. in the second place "consumers' welfare" is stressed, however, this is a consumers' welfare which "is at the heart of well-functioning markets" and its main components are: "price, choice, quality, diversity, affordability" and only in the last position - "safety." Only the third objective still resembles the traditional

165 J. Stuyck, 'European Consumer Law...

166 COM(2007) 99 final.

conception of understanding consumer protection, that is, the Commission intends to protect consumers also "from the serious risks and threats that they cannot tackle as individuals".

However, the tendency to perceive a consumer as a market actor with merely economic interests, whose 'transactional' performance European law seeks to further thus promoting the 'smooth functioning of the internal market', is also perceptible in the Directive 2005/29[167] 'concerning unfair business-to-consumer commercial practices'.[168]

This tendency is still current, and one of the main manifestations of such tendency is the choice made by the Commission with regard to a shift from minimum to maximum harmonization which is present in the recent pieces of consumer credit legislation, even though the notion 'consumer – citizen' still exists. Howells[169] characterizes the shift in the EC law from the minimum to maximum harmonisation approach - as a shift of the Community law being initially a "benevolent friend of the consumer guaranteeing minimum rights," to "the guardian of trade interests." This clearly shows what the EU legislator has at heart nowadays.

Reifner,[170] considering the consumer protection issue in the new consumer credit proposal,[171] aptly labels this recent choice made by the Commission as a dangerous policy shift from 'consumer protection' to the 'consumer advantage'. But actually - it has to be stressed – that this renaming already took place in the Green Book on Financial Services: Protecting Consumer Interests[172] from 1996. In this report, the notion 'consumer protection' was replaced by that of the 'consumer advantage', and, as was also argued in legal doctrine, any harmonisation at all in this area was seen as impeding the higher national consumer protection standards. Reifner[173] even argues that the word protection should be abolished, and instead, should be seen as consumer empowerment.

The tendency to seemingly harmlessly rename the existing and commonly accepted notions was also continued in the DG Market's action programme on financial services[174] two

---

167 OJ L 148, 22 of 11 June 2005.

168 M. Everson, C. Joerges, 'Consumer Citizenship in Postnational Constellations?'.

169 G. Howells, "The Rise of European Consumer Law – Whither National Consumer Law?" 28 Sydney Law Review 63 (2006).

170 U. Reifner, 'Proposal for a Directive of the European Parliament and of the Council on the harmonisation of the laws, regulations and administrative provisions of the Member States concerning credit for consumers Expertise and Alternatives developed for the Verbraucherzentrale Bundesverband e. V. (vzbv), the Federation of German. Consumer Organisations, available at: www.ecri.be/media/documents/ Reifner-consumer_credit_directive.pdf .

171 COM(2002) 443 final.

172 COM (96)209.

173 "Reifner (2006) - Renting a Slave – European Contract Law in the Credit Society. Paper presented at the Conference on Private Law and the Many Cultures of Europe University of Helsinki Faculty of Law Department of Private Law Helsinki,14 pp.

174 COM(1998) 625 final version 28.10.1998.

years after the Green Book was issued (i.e. in 1998). This referred to the 'user of financial services' while it continued to demand the 'freedom of choice for consumers' and, in the name of the 'users/consumers', asked for the 'abolition of all restrictions on cross-border consumer financial services'.

Reifner[175] claims that confusion of users and consumers is not accidental. It is in fact a calculated move which shows that ideologically the EC legislator saw consumers merely as players in the market operating on the demand side who would profit from the best market in the same way as suppliers do. It demonstrates that the Commission perceives consumers as different actors on the market scene than they really are. And, in fact, in the oversimplification of market relations, reducing them only to the 'commercial' ones, and trying to explain them with notions borrowed from pure economic theories, such an approach does not cover all the complicated and complex relations that exist on the market and concern, inter alia, consumers.

Similarly, Krämer[176] expresses criticisms regarding the emergence of an 'EU' consumer: Krämer claims that such an approach reduces the citizen to an economic subject, to "a nearly parasitic 'middle-class' shopper" whose main and only concern is to get the best bargain at the lowest price.

Micklitz[177] reproaches the European Commission for introducing a specific normative concept which ties the consumer into the EC's new policy objective, namely to make Europe the best economic player in the world. In other words, the European Commission takes advantage of the consumer by treating him as a tool in reaching the Lisbon Agenda 2000 objectives. The same thing happens in relation to the whole concept of consumer protection. By expecting consumers to behave in a particular way (and here economic efficiency seems to play the key role) and by training them accordingly, the EC makes them equal, reducing them to 'shoppers'. Such an approach obviously entails the necessity to remove the fragmented domestic consumer law regulations, since consumer protection – as well as the other branches of law – is an element of the complex strategy, and as such has to serve international competitiveness.

Garcia Porras and van Boom[178] notice the shift of the meaning of the notion 'consumer' in the recent EU consumer protection legislation, also on the consumer credit level. This is expressed by the shift from the (above mentioned) social market approach towards the neoliberal approach "by gradually moving away from a conception of consumers as *objects* of European law, towards a notion of consumers as regulatory subjects by substituting 'con-

---

175 U. Reifner, 'Proposal for a Directive of the European Parliament and of the Council on the harmonisation of the laws...'.

176 L. Krämer, "The European Union. Consumption and Consumer Law", in L. Thévenoz and N. Reich (eds.), Droit de la consummation – Konsumentenrecht – Consumer Law. Liber amicorum Bernd Stauder, Baden-Baden, 2006, pp. 177-94, p. 177 in N. Reich, "Crisis or Future...

177 H.-W. Micklitz, "The Targeted Full Harmonisation Approach..., p. 81.

178 C.I. Garcia Porras, W. H. van Boom, "Information disclosure...

sumer protection' with a broader notion of 'consumer policy', in which consumers are empowered with tools that support their role as accountable and active actors, rather than as passive subjects that need to be protected against themselves."

The new understanding of the role and position consumers have on the market i.e. putting consumers on a par with all the commercial market players and thus appointing them as active 'regulatory subjects' seems to be one of the manifestations of an attempt to change the paradigms of consumer law in a sense of shifting the responsibility, since now an educated, well-informed consumer should be fully responsible for his failure. In other words, the automatic and (in a way) natural consequence of treating consumers and professionals as identical market actors, (with a minor exception of the necessity to provide consumers with the certain set of information), is that no 'extenuating circumstances' are conceivable in case of a consumer's failure. Assuming that the bargaining power of both parties is equal, there is no point in granting one party (who happens to be called 'consumer') any 'handicap'.

Undoubtedly, in the recent EC consumer protection legislation a certain tendency is clearly perceivable, i.e. this is a trend which diverts from the idea of protecting a vulnerable consumer in the sense of granting him a certain 'handicap' so as to account for his special personal needs determined (inter alia) by his national and social identity. Such trend on the other hand, leans towards a consumer-market player; a consumer–"best-bargain-seeker" who as a purely economic subject belongs to a huge homogenous group labelled as the 'European consumers'. Undoubtedly, one of the manifestations of the above outlined tendency is the shift from minimum to maximum harmonisation. Most of the academics who make an effort to scrutinize the reasons for such a change of views on the EU level, stick to a thesis, according to which, the EU legislator remains under the persuasive influence of the professional side, which in turn finds the maximum harmonisation approach unquestionably beneficial. Unreservedly, such an explanation is very true, since, at least, in the field of consumer credit, during the process of designing the shape of the new directive, financial service providers did not remain inactive; on the contrary they lobbied the EC legislator rather firmly. Such a thesis, in a way reflecting the reality, is not in my opinion a complete one. One can argue that the EU legislator, no matter how "institutionalised" it seems to be, still at the end of the day consists of the individual private persons who first and foremost are simply consumers. Consequently, being consumers themselves they presumably understand the concerns of this group and view the major market issues from the demand perspective and therefore, they can perfectly represent other consumers. However, this is only a theoretical assumption, which like in the case of any political representation theories, is only partially true.

The problem of representation - being a result of the phenomenon that even free and democratically elected decision makers derive mostly from the intellectual and financial elites of the respective society and in fact are not capable of representing the society entirely due to a different perception of reality - is known to political science and worked out on the national levels. Here however, on the EC level the representatives seem to depart even further from the represented citizens of the European states (i.e. the gap between 'Euro-crats' and European politicians and the members of the society of the respective 27 member states is very wide). Without going into detail and elaborating on the political dimension of the European Community (since this is not the purpose of this paper), I would like to stress that one should be aware that whereas the level of affluence, education, and the understanding of the law, the national traditions and habits etc. – are all indicators which differ significantly viewed both from a national perspective (especially since the last two EC enlargements), but also from the social perspective. The EC officials no matter how hard they try, cannot deny the simple fact that their reality is different. They live their lives on a certain relatively similar standard, and mostly have a similar level of education: both their knowledge of foreign languages, as well as their awareness of law exceeds that of the average citizen. Moreover, the fact that they decided to move away from their homelands indicates finally that they feel like citizens of Europe, i.e. everywhere within the EC they make themselves at home. Thus they can be considered capable and willing to take the advantage of the internal market, as well as capable of seeking the best bargain and finally, they represent the group of consumers the recent EU legislation is designed for. From the perspective of the Brussels officials the reality is a unified, common Europe with a single internal market, and this is – in my opinion – the main reason for the shift in the EC legislation from the minimum to maximum harmonisation and for perceiving the consumer as a confident market player.

Hence, an evaluation of the recent EU legislative activity allows, on the one hand, to come to a conclusion that Brussels ignores the existing EU law definitions of the consumer, since the EU legislator more and more often identifies consumers with commercial entities i.e. economic market players, and moreover that the EU legislator decided to totally subordinate consumer welfare to the overriding goal of the EU, that being the realisation of the idea of the internal market. Nevertheless, it is true in a way that from Brussels' perspective, the perfectly functioning European common market is the most apt tool in striving for consumers' well-being. The question remains to be answered, however, as to whether this is an objective statement or just wishful thinking.

Indeed, one can observe that the EC legislator managed to reconcile his view of consumer protection (this goal is still undeniably present in the Treaty) with an argument that limiting such protection is to the advantage of the consumer. In this connection the liberalized services and the completion of the internal market are - according to the Commission's view - a form of consumer protection in themselves, so that as a result, maximum harmonisation would not conflict with Art. 153. So, according to Reifner, in order to implement Art. 59 (which lays down the free flow of services) and Art. 3 paragraph 1(t) effectively, it would therefore suffice to justify maximum harmonisation and to promote the interests of consumers.

As a matter of economic theory, it is not contentious to affirm that the EC law of market integration does and will benefit a consumer, and in this sense, these legal regulations can be rated among consumer protection laws. And here there is a space for a negative law: the provisions of the EC law directed at the prohibition of the national measures or practices which are harmful for the cross-border transactions.[179] At present, the legal provisions of the individual member states creating impediments to the functioning of the internal market can be tolerated in only one case, namely, where these provisions serve an interest of sufficient importance to override the principles of an internal market, and the second requirement is that they have to be proportionate to achieve that objective. The objective of efficient consumer protection is just such a justification. And many ECJ cases illustrate the foregoing: collisions between national consumer law and the EC law of market integration. Weatherill[180] calls this "the clash of competing consumer interest: the Community-driven notion of free trade versus the national choice about protection." Since the negative law approach endorses the rejection of national provisions in favour of Community regulations, this thereby means that there is a preference for the consumer advantages of the internal market (with its free trade principles) over the advantages for the consumer of any home-state's regulation which still impedes this market. However, when a member state upholds its law, this means that such a state maintains certain powers and responsibilities which are not repealed by the process of market integration, and then as a result, the process of market integration is withheld. At this point the need for a positive law approach appears.[181]

Member states handed over their legislative entitlement in the field of consumer protection to the European legislator, which in consequence deprived them of their autonomy in regulating that area. Nevertheless, Micklitz[182] argues that by being a driving power of the consumer protection legislation, the European Commission has not simply extended the member states' social welfare philosophy to the European level. To the opposite, he claims that the European Commission has begun gradually to submit consumer law to the internal market philosophy. The clear manifestation of such a "market driven consumer policy" is - according to Micklitz - the shift from the minimum to maximum harmonisation, which after all is in line with 'plaiting' the consumer into a project dictated by the Lisbon Agenda 2000 i.e. to make the European Community the strongest world economic power.

On the whole, there is a sharply defined line between "European – *market behaviour* – consumer law" and "national consumer *protection* law", although that general rule does not necessarily apply to all the member states, and at the EU level that observation is not con-

---

179 H.-W. Micklitz, S. Weatherill, 'Consumer Policy in the European Community: Before and after Maastricht' in 'European Consumer Policy after Maastricht', N. Reich and G. Woodroffe (Ed.), Kluwer Academic Publishers, 1994, p. 6.

180 S. Weatherill, 'EU consumer law and policy'..., p.39.

181 H.-W. Micklitz, S. Weatherill, 'Consumer Policy in the European Community..., p. 6.

182 H.-W. Micklitz, "The Relationship Between National and European Consumer Policy – Challenges and Perspectives" in C. Twigg-Flesner, D. Parry, G. Howells, A. Nordhausen (ed.), "The Yearbook of Consumer Law 2008. Markets and the Law", Ashgate 2008.

firmed by some of the ECJ judgments.[183] Still, Micklitz stresses the distinction between European consumer law, which is a consumer law without a social protective outlook, and which expects a consumer to be attentive and self-responsible, and on the other hand, the national consumer law having a protective character.

Similarly, the authors of the Manifesto on Social Justice in the European Contract Law[184] reproach the European legislator of not taking into consideration social justice when harmonising contract law, and criticize that the only source of inequality that the EC Directives in reality deal with are informational asymmetries between contracting parties. According to the authors, 'social justice' is understood as being crucial for European contract law value, which represents a compromise between freedom of contract and solidarity.

G. Majone[185] seeks the answer to the "social deficit" in Europe's "regulatory state" without interventionist/social adjectives, but it is the "state" whose task is to correct market failures in order to increase the economically defined welfare of consumers/citizens.

Somma[186] reproaches the EC legislator with creating a model for social justice which, on the one hand, aims directly at avoiding market failures, but however, on the other hand, rebalancing social weaknesses is for that model a very minor indirect goal. The author supports the proposition conveyed by the Manifesto to develop European contract law in line with the social and economic rights from the Nice Charter of Fundamental Rights. However, Somma stresses the condition for such contract law, that is, the exact similarity of the fundamental rights included in the Charter and those recognised constitutionally by the individual member states, as he observes that constitutions of member states contain the invocation to social values: solidarity, public interest etc.

Joerges and Rödl[187]discussing the 'social deficit' of Europe invoke F. Scharpf's[188] thesis according to which democracies which prove to be unable to resolve problems of economic and social stability risk the loss of social legitimacy.

How Far Should the Legislator Go in Interfering?

According to Ramsay,[189] the three fundamental questions one seeks to answer when discussing consumer protection are: 1) Why do consumers need protection; 2) When ought

183 H.-W. Micklitz, "The Relationship Between National and European Consumer Policy...

184 Study Group, "Social Justice in the European Contract Law: a Manifesto", (2004) 10 European Law Journal 661.

185 E.g. G. Majone, „Regulating Europe: Problems and Perspectives" in Jahrbuch zur Staats- und Verwaltungwisselschaft 3 (1989), p. 159-177 in Ch. Joerges, F. Rödl, '"Social Market Economy" as Europe's Social Model?', EUI Working Paper LAW No. 2004/08.

186 A. Somma, "Social Justice and the Market in European Contract Law", ERCL 2/2006.

187 Ch. Joerges, F. Rödl, '"Social Market Economy...

188 F. Scharpf, "Economic Integration, democracy and the weather state", Journal of European Public Policy 4 (1997), p. 18-36.

governments to intervene to protect consumers and, lastly 3) How ought governments to intervene.

Although, tracing back to Roman law epoch in the past, consumers have been treated in a special way in many legal systems, the concept of contemporary consumer law (in the form that it is used nowadays) poses a rather new issue. Only in modern times has the protection of employees, tenants, patients and finally, consumers changed the paradigm of the civil law: before the freedom of contract was perceived as the only prevailing value of contract law; today the same importance has been attributed to the protection of the weaker party.[190]

Already in the 19th century the legislator departed from the freedom of contract as a strictly understood principle of contract law and introduced some protective tools – initially, advantages for tenants and workers.[191] The motivation for that was a perception that freedom of contract cannot guarantee acceptable results for all the participants of legal relations, or in other words: there was a need to restrict one person's freedom in order to safeguard the freedom of the opposite party.

Consumer protection greatly changed the paradigms of private law and of the relationships hitherto known to the market economy. There are even theories that consumer protection ideology is characterized by hostility to the market economy. The critic towards the performance of markets (i.e. the natural processes taking place in the markets as a result of interaction between market forces) are accompanied by "an unquestionable faith in the ability of governments to intervene in the consumer's interest."[192]

Still in the 21st century, it is not controversial, even for the strongest supporters of the free market that one of the most relevant roles that the law should play, especially in financial services, is to protect a weaker party of a contract.[193] Nevertheless, economic freedom requires the legitimate justification of the provision limiting freedom of contract.[194] Such a justification of the state/Community intervention can be market failure, but the non-market goals can also be reasons for interfering.

---

189 I. Ramsey, "Framework for Regulation of the Consumer Marketplace", Journal of Consumer Policy, 8 (1985) 353-372.

190 E. Hondius, 'Consumer Law and Private Law: the Case for Integration' in 'Neues Europäisches Vertragsrecht und Verbraucherschutz: Regelungskonzepte der Europaeichen Union und ihre Auswirkungen auf die nationalen Zivilrechtsordnungen', edited by W. Heusel, 1999 Bundesanzeiger Verlagsges., Köln.

191 T. Hartlief, "Freedom and Protection in Contemporary Contract Law", Journal of Consumer Policy 27: 253 – 267, 2004.

192 See inter alia: R. Parish, "Consumer Protection and the Ideology of Consumer Protectionists" in A.J. Duggan and L.W. Darvall (eds.), "Consumer Protection Law and Theory" (Sydney, The Law Book Company, 1980, p. 229.

193 See P. Cartwright in 'Consumer Protection in Financial Services', P. Cartwright (Ed.), Kluwer Law International 1999, p.7.

194 See M. Freidman, 'Capitalism and Freedom', University of Chicago Press, 1962.

The major justification for the state/Community interfering in the market mechanisms with the consumer protection provisions is certainly the necessity to balance the power of both parties to a contract, characterized by a weak, vulnerable consumer, and a strong professional.

According to the Judgment of the Polish Constitutional Tribunal on bio-components in gasoline and diesel (K 33/03),[195] the purpose of consumer protection is to safeguard the interests of the weaker participant of the market, whose knowledge and orientation are very limited in comparison to that of the professional. The idea of consumer protection is not to grant the consumer additional special privileges, on the contrary, the purpose of this legislation is to secure the proper market practices, where a consumer has enough knowledge and has access to the necessary information, and thanks to which, in reality he can make free, unrestrained choices, which are moreover in compliance with his own interests. That is why, the Tribunal stresses the principle of transparency, publicness, and true availability of the clear, complete and comprehensible commercial information, and calls it "protection via information." The burden of providing the consumer with such information lies on the professional party.

According to the document of the UK's Department of Trade and Industry, "A Fair Deal For All: Extending Competitive Markets: Empowered Consumers. Successful Business." (2005), the criteria (the rationales) for 'intervening' in consumer markets in the form of introducing consumer policy are: market failure, equity (i.e. the protection of vulnerability), whether or not an item is a necessity of life, and finally, externalities (i.e. the effects of consumption on third parties).

Ramsey[196] scrutinizes two main goals standing behind the regulation of the consumer marketplace: 1) "the improvement of economic efficiency by remedying market failures" and 2) equity. The requirement to be fulfilled for an intervention to be 'efficient' is that the economic benefits should outweigh the economic costs; moreover one should also consider the impact of intervention on the behaviour of those affected. On the other hand, the notion of 'equity' stands for "distributive and corrective justice considerations and a concern for public values." Ramsey does not assume a necessary mutual exclusivity of these two objectives, however, at the same time he does not preclude the potential conflicts nor trade-offs between them. The major concern which follows from the issue of 'distributive justice' is the effectiveness and fairness of the use of consumer protection rules to achieve distributional goals. Next to distributive justice, the idea of 'corrective justice' stands for the protection of individual entitlements (i.e. here the justification of regulation is a protection for the new 'social rights'). Economic market failure analysis rejects the redistribution role of consumer protection provisions because of their backfire-effect, i.e. business will pass along the increased costs of any redistributive measures to consumers or, prevented from doing so, will

195 Judgement from April 21st, 2004. Available at: http://www.trybunal.gov.pl.

196 I. Ramsey, "Framework for Regulation...

cease dealing with consumers - e.g. the restrictive consumer credit rules might force a low-income consumer to turn to predatory lenders.[197]

In contemporary analysis of consumer credit policy, Ramsay[198] notices the dominance of the 'market failure model', i.e. the model of a sharp distinction drawn between those rules which 'facilitate the functioning of the markct', and those which distribute resources or rights between consumers and creditors. In other words, the problems arising on the consumer credit market may have two sources; these are various market failures, and a significant stratification of the society which is the result of unequal income distribution, poor education etc. And whereas applying consumer protection tools as a remedy to overcome the first cause of problems – the market failures – in general does not encounter any opposition, using consumer protection provision for fighting against the second group of causes – is often strongly questioned.[199] Some lawyers however reject this thesis stating that the main sources of the problems in the consumer credit field are inequalities of class, gender, race etc., rather than the rules of market transactions. Ramsay defends the opinion that the main issues, when it comes to consumer credit regulation, are distributional, having as a goal – the achievement of certain values such as: security, autonomy and equal access to credit markets.

However, at the same time he invokes the views on consumer credit legislation associated with law and economics[200] which argue that the terms of consumer credit contracts are a futile and unfair remedy for the worse off consumers, since the credit providers will find methods to avoid conforming to these rules, and as a consequence the most disadvantaged consumers can be excluded from the official credit market entirely.

According to Howells,[201] one can no longer imagine a market functioning completely without any state control. The justification for state intervention concerns not only consumers', but also the whole society's well-being: first, the consumers as vulnerable actors on the market expect and have a right to be protected and second, the state should prevent society from suffering the external costs that arise when a consumer suffers harm. In the other words, the purpose of the regulator's intervention via introduction to the legal order consumer protection provisions is not solely the good of a particular consumer; on the contrary by creating the legal framework for consumer protection, the state/Community prevents the whole society from experiencing negative consequences related to the harm of an individual. Each consumer is an element of the whole, so as a consequence his failure is sensed and

197 See: Cayne, Trebilcock, "Market Considerations in the Formulation of Consumer Protection Policy." University of Toronto Journal, 23, 396-430, 1973.

198 I. Ramsay, "Consumer Credit Law, Distributive Justice and the Welfare State", Oxford Journal Law of Legal Studies, Vol. 15, No. 2. 1995, pp. 177-197.

199 See R. Goode (ed), "Consumer Credit" 1978, at 98.

200 See D. Cayne and M. Trebilcock, „Market Considerations... and A. Schwartz, "Justice and the Law of Contracts: A case for the Traditional Approach" (1986) 9 Harvard Journal of Public Policy 107.

201 G. Howells, "The Potential and Limits...

recognized in a negative way by the whole society. On the other hand, however, before making an effort and launching the legal intervention, the legislator should consider the costs and gains of such intervention, i.e. he should attempt to compare the welfare gains which would be that of moving a market closer to the competitive outcome due to an intervention, with the administrative costs to the state and the costs to the firms of compliance with the newly introduced legal requirement.[202]

The additional justifications for state intervention in the credit market can be found in the Crowther Committee's Report, the document which gave rise to the Consumer Credit Act 1974. Apart from market failure, the report justifies provisions on consumer protection with: the social context difficulties for consumers in obtaining redress through 'lack of energy and initiative'; problems for those who lack the ability to budget and to manage their income, especially with regard to the indigent, who are peculiarly vulnerable to 'harsh and oppressive terms'.[203]

Unquestionable consumers of financial services need and expect to be protected by one of numerous legal mechanisms. In addition, there is no need to give any sophisticated explanation for the fact that this group of consumers is dearly particularly vulnerable, but also very diverse. Although, according to Wilhelmsson,[204] the mandatory regulations of inter alia consumer law are being justified in general with reference to the need to protect the weaker party, he notices a certain "trap", namely that the definition of the weaker party is formalized in a way that allows parties of the same class, who might be in fact in a stronger position, to take advantage of the protective provisions. In the same vein, Hartlief[205] stresses that consumers are protected via law as a category regardless of whether or not a certain person indeed is vulnerable in a certain legal relation and indeed needs this protection.

It is indisputable that consumer protection law – no matter how one classifies it, within which branch of law – has an interventionist character. However, when it comes to the aims of these legal regulations, a heated debate ensues. Some lawyers describe the aim of public intervention with 'market failures', claiming that these provisions intervene in the market in order to place the consumer in a better position than he would find himself without any intervention; others – with 'equity', i.e. distributive and corrective justice premises and public values. No objective measures probably exist to give an objective, unbiased answer to the issue sketched out above. Although the introduction of the consumer protection provisions to legal systems took place in the 1960s, the heated discussion is still ongoing and the questions posed above are still open to answer: On the one hand, what are the adequate

202 A. Schwartz, L.L. Wilde, "Intervening in Markets on the Basis of Imperfect Information: a Legal and Economic Analysis", University of Pennsylvania Law Review 1978-1979, Vol. 127: 630.

203 P. Cartwright in "Consumer Protection..., p. 13.

204 T. Wilhelmsson, "The Philosophy of Welfarism and its Emergence in the Modern Scandinavian Contract Law" in Ed. R. Brownsword, G. Howells, T. Wilhelmsson, "Welfarism in Contract Law", Dartmouth Publishing Company Limited, 1994, p. 91

205 T. Hartlief, "Freedom and Protection...

measures for efficient consumer protection, and, on the other – what are the adequate measures to maintain the proper functioning of the free market? And, furthermore, where are the limits for interfering in the market, or to draw up the issue from a different perspective - is it really beneficial for consumers to introduce or to keep these very high consumer protection standards? These problems require an adequate and effective solution: the Community legislator and academics attempt to do so by testing different methods and approaches, but so far the debate has not cooled down.

An ambiguous answer to the concerns about the boundaries of protective measures can be found in the Council's Resolution on Consumer Policy 1999 to 2001,[206] which declares that the choice of protective measures should be based (inter alia) on: the analysis of the objectives to be achieved; the potential costs and benefits of action or lack of action, and the developments on the market in order to make the best choice between different legislative and non-legislative solutions. According to the generally approved principle of proportionality, consumer measures should not be more restrictive than is necessary to achieve the accepted level of consumer protection. If one assumes that the internal market serves the consumers' interest (and according to, inter alia, Pelkmans[207] that this statement is true), then a conclusion can be drawn that protective measures which interfere in the free market may be necessary only where the market does not provide for a just equilibrium between business and consumers, because every protection involves costs.

The question as to how far should and can the state intervene in the economy, but also in lives of its citizens has been posed by many politicians, by varied leaders coming from very different backgrounds, representing different circles and view points, and finally by academics - representatives of various disciplines: lawyers, economists, sociologists, philosophers, etc. One could even dare to say that this problem poses one of the most frequently asked questions from the dawn of history. In the attempts to finding the unique perfect solution, one is always exposed to contradictions – that is, to the tension between advantages and disadvantages in the aftermaths of public intervention. Hence, consequently, the attempt to resolve the problem boils down again to the statement concerning principles that prevail in a discussion and the type of regime one favours.

In the literature, one can find views expressed by the purely liberally inclined writers who favour the stance that the parties to a contract should be left to their own devices, no matter how glaring the imbalance in their positions is. Others are poles apart, they emphasize the 'social' function of private law, and accept or favour the variety of restrictions of freedom of contract and the need for the courts to step in and protect the weaker party.[208]

---

206 O.J. 1999, C 206/1, recital 7.

207 Pelkmans, 'Consumer Interest in the EC Competition Regime. An Economic Perspective", in Goyens (Ed.), 'EC Competition Policy and the Consumer Interest' (Cabay Louvain-la-Neuve, 1985), p. 22-69.

208 See B. Markesinis, H. Unberath, A. Johnston, „The German Law of Contract. A Comparative Treatise", Oxford and Portland, Oregon, 2006.

State intervention has definitely the strong and undeniable capability to improve the economic welfare, and naturally also the welfare of consumers. However, by having this obviously positive effect, the intervention can go beyond a very thin line and then, instead of a welfare state, one obtains a social compulsion, and in fact the absolutist 'police' state as a final product: the state with a strong interference in the lives of its citizens. The trap of overregulation of citizens' lives is very imaginable and apparently plausible.

At this point one can start a discussion which poses a political-economic never-ending story of what overregulation signifies in reality, starting from big, loftily sounding "watchwords" like restricting individual freedoms and reducing individuals to a tiny part of state-run economic machine.[209] At the moment, it should not be ignored that the state associated with paternalistic and bureaucratic practices entails in the long-run a significant number of side effects, problems like de-skilling of individuals and cutting off their self-help potential which leads to perpetualisation of poverty,[210] - so in conclusion, such practices can bring about counter-productive affects. So is it as simple as that? Are there only two political alternatives: freedom or socialism? Is a society, in which socially secure individuals still experience their freedom imaginable at all?

In order to deliberate the title issue, one should first discuss what is understood under the notion of 'consumer'. Although the definition of 'consumer'[211] does not raise any fundamental disputes, still the entire construction of the subject is quite ambiguous. One can distinguish two major views on consumers, namely consumer as an 'economic actor' and as a 'political actor'.[212] Thus, simplifying, a legislator designs protective provisions either for the sake of an 'economic actor' i.e. a market player, a rational maximizer of his own utility who should bear the share of market risk on a par with his professional contractual partner; or for the sake of a 'political actor' who requires a state/Community to protect his safety interests.

The distinction outlined above suggests a few questions in the field of consumer credit. One can try to discuss the character of a goal the EU legislator is aiming at i.e. the protection of consumer interest, that is: should the legislator create the perfect condition for the variety of credit offered? Should he open the EU market for all credit providers, and consequently also for usury? Or inversely, should the legislator in a paternalistic way limit consumer choice by eliminating from the consumer credit market the most "dangerous" credit providers and at the same time limit consumer choice and what follows from it, i.e., the deprivation of a group of the poorest consumers without credit-worthiness of the possibility of being granted credit? One can reduce this issue to posing a question of whether or not consumers (natural

---

209 W. Eucken, "What Kind of Economic and Social System" in "Germany's Social Market Economy: Origins and Evolution", Ed. Alan Peacock and Hans Willgerodt, p. 35.

210 Steffen Mau, „The Moral Economy of Welfare States. Britain and Germany Compared.", EUI, Florence, 2002, p. 174.

211 See charter above.

212 The different meanings of the notion 'consumer' I discussed extensively in the chapter 'Internal Market and Consumer Protection'.

persons lacking special training and knowledge, with no further experience in business, applying for the credit maybe for the first time in their life) can be considered as the best judges of their own interest. If the answer to this question is a negative one, then again, all can be narrowed down to the discussion on the limits of state or community intervention: that is, how much intrusive intervention can market actors tolerate, how far, and how deep can paternalism reach within a citizens' life?

There is the alternative between granting unrestricted freedom to citizens in the economic sphere of their lives and between regulating, controlling and to a large degree restricting their room for free choice. This choice finds its expression in the two opposing trends existing on consumer markets since 1970s, namely liberalization and regulation. The major goal of liberalization is to foster greater competition and improve trade, and due to these outcomes, liberalization provides, in the end, better choice - hence it maximises economic profits for market players. On the other hand, regulation is usually considered to protect safety interests of market players by ensuring protection against different kinds of risk market actors encountered in the market place. However, although the two trends exist in tension, both of them share a common goal of improving consumer welfare. On the one hand, consumer advocates object to the abolition of tariff barriers to trade, and to setting free financial markets etc., since the completely free market, in their opinion, confronts consumers with potentially dangerous products and business practices from less regulated markets abroad. On the other hand, the advocates of liberalization strive for abolishing the majority of restrictions, as only then, in the conditions of market freedom, all the market actors (including consumers) can enjoy the benefits of healthy competition. The result is a difficult trade-off in which policy makers have to balance the costs and benefits of greater liberalization and greater protection.[213]

The discussion about the limits of the state's interference is a theoretical discussion about the welfare state, about consumer protection and the limits of the principal contract rule – freedom of contract. The economic and legal literature, as well as the world's history propose very different models of balancing the opposing notions, i.e. liberalization (freedom of contracts, thus no minimal or no public interference in the private law relationships between market actors), and regulation (i.e. when a state at the very most only partially respects freedom of contract and interferes in the private law relationships for the sake of changing the balance between the powers different actors enjoy). These models are linked to different models of contracts and are characterised by very different outcomes when it comes to the issue of distribution of wealth.

Brownsword[214] distinguishes three models of the above sketched 'balancing' and calls them Welfarism models. When the first model is applied - namely, Welfarism I - the state is to establish and maintain minimum conditions of non-interference. While individuals are left

213 See more: G. Trumbull, "Consumer Capitalism..., p. 22.

214 R. Brownsword, "The Philosophy of Welfarism"..., p. 30-31.

free to make their own decisions and in general to get on with their lives, some would succeed taking advantage of their skills, and others would fail. In case of Welfarism I, welfare may be distributed very unevenly, so as a result, prosperity would neighbour with poverty. The state is to guard the freedom of contract and to secure the minimal conditions of non-interference.

Welfarism II - second 'balancing' model - according to Brownsword, draws a line below which citizens must not be allowed to sink, however above the line free competition is left to operate. Welfarism II assumes that the state's task is not only to secure the minimum conditions of non-interference, but also the state should actively combat the negative side effects of functioning of the society like poverty, squalor etc. Brownsword cites Churchill's idea which expresses the sense of Welfarism II:

> "We want to draw a line below which we will not allow persons to live and labour, yet above which they may compete with all the strength of their manhood. We want to have free competition upwards; we decline to allow free competition to run downwards."[215]

According to the third of Brownsword's Welfarism models, the state prevents the situation in which some citizens reach the top of financial success, while others, at the same time, experience misery. Through an attempt to make the worse-off better off, Welfarism III causes a situation in which there are no obvious winners and losers.

Starting from the most liberal supporters of Welfarism I, according to Adam Smith,[216] the interest of the consumers are guaranteed most efficiently and comprehensively by the "invisible hand." The distribution function of the market as a provider also serves the consumer. Hence, the market can be defined as a consumer protection tool. If one assumes that only in the conditions of free competition and freedom of contract, market can properly fulfil its functions, then private autonomy is a sine qua non of the proper competition and as such should be protected by the legal system. Although according to Smith, one of the three functions of the State is a duty to protect the citizens from oppression, force, and fraud, and to make provisions for administering the system of justice to that end,[217] he states that there is a natural harmony between private and public interest in 'the system of natural freedom', whereas the interference with this system distorts the natural harmony in the interest of selected groups.[218]

---

215 W.S. Churchill, "Liberalism and the Social Problem", Hodder and Stoughton, 1909, London, p. 82.

216 J. Drexl, "Die wirtschaftliche Selbstbestimmung des Verbrauchers", Jus Privatum, Beiträge zum Privatrecht", Band 31, Mohr Siebeck, Tübingen, 1998, p. 94.

217 P.S. Atiyah, The Rise and Fall of the Freedom of Contract, Oxford 1979, p. 302.

218 Ibid., p. 299.

Also Hayek[219] extols the efficiency of the spontaneous order in the market. According to this author, the market, having an inherent capacity for self-correction, will deliver outcomes superior to a programme of public intervention, so consequently he criticizes state intervention for adjusting the operation of the market in the (alleged) public interest. To explain his reluctance towards the State-run activities, Hayek refers to the problem of a lack or a shortage of the right information on the side of a legislator in comparison to the market choices. Finally, Hayek accuses these few who enjoying transient power introduce state intervention of wresting extra benefits for themselves at the expense of the whole society. This view is strongly related to the idea of constitutional protection from state interference granted to individual freedoms in the market and in society.

The idea of supporting economic freedom as a means to reach a common welfare was developed later on by two authors, Tesón and Klick.[220] According to them, the philosophers (a collective qualification of the believers in the philosophical literature on global justice) and the advocates (believers in the literature on socio-economic rights) ignore and even sometimes reject the crucial fact that, generally, free trade actually helps the poor; free trade is an effective tool in the fight against poverty. Tesón and Klick believe that free movement of goods, services, and persons will go a long way toward alleviating world poverty, so as a consequence they state that any theory of global justice should encourage and promote the establishment of free trade. They point out a certain misperception that often shifts the discussion about the effects of trade imperceptibly from the question of whether trade helps the poor to the question of whether trade increases or reduces inequality. Consequently, such an approach may lead to over-protection, thus may hamper the chances for the poor to participate in the market. Now, if one understands free trade in the field of consumer credit as opening the national markets to all credit providers, then, following Tesón and Klick's reasoning, such an opening should be supported by defenders of the welfare state and of laissez-faire economics alike, as a factor "stimulating growth and making public expenditures, on social programmes and similar schemes, to alleviate the plight of the poor." And this is again very much in line with the EU legislator reasoning, since in the new consumer credit Directive it was decided not to restrict the consumer credit market, and to keep it open to different service providers, including predatory lenders.

Also in line with the recent EU legislator's move is Straetmans'[221] thesis, according to which, the only right which a consumer can claim is to choose freely on the market.

---

219 Hayek, „Law, Legislation and Liberty", Routledge and Kegan Paul, 1973, 1976, 1979 in G. Howells, S. Weatherill, "Consumer Protection Law", Ashgate, 2005, p. 78.

220 Fernando R. Tesón, Jonathan Klick, „Global Justice and Trade: A Surprising Omission". Available at: http://works.bepress.com/cgi/viewcontent.cgi?article=1000&context=jonathan_klick.

221 G. Straetmans ph.d. thesis defended at the Katholieke Universiteit Leuven in 1998: Consument en market: onderzoek naar de rechtspositie van de consument op de Europese interne markt (Kluwer, Studiecentrum voor Consumentenrecht, Deurne, 1998). In J. Stuyck, 'European Consumer Law after the Treaty of Amsterdam...

Straetmans claims that the interests of business and consumers often go together, and furthermore that market stability is guarded by market self-regulatory forces and it benefits all market actors. Thus, the only way to achieve a better level of consumer protection is through information duty.

The other voice of the advocate of unlimited contract freedom comes from Sir Jessel MR in the case Printing and Numerical Registering Co. v. Sampson,[222] who forewarns of declaring that a certain contract is void, as he requires that "men of full age and competent understanding shall have the utmost liberty of contracting and that their contracts, when entered into freely and voluntarily, shall be held sacred and shall be enforced by Courts of Justice".

K. Zweigert and H. Koetz[223] join the believers of an unlimited contract freedom. They emphasize that liberalism, although strongly criticized these days, "was a great emancipator which unleashed an astonishing amount of creativity." What is very often forgotten is that the freedom of contract not always had its place among the general principles of a given legal system. The authors have in mind extended periods of society evolution when an individual's rights and duties were determined by his birth etc. As a consequence, when one focuses on contract law from such a historical perspective, one can easily find the answers to the question: why, or more precisely, on what grounds contracts are nowadays granted with the legally binding force. So the aim of the present contract law is to protect the freedom and the capacity of self-determination of any individual, so that until the limits determined by the infringement of the freedom of others, one can act without constraint, prescription, governmental or social pressure.

Nowadays, the neo-classical approach, which reflects ideas included in Brownsword's Welfarism II, assumes that there is no need for government intervention in case the adequately informed consumers and in case no substantial market failure exists. Extolling consumer sovereignty, they consequently reject any manifestations of paternalism.[224] Certainly, this approach is shared by the EU legislator, which is clearly shown by the example of the new consumer credit Directive which introduces – as the main tool of consumer protection – information disclosure duties, and at the same time, attempts to keep consumer financial markets open to all kinds of service providers, and free from nearly any coercion.

At the opposite pole is Brownsword's Welfarism III which assumes a strong public authority intervention in the market in order to level the society economically. Here, however, one cannot limit the discussion only to strict market issues nor merely to the problem referring to limitation of the freedom of contract. One cannot possibly disregard the problem of

---

222 G. Jessel MR in Printing and Numerical Registering Co. v. Sampson (1875) LR 19 Eq. 462, 465cited in K. Zweigert, H. Koetz, "Introduction to Comparative Law", Clarendon Press, Oxford 1998, p. 325.

223 K. Zweigert, H. Koetz, "Introduction to Comparative Law", Clarendon Press, Oxford 1998, p. 325

224 I. Ramsay, "Consumer Law and Policy: Text and Materials on Regulating Consumer Markets", Hart Publishing, 2007, p. 78.

limitation of individual freedoms the Welfarism III must entail. Hence, the discussion as regards Welfarism III must be considered on two levels: 1) on the market platform (i.e. violations of the contract law principles) and, 2) on an individual freedoms level (i.e. violation of personal autonomy).

Individual Freedoms v. State Intervention

Whereas, the Brownsword's Welfarism model refers mainly to the relation between public authorities - public regulation versus the freedom of the individual actors to make their sovereign choices in respect to contract law relationships - Freinberg,[225] however, identifies four ways of treating the relationship between personal autonomy and personal good. The first way, advocated by paternalists, derives the right of self-determination entirely from its conductibility to a person's own good. The supporters of this approach deny that the right to self-government is ultimate, basic or natural. They see it as entirely derivative and instrumental, so consequently a person is allowed to exercise a right to self-determination only because, and insofar as, it promotes his good to do so. As a result, state intervention can operate against the will of a person (every citizen, even those competent and fully conscious) acting fully voluntary in order to protect him from harmful consequences of his choices. Such an approach poses a danger of authoritarian imposition of others' preferences regarding the collective or individual good.

The second view assumes that any harm a person might do to his own good taking the advantage of his free choice in a foolish manner "would in every case necessarily be outweighed by the greater harm done by outside interference and direction."

According to the third view, personal autonomy prevails as a non-derivative and morally basic right, more important than personal well-being and consequently, even if a person is likely to harm his own good, others have no right to intervene. So legal intervention can be exercised only to prevent a person from making choices harmful for his own good in a substantially non-voluntary manner.

According to the fourth (compromise) view there is a coordination between personal autonomy and personal good/self-fulfilment without gradation or superiority between them. Consequently, most of the cases allowing a person to make his own choices, deliver the best value for the person's own good. Freiberg notices that whereas the third view is definitely hostile towards paternalistic intervention, the first as well as the fourth views are most attractive to the paternalist.

There are many different definitions of paternalism. Hartlief[226] defines paternalism as a situation where legislators in the contractual relations assume to know better than the par-

225 J. Freinberg, „Harm to Self", 1986, p. 58 in M.J. Trebilcock, "The Limits of Freedom of Contract", Harvard University Press, 1993, p. 148.

226 T. Hartlief, "Freedom and Protection...

ties themselves what is more favourable for them. In the literature, two manifestations of paternalism are distinguished: 1) the situations where intervention accords with an individual's real preferences, in case they are blocked, and 2) the situations where public authority overrules the real preferences of a person. However, even in the second group the substitution of governmental judgments for the judgments of an individual can be in some instances justified - i.e. certain individuals may wish to be protected from themselves ('rational paternalism').[227] Trebilcock[228] poses a question of whether or not "exchanges which appear to reflect parties' present preferences are really in their own best interests" and, "whether the collectivity through its legal instrumentalities is entitled to substitute its judgments for those of the individuals involved."

Dworkin,[229] however, perceives paternalism from a quite different perspective. On the one hand, similar to the foregoing views, under the notion of paternalism he understands the interference with a person's liberty of action, on the other, the author emphasises the role of justifications, namely - the state's interference is justified by reasons referring *exclusively* to the welfare, good, happiness, needs, interests or values of the person being coerced, community values and, finally, distributive justice, ensuring that for those who are the most vulnerable in the society, a particular protection is granted. Similarly, the distribution of the resources can be based on what is just, rather than what is economically efficient. For Ogus,[230] paternalism is an ideological issue concerning the balance between distributive justice and market efficiency.

Paternalism assumes a variety of very different forms. Through history, there have been many types of paternalism which were seriously warped. The other extreme, as far as state intervention is concerned, was the experience of the centrally-planed economies. In the considerations about freedom understood both as an economic right (being part of the contract law), as well as the right of the individuals to self-determination, and about the factors which threaten this freedom, one cannot ignore the rise of the ninetieth century communistic ideas and consequently, the twentieth century transformation of the state, which caused the fact that the control of the modern industrialized economy became a state's domain.[231] Those new trends posed a consistent reply as a reaction to the reality at the time, particularly to the distorted capitalistic relationships, which in theory were characterised by the freedom of contract, in practice, however, they were based on 'jungle rights', as the parties had nothing but an equal bargaining position. This was followed by the central power authorities coming into being and causing the threat to crush the individual persons. The effect was that everything became decided, recorded, checked and officially supervised by the state de-

227 I. Ramsay, "Consumer Law and Policy..., p. 100.

228 M.J. Trebilcock, "The Limits of Freedom..., p. 147.

229 R. Dworkin, 'Paternalism', in R. Wasserstrom (ed.), 'Morality and the Law', Wadsworth, 1971, p. 108.

230 A. Ogus, 'Regulation: Legal Form and Economic Theory', Clarendon Press, 1994, p. 46.

231 W. Eucken, "What Kind of Economic and Social System" in "Germany's Social Market Economy: Origins and Evolution" Ed. A. Peacock and H. Willgerodt, p. 35.

partments. Since the state managed to spread its control over the entire economic life of a person (thanks to the combination of economic and political power), an individual became "a tiny part in the anonymous, state-run economic machine"; an object deprived of his character as a person. Finally, Eucken[232] asks whether it is possible to preserve the freedom of the individual in the industrialized economy. The question – to simplify – can be boiled down to the problem of finding an economic system in which individuals are more than just a tiny part of the machine.

On the other hand, Freinberg's[233] second view regarding the harm of public intervention in individual autonomy is fully supported by Mill.[234] The latter stated directly his reluctance towards any restrictions of men's freedom:

> "His own good, either physical or moral, is not a sufficient warrant [for invading his liberty]. He cannot be rightfully compelled to do or forebear because it will be better for him to do so, because it will make him happier, because in the opinion of others, to do so would be wise ... these are good reasons for remonstrating him, or reasoning with him, or persuading him, or entreating him, but not for compelling him or visiting him with any evil case he do therwise."

The contemporary author, Van den Bergh,[235] also represents Freinberg's[236] second view, while discussing the disadvantages of public intervention in the form of consumer protection regulations. Justifying his reluctance towards consumer law, the author indicates that protectionist provisions are based on the assumption that a consumer is a person not really able to make an adequate judgment and, consequently, such an assumption allows the legislator to act as a "benevolent dictator" who has a better knowledge than the consumer of what is to the benefit for him, and what unquestionably clashes with the principle of consumer sovereignty, and I would add, that also clashes in a way, with a general notion of human dignity.

In a similar view, Ramsey[237] warns that paternalism is "a slippery" rationale for intervention in the market, as this ideology assumes the general distrust that individuals are capable of acting rationally, and of evaluating provided information. Finally, it assumes that the authorities would secure well-being for individuals much better than the individuals would have done if otherwise acting independently. Additionally, one may encounter difficulties in drawing a borderline between cases where the justification of the authorities' intervention is an appeal to real preferences of an individual, and those cases where authorities overrule these real preferences, substituting them by their own choices. According to Ramsey, only the latter fits the notion of 'paternalism'.

---

232 Ibid.

233 J. Freinberg, „Harm to Self", 1986, p. 58 in M.J. Trebilcock, "The Limits of Freedom..., p. 148.

234 J.S. Mill, "On Liberty", 1956, 13.

235 R. Van den Bergh, „Economische analyse van het consumentenrecht", Ars Aequi, 39 (10), 1990, 787-793 in T. Hartlief, "Freedom and Protection...

236 J. Freinberg, „Harm to...,p. 58.

237 I. Ramsey, "Framework for Regulation...

There are a substantial number of advocates of Freinberg's[238] third view, which assumes that individual autonomy is an original human right and as such should be left free from any coercion even though legal intervention is considered acceptable in certain circumstances.

First and foremost, it is deeply ingrained in the theory of natural rights which describes the certain universal objective rights as not being contingent upon the laws, customs, or beliefs of a particular society, but deriving from the nature of man. The theory introduced initially by the Stoics of Late Antiquity, was then taken over by subsequent philosophers, inter alia Grotius, etc. and followed by the precursors of social contract thought – which tries to explain the ways in which people form nations and maintain social order by giving up some rights to an authority in order to receive or maintain social order. In other words, social contract idea assumes that legitimate state authority must be derived from the consent of the governed citizens.

Hobbes - who as a first modern philosopher articulated in the 17th century a detailed contract theory with its 'social contract' idea – claimed that the 'social contract' is a result in fact of a pragmatic self-interest. He presented a process of forming a contemporary society according to which, the individuals in a state of nature ceded their individual rights to create state sovereignty, in return for their protection.

Later on, Hobbes's successor, Locke argued that persons in a state of nature would willingly come together to form a state i.e. that individuals would agree to form a state that would provide a "neutral judge", and that could therefore protect the lives, liberty, and material possessions of those who lived within it. The conclusion that Lock drew thereof is that state laws could only be legitimate if they sought to achieve the common good.

Rousseau continuing the divagations about the status of the legal provisions in society stated that law, provided that it is voted by the people's representatives, is not a limitation of individual freedom, but its expression. The same is true for the enforcement of law which is not a restriction on individual liberty, since the individual explicitly agreed to be constrained if, as a private individual, he did not respect his own will as formulated in the general will.

This is very much in line with the views represented by 'social liberalism' or 'social justice liberalism' which values political freedom and assumes that the state should as far as possible leave individuals alone to make their own decisions on how to live their lives, but at the same time it further advocates that liberalism requires a commitment to a fair distribution of wealth and power, which in turn leads to support for redistributive taxation and public services as ways of fairly distributing wealth and for democracy as a way of fairly distributing power.[239] Fairness – in 'social liberalism', according to Howarth - can be seen both as a

---

238 J. Freinberg, „Harm to Self", 1986, p. 58 in M.J. Trebilcock, "The Limits of Freedom..., p. 148.

239 D. Howarth, "What is Social Liberalism?" in D. Brack, R. S. Grayson, D. Howarth eds, Reinventing the State: Social Liberalism for the 21st Century, 2007, Politico's Publishing.

condition for the legitimacy of the state itself (the characteristic 'social contract' view) and as a condition for meaningful freedom.

Having said that, one can conclude that according to the views presented above - all the tools applied by the legislator in order to intervene in the consumer credit market should be scanned on the background of the estimation of whether the society can afford the long-term costs which they bear, and whether the legislator's activity is necessarily directed to reaching the common good.

In the literature, there are many more moderate voices of the authors who are trying to find a balance between these two extremes (i.e. liberalism characterized by Welfarism I, which excludes almost any public intervention, and centrally steered economy which can assume a face of paternalism or a 'police' state). These are 'social-oriented' writers supporting the ideology of providing the weaker party with a certain amount of protectionist provisions in order to establish the equilibrium between parties to the contract, however, at the same time, they are cautious of interfering in principle individual freedoms. Wakley[240] stresses the problem with a telling question: "What was the Legislature for if it was not to protect the weak against the strong?" In a similar vein, Goodin speaks of "moral collectivism" which represents a duty for society, that is, a peculiar 'national debt', to alleviate the negative consequences of poverty.

According to Howells and Weatherill,[241] the participation of the State in private law is not controversial anymore. However, the modern debate concerns "the appropriate intensity of state participation in the economy and in society." Howells and Weatherill stress that state intervention can be perceived as hostile to individual freedom – a clear example of the unquestionable superiority of the Western free market over the Eastern State-run economies. However, it is not only about pure economic efficiency; minimal state intervention is identified with individual rights and democratic freedom.

In Wilhelmsson's[242] description of the Welfare State, this notion includes a combination of a belief in market forces and in private enterprise, as the instruments required creating the conditions of welfare, and at the same time a further believe in the state's intervention in the market forces in order to secure goals connected with redistribution and social security. For Wilhelmsson, the Welfare State balances continuously between market-oriented efficiency and solidarity-based interventions of the state. At the same time, Wilhelmsson perceives that there is an open question about the areas and the means of this intervention.

---

240 R. Wakley, Speech on the Ten Hour Bill. Hansard's Parliamentary Debate. House of Commons. 3d ser., 86: 1045-50 in R. E. Goodin, "Protecting the Vulnerable. A Reanalysing of Our Social Responsibilies", The University of Chicago Press, Chicago 1985.

241 G. Howells, S. Weatherill, "Consumer Protection Law", Ashgate, 2005, p. 4.

242 T. Wilhelmsson, "The Philosophy of Welfarism and its Emergence in the Modern Scandinavian Contract Law" in Ed. R. Brownsword, G. Howells, T. Wilhelmsson, "Welfarism in Contract Law", Dartmouth Publishing Company Limited, 1994, p. 67.

In the same vein, Collins[243] draws a clear distinction between contract law being an inherent element of the market economy and the Welfare State which comes into being as a result of "a partial loss of faith in the market mechanism as the institutional techniques for achieving social goals." In the Welfare States, market mechanisms are being replaced by regulatory controls and bureaucratic administration whose purpose is to eliminate phenomenons like poverty, hunger, homelessness, etc. without, however, challenging the proper functioning of the market. The Welfare State by redistributing wealth relies on the market outcomes, but at the same time enables worse off citizens to participate in this market. At the same time, Collins observes a certain fact: "when lawyers try to control the contents of contracts, the law begins to go against the current of market forces."

Scheiber[244] represents similar views. He draws a picture of the evolution of economic liberty. He remarks that the ideas of economic liberty and the logic and rhetoric of the freedom of contract has been exploited by both: the liberal thinkers supporting economic individualism as well as the defenders of state intervention, in the discussion on "negative" as well as "positive liberty." "Positive liberty" - defined by Scheiber – justifies states' interventions by stating that (inter alia) regulatory regimes and redistributive social programmes etc. are necessary instruments which reconcile social realities with primary ideas of contract law. Scheiber stresses that advocates of the "positive liberty" sought to link interventionist objectives with freedom of contract, and with economic liberty.

As E. Posner[245] has rightly pointed out, the state has two commitments: 1) maintaining a free market (thus e.g. enforcing property rights and contracts) and, 2) preventing all citizens from falling behind a minimum welfare level. After a long and in-depth reasoning, he concludes that "laws restricting freedom of contract are best understood as a legal mechanism for restricting the extension of credit to high-risk borrowers, particularly the poor, and that this policy is broadly consistent with the goal of marinating the welfare system within a free market." Consequently Posner remarks that the support of the policy of poverty reduction through the welfare system goes perfectly along with the support for restrictive contract law.

Already in the field of consumer credit, F. Figueira doubts whether the market can function properly if consumers do not know how to make the best choices; if they do not understand financial services. If one makes an assumption that markets depend on the ability of consumers to play their role by making informed choices between different products, then can one talk at all about market equilibrium? This is especially problematic – according to F.

243 H. Collins, "Disclosure of Information and Welfarism" in Ed. R. Brownsword, G. Howells, T. Wilhelmsson, "Welfarism in Contract Law", Dartmouth Publishing Company Limited, 1994 p. 102.

244 H.N. Scheiber, "Economic Liberty and the Modern State" in Ed. H.N. Scheiber, "The State and Freedom of Contract", Stanford, California, 1998, p. 123.

245 E. Posner, "Contract Law in the Welfare State: a Defense of the Unconscionability Doctrine, Usury Laws, and Related Limitations on the Freedom to Contract", Journal of Legal Studies, vol. XXIV (June 1995).

Figueira[246] - at a time when people depend more and more on financial services to maintain their lifestyle, as the responsibility for financial decisions is shifted away from the government, to individuals.

In the discussion of the state's intervention, one cannot ignore the famous German example for a reconciliation of seemingly contradictory interests in the history of economy, an example of a success in finding the right balance between state and private realms, namely 'social market economy' ('soziale Marktwirtschaft'), where the structural elements were based on the fundaments of capitalism (private ownership of the means of production, free-enterprise, initiative for the entrepreneur, unrestricted competition) and, on the other hand where a certain degree of social stability was guaranteed.[247] Erhard, based on the mixture of the neo-liberal and Keynesian economics, as well as the liberal, social and political theories and the Catholic social teachings and finally the tradition of local self-government, managed to create a free-market economy developed on the basis of a centrally planned system for the satisfaction of critical social needs; and Karl Schiller's 'Marketbeeinflussung' meant state intervention in the market, which was not however state control of the market.

The philosophy which stood behind this economic model was ordoliberalism, defined by Joerges and Rödl[248] as the solution for the complex problem of how to maintain a stable liberal market economy, to guarantee its inherent individual freedoms and to avoid both, "market failures" and "state failures." Ordoliberalism was based on a legal regime which had to guarantee private contract autonomy, and individual property rights etc. Thus, it acknowledged the state's important function in ordering the economic sphere, and transformed the liberal idea of state intervention in itself into state intervention, being a fundamental element of the institutional reality.

Müller-Armack[249] understands ordoliberalism as a combination of the principles of market freedom with the principles of social balance. The author stresses the beneficial function of the economy based on ordoliberal principles for the consumers whose needs and interests it is able to satisfy. However, the crucial difference between "social market economy" and mixed economies with elements of planning were not social goals, but the instruments which were applied to achieve those goals, since in Müller-Armack's model, all social state policies were subordinated to the functionality of market mechanism.

Joerges and Rödl[250] object to a statement that the "social market economy" is equivalent to the 'social state' and is fully adequate to express the desired fundamental social

---

246 F. Figueira, "The European Commission and Financial Capability: Simplifying Financial Services", ECRI Policy Brief No. 2/July 2007.

247 R.A. Isaak, "European Politics. Political Economy and Policy Making In Western Democracies", St. Martin's Press, NY, 1980, p. 44.

248 Ch. Joerges, F. Rödl, '"Social Market Economy...

249 Müller-Armack, "Soziale Marktwirtschaft" in v. Beckerath et al., Handwörterbuch der Sozialewisseln-schaften, Vol. 9 (1956) in Ch. Joerges, F. Rödl, '"Social Market Economy...

250 Ch. Joerges, F. Rödl, '"Social Market Economy...

character of the future European Union. They invoke the German constitutional literature, according to which, the 'social market economy' is defined as an approach to fulfil the task of the German state to perform as a 'social state'. It has been argued, though it is not indisputable, that the 'social market economy' is the only approach which does not conflict with the fundamental rights of the German constitution, like freedom of contract or guarantee of property rights. According to other scholars[251] the idea of 'social state' is explained by the state's task to intervene into the sphere of society with social aims.

Drexl,[252] who can be rated among ordoliberal thinkers, proves that consumer protection can go in line with a free and social market. The author makes different assumptions: not a presumed social inferiority of the position of a consumer, but the identification of specific situations where a consumer's self-determination, which is based on private autonomy and competition, is affected. The application of the specific consumer measures is conceivable in circumstances when the basic principles of freedom and competition fail in guaranteeing the consumer's self-determination, then however, the principle of proportionality determines the intensity of these measures i.e. they should not be more restrictive of personal freedom than is necessary to achieve the required level of consumer protection.

Contract Law v. State Intervention

In discussing the two goals of consumer credit regulations (i.e. curing the market failure and distributional goal), at the same time, Ramsay[253] touches upon the other problem, that is: "(r)ecognition of the distributional role of the law in constituting the credit market, and affecting market values, undermines the distinction between the supposedly private, natural and non-political world of the market and the public world of politics and state activity." The goal of introducing a consumer credit law was to reshape the paradigms of consumer credit contracts law, and to change the balance of power of that market, i.e. moving the market from a credit providers' to a consumers' market. In line with the above-mentioned goal, the idea was to protect low-income and disadvantaged consumers and to redistribute power and resources generally from creditors to consumers.

The main assumption of the classic contract law theory is that contracts are institutions based on competition, and all the means adopted by legal systems, which aim at protecting one party of the contract against the other, can be perceived as a threat to the core idea of

251 See e.g.: K. Hesse, „Grundzuge des Verfassungsrechts der Bundersrepublik Deutschland", 20th edition, Heidelberg, C.F. Muller Verlag, 1995, para. 209 ff.

252 J. Drexl, Habilitationschrift, Publisher with the title Die wirtschaftliche Selbstbestimmung des Verbrauchers., Tübingen, J.C.B. Mohr, 1998. In J. Stuyck, 'European Consumer Law after the Treaty of Amsterdam...

253 I. Ramsay, "Consumer Credit Law, Distributive ...

contract law. Stuyck[254] asks whether consumers should be protected by specific measures which depart from the fundamental principles of private law.

In Brownsword's[255] models of contracts, built on the base of the three models of Welfarism, Contract I resembles the above description. It relates to Welfarism I,[256] and as such complies with the theory of the classical model of contract in which contract is the outcome of the free agreement of parties who are motivated merely by self-interest, so the law is only required to establish the proper rules equal for every party which allow such a self-interested, free from coercive interference, competitive dealing to take place. Smits[257] calls it: contract law governed by the old principles, i.e. by the 'morality of trade', which means that a party to such a contract only takes care of satisfying his own interests.

One can position Brownsword's[258] Contract II, as one step further, related to Welfarism II, which resembles the above described transaction, however, in the case of Contract II, the free competition must run only upwards not downwards. In other words, the parties to the contract should be protected against outcomes which threaten to push them below the Plimsoll line – an expression borrowed from the maritime vocabulary. The Contract II idea assumes some intervention of public authority, e.g. protection of those who are not even minimally prepared for the contract competition, or who are in general, vulnerable.

Next, the Contract III in Brownsword's[259] division assumes that parties should deal with each other from roughly equal positions. It follows from this that the state should provide a contract law which can compensate for the lack of an equalising agency. This reflects a rather common view on the role of consumer protection and state's interference in freedom of contracts.

The second type of contract, according to Smits' division (Smits distinguishes only 2 types of contracts),[260] poses contract law governed by the "morality of the welfare state" which is no longer about making profit, but the goal of such a contract is to facilitate "living, working, life and health." This type of contract fulfils a description of, again, Brownsword's[261] Contract IV. First of all, the Contract IV idea does not state that a contract is the outcome of self-interested competitive transaction - inversely by striking a contract, a party weighs his own interests equally with the interest of the other party. Thus, this type of contract represents a concept very remote from what is classically perceived as a contract, namely in place

254 J. Stuyck, 'European Consumer Law after the Treaty of Amsterdam...

255 R. Brownsword, "The Philosophy of Welfarism" ..., p. 36

256 See above.

257 J. Smith, „Towards a multi-layered contract law for Europe", in S. Grundmann and J. Stuyck "An academic green paper on European contract law", The Hague 2002, p. 391.

258 R. Brownsword, "The Philosophy of Welfarism"..., p. 36.

259 Ibid.

260 J. Smith, „Towards a multi-layered contract law..., p. 391.

261 R. Brownsword, "The Philosophy of Welfarism" ..., p. 36.

of competition there is an other-regarding cooperative business, a joint-venture. Hartlief[262] also takes note of this new tendency in the evolution of the case law in the Netherlands. He observes a new guiding principle in the case law, according to which the parties to the contract have to take into account not only their own interests, but moreover the legitimate interests of the other party. Hartlief explains this new phenomenon as duties of care which derive from the principles of good faith and fair dealing, as the obligation to inform, to warn the opposite party or even to investigate whether the other party is aware of his activity. Consequently, such 'altruism' means that the duty to take care of the other party seems to have priority over the duty to take the responsibility for the party's own acts. At the same time, the author sees a menace in such a distinction (i.e. a distinction on contracts governed by self-interests and those governed by duty of care), since according to him, a major part of the contracts would have to belong to the second type – contract ruled by the "morality of the welfare state" principle. He also stresses that the result of consumerist legislation is the fall of the ancient principle *pacta sunt servanta*, since nowadays one can end the contract without having a good justified reason for doing so.

In the literature, there are positions which confirm that contract law, and thereby relationships on the market, do not necessarily have to be based on pure competition. For instance, Whitman[263] rejects the popular perception of the conflict between "consumerism" and "producerism" as the conflict between two different classes of real existing persons, with two different conflicting sets of interests. Whitman explains his criticism by stating that all productive members of the society are both "consumers" and "producers." In this way, he gives an example of a worker - being once a producer and once a consumer.

Undoubtedly, contract law is still at present, and also in the relatively near future will be governed by the dogmas of competition. In addition, there will be always advocates of the pure freedom of contract. One can, however, ask the question as to whether a contract - in which one party has a significantly weaker position – is still a competitive contract. Is it a competitive contract and is the principle of freedom of contract preserved in the case in which business power replaces consumers' sovereignty, like in certain sectors of the modern consumer economy, where business and more specifically, large corporations, have managed to gain power over the market. The other question following from that is whether the market actually responds to individual preferences by offering its customers what they want to obtain. Furthermore, is not it true that – as Galbraith[264] claims - the major goal of private producers is to sustain continued demand for the new forms of private consumption, often at the expense of the provision of public services. Hence, it seems that certain ingrained principles of market mechanisms have been already violated without the public authority intervention.

---

262 T. Hartlief, "Freedom and Protection...

263 James Q. Whitman, "Consumerism versus Producerism...

264 J.K. Galbraith in I. Ramsay, "Consumer Law and Policy..., p. 34.

For Atiyah,[265] protective consumer credit legislation is a picturesque example of a state's interference with the freedom of contract. Such interference, however, does not in reality harm that freedom of contract. The author gives an example of information duty or cooling-off provisions, which serve to ensure that the consumer concludes the contract with a full understanding of its content, and with an awareness of the seriousness of the obligation, and can be paradoxically perceived as an aid to the competitive market.

According to Atiyah,[266] the proposition that a party who enters a contract is the best judge of his own interest is a good starting-point for laws and institutional arrangements, but at the same time it does not square with human experience. Similarly, it is often repeated that preventing a person, even in his own interest, from entering a certain contract poses a questioning of his moral autonomy. Nevertheless, a grossly unfair contract secured for a professional at the expense of a vulnerable person unaware of the seriousness of his obligation can have only very negative consequences, thus should not be accepted by the legal order.

The principle of freedom of contract, or speaking widely, the principle of 'the purity' of contract law is not, or should not, stand for an idea per se; an idea in its own right, in isolation from the social-economic reality. This principle should have rather utilitarian meaning. The law itself should serve the society, and should not be only a hollow collection of watchwords. The historical experience shows that it is feasible to reconcile paternalistic interference with the free contract principle. There should be no tension between the freely operating market and the Welfarism's ideas.

There is a question as to whether a contract is an outcome of a self-interested competitive activity or an outcome of "a transaction in which both sides have weighted their own interests equally with the interests of the other side" - a transaction which is "an other-regarding cooperative business; an instrument of social solidarity, representing a joint venture, with both sides concerned that their contract should genuinely further one another's interest".[267] The second description means that a contact consists of both respect and concern as each of the parties has their own goals when entering the contract, and these goals have to be respected, but at the same time each party is also concerned with promoting the other's interests, provided that this is compatible with one's own interest in the contract.[268]

The market cannot be a zero-sum game, in which one player gains exactly what the other player loses, in other words, the situation where there is no cooperation between players is not positive and does not guarantee long-term profits for any of the competing

265 P.S. Atiyah, "Freedom of Contract and the New Right" in P.S. Atiyah, "Essays on Contract", Clarendon Press, Oxford, 1986, p. 358.

266 P.S. Atiyah, "The Liberal Theory of Contract" in P.S. Atiyah, "Essays on Contract", Clarendon Press, Oxford, 1986, p. 148.

267 R. Brownsword, "The Philosophy of Welfarism...,p. 36.

268 Ibid., p. 37.

parties. The market should be a variable-sum game whereby cooperating players can gain more than either could gain by staying by himself.

However, since these theoretical ideas are still very far from what one can encounter in the every day market relationship, at least the legislators should not feel prevented from introducing provisions which would restore the right balance, i.e. which would level the bargaining position of a consumer with the bargaining position of the professional.

Costs of Intervention v. Costs of Lack of Intervention

Michael Pertschuk,[269] former Chair of the US Federal Trade Commission and a consumer advocate noticed: "Economists are very good indeed at framing questions that lawyers and consumer advocates have not asked. (...) They ask, 'What do you think you are accomplishing with this rule? Who will benefit, who will pay? What else will happen as a result of this rule; who among competitors will be the winners and who the losers? In curing this marketplace failure, what others may you inadvertently cause, and what healthy market signals will you distort? Is there a less intrusive, less costly way to remedy the problem?"

And these are the questions which are being very often passed over in the discussions about consumer protection regulations. Various legislators, including that of the EU, hang in the balance of the arguments of the business side and the argument of the consumer advocates, however, what is very often missing is an honest, decent scrutiny and calculation of the pros and cons of introducing consumer protection regulations. Since every legal provision entails certain side effects, the duty of a legislator is to take such side effects into consideration in the process of making legislative decisions. Sometimes designing a new legislation piece resembles the struggle between the arguments of two opposing parties having mutually exclusive interests and a legislator, occupying the chair of a judge, tries to somehow balance these opposing arguments in order to, at least partially, satisfy both parties' demand. Then, like in a court, what is known from practice, often the arguments which prevail are those of the party who is simply stronger, or who has better lawyers, or whose voice is better audible. Whereas a legislator should have a global view; he should make his own estimation, by taking into account a long-term perspective and long-term development, since the outcomes which for both parties may seem to be beneficial *hic et nunc*, can bring for the whole society a substantial harm in the long-run. Finally, not all parties have sufficient means to loudly express their positions – the power of consumer organisation is understandably relatively weak, especially when compared to the business side – which was forcibly perceivable in the discussion during the process of designing the new shape of the consumer credit regulation. In this respect, perhaps the EU legislator should step down from his comfortable pedestal and less superficially take into consideration the interests of consumers. The EU legislator, instead of focusing on striking a balance between internal market

269 Cited by: I. Ramsay, "Consumer Law and Policy...

(market efficiency) and consumer protection, should take into account all side effects and costs of introducing a new regulation. And this is not a 'neo-liberal' discourse aiming at proving how much cost consumer protection provisions entail, even though none can deny this. On the contrary, actually a lack of consumer protection in a long-term (and this is also what should be of great interest to the legislator) costs even more, and this is currently not really being adequately analysed.

An appeal to take into account the costs of intervention is stressed very often in the literature. Trumbull talks about a difficult trade-off in which policy makers have to balance the costs and benefits of greater liberalization and greater protection.[270] Already mentioned above Schwartz and Wilde[271] express the necessity for a legislator to compare the welfare gains which is moving a market closer to the competitive outcome due to an intervention with the administrative costs to the state and the costs to the firms of compliance with the newly introduced legal requirement, since only then is the intervention "efficient" that is, in the case where the economic benefits outweigh the economic costs. Ramsey[272] urges the legislator to consider also the impact of intervening on the behaviour of those affected.

The issue which seems to be very often neglected or passed over is the fact that actually protection involved economic costs. This is a pragmatic, though very strong argument, although totally devoid of any ideology, which supports the liberal idea of letting the market function naturally; that is, one has to keep in mind that when a legislator introduces protective provisions, there must be also someone who bears the costs. This is a real public cost. First and foremost, protective requirements undeniably cause an increase in costs for producers and service providers and then the natural market consequence is an increase in prices for goods and services; and secondly, consumers are treated as a homogenous group where each member of the group is perceived as an inexperienced and vulnerable individual, hence, in effect every consumer has to pay a higher price. So the legislator should keep in mind that when attempting to change economic relations by restoring a balance, the consumer will be the one to pay for such a change. Thereby, for example Pelkmans states that protective regulations, interfering in the market mechanism can be justified only in case the market itself does not provide a just equilibrium between consumers and professionals. Similarly Hartlief,[273] who denies being against consumer protection, claims to believe that protectionist regulations can be justified with a market failure, but at the same time he encourages to find what type of market failure in reality poses a decent justification. Thus following law and economics, the author states that the regulation from above is justified when market solutions fail. Discussing the cost-benefit analysis, Ramsey[274] rejects a traditional ap-

270 See more: G. Trumbull, "Consumer Capitalism..., p. 22.

271 A. Schwartz, L.L. Wilde, "Intervening in Markets on the Basis of Imperfect Information: a Legal and Economic Analysis", University of Pennsylvania Law Review 1978-1979, Vol. 127: 630.

272 I. Ramsey, "Framework for Regulation...

273 T. Hartlief, "Freedom and Protection...

274 I. Ramsey, "Framework for Regulation...

proach of economists assessing exclusively 'the aggregate benefits to society' (in order to classify the intervention as an efficient one the aggregate benefits have to exceed the costs) and stresses the importance of assessing the distributional impact of the costs and benefits amongst different groups.

And yet, apart from the costs, extended protection provisions may have some side effects, difficult to foresee or prevent. Pelkmans[275] indicates the example of irresponsible behaviour being a problem in itself, but as, also having more serious consequences.

According to Hartlief[276] unquestionably "[p]rotection comes at a price." By price, Hartlief means the harmful influence of the protectionist provisions on the behaviour of a protected party as e.g. the burden of responsibility is being to a certain extent moved from consumers' to the opposite side, which consequently may pose an incentive for careless behaviour. Hartlief[277] lists also other negative side effects of protectionist policy for instance: a shortage on the market, and a decrease in the competitive position of the industry of a specific nation.

The other significant result of the introduction of protectionist provisions, especially mandatory formal requirements and cooling-off periods, may be a change in attitude towards the importance of the binding force of contractual obligation.

When it comes to financial costs of the protectionist measures, Parish[278] claims that most of these costs are either very difficult or impossible to ascertain, since apart from the 'direct' costs incurred by the regulatory agency, all the rest – born by regulated professionals in complying with the protective rules, or born by consumers in case the professionals pass the costs incurred by them to their clients – are almost undetectable.

In the field of consumer credit, Kösters, Paul and Stein[279] express their surprise that the political discussion concerning the protection of consumer-borrower hardly ever mentions the economic costs involved or even seems to assume that the protection can be put into effect completely free of charge. The authors advocate the idea of consumer protection in the field; however claim that from an economic point of view, regulation that exceeds a certain level can be counterproductive. Overprotection could weaken the so called "spirit of competition" and could promote irresponsible actions by consumers. The authors warn against over-regulated markets which cause an increase in the administrative costs for the credit institutions which in turn results in an increase of prices, and at the end of the day, in a decrease of the demand rate, which might result in the growth of the indexes of unemployment and economy.

---

275 Pelkmans, 'Consumer Interest...

276 T. Hartlief, "Freedom and Protection...

277 Ibid.

278 R. Parish, "Consumer Protection and the Ideology..., p. 229.

279 W. Kösters, S. Paul, S. Stein, "An economic...

Harlief[280] brings up the question of, whether all consumers are in reality willing to pay this increased price; whether well-informed consumers would not prefer to pay less being less protected at the same time. If this is true, then mandatory protection would not allow them to make such a choice. Paradoxically, in consequence those who were supposed to be protected by the law, would be deprived of the possibility to take advantage of these protectionist provisions, since as a result of the above mentioned increase in prices, some goods and services may simply no longer be available for a certain (poorer) group of consumers.

Nearly three decades earlier, Atiyah[281] conduced a very similar reasoning, however some remarks he came up with are different. Like Hartlief, the author of "Essays on Contract" points out that a well-informed consumer, completely aware of the contract law provisions does not accept protective regulations which at the end of the day cause him to pay more. Atiyah sketches a probable situation, in which the 'beneficiaries' of such consumer protective rules may not always appreciate the value of these benefits. Atiyah compares the consumer protection regulations to a special compulsory insurance, and since someone has to bear the costs of such protection, it is the consumers themselves who pay in the end, in the form of increased charges. It is fair when a consumer really needs such protection and takes advantage of their right to same. However, it is conceivable that a consumer (well-informed, aware of the contract terms etc.) does not want to pay for something which is useless from his perspective. Atiyah emphasizes – as distinct from Hartlief - that such a situation not only distorts the operation of the market, but it also interferes with the private rights of the consumers to make the choices concerning their money.

Ramsay[282] is however of a different opinion. Consumer law – often labelled as a distribution of power and resources from producers to consumers: low prices, policies of loss-spreading – shifts risk from consumers to producers. Even if a backfire-effect happens and some of these costs are passed along to consumers, still consumers are willing to pay for this insurance, thus poor and disadvantaged consumers in the end might benefit.

Due to all the above mentioned side effects of public authority intervention, to recapitulate, Harlief[283] proposes to abandon the traditional consumer protection legislation via changes to contract law, and to introduce protection via competition law, since "competition will give incentives to deliver optimal quality of products and services through innovation, a variety of differentiated supplies, and an excellent price/quality relationship," provided that the consumer has an adequate overview of the market offers and moreover is able to compare these offers. Although the author does not state it explicitly, his views suggest that the best way of protecting consumers on the credit market is to 'arm' them with all the relevant information and to offer them financial education.

---

280 T. Hartlief, "Freedom and Protection...

281 P.S. Atiyah, "Freedom of Contract and the New Right..., p. 358.

282 I. Ramsay, "Consumer Law and Policy..., p. 88.

283 T. Hartlief, "Freedom and Protection...

Not far from Hartlief's views is Stuyck[284] who stresses – contrary to earlier views – that the consumer interest may be better served by a proper functioning of the market and by developing the dialogue between consumer organisations and business (e.g. voluntary agreements). This is why – similar to Pelkmans[285] – Stuyck claims that measures of consumer protection which restrict the functioning of the market should be specially justified, or, in other words, they must be proportionate to the objectives pursued.

Kösters, Paul and Stein[286] defend the thesis that competition offers consumers the best protection from an economic point of view, proving that a "spirit of competition" from both lenders and borrowers is the main prerequisite for fostering competition.

Cayne and Trebilcock[287] are also sceptical towards consumer protection and argue that it is senseless to interfere in freedom of contracts as consumers would not be better-off anyway: consumers would pay the potential cost of the intervention or the professionals would simply refuse dealing with that 'protected' group.

Even if one disagrees with Hartlief and Stuyck, the problem of overregulation should still be taken into account. It must be kept in mind that the market, although a living organism, vulnerable to diverse external influences, nevertheless, still has its own strong mechanism. This is also true for the EC market. Therefore, if a legislation crosses a certain borderline of a welfare's 'socialist' intervention into the market, such a public activity may turn out to be seriously harmful for – so called 'beneficiaries' – of the intervention. In other words: overly strict consumer protection rules lead to difficulties for the business side, and for financial service providers to design products, thereby limiting innovation, making credit more expensive and less accessible, and thus it favours the underground lenders and in fact exacerbates the situation of consumers. This finally, as a consequence, paradoxically effects in a negative way the interest of consumers. Too much market intervention dedicated to consumers' good can become counter-productive from the consumers' perspective.

In the field of the European consumer credit, there are several side-effects which consumer protection legislation as such, as well as a lack of this legislation, will encounter. Unquestionably, by introducing protective provisions, the legislator should be aware of the fact that, by the same token, he violates the market mechanisms.

Moreover, the negative consequence of introducing a substantial amount of duties imposed on the business side (like e.g. information disclosure duties) means, firstly, that these additional costs for credit providers will be passed onto their customers, and secondly, that a consumer overwhelmed by the multitude of such information, will ignore all of it and, at the end of the day, will not take advantage of same.

---

284 J. Stuyck, 'European Consumer Law after the Treaty of Amsterdam ...

285 Pelkmans, 'Consumer Interest...

286 W. Kösters, S. Paul, S. Stein, "An economic analysis...

287 Cayne, Trebilcock, Market Considerations...

A very complex issue (also, as far as the potential costs are concerned) is that of opening the European credit market for all credit providers, including those described as predatory lenders, and not regulating the phenomenon of usury at all. These two legislative solutions, on the one hand, may cause a much bigger risk of consumer insolvency. Nevertheless, on the other hand, restricting the market only to mainstream providers who would establish a price of credit on a legally acceptable interest level could entail a risk of excluding a certain group of consumers from the official market and push them in the realm of the then underground thus more harmful predatory lenders. Both consequences seem to pose a risk of a potential harm for society.

Furthermore, the lack of consumer bankruptcy regulation in the new Directive, the lack of a right to a bank account, and the lack of a right to credit will unavoidably contribute to social exclusion and thereby to the elimination of certain consumers from the market. And both of these side effects have very serious consequences: first in the negative outcome for the economy which will be noticeable for the other (not directly afflicted) members of society; and second in the costs the whole society will have to pay due to supporting financially those who failed; and third, in the very long term, in the risk that social exclusion may be 'inherited' by the next generations, thus the problem would expand instead of diminishing.

There are also several other minor examples of the side effects potentially stemming from regulation, overregulation or lack of regulation like even conveying certain messages via financial education programmes, for example, the adoption in practice of the rule 'first save then spend' may have negative consequences for the development of the economy; or adopting the responsible lending principle with its shift of responsibility - may induce some consumers to careless behaviour etc.

Conclusions

European consumer protection policy has gone through different phases over the years: initially a by-product of internal market policy, it has evolved into one of the crucial goals of the united Europe, with consumers having their rights recognised in the Treaty. In a sense, the emancipation of the consumer protection 'dogma' came to an end when the EU legislator perceived consumer policy as a tool in the realisation of the idea of the internal market. The positive interdependence between a stronger, empowered, confident consumer and the blooming common market is unquestionably correct. The thesis according to which -the open, unrestricted internal market will benefit the EU-wide bargain-seekers is easily defendable. Furthermore, nobody denies that the EU-wide active consumers are the driving force of the development of the European economy. Globalisation, cross-border offers, wider choice, greater opportunities etc. – all these watchwords certainly pave the way for consumers' welfare. Nothing better serves consumers than effective competition combined with 'healthy' market mechanisms, since there is nothing more sensitive to the swinging moods of the demand side than an attentive - even to all the most trifling signals - supply. Consequently, one should accept the statement that the internal market is the best tool to ensure adequate consumer protection. This reasoning gives the EU legislator a new rationale in relation to consumer protection provisions: it is no longer the restoration of balance; instead, at present the justification is the efficient single market. This is all true, and denying it may resemble a fight against windmills. The only piece of the puzzle which somehow does not fit that is, the only problem which remains, is that not all EU citizens can be rated among the category of these confident 'shoppers', and active market players. Thus, not all consumers will possibly profit from the internal market.

Perhaps one mistake made by consumer protection regulations lies in a certain simplification that was adopted for the sake of such a legislation, namely that consumers are a homogenous group of people, who apart from concluding contracts for their private purposes, have many other common features. And when one does not limit oneself to a very superficial glance at the issue, it becomes possible to perceive that within this one general category there is a huge diversity, and there is no reasonable justification for putting an equal sign between all the members of the group. Therefore, if one explores deeper into the reality of this general category – i.e. consumers - one will easily distinguish these participants who indeed cannot handle their own responsibility; who cannot take proper care of their economic interests and, who definitely and undoubtedly indeed need to be protected - as they are characterized by such features as vulnerability, helplessness, unawareness of law and market mechanisms, susceptibility to marketing tools/manipulations, etc. Hartlief[288] suggests that a legislator should only address these vulnerable consumers, and only in the context of general rules of contract law via old good institutions like mistake, fraud, duress etc. The majority of authors, however, see the need for a firm legislator's activity in designing consumer protection legislation, beyond the realisation of the internal market idea. This is why, for example, a statement by Garcia Porras and van Boom[289] may rise a loud, well-earned criticism when they claim that exposing consumers to financial risks may be a good thing, because such an experience provides consumers with a lesson of *market skills* and self-control (unless a consumer is *particularly* vulnerable or the product is *particularly* harmful).

In the discussion on how much state interference should be allowed, one should primarily answer the question of what is supposed to be the goal of that interference, namely is the goal of intervention to secure the citizens a fair amount of autonomy or is it to level all the members of the community and to create a completely egalitarian society? The first option assumes that a citizen is provided with a freedom of choice in the conditions of fair opportunity,[290] whereas the latter solution entails a significant risk.

---

288 T. Hartlief, "Freedom and Protection...

289 C.I. Garcia Porras, W. H. van Boom, "Information disclosure...

290 H. Collins, "Disclosure of Information ..., p. 103.

Nowadays, contrary to the nineteenth-century beliefs, it's obvious that if citizens are left to look after themselves, after their own interests, if they are left completely free to make their own decisions regarding market choices, many of them will fail; there will always be losers, and – what Atiyah rightly recons – the losers will often be the same people in many different fields of activity.[291]

With regard to contract law, one should not forget that the main principle of this branch of law is the freedom of contracts which is violated not only when public authorities interfere but, first and foremost it is violated glaringly when parties have completely different bargaining positions, thus provisions which would restore the right balance between bargaining powers of both parties do not seem as such to violate freedom of contract at all. And secondly, one should not forget that next to the old, there are also new principles of contract law which assume that cooperation is better than competition and better than taking into account merely one's own interests. The contractual relationships which are based on trust and on mutual understanding of each others' interests and supporting them in the long run can bring measurable profits and can decrease the risk of failure.

Going back to the pragmatic argument concerning costs of protective regulations - from the wider perspective of the society as a whole, i.e. a very complicated organism - introducing even strongly protective consumer provisions and restricting the freedom of contract principle bears less costs than rescuing "drowning bankrupts." In some, special (exceptional) circumstances paternalism is the only solution (i.e. - the most efficacious and paradoxically the cheapest one). The state's intervention - from the state's point of view - can be a very far-reaching step, because in many cases, if the state does not intervene at the moment of the conclusion of the contract, then it is actually the state itself who may possibly bear the responsibility when one party fails. Since one of the roles of the contemporary state is to provide help for the poorest members of the society, nowadays the state is strongly committed to help those who cannot properly take care of their own interests. Furthermore, redistribution does not necessarily have to be seen as a pure socialist idea. In a broader perspective redistribution should be recognized as the proper preparation for the future productivity. According to Atiyah,[292] any contract which affects a person's ability to care about their interest, may potentially effect the public interest.

As has been pointed out above, every intervention into the market stemming from the authorities requires a decent justification, since every intervention causes the costs to be born by the whole society. The cost which should be considered is not only the cost per se (i.e. the financial burdens imposed on the members of the given society needed in order to realize such intervention), but this is also an infringement of the original private law paradigms, and on the top of this a big number of the side effects. Nevertheless, on the other

291 P.S. Atiyah, "Freedom of Contract and the New Right..., p. 358.

292 P.S. Atiyah, "Freedom of Contract and the New Right..., p. 358.

hand, the lack of intervention in certain fields may bear even more significant costs for the whole society.

In the field of consumer credit, on the European level, the discussion about liberalization (i.e. no public authority intervention), versus regulation (i.e. protection), is reflected clearly by the tension between two goals of the European Union - i.e. internal market (in other words: market efficiency goal with a boosted competition, maximized choice between offers from different providers, including those from abroad, as well as predatory moneylenders) versus consumer protection (in other words: regulation of the credit market for the sake of consumers' safety, and of preserving certain social values, as well as for the sake of taking into account national habits, traditions etc.).

State intervention is needed, however, as the one which violates the major principles of contract law, which interferes in individuals freedoms, and on the top of it, as the one which entails costs for the whole society, it requires a decent justification, which is a common good. Thus every public authority intervention should be scanned on the background of the estimation of whether the society can afford the long-term costs which they bear, and whether the legislator's activity is necessarily directed at reaching the common good. The pure neo-liberal approach adopted by the EU legislator in the new consumer protection legislation – giving the arm to the consumers in the form of mandatory information disclosure duties and the right to withdrawal, but at the same time opening the consumer credit market for basically all the providers, not taking into account the responsible lending principle, ignoring the problem of consumer insolvency, in other words, taking into account merely consumers economic interests, depriving a significant number of consumers from hitherto enjoyed protection due to introduction of the maximum harmonisation approach - is absolutely in line with the premises of the internal market ideology. However, a thesis according to which, the internal market is really the common good, is greatly questionable.

Harmonisation of Consumer Credit Legislation

Article 3 of the Treaty (before December 2009) set three objectives for the European institutions: free movement of capital and services, harmonization of the law, and consumer protection. However, it must be kept in mind that none of these goals can be directly sacrificed for the sake of the others, although harmonization, in comparison to the other two objectives, is rather a technical means for accomplishing them. Consumer protectionists stress that the European law and its harmonization cannot be compared to the unification of the American legislation, because in the case of the United States the idea of a unified nation prevails and as a consequence it is a federal law which dominates.[293] However, the European Union with its subsidiary principle is an organism which gathers together countries of cultural diversity, and this is unconditionally reflected also in the sphere of legal regulations, so that it can be said that consumer protection is 'a part of the cultural heritage'.

Presented in 1958 as a remedy for the problems created by differences in the national regulatory regimes, harmonisation is 'the key to the creation and development of the European common market',[294] and 'involves the adoption of legislation by the community institutions that is designed to bring about changes in the internal legal systems of the member states'.[295] It aims not only at liquidating differences in the legal systems of the respective member states, but furthermore, to foster convergences through the common policy goals;[296] in other words, it is the triumph of centralized rule-making over local autonomy.[297]

Harmonisation is considered to be one of the most effective instruments for economic operators, as well as for national administrators.[298] G. Davies describes the goal of harmonisation as 'the creation of harmony'.[299] In order to achieve this objective, the application of the harmonisation method causes the elimination of problematic disparities between national legal regulations and leads to similar (but not necessarily identical) laws, so that they can 'smoothly fit together'. The ECJ, in the case concerning the validity of the Directive 98/44/EG on the legal protection of biotechnological inventions (Case C-377/98, Netherlands v. European Parliament and Council [2001] ECR I-7079), stated: 'The purpose of harmonisa-

---

293 Udo Reifner, Proposal for a Directive...

294 C. Cosgrove Twitchett, "Introduction", in C. Cosgrove Twitchett (ed.), "Harmonization in the EEC, St Martins Press, New York 1981, p. 1 in M.P. Egan, "Constructing a European Market. Standards, Regulation, and Governance", Oxford University Press, New York 2001, p. 62.

295 D. Daswood, "The Harmonization Process", in EEC, St Martins Press, New York 1981, p. 7 in M.P. Egan, "Constructing a European Market. Standards, Regulation, and Governance", Oxford University Press, New York 2001, p. 62.

296 M.P. Egan, "Constructing a European Market...", p. 62.

297 S. Weatherill, "Cases and Materials on EU Law", New York 2006, Oxford University Press, p. 622.

298 The Commission's Second Biennial Report on the Application of the Principle of the Mutual Recognition in the Single Market, COM (2002) 419, para 3.

299 G. Davies, "European Union. Internal Market Law", Cavendish Publishing Limited, London 2003, p. 145.

tion is to reduce the obstacles, whatever their origin, to the operation of the internal market which differences between the situations in the member states represent.' In the later judgment (Case C-380/03, Germany v. European Parliament and Council [2006] ECR I-11573), the ECJ stated that consumer protection rules may distort competition by imposing different regulatory standards on traders and different intensities of consumer protection. Therefore, the Court advocated harmonization as a tool applied in order to improve and intensify protection, and as such harmonisation does not necessarily result in a 'levelling down'.

Harmonisation resulting from the directives generally represents a form of limited intervention; thus member states are required to adapt their legal regulations only to a certain extent – as far as necessary to achieve the objectives set out in the relevant Treaty provisions, which serve as a legal basis for a directive. The directives, while restraining their fetter role to only certain objectives, leave member states a wide choice of the 'form and methods', which result in changing the national laws to a certain necessary extent, and respecting the characteristic features of national regulations.[300]

The extent to which member states are required to adapt the EU law depends on the methods of harmonisation passed by the EU legislator, whether this be a maximum or minimum harmonisation.[301,302] However, nowadays the Commission[303] considers three options in regard to harmonisation, i.e. full harmonisation (as the first option); next minimum harmonisation with a mutual recognition clause; followed by minimum harmonisation combined with country-of-origin principle.[304]

In case of a maximum harmonisation, or a 'total' one, member states are not allowed to maintain or adopt the regulations which vary from those adopted in a directive. This means that in practice, member states' legislators no longer have competence to set up new

300 S. Prechal, "Directives in EC Law", Oxford University Press, New York 2005, p. 4.

301 Ibid., p. 44.

302 Some authors distinguish also 'internal harmonization' in other words – mutual recognition, judicial harmonization – 'negative' or 'positive' one and then legislative harmonization what is the notion considered in this paper. In legislative harmonisation we can differentiate – apart from 'minimum' and 'maximum' – also the 'optional' harmonisation (which refers to the situation where national legislation may comply with Community rules, but does not have to, national standards internally may be higher or lower than Community ones) and 'partial' harmonisation (when only some certain aspects of the field are harmonised) .

303 Green Paper on the "Review of the Consumer Acquis", (COM (2006) 744 final from 8th February 2007).

304 This selection may rise several doubts, keeping in mind that both minimum harmonisation options are explicitly not consistent with the Rome I Regulation (EC) 593/2008 which excludes the mutual recognitions as well as country-of-origin approach as it guarantees consumer a "minimum protection clause" of his country of residence, and secondly none of the options takes into consideration so far existing in the most of consumer protection directives traditional minimum harmonisation approach in N. Reich, Chapter: "Economic Law...

laws in this area; in fact all the laws in a certain field originate with the Community's legislator.[305]

On the other hand, the minimum harmonization formula allows member states to set stricter rules than those established in a directive; all the same, these national laws have to be consistent with the primary Community law, especially with respect to the Treaty provisions on free movement. Obviously, if such stricter rules for protecting consumers already exist, they do not need to be changed. In other words, the Directive only sets minimum standards and as a minimum measure these standards do not prevent member states from adopting the stricter rules.

The minimum harmonisation is considered to be the most adequate measure of reconciling the Common Market with consumer interests.[306] It has been a standard component of directives on consumer protection since the beginning of the 1970s, but only in the Single European Act did it become "institutionalized" through its express incorporation into the Treaty on the European Union.[307]

While the Commission had previously advocated the minimum harmonization approach in consumer protection legislation, at the beginning of the new century it started recommending the maximum model as the only one adequate to provide the basis for completing the internal market goal. In the recent consumer policy documents issued by the Commission, the issue of total harmonization is the most central and controversial problem. The Commission put forward an ambitious plan to progressively up-date and adapt all the consumer directives from minimum to full harmonization measures, in order to 'minimise variations in consumer protection rules across the EU that create fragmentation of the internal market to the detriment of consumers and business'.[308] In the recently issued Explanatory Memorandums, the EC legislator gives plenty of examples in order to prove the advantages of all the predicted effects of the total harmonisation approach. The arguments that maximum harmonisation would create the conditions for a genuine internal market to operate freely, as well as ensure a high level of consumer protection by establishing a set of modern rules that guarantee consumers a good level of protection no matter in which member state they enter into contract, are followed by others, that is, the conviction that total harmonisation would result in increased competition within the single market, which means higher quality products for consumers at highly competitive (lower) prices and a better comparability of offers. Finally, the common set of rules will create a pan-European market (i.e. – it will provide European-wide choices for consumers with its first step – mandatory Pan-European Info Box), and as a consequence will release economies of scale and reduce transaction

305 G. Davies, "European Union...", p. 146.

306 K. Mortelmans, "Minimum Harmonization and Consumer Law", 1988 ECLJ 2, p. 5 in S. Weatherill, "Cases and Materials ... , p. 643.

307 M. Dougan, "Minimum Harmonization and the Internal Market", p. 853.

308 Consumer Policy Strategy for 2002-2006, COM (02) 208, OJ 2002 C137/2.

costs. For the banking institutions, maximum harmonisation will allow them to enter market financial products cross border without making further adaptations to the legal environment – achieving economies of scale (using the same IT support or with the same procedures to be respected in order to comply with the rules relevant for a respective consumer). Furthermore, the advocates of total harmonisation ensure that the effect would also be a reduction of 'red tape' at the national level.

Micklitz and Reich[309] foresee a danger that if no legislative action is taken in the field of European consumer law, the significant costs incurred by business to comply with the fragmented legal provisions existing in member states will continue to be passed on to consumers in the form of raised prices, and in a worse case scenario, businesses will continue refusing to sell cross-border, or will create geographical discriminations between consumers depending on their country of residence. Just that prediction could be incentive enough to introduce the maximum harmonisation approach on the EU level.

Furthermore, it is a commonly accepted statement that a more competitive and efficient European market will bring benefits for consumers; however, one must also take into consideration that the move towards total harmonization will 'bring about a considerable re-shaping of the bargain that has hitherto underpinned the development of a consumer policy for the EC'.[310] And the result of such a re-shaping will definitely not be favourable from the consumers' perspective.

Results of Minimum Harmonisation

Since the Directive 87/102/EC on consumer credit is based on minimum harmonisation (Article 15 states the minimum harmonization rule: "This Directive shall not preclude member states from retaining or adopting more stringent provisions to protect consumers consistent with their obligation under the Treaty"), member states vary in the extent to which they go beyond the required provisions. The reports and consultations show that there are enormous differences between the laws of the various member states in relation to credit for natural persons in general, and particularly in relation to consumer credit, and what is evident nowadays is that, in fact a European credit market does not exist.[311] Such a situation constitutes obstacles to the internal market, which as a result discourages moneylenders from extending their offer to all of Europe.

309 H.-W. Micklitz, N. Reich, "Cronica de una muerte anunciada. The Commission Proposal for a <Directive on consumer rights>", CMLRev Vol. 46, Nr. 2, April 2009, pp. 471-519.

310 S. Weatherill, 'EU consumer law and policy'..., p.25.

311 Cross – border consumer lending in the EU is estimated to be between 2 and 5 % of total number of consumer loans in 2002 - K. Lannoo, A. de la Mata Muňoz, „Integration of the EU ...

According to the European Credit Research Institute Research Report No. 1,[312] the Directive, which had as its objectives to bring a common level of protection to consumers and to improve cross-border trade, has succeeded in the former but not in the latter. By insisting on the need for a high level of consumer protection, it has made cross-border provision of consumer credit almost impossible. As a result of permitting member states to retain or adopt more stringent techniques for protecting consumers, a distortion of competition has arisen between creditors in the internal market and restriction of the scope of consumers obtaining credit in other member states. Nowadays, Europe deals with a segmentation of the internal market into separate national markets and discrepancies in consumer protection. A logical consequence of this is that such distortions and restrictions in turn affect the volume and type of credit sought, as well as the purchase of goods and services. Differences in legislation and banking/financial practices also mean that with regard to consumer credit, the consumer is unable to enjoy the same degree of protection in all the member states.

The consequence of such an approach is that consumer credit legislation has become re-nationalized and caused complex fragmentation of consumer credit regulations; in addition, national regulations have become too excessive in terms of consumer protection. According to G. Davies,[313] most things that have to do with consumer finances are national. The author even asks if it is a coincidence that levels of consumer satisfaction are also markedly low in this field, and that banks are constantly accused of anti-competitive practice.

Reich[314] criticizes the application of directives for consumer protection purposes, since the case of minimum harmonisation approach proved that the differences in the level of protection among member states were not only considerable, but in many instances even greater than before "harmonisation."

At present, although cross-border trade exists, there is a wide diversity between the markets, where levels of consumer credit vary considerably, although all admit that the market for credit has a huge potential to develop. The evolution of individual national 'lending cultures' has proceeded in many diverse ways – as indicated above – so that there are substantial discrepancies regarding the market structure. Such discrepancies include: the tools serving for incurring the debt, the entities acting as credit providers (banks or other financial institutions), the importance of consumer credit or generally the importance of loans in financial managing, etc. The data[315] shows that whilst the UK market amounts to ca. € 230 billion, on the contrary in Italy it reaches only € 40 billion. The average use of credit per

312 N. Diez Guardia, European Credit Research Institute Research Report No. 1 available at: http://www.ecri.be/media/research_report/ECR1en.pdf.

313 G. Davies, "European Union...", p. 93.

314 N. Reich, "A European Contract Law, or an EU Contract Law Regulation for Consumers?", Journal of Consumer Policy (2005) 28:383-407.

315 The data come from the years 2004, 2005, thus naturally from the periods preceding the world financial crisis of 2008, however they were relevant and current for the discussion which preceded the adoption of the new CC Directive.

household in Spain amounts to € 942, and in UK reaches the level of almost € 18,000.[316] Also when compared to gross domestic product, e.g. again in the UK consumer credit represents about 15 % of GDP, whereas in Italy consumer credit hardly reaches 4 % of GDP.[317] Of course these are all extremes and the figures for almost all EU countries fall somewhere in between, but it should also be stressed that most of the statistics still do not take into account the indicators available from the EU newcomers.[318]

As shown above, the financial market is very localized. Obviously, apart from legal differences (different levels of consumer protection), we can indicate other powerful obstacles: geographical distance, consumer preferences for local banks, taxation, interest differentials, price differentials, different economic structure and frameworks, habits, tradition, feelings of trust and confidence, language barriers, culture, etc. Certainly, it does not make any sense to fight against these obstacles, because they limit market integration even in the 'world of perfect legal regulations'; in fact, only an effective marketing policy of the creditors could improve the situation in this respect.[319] Nevertheless, many strongly believe that a consumer needs to have a choice - there should be no barriers stemming from legal regulations, and all the obstacles linked to laws need to be identified and eliminated using the measures foreseen in Art. 3 of EC Treaty.

However, one can also identify the positive, non isolated views on minimum harmonisation included in the first Consumer Credit Directive which, as an act decided unanimously after lengthy negotiations, offered consumers a rather low level of protection, however, thanks to Article 15 the Directive's provisions did not in reality harm the situation of the consumers – borrowers.[320]

---

316 Explanatory Memorandum of Amended proposal for a Directive of the European Parliament and the Council on Credit Agreements for Consumers amending Council Directive 93/13/EC COM (2005) 483 final 2002/0222 (COD).

317 ECRI Statistical Package (2004).

318 The year 2008 bringing the world financial crisis had an enormous impact on the real annual growth rates of total credit to households in the European Community. The index was negative in Germany, Italy, UK, Netherlands, Ireland, Latvia (2008). Real growth rates of the EU 27 retail credit market have dropped for the third consecutive year. The increase of 0.75% in 2008 was the smallest in the last 12 years and well below the average compound annual growth rate of 5.1% since 2000. In more than three-quarters of the EU member states, credit granted to households in 2008 grew at a slower pace than in 2007, when the then-looming credit crunch started to drag on real annual growth rates. For two thirds of the countries, the year 2008 brought about the second consecutive drop, with the retail credit market in six countries even shrinking in relation to the previous year. Until 2008, real negative growth was a phenomenon that in Europe only appeared in Belgium and Germany. Source: Lending to Households in Europe (1995-2008), ECRI Statistical Package 2009, ECRI, Brussels. Available at: http://www.ecri.be/new/system/files/2009StatisticalPackage_KeyFindings.pdf.

319 K. Lannoo, A. de la Mata Muňoz, „Integration of the EU Consumer Credit Market"...

320 P. Rott, Chapter 5 'Consumer Credit' in H.-W. Micklitz, N. Reich, P. Rott, "Understanding EU...

Full Harmonisation and a Confident Consumer

In recent activities at the European level, one can easily notice a strong tendency to replace the minimum harmonisation approach by that of maximum harmonisation (e.g. EC-Commerce Directive 2000/31/EC, Distance Marketing of Financial Services Directive 2002/65/EC), which is compatible with the strong tendency to foster the EC-wide internal market.[321]

In its Green Paper on European Union Consumer Protection[322] the Commission stressed the importance of benefits consumers can reap from the internal market. However, the pre-condition for that is "easy access to goods and services promoted, offered and sold across the borders." Furthermore, the document in its pro-harmonisation canvassing comes to the conclusion that "[i]t is the cross-border movement of goods and services that allows consumers to search out bargains and innovative products and services and thus ensures that they optimise their consumption decisions. This cross-border demand increases competitive pressure within the internal market and allows for a more efficient and competitively priced supply of goods and services. This virtuous circle can only be achieved if the regulatory framework in place encourages consumers and businesses to engage in cross-border trade. Different national laws on commercial practices relating to business–consumer relations can hinder this evolution." Much later, in the explanatory memorandum of the Proposal on Consumer Rights[323] which makes an attempt to explain the rationale of adopting the full harmonisation approach to the consumer contracts covered by the Proposal, one reads that the legal fragmentation problem cannot be solved by the member states individually, and that only a coordinated Community intervention can contribute to the completion of the internal market by solving this problem.[324]

The first step in the Commission trail towards the totally harmonised consumer protection legislation was the Directive 2002/65/EC on the distance marketing of financial services. That move was backed by the Commission's statement that in that specific field only maximum harmonisation could ensure the realization of the idea of the internal market. A similar tone concerning the shift between different methods of harmonisation was perceivable in the Consumer Policy Strategy 2002-2006[325] where the Commission introduced full harmonisation as the new objective of its politics on commercial practices and on consumer contract law, as well as in Green Paper on the Review of the Consumer *Acquis.*[326] In its Communica-

321 P. Rott, Maximum Harmonisation and Mutual Recognition versus Consumer Protection: The Example of Linked Credit Agreements in EC Consumer Credit Law, EuLF 2006, I-61-I-68.

322 COM (2001) 531 final.

323 COM (2008) 614 final.

324 H.-W. Micklitz, "The Targeted Full Harmonisation..., p. 53.

325 COM(2002).

326 COM(2006) 483 final.

tion on Consumer policy strategy 2002-2006,[327] the Commission emphasises the importance of the consumers' comparable opportunities to fully benefit from the potential of the internal market in terms of greater choice, lower prices, and the affordability and availability of essential services. The Commission seems to ignore the specificity of the consumers' protection stating that barriers to cross-border trade should be overcome in order to allow the consumer dimension of the internal market to develop in parallel with its business dimension. Consequently and consistently, the aim of the EU consumer policy is to create "a coherent and common environment ensuring that consumers are confident in shopping across borders throughout the EU." In the same vein, the Communication from the Commission to the Council, the European Parliament and the European Economic and Social Committee on EU Consumer Policy Strategy 2007-2013 Empowering consumers, enhancing their welfare, effectively protecting them from 2007[328] - mentions "full harmonisation" as a means to achieve better consumer protection regulation, and at the same time, a means to improve the internal market. However, the controversial debate regarding the harmonisation method in the unfair commercial practices Directive[329] has been resolved by the full realization of the country of origin principle.

The Proposal for a Directive of the European Parliament and of the Council on the Harmonisation of the Laws, Regulations and Administrative Provisions of the member states Concerning Credit for Consumers[330] - being a response to an alleged failure of the minimum harmonization approach of the Directive 87/102 - foresaw the total harmonization of credit provisions. The declared aim of the Proposal was to secure the maximum harmonisation with regard to the credit on offer to consumers by guaranteeing them a high level of protection. All the types and forms of credit that were available to private individuals would, in principle, be harmonised. The Proposal also covered surety agreements. The harmonisation being sought for these agreements would focus mainly on the information to be provided to consumers concluding such agreements, even if they guaranteed credit that was granted for employment-related purposes. Member states were not entitled to have other provisions in place in relation to the areas covered by that Proposal unless otherwise stipulated.

According to the amended proposal for a directive of the European Parliament and of the Council on credit agreements for consumers amending Council Directive 93/13/EC,[331] the actors on the consumer credit market would have had to deal with four sets of rules, if the proposal were to be adopted:

327 Communication from the Commission to the European Parliament, the Council, the Economic and Social Committee and the Committee of the Regions Consumer policy strategy 2002-2006 (COM(2002) 208 final) (2002/C 137/02).

328 COM(2007) 99 final.

329 2005/29/EC.

330 COM(2002) 443 final.

331 COM(2005) 483 final/2.

(1) Those rules that are fully harmonised - Article 21(1): member states cannot depart from the harmonized provisions, neither by adopting stricter rules nor by adopting less strict rules, both with regard to domestic situations and cross-border situations. According to the preamble the full harmonization only applies to the harmonized provisions (Recital 9).

(2) Those rules that are not harmonised but where the trader, under the principle of mutual recognition, can rely on his own member state's law if this is more generous than the law of the member state where the consumer is domiciled (with regard to the implementation and application of certain provisions - i.e. right of withdrawal, linked transactions, overrunning and intermediation) - Member Sates shall not restrict freedom of establishment and the free provision of services, albeit with the exception of measures on grounds of public policy – Article 21 (2).

(3) Those issues that remain in the competence of the member states - the elements which are not explicitly dealt with in the text of the Directive (e.g. joint and several liability of the seller or supplier of services and the creditor; right of withdrawal from the contract of sale of goods or supply of services if the consumer exercises his right of withdrawal from the credit) are not harmonized and are left to the national legal systems (5.11 of the Explanatory Memorandum); and

(4) Issues where the reach of maximum harmonisation is unclear.

In the opinion of the authors of the above mentioned analysis,[332] the last category is problematic from both a creditor's and a consumer's perspective, as it can be in these cases time consuming to determine whether the law of the creditor, or the law of the consumer is applicable, assuming that both contracting parties are coming from two different member states.

The newly adopted Directive[333] in its Deliberations states that in order to facilitate the emergence of a well-functioning internal market in consumer credit, it is necessary to make provision for a harmonised Community framework in a number of core areas. The EU legislator assumes that there is a need for a CCD which is able to adapt to future forms of credit and which allows member states the appropriate degree of flexibility in their implementation; especially keeping in mind that the market in consumer credit is constantly developing as well as the mobility of European citizens is continuously increasing. On the one hand, the EU legislator has chosen full harmonization as the sole means to guarantee a high and common level of protection to all consumers EU-wide and to create a genuine internal market. According to Article 22 (1), "[i]nsofar as this Directive contains harmonised provisions, member states may not maintain or introduce in their national law, provisions diverging from those laid down in this Directive".

332 F. Alleweldt (Project Director) et al. Broad Economic Analysis...

333 Directive 2008/48/EC of the European Parliament and of the Council of 23 April 2008 on credit agreements for consumers and repealing Council Directive 87/102/EEC.

But on the other hand, as it is expressed in the Directive's Deliberations, that there are no limitations for member states in the field of consumer credit in the areas which are not harmonised; i.e. where the Directive does not provide restrictions, member states should remain free to maintain or introduce national legislation. The leeway for member states concerns inter alia maintaining or introducing national provisions on joint and several liability of the seller of goods or the supplier of services and of the creditor, maintaining or introducing national provisions on the cancellation of a contract for the sale of goods or supply of services if a consumer exercises his right of withdrawal from the credit agreement.

Full harmonisation is undoubtedly a substantial solution in the case of many parts of the consumer credit legislation;[334] however it totally restricts the freedom of member states to legislate on consumer protection as far as the totally harmonised issues are concerned. This is the reason why full harmonisation is so necessary for access to databases and information systems, as well as in relation to the right of withdrawal, and exclusion of mortgages, although whether this method is proper for all the provisions of consumer credit legislation is questionable. Particularly since already nowadays it is sometimes stressed that Brussels – being mainly influenced by a Northern European approach - interferes too deeply with the national legislation, irrespective of the specific social, economic or legal contexts of the member state, and cannot resist the temptation of regulating everything in detail.[335]

Unquestionably, maximum harmonisation will create a common ground for the market to operate freely – enabling a smooth cross-border supply and demand of consumer credit. However, the whole process of passing a piece of EU legislation containing a maximum harmonisation approach is time-consuming, burdensome and politically difficult, but, apart from this, total harmonisation often meets with disapproval for many other, content-related reasons.

First of all, a directive which is based on total harmonisation should guarantee the highest level of consumer protection that can be found in the national law regulations.[336] However, due to the process of levelling the legal provisions in the EU arena, such process actually brings into effect the lower standards of consumer protection (adoption of the lowest common denominator) in the member states which used to boast of highly protective regimes. As a result, from the consumers' point of view their hitherto guaranteed rights are lessened. Simultaneously, the maximum harmonisation provision will force some member states to fall behind the existing high level of protection granted to their citizens. For consumers in some member states, there is also a risk of depreciation in standards of protection

334 The Eurobarometer opinion poll (Eurobarometer 56.0, December 2001) reveals that a majority of consumers (53%) consider consumer protection as a proper matter for full harmonisation throughout the EU.

335 R.M. Gelpi, F. Julien-Labruyère, "The History of Consumer Credit...", p. 148.

336 This would be consistent with the Community consumer policy strategy for 2002 to 2006, the Council resolution on Community consumer policy strategy 2002-2006, OJ 2003, C 11/1 and the Commission's Communication on consumer policy strategy 2002-2006, OJ 2002, C 137/2, No. 3.1.

from market failure and/or market inequities. The maximum harmonization approach also means that consumer protectionists will have only very limited and weak tools to secure effective protection – namely, influencing the political debate and then striving to ensure that the relevant rules are faithfully interpreted and applied in this pro-consumer manner.[337]

Micklitz and Reich[338] are very reluctant towards the recent trend in the EC legislator's approach and describe full harmonisation in the field of consumer contract law as a "toxic package" as it implies a complete shift in jurisdiction as far as national law is concerned to the EU with little room for manoeuvre for the domestic legislature, judicature and to some extent the executive.

In a similar vein, Howells[339] makes a remark that in case of maximum harmonisation approach, the only concern of businesses is to lobby for a EC law, that is appropriate for their interests, whereas the domestic legislators are deprived of any legislative means to react to any remaining consumer concerns.

Micklitz[340] stresses additional danger which might be caused by the maximum harmonisation approach, namely the specific competence shift, the loss of competences, or more precisely, autonomy of national courts with regard to interpretation and decision in the open issues, since due to maximum harmonisation national courts will be obliged to refer all these issues to the ECJ. In the circumstances where member states are deprived of taking complementary legislative measures, the European Court of Justice captures the role of the key player in deciding on the issues left open by the EU act assuming full harmonisation approach.[341] Apart from the ECJ, the European Commission would also start playing a significantly more dominant role; here too to the detriment of the domestic courts, since again due to maximum harmonisation in order to amend any single provision in the directive, the European Commission would have to step in as the only institution which has the legislative initiative.[342]

However, in general, Micklitz and Reich[343] do not present an entirely hostile attitude towards full harmonisation. They postulate yet to conduct a careful analysis of the implications of full harmonisation with regard to each individual measure, as they stress that from a professional's perspective, entry in a foreign market - being a "journey into the unknown" - entails a corresponding risk, which to some extent this professional shares with his consumers.

The fact that - the maximum harmonisation decreases the risk both for money lenders as well as for consumers, poses an unquestionable advantage of this approach. That is, ac-

337 S. Weatherill, 'EU consumer law and Policy"..., p.25.

338 H.-W. Micklitz, N. Reich, "Cronica de una muerte anunciada..."

339 G. Howells, "The Rise of European Consumer Law...

340 H.-W. Micklitz, "The Targeted Full Harmonisation Approach..., p. 59.

341 H.-W. Micklitz, N. Reich, "Cronica de una muerte anunciada..."

342 H.-W. Micklitz, "The Targeted Full Harmonisation Approach..., p. 59.

343 H.-W. Micklitz, N. Reich, "Cronica de una muerte anunciada..."

tors from both groups do not need to explore legal systems of the other country when seeking to attract consumers from that country (in case of creditors) and when borrowing money in that country (in case of consumers).

All in all, total harmonization means a greater clarity regarding the rules of the game on the market, where everybody with due diligence knows or can easily learn them, and it concerns not only professionals, but also and above all consumers. Needless to say, such an approach fits perfectly with the idea of globalization, at least in the EU scale, which means a global internal market goal.

Similarly Reich[344] - considering the issues of the competences in the EU in the consumer protection field to be linked tightly to the discussion on total and minimum harmonisation - advocates the older minimum harmonisation approach in accordance with Art. 153(5), however leaving technical aspects fully harmonised EU-wide. As a positive effect of the total harmonisation approach he indicates the fact that such an approach requires member states to enact the protective provisions of a directive fully, thus in compliance with the general principles of Community law.[345] Although the author criticizes the simple allocation of 'market aspects' to the realm of the European Union and of 'social aspects' to the exclusivity of the member states, at the same time he supports the 'constitutional responsibility' of the Community to establish and enhance the functioning of the internal market and of the member states to safeguard (inter alia) the social well-being of their citizens as a justification for such a division. Still Reich claims that the EU also has 'social purposes',[346] as well as the member states' obligation is also to support market building. These tasks stem from the basic constitutional obligations of the EU and member states to mutual support and trust. For these areas, Reich proposes the minimum harmonisation approach.

There are certainly few positive features of the maximum harmonisation approach. One of them is that it will plausibly have a favourable effect in the form of preventing or making impossible a (so far present) 'dumping' activity between member states: in the circumstances where the consumer credit directive contains only minimally harmonised provisions, individual member states, by not going further with protecting provisions than the mandatory minimum, can attract credit institutions to establish their premises in the low-protection country to the detriment of consumers.

Micklitz[347] discusses the competences of the European Community with regard to the field of private law. According to Article 95 EC (at present Article 114), the EU legislator has a competence to take measures to complete the internal market at a high level of consumer protection and to support, supplement and monitor the consumer policy by the member

344 N. Reich, "Crisis or Future of European Consumer Law?" in "The Yearbook of Consumer Law 2009", D. Parry, A. Nordhausen, G. Howells, Ch. Twigg-Flesner (eds.), ASHGATE 2008.

345 Ibid.

346 Reich deduces it from Case C-437/05 ITF & FSU v. Viking at al. [2007] ECR 1-(11.12.2007) at para. 79with regard to worker protection and social action.

347 H.-W. Micklitz, "The Targeted Full Harmonisation...

states - Article 153(2) b), however the Commission deduced, basing on the Tobacco I judgment,[348] that the Article 95 requires the full harmonisation approach. And, in a Tourist Guide case,[349] the ECJ ruled that generally consumers profit more from deregulation and cross-border competition than from exclusionary local regulatory practices.

Bearing in mind the provision of Article 95(3) EC,[350] one can raise the question as to whether full harmonisation does not actually contradict the Treaty. One can also pose a general question: is the European Community legitimated at all to impose restrictions on hitherto existing consumer protection provisions? There is an alleged[351] remedy in Article 95(4) EC which provides for a situation where if 'a member state deems it necessary to maintain national provisions' while the EC legislator adopts a harmonisation measure, Article 95(4) et seq. is considered to be the only means for such a member state to 'escape <upwards> from an agreed harmonized rule'.[352] In other words, Articles 95(4) and (5) EC allow the member state's legislator to maintain or adopt a higher level of protection once the European Community has totally harmonized a certain field of law. However, Art. 95(4) refers only to 'national provisions on grounds of major needs referred to in Article 30, or relating to the protection of the environment or the working environment' and consumer's financial interests are not mentioned in Article 30 EC. Thus, the member state's legislator is not legitimated in the case of consumer credit provisions to maintain or adopt a higher level of the protection of the consumer's financial interests, once a total harmonization measure has been enacted.[353]

The full harmonization approach may alarm highly protective member states, which as a consequence may block any further development in the field of consumer law. Hence, P.

---

348 ECJ Case C-376/98 (2000) ECR I-8419.

349 Case C-154/89, Commission v France [1991] ECR I-659.

350 After the Treaty of Lisbon, in consolidated versions of the Treaty on European Union and the Treaty on the Functioning of the European Union (2008/C 115/01) Official Journal C 115 , 09/05/2008, the content of the Article 95 TEC was moved to Article 114 "1. Save where otherwise provided in the Treaties, the following provisions shall apply for the achievement of the objectives set out in Article 26. The European Parliament and the Council shall, acting in accordance with the ordinary legislative procedure and after consulting the Economic and Social Committee, adopt the measures for the approximation of the provisions laid down by law, regulation or administrative action in Member States which have as their object the establishment and functioning of the internal market. (...) 3. The Commission, in its proposals envisaged in paragraph 1 concerning health, safety, environmental protection and consumer protection, will take as a base a high level of protection, taking account in particular of any new development based on scientific facts. Within their respective powers, the European Parliament and the Council will also seek to achieve this objective."

351 Some literature considers Article 95(4) EC as a real solution.

352 S. Weatherill, "EU Consumer Law and Policy", p. 68.

353 P. Rott, "Minimum Harmonization for the Completion of the Internal Market? The Example of Consumer Sales Law.", Common Market Law Review 40: 1107-1135, 2003.

Rott suggests amending Article 95(4) and (5) (at present Article 114)[354] by introducing a respective escape clause as a compromise between the establishment and functioning of the internal market and the principle of minimum harmonization. The goal of such a clause would be to allow – for important reasons supported by social science - a higher level of protection in national legislation and, as a result, to establish a European Community high level of consumer protection with no need to force member states to give up any instruments for the protection of their consumers. Even if one does not consider total harmonisation as a breach of Art. 95 (which legitimizes the Community to legislate where it is necessary for the approximation of the national laws, the laws whose object is the establishing and functioning of the internal market),[355] it is usually agreed that the Commission's new approach contradicts Art. 153 of the Treaty.[356]

---

354 Article 114: "4. If, after the adoption of a harmonisation measure by the European Parliament and the Council, by the Council or by the Commission, a Member State deems it necessary to maintain national provisions on grounds of major needs referred to in Article 36, or relating to the protection of the environment or the working environment, it shall notify the Commission of these provisions as well as the grounds for maintaining them. 5. Moreover, without prejudice to paragraph 4, if, after the adoption of a harmonisation measure by the European Parliament and the Council, by the Council or by the Commission, a Member State deems it necessary to introduce national provisions based on new scientific evidence relating to the protection of the environment or the working environment on grounds of a problem specific to that Member State arising after the adoption of the harmonisation measure, it shall notify the Commission of the envisaged provisions as well as the grounds for introducing them."

355 See: Case 376/98 Germany v. Parliament and Council (Tobacco Advertising) [2000], ECJ 5 Oct. 2000, ECR I-8419.

356 Art. 153 of the Amsterdam Treaty (after the Treaty of Lisbon, in consolidated versions of the Treaty on European Union and the Treaty on the Functioning of the European Union (2008/C 115/01) Official Journal C 115 , 09/05/2008, the content of the Article 153 TEC was moved to the Article 169 and Article 12) states in clear terms the principle of minimum harmonisation as it applies to national consumer protection law: "Member states cannot be prohibited to keep or develop stricter measures of consumer protection than provided for by paragraph 4" The notion of "measures" covers all kind of actions, including legislative measures in the member states. The Commission itself addresses the articles contained in this Directive as "measures." Art. 153 is only the most distinct expression of the high value the Treaty attributes to a high level of consumer protection.
Article 153 "1. In order to promote the interests of consumers and to ensure a high level of consumer protection, the Community shall contribute to protecting the health, safety and economic interests of consumers, as well as to promoting their right to information, education and to organise themselves in order to safeguard their interests. 2. Consumer protection requirements shall be taken into account in defining and implementing other Community policies and activities. 3. The Community shall contribute to the attainment of the objectives referred to in paragraph 1 through: (a) measures adopted pursuant to Article 95 in the context of the completion of the internal market; (b) measures which support, supplement and monitor the policy pursued by the Member States. 4. The Council, acting in accordance with the procedure referred to in Article 251 and after consulting the Economic and Social Committee, shall adopt the measures referred to in paragraph 3(b). 5. Measures adopted pursuant to paragraph 4

Moreover, the additional problem with the new maximum harmonisation approach refers to the fact that achieving maximum harmonisation in the field of consumer law on the basis of Article 153 EC seems to be very difficult if not completely inconceivable, since the provision requires the agreement to be reached between all member states.[357] The natural consequence of that fact is that the maximum harmonization has to be based on internal market policy rather than on consumer protection, which in turn, causes a natural shift i.e. from consumer protection policy to internal market policy as a Community's primary policy. And as Unberath and Johnson[358] rightly notice even the ECJ - who would be more prone to foster consumer interests - is tied up by the legislative decisions, and in this respect jurisprudence competences are very limited.

The prevalence of the maximum harmonization approach in the European consumer protection legislation may lead to the situation where "considerations of economic efficiency, facilitation of cross-border trade, or other factors relating to the elimination of trade barriers get to take the upper hand over consumer interests."[359] On the other hand, the opposite approach i.e. adopting the new EC consumer protection legislation with a maximum harmonisation approach at the highest protective level would bear a risk of stifling the development of trade and commerce within Europe.

The critical view on the new EU tendency to completely harmonise the entire field of consumer law is represented by Reich as well.[360] The author claimed - building the postulates for the future ECCLR (EU consumer contract law regulation) - that complete harmonisation of consumer contract law is an illusion and should not even be a goal of EU policy, according to Art. 153 (5).

Furthermore, this method of harmonisation does not take into account the cultural and historical diversity of consumer habits in respective member states.[361] Howells[362] stresses the significant differences still existing in the national consumer protection culture. As a 'one-size-fits-all' solution for heterogeneous and fast-changing credit markets, it simply 'downplays local traditions',[363] cutting across the principle of the cultural and historical di-

shall not prevent any Member State from maintaining or introducing more stringent protective measures. Such measures must be compatible with this Treaty. The Commission shall be notified of them."

357 V. Mak, "Review of the Consumer Acquis: Towards Maximum Harmonization?", ERPL 1-2009[55-73].

358 H. Unberath, A. Johnson, „The Double-Headed Approach of the ECJ Concerning Consumer Protection", CMLR 44 (2007): 1237 at 1244, 1274.

359 V. Mak, "Review of the Consumer Acquis..., p. 65.

360 N. Reich, "A European Contract Law...

361 According to consumer protectionists, the variations which depend largely on the cultural heritage of each country are inter alia the way variable rate credit is adjusted to market conditions, contracts are terminated, payments on arrears are compounded, default interest rates are capped or damages are calculated in case of default.

362 G. Howells, "The Rise of European Consumer Law...

363 K. Lannoo, A. de la Mata Muňoz, „Integration of the EU Consumer Credit Market...".

versity underlying the EU. As total harmonisation does not distinguish between the different types of rules, it obviously also sacrifices the cultural diversity in favour of the unified markets. As social rights rely heavily on moral persuasion, it thus undermines the effectiveness of solidarity rules in the member states and will therefore not prevent overindebtedness but will even weaken structures which act as a barrier to overindebtedness in most continental European states. And this argument in the case of consumer credit appears to be one that is very important since – as has been stated above – credit relations seem to be deeply ingrained in national habits and practices and are based on trust.

There is also a risk that member states might not be allowed to take immediate action if unforeseen problems arise, especially when one takes into consideration the specific character of the credit market – that is, a fast development of products and tools, as well as susceptibility to many factors which depend again on the performance of the worldwide and national economies, but also on unpredictable ('moody') floating living style. Already the whole legislation process (which lasted five and a half years – taking as a starting point the adoption of the first proposal in September 2002) demonstrates that the agreement between 25 (now 27) parties is not only difficult to reach, but that it is also very time consuming. Now, in the case of any substantial changes in the credit market, the national legislator is not only entitled, but also obligated, to introduce the appropriate instant reaction. However, the question must be asked, as to how quickly would be the reactions of 25 (now 27) countries to some major problems?[364]

Furthermore, total harmonisation is reproached for eliminating competition among national regulations and causing for the domestic legislators the loss of not only legislative power, but also of the possibility of contributing creatively to the legislative procedure – the EU institutions (i.e. a small number of EU civil servants) are not capable of achieving a greater degree of creativity than 25 (now 27) different national legislators.[365]

Howells,[366] paraphrasing the famous 'confident consumer' notion, claims that with its strive for maximum harmonisation, the Commission uses/abuses the image of the 'underconfident businessman' as a justification for the fact that shift is the assumption of professionals' reluctance to risk exercising their activity in other states if the legal regimes are not identical.

The author[367] rightly notices that with regard to big businesses, which are typically interested in cross border trade, they often adopt the highest level of consumer protection, thanks to which, they are consequently able to adopt a common approach, hence for them the information gap between diverse domestic regimes in reality does not pose a problem.

---

364 P. Rott, 'Consumer Guarantees in the Future Consumer Credit Directive: Mandatory Ban on Consumer Protection?', European Review of Private Law 3-2005, Kluwer Law International, p. 383.

365 K. Lannoo, A. de la Mata Muňoz, „Integration of the EU Consumer Credit Market...

366 G. Howells, "The Rise of European Consumer Law...

367 Ibid.

Similarly Wagner[368] disproves the argument of the business side according to which minimum harmonisation presumably distorts the competition, since – he claims – the same contract rules apply to all products on the market.

Howells[369] proposes a different approach towards the goal of bringing together various member states' legal regimes in contract law. He claims that business in fact does not require a complete uniformity in order to act cross border, however, the author believes at the same time that member states' laws can evolve in a similar direction. The national rules which catch business by surprise should definitely be excluded from the national legal regimes and in this respect Howells would opt for harmonisation. He also advocates the idea of bringing laws into a similar structure, accompanied by the promotion of a common legal and trade culture.

Moreover, there is another disadvantage which can potentially be brought by the present approach, namely adopting total harmonization would also modify the activity of the national consumer associations, and thereby they would stop putting pressure on the national legislation as they do today. The same pertains to the lobbing activity of the credit providers. As a solution, the author[370] puts forward an alternative approach for the smooth harmonization of laws – a modified, more flexible legislative procedure with the respective countries playing a direct role from the beginning of the process, thus, a variation of the Lamfalussy approach. The main advantage of applying this approach to consumer financial services law is that the legislative process would be eased, but it would also stimulate market integration, thereby involving member states to a much greater extent - 'member state officials would jointly propose and discuss details of implementing laws'.

Developing the CCD as a framework directive in combination with a comitology procedure, which could be modelled according to other directives employing the comitology procedure, or by using the Lamfalussy approach, has been presented by the Broad Economic Analysis of the Impact of the Proposed Directive as an Option 2 of the possible solution. The authors of the Analysis quote the recent evaluation of the Financial Services Action Plan which concludes that "the new approach to the preparation of legislation introduced under the Lamfalussy process brought significant improvements in terms of consultation, institutional co-operation, and (potentially) greater flexibility to respond to market events, and there is a general appreciation of the quality of the measures finally introduced."[371]

In order to strike a balance between two often opposing goals of the contemporary European legislation: the consumer protection and the single market, the European Financial

368 G. Wagner, "The Economics of Harmonization: the Case of Contract Law" (2002) 39 Common Market L. Rev 995 at 1004-5.

369 G. Howells, "The Rise of European Consumer Law..., at 70.

370 Ibid.

371 European Commission, FSAP Evaluation - Part I: Process and implementation, 2007, (http://ec.europa.eu/internal_market/finances/docs/actionplan/index/070124_part1_en.pdf), p. 33.

Services Round Table[372] suggested finding a compromise between a total and minimum harmonization approach - i.e. the targeted harmonisation of a few main issues (key points), leaving the rest for national legislation via mutual recognition. The recommended idea would be to identify various principles for a distinction between key and non-key issues which should become the guiding principles for further harmonization. As soon as these essential rules are determined, they should be fully harmonised across the European Union – 'targeted full harmonization'. Such a full harmonisation of these key rules would intentionally facilitate further integration. The remaining non-essential areas should be subject to mutual recognition, the home country principle – providing that those viewed as essential and non-essential would be analysed case-by-case for different product types. However, in some exceptional cases, legal uncertainties might remain because products and services would need to comply with those host country rules which possibly do not fall under the mutual recognition principle.

The other difficulty that might result from such an approach is that since non-essential issues are not directly regulated by European law, the differences in national laws might remain so huge that member states might find it difficult to mutually accept the other countries' rules. As a solution to this problem the EFR suggests the examination of national exceptions by respective member states to find out whether these national provisions are justified by real needs. Then, member states could agree on a minimum standard of non-essential issues, to reach a certain common denominator for these issues. Another mechanism could also be the 'comply or explain' principle. The principle - borrowed from the field of corporate governance - obliges companies to justify any deviation from corporate governance codes, in other words a company must either follow each of the recommendations that make up the Code, or explain why it has chosen another solution. In the consumer credit regulation's field, the 'comply or explain' principle would mean the European harmonization of also the 'non-essential issues' combined with an imposed obligation on the member states to justify departing from adopted, harmonised provisions.

Consumer protectionists claim that, depending on the kind of consumer protection one considers, different forms of harmonization of the laws is preferred.[373] While rules on social consumer protection (i.e. protection of culture and social standards) require a special application of the minimum harmonization principle, consumer protection in the form of information (protection of competition, information and rational choice) addresses products which are already highly standardized in the European Union through the globalization of the economy. Consumer protectionists indicate the division drawn above as a reason why the harmonization of consumer protection rules can be attributed neither to maximum nor to minimum principles. Decisions referring to the way in which the laws are harmonized should be based on the type of problems the legal regulations seek to address. The provi-

372 Consumer Protection – Consumer Choice, European Financial Services Round Table, January 2006.

373 U. Reifner, Proposal for a Directive...

sions responding to the personal needs of consumers and their specific consumption patterns are linked to the culture of the nation concerned. In the case of the provisions linked to transparency and the price disclosure of the standardized products, they have a more technical impact and should be standardized in order to make market control more efficient. Those national rules on social consumer protection differ significantly, considering their scope, intensity and sanctions, and actors.[374] Social consumer protection represents one of the principles of the Treaty and has its roots in the subsidiary principle, which supports cultural diversity in the process of market integration; it is much more than an advantage or a benefit to the consumer, and needs to be adapted to diverse conditions and diverse environments (different countries).

Wilhelmsson[375] poses a question of great importance: i.e. whether the increasing approximation and a predicted maximum harmonization of large areas of substantive consumer European law is really a necessary tendency for consumers. If the answer to this is 'yes', then it is justified through the combination of the consumer (reduced to a cross-border shopper) interest argument and internal market reasoning.

Studying the EU institutions' documents on a 'confident consumer', it is difficult to resist the impression that Wilhelmsson is actually right. Initially, both action plans from the Commission for 1990-92[376] and for 1993-95[377] emphasise the necessity of building a 'confident consumer' in order to support the creation of the internal market. Later on, in its Communication on Consumer policy strategy 2002-2006,[378] the Commission expresses the aim of the EU consumer policy which is to set "a coherent and common environment ensuring that consumers are confident in shopping across borders throughout the EU." To this end it is crucial to ensure consumers the comparable opportunities to fully benefit from the potential of the internal market in terms of greater choice, lower prices, and the affordability and availability of essential services. In another Communication of 2005 on "Healthier, safer, more confident consumers: a Health and Consumer Protection Strategy,"[379] the Commission explains that consumer confidence is a basic requirement of markets in the sense that the internal market cannot function properly without consumer confidence. And furthermore, the later document (of 2007) of the Commission, the Green Paper "On the Review of the

---

374 Some countries characterise with a greater informal consensus on solidarity than others, some use administrations and others have an abundance of courts and judges, while others again have strong NGOs or central commissions in which all market players participate.

375 T. Wilhelmsson, 'The Abuse of "Confident Consumer" ..., 317.

376 COM (90) 98.

377 COM (93) 378.

378 Communication from the Commission to the European Parliament, the Council, the Economic and Social Committee and the Committee of the Regions Consumer policy strategy 2002-2006 (COM(2002) 208 final) (2002/C 137/02).

379 (COM (2005) 115 final).

Consumer Acquis"[380] adds that consumers' confidence in the internal market must be stimulated by ensuring a high level of protection across the EU. The Green Paper was followed by the next Communication "EU Consumer Policy strategy 2007 – 2013, Empowering consumers, enhancing their welfare, effectively protecting them", where the Communication states that only the consumers – who are confident, well-informed, empowered and equipped with effective protection from the circumstances they cannot tackle as individuals - can play an important role in the modern economy. And finally, the recent Report (from 2008) of the European Parliament on protecting the consumer: improving consumer education and awareness on credit and finance,[381] underlines in the same vein that empowered and educated consumers help to foster competition, quality and innovation within the banking and financial services industries, and recalls that educated and confident investors can provide additional liquidity to capital markets for investment and growth.

The advocates of the total harmonisation approach prove that harmonization contributes to increase in the confidence of consumers in their possibilities to make use of the internal market. According to this view, a confident consumer and the single European market are mutually interacting elements: a confident consumer contributes to the strengthening of the internal market, but at the same time, the stronger and more integrated (harmonised) market, the more confident the consumer. They also explain why it makes sense to harmonise the law of respective member states – in order to make sure that consumers are not scared or prevented from the internal market activities by differences in national consumer law, and - going even further - one can claim that the reason why the EU legislator introduces protectionist regulations is the assumption that a more confident consumer would make greater use of the internal market.

Notwithstanding, this concept is not completely indisputable. There are voices which argue that the whole idea of encouraging a 'confident consumer' to become an actor on the internal market stage aims in fact at constructing the single market; in other words, consumers only have a utilitarian function namely they are expected and supposed to make the internal market work.[382] So, by definition, the interaction is in fact only one-sided. Weatherill[383] even states that it seems nowadays "as if consumer confidence has become the wonder weapon to justify EU competence in the field of consumer law." Reich[384] admits that consumer confidence being important for an internal market, should however not, due to this, serve as a pretext for sticking only to market forces in order to achieve a result of a con-

---

380 (COM (2006) 744 final).

381 European Parliament, "Report on protecting the consumer: improving consumer education and awareness on credit and finance", 18 November 2008, (2007/2288(INI).

382 H.-W. Micklitz, 'Zur Notwendigkeit eines neuen Konzepts für die Fortentwicklung des Verbraucherrechts in der EU. Verbraucher und Recht, No. 18, 2-12 (2003).

383 Weatherill, "European Private Law and the Constitutional Dimension" in Cafaggi (ed.), "The Institutional Framework of European Private Law", Oxford University Press, 2006), p. 105.

384 N. Reich, Chapter: "Economic Law...

fident consumer. On the contrary, in order to reach such a goal, the active support measures should be adopted and the idea of full harmonisation should be abandoned.

Furthermore, in Wilhelmsson's opinion,[385] the harmonisation of laws does not considerably influence the confidence of the consumer, so, in other words, the change in the Commission's approach towards maximum harmonisation cannot be justified only by referring to promoting this confidence. The author also indicates other measures that could play a more meaningful role in striving for this aim i.e. the confidence of consumers. So the answer to the question of whether this shift towards total harmonization can be justified with reference to consumer confidence is negative. Therefore the proposed change is based on the needs of business rather than on the needs of consumers. Wilhelmsson also claims that it is not acceptable to use the consumer-confidence argument as a justification for the substantive approximation and harmonisation measures, because common sense (i.e. doubts about consumers' good knowledge of their rights even on a national level, and about the impact of such a lack of knowledge on their behaviour – and here the argument is that this lack of domestic legal provisions does not deter consumers from shopping in their home state) and self-evident knowledge about how consumers act in the marketplace do not allow for such reasoning.

As a matter of fact, there are a few counterarguments to this approach. First, in the sector of credit or generally in some sectors of high value, consumers have acquired a practical knowledge (often thanks to their own experience or those encountered through the others), but they suspect that they lack this knowledge in other member states. Another counterargument is based on 'nationalistic' beliefs: there is the strong conviction of a number of consumers that the legal system of their own state is more protective than that of others, nevertheless, this is the case – as the Consumer Survey shows – in only some European countries. Therefore, these two arguments can prevent consumers from cross-border actions, and, according to T. Wilhelmsson, they are indeed the arguments for the need of a minimum harmonisation, but they definitely do not support the maximum one. Thirdly, what Wilhelmsson presented is probably a generalisation which is too advanced: undoubtedly there is a group of consumers who benefit from the internal market, and who will even reap more profits in the condition of fully harmonised regulations, however, certainly they are not the majority.

In the atmosphere of a heated debate about the appropriate form of consumer protection for EU legislation, G. Howells and T. Wilhelmsson[386] believe that since the Commission is turning from the minimum to maximum harmonisation approach, there is a strong need for a fundamental reassessment of what role Community consumer law should play in such approach and what principles it should be based upon.

---

385 T. Wilhelmsson, 'The Abuse of "Confident Consumer" ...

386 G. Howells, T. Wilhelmsson, 'EC Consumer Law: Has It Come of Age', E. L. Rev. 2003, 28(3), (370-388).

It has to be stressed that by introducing the total harmonisation approach, the Commission is striving to remove the freedom of the member states to develop their own, more protective, consumer policy. Rebutting these attempts of the Commission, G. Howells and T. Wilhelmsson claim that it is impossible to leave consumer policy entirely in the hands of the European Union. Furthermore, they state that neither the benefits of the total harmonisation to trade nor to consumers, outweigh the negative effects of this newly presented approach. According to the authors, there is no convincing argument to support the idea that renouncing the maximum harmonisation approach to consumer law would relevantly influence in a negative way the development of internal market. They admit that one can find areas where certain national regulation divergences may hamper cross-border trade and competition, but still these do not prove the necessity for harmonising the laws; the adequate solution is then, in their opinion, to address the problems through targeted measures. Also, they stress that in many cases hindrance in cross-border trade is simply a lack of sufficient information on national laws, in which case some transparency measures concerning national legislation and practices seem to be sufficient remedies. However, it must be kept in mind that even if the Commission launches a total harmonisation approach, the matter of national interpretation, practices and procedures to overcome – still remains.

Finally, G. Howells and T. Wilhelmsson claim that from the consumers' perspective, total harmonisation is definitely detrimental.[387] Consumers do not require identical rules in all member states, since they are very often not even aware of their national legal regulations.[388] Instead of unified provisions on a low protective level, they need to be provided with protection corresponding to their expectations. Moreover, G. Howells and T. Wilhelmsson[389] stress that national cultural traditions are much the greater obstacle to introducing total harmonisation within consumer law than different areas of legal regulations which mainly deal with business, because the consumer law concerns people with their national habits and traditions.

The next argument against maximum harmonisation is that the adoption of such an approach would create a serious confusion in the field of consumer law. Hitherto, under the minimum harmonisation approach, there has been a possibility to introduce more protective provisions than these offered by the Directive. Hence, at the time of designing the EU law, there was no strong need to strive for perfect legal provisions as every national legislator could improve the existing provisions by introducing more protective regulations to the domestic legal order. As a result of this, one can elaborate on many weaknesses in the Community legislation which have not been probed. When the Commission prohibits member states from introducing more protective regimes and, as a result, the Community's provi-

387 Ibid.

388 T. Wilhelmsson, 'The Abuse of "Confident Consumer" ...

389 G. Howells, T. Wilhelmsson, 'EC Consumer Law...

sions will be the sole source of consumer protection, consumers will be left with these weak rules.

Micklitz[390] expresses a similar category of complains. Discussing the full harmonisation approach adopted in the Proposal on Consumer Rights,[391] he explains that "EC secondary consumer law demonstrates that the conflicts where an agreement was difficult to achieve are often hidden in the rather cloudy wording of the respective rules, or are transferred into the recitals, sometimes even in contradictory forms," and in case of the minimum harmonisation approach it was never of great importance, however simultaneously with introducing the total harmonisation approach which assumes that the Member Stats' legislators have to retreat in order to give way to EC provisions, the relevance of these uncertainties in EC secondary consumer law increases significantly.

Furthermore, Micklitz finds that the main problem is how to define the scope of fully harmonised rules; how to define the pre-emptive effect of secondary Community law. That difficulty in defining such scope and effect can be explained by the fact that "contrary to CCP, there is no single provision in the EC-Treaty to be interpreted, rather a whole series of rules and recitals which often lack a clear cut picture."

Reifner[392] stresses that the issue of consumer protection in consumer credit contracts, already mentioned in the Old Testament of the Bible and in the Koran, is clearly not merely an economic principle. Reifner calls it 'social consumer protection' and claims that it is certainly not the same as an 'economic advantage' or an 'economic benefit' for consumers, since it forms part of the area of social relations and protects the effective income of consumers. The distinction between these two notions is made clear in the Treaty. According to this leading consumer advocate, 'social consumer protection' is therefore one of the principles in the Treaty, derived from the subsidiarity principle, and upholding cultural diversity in the process of economic integration. Hence, there is a requirement for diversity: 'this kind of consumer protection needs to be adapted to different situations in different countries where different practices and structures create quite different hazards for consumers'. Since the European Community is still not equivalent to a total unification in language, habits and preferences, also in the consumer credit field or more generally in the consumer protection regulations, the European Community should not impose these 'brand new', artificial rules on member state citizens, but should "refer to national developments and extend the best of it to those who have nothing, by trying to keep up a minimum standard in all countries alike." Especially since the addressees of the provisions are consumers who will only be aware of the law in their own language, based on their own culture and conceived as a part of the existing rules in their respective societies. This is because – as Reifner also states in his paper – that the principal feature of consumer protection law is that consumers assume it to

390 H.-W. Micklitz, "The Targeted Full Harmonisation...

391 COM (2008) 614 final.

392 U. Reifner, Proposal for a Directive...

be valid, without knowing the laws verbatim. And this is also the reason why the Rome Treaty on international private law implements the host country control principle for consumer law.

In the discussion of full harmonization between its advocates and opponents, one relevant problem is usually put aside, namely the fact that consumer lending is also affected by other sorts of laws and policies that are currently not harmonized (e.g. laws regarding debt collection or personal bankruptcies), and that all of these regulations constitute additional legal obstacles to the creation of a single market in the field of consumer credit. So the natural conclusion which follows is that total harmonization would contribute to the achievement of a Single Market, but would not in itself be enough to bring about substantial changes in the field. Furthermore, after a very long period of negotiations concerning the consumer credit Directive, it has become evident that it is not politically viable to introduce full harmonization in such a specific field. So in fact the only solution is the targeted harmonization of the few main issues. However, the market of consumer credit requires long-term actions. A suggested step is to increase interstate cooperation on the application of comitology, which would speed up the process of legal convergence, and as a consequence lead to legal harmonization being achieved.[393]

Furthermore, alongside the maximum harmonisation approach, another contentious issue brought up by the modified CCD proposal, is a mutual recognition tool. In Article 21 (2) the Proposal foresaw mutual recognition for some issues to be introduced, giving leeway to national implementation in order to prevent new and additional barriers to the internal market. Those issues were, among others: early repayment, linked transactions, overrunning and intermediation, and a few information obligations. According to such Article, member states could not restrict the activities of creditors established in another member state and operating within their territory in accordance with that Proposal either through freedom of establishment or free provision of services. So in the case of adoption of the Proposal, for an activity in another member state than the one he was established in, a creditor would only have had to comply with legal requirements of his member state of origin, and not with those of the host member state. In other words, creditor would had been only bound by the law of the member state of his own place of business, and due to this, would not have needed to be acquainted with the corresponding rules of the member state where the consumer is domiciled. According to the Commission's explanation, the principle of mutual recognition would not apply to the admission or supervision of money-lenders as service providers; rather, such principle would find its application to the field of consumer protection in private international law. Stuyck and van Dyck describe this tool as a special passport for credit products: once these products comply with the home country laws and practices, they can

393 A. de la Mata Muñoz, Commentary, The EU Commission amends its Proposed Consumer Credit Directive. European Voice, December 2004 – January 2005, http://www.ecri.be .

be exported to any other member state.[394] The country of origin principle – appearing for the first time in the 1984 Commission paper on 'Television without Frontiers' – means that professionals may establish their premises in the legal environment most favourable for them i.e. 'in the environment most favourable for them' with regard to consumer issues, therefore businesses may choose a country with the lowest regulatory standards and keep to these standards also when conducting business in other countries. All in all, such an arrangement would most probably eventually lead to competition between the legal orders of the different states and, at the end of the day, to a 'race to the bottom'.[395] While total harmonisation aims at creating one single law for all member states, mutual recognition does allow for differences in the legal systems.

Although in general, in the literature both notions - the principle of mutual recognition and the principle of country of origin - are treated as synonyms, the European Court of Justice distinguishes between mutual recognition and the country of origin principle and explained the difference between them in two rulings.[396] According to the ECJ, the mutual recognition – contrary to the country of origin principle - cannot be applied against either mandatory legal requirements or public policy of the host country, provided these requirements serve objectively justifiable goals (e.g. consumer protection, fairness of commercial transactions).[397]

From creditor's perspective, the principle of mutual recognition is optimal since it allows him to comply only with his own member state's law. Both mutual recognition as well as the country of origin principle would be welcomed by those money lenders whose premises are placed in the countries of low-standard jurisdictions. In other words, those creditors that are located in high-standard jurisdictions may fear cross-border competition from those located in low-standard jurisdictions. Also those creditors who do not invest in branch networks in other member states would find both mutual recognition and the country of origin principle attractive (contrary to those who did invest in branch networks in other member states and would fear cross-border competition from those who did not).[398] It is conceivable also that as a presumable consequence of introducing mutual recognition to the EU legal system, the competition between national legislations would result in delocalisation of professional enti-

---

394 J. Stuyck, T. van Dyck, Consumer Credit Directive, Briefing Note, requested by the European Parliament's Committee on Internal Market and Consumer Protection, IP/A/IMCO/NT/2006-16, PE 373.567.

395 N. Reich, "Crisis or Future...

396 Case 120/78 Cassis de Dijon [1979] ECR 649; Case C-55/94 Gebhard v Consilio dell'Ordine degli Avvocati e Procuratori di Milano [1995] ECR I-4165.

397 Since the borderline between the mutual recognition and the country of origin principle is of rather little importance and most of the authors use the two notions interchangeably, and further, there are views according to which the Proposal, although naming the suggested approach "mutual recognition" in fact meant country of origin principle (see: Reich below "Crisis or Future...) in my work I decided follow this tendency.

398 S.M. Franken, "The Political Economy...

ties to the member states where legislation is more flexible (i.e. more business-friendly). However, in the case of a conflict, it would still be the courts of the member state in which the consumer is domiciled that would apply the law of the trader's place of business. One could imagine in this place a certain risk, namely that these domestic courts would apply the trader's law (the law of the country where a professional is based) in a way that in all probability differs from the attitude of the courts in the trader's member state.[399]

On the other hand, the authors of the Broad Economic Analysis[400] scrutinized also the consumer's perspective and state that the principle of mutual recognition means that the diligent consumer who is aware of this principle will have to research the different national implementations of the proposed Directive in order to find out the differences. The consumers who would need advice in the preparation of contracts, would experience significant difficulties with this activity because their choice would be limited only to e.g. lawyers, who are familiar with the law from other member states. Also the activity of consumer organizations would encounter major obstacles since they would have to specialize in several legal provisions of other member states. As a consequence, a consumer would be burdened with the related transaction costs (it is very probably that the overall information costs are higher in comparison with a situation, in which only national rules apply) and furthermore unaware of this principle, such a consumer would only find out about it once it was too late, which means that he might conclude a credit contract on the basis of false assumptions. It has to be stressed that such an approach would certainly be an impediment for creating consumer confidence. Moreover, consumer organisations note that lenders would provide credit cross-border from the member state with the lowest consumer protection, and thereby erode both consumer protection and consumer confidence.

Stuyck and van Dyck[401] observe a potential pitfall: once a credit product is "passported" to other member states, it is not entirely clear how mutual recognition would practically work. They ask if, in the case when the law of the host country is chosen, the creditor can still invoke the law of his home country. Differently, when the credit contract does not contain any law clause, it would seem – according to the authors - that national courts of the host country would be required to dis-apply the national implementing provisions that would or could restrict free movement: "if areas mentioned in the mutual recognition clause are concerned, the host member state has to ensure that the said standards would not apply to the contract. Either the law chosen by the parties, or, in the absence of such a choice, the requirements of the creditor's home country law would continue to apply." Stuyck and van Dyck expect that such "dis-application" would lead to a major legal uncertainty.

---

399 F. Alleweldt (Project Director) et al. Broad Economic Analysis...

400 Ibid.

401 J. Stuyck, T. van Dyck, Consumer Credit Directive...

According to Reich,[402] the combination of these two rules: a prevailing total harmonisation approach and the country of origin principle, would mean that cross-border credit could exist only if complying with harmonised EU-wide provisions and the rules of the country of establishment of the credit provider, moreover the controlling authorities would be those of the country of the business premise.

Another problem would be caused by the fact that the relationship between the principle of mutual recognition and private international law is not clarified in the proposed Directive. Stuyck and van Dyck[403] raise the question of whether the home country control principle can be overruled by choice of law rules. Compliance control of the creditor, taken seriously, would imply that the law of the home country applies, regardless of whether the parties have chosen the law of the host country or not. According to the authors, such a far-reaching consequence of the principle of mutual recognition would have to be explicitly laid down in the proposed Directive.

Moreover, the authors foresee – supposing the new Proposal with the mutual recognition provision is adopted - a need for an administrative convergence, since the proposed shift of compliance certainty requires convergence of the "quality" of, and standards used by, the administrative authorities monitoring, interpreting and applying the consumer credit laws of the country of origin. They stress that the Regulation (EC) no 2006/2004 of the European Parliament and of the Council of 27 October 2004 on cooperation between national authorities responsible for the enforcement of consumer protection laws, would not suffice in the consumer credit field, where current administrative practices vary considerably and often reflect different sorts of policy choice.

Furthermore, Reich[404] notices that the same Proposal, suggesting the mutual recognition principle in areas not harmonised 'in order to avoid additional burdens on creditors', at the same time did not even consider consumer interests. Reich continues that while the Commission refers to 'mutual recognition', in fact it means the country of origin principle. Thus, he concludes that consumer protection was set aside in favour of creditors protection.

Micklitz[405] calls attention to another significant threat to consumer interests as a result of adopting maximum harmonisation combined with the country of origin principle, i.e. he warns that such a solution would affect the level of enforcement of consumer protection legislation i.e. "(t)he country with the lowest enforcement level could then become the 'leader' in giving shape to the interpretation of the rules of the UCPD."

Similarly, though drawing attention to different aspects, Rott joined in the criticism of the new proposed approach. The mutual recognition rule applied to consumer credit would

402 N. Reich, "Crisis or Future of European Consumer Law?" in "The Yearbook of Consumer Law 2009", D. Parry, A. Nordhausen, G. Howells, Ch. Twigg-Flesner (eds.), ASHGATE 2008.

403 J. Stuyck, T. van Dyck, Consumer Credit Directive...

404 N. Reich, "Crisis or Future...

405 H.-W. Micklitz, Chapter: "Unfair Commercial Practices and Misleading Advertisement" in H.-W. Micklitz, N. Reich, P. Rott, "Understanding EU...

turn the provisions from the Rome Convention on the Law Applicable to Contractual Obligations and the Rome I Regulation upside down, since in case of differences in consumer protection rules from one member state to the other, the less protective regime of the country in which the professional is domiciled would apply.[406]

At this point it should be also noted that in case of adoption of the proposal for CCD containing mutual recognition provisions, in the view of the Rome Convention on the Law Applicable to Contractual Obligations,[407] as well as in the view of the newly adopted Regulation on the Law Applicable to Contractual Obligations (Rome I),[408] a very questionable situation would take place. According to the Article 5 of the Rome Convention on the Law Applicable to Contractual Obligations, the choice of law by the parties to the contract may not deprive a consumer of the protection of mandatory provisions of the law of the country of the consumer's habitual residence, and in the absence of a choice of law, a consumer contract is governed by the law of the country of the consumer's habitual residence. Thus, a "passive" consumer dealing with a creditor in the consumer's home country may not lose the protection afforded to him by the mandatory consumer protection laws of his own country, and - as Rott[409] stresses – the consumer credit laws of the member states are usually mandatory.

The same provisions were placed in the successor of the Rome Convention, namely in the Regulation (EC) No 593/2008 of The European Parliament and of the Council on the Law Applicable to Contractual Obligations (Rome I). According to the Art. 6 of Regulation, in case of a "passive" consumer (when a professional pursues his activities in the country where the consumer has his habitual residence), a contract concluded between the consumer and such a professional shall be governed by the law of the country where the consumer has his habitual residence. Moreover, when parties to such a contract choose the law applicable, such a choice may not, however, have the result of depriving the consumer of the protection afforded to him by provisions that cannot be derogated from agreement by virtue of the consumer's home country law. It was argued[410] that out of two possible solutions, namely full application of the law applicable to the professional or the law applicable to the consumer – only the latter would be truly compatible with the principle of high consumer protection. The DG Justice, Freedom and Security stressed also the economic fairness for that solution, i.e. the professional dealing cross-border on regular bases would spread the cost of learning

406 P. Rott, Chapter 5 'Consumer Credit' in H.-W. Micklitz, N. Reich, P. Rott, "Understanding EU...

407 Opened for signature in Rome on 19 June 1980 (80/934/EEC).

408 Rome I was adopted as Regulation (EC) 593/2008 on 17 June 2008. The Regulation will enter into force 18 months after its publication in the Official Journal. From that date, it will take the place of the Rome Convention 1980. That is the instrument that currently determines the law applicable to international contracts.

409 P. Rott, Maximum Harmonisation and Mutual Recognition versus Consumer Protection...

410 COM (2005) 650 final.

about other member states' legal system over many transactions, whereas for the consumer it would mean that the whole effort would only fall under a single contract.[411]

The Commission,[412] in reaction to the potential confusion junction of the provisions foreseen in the Proposal and in the Rome Convention, stated that the host member state has to ensure that the said standards (i.e. coming from consumer's home country legal system and at the same time restricting creditor's activity by being higher than creditor's home country standards) would not apply to the contract. Either the law chosen by the parties, or, in the absence of such a choice, the requirements of the creditor's home country law would continue to apply.

Consequently, in case of adoption of the Proposal containing mutual recognition principle, the consumer would be protected by the consumer credit law of his own country, and only where the principle of mutual recognition of the proposed Consumer Credit Directive would apply, could the creditor rely on his own law. Thus, the laws of the two member states would both be applicable, each restricted to specific issues of consumer credit law. That would undoubtedly create a serious legal disorder and would weaken consumer confidence.

The idea of mutual recognition was strongly criticised in the literature. Because of the problems depicted above, neither consumer organizations nor most of the banking associations were favourable to mutual recognition.[413] Additionally, the authors of the Broad Economic Analysis,[414] concluding the observations on full harmonisation and mutual recognition for certain issues, stated that if adopted, the Directive containing mutual recognition "could lead to a 'regulatory' mix that creates confusion among consumers and affects consumer confidence adversely." They stressed that the principle of mutual recognition would add a further level of complexity because of the variety of legal orders that could apply to one contract. Rott[415] remarks that the principle of mutual recognition would turn the rules of private law upside down, since it deprives the consumer of the protection that private international law has offered until now, and at the same time the Proposal did not foresee any obligation for the creditor to inform the consumer about the fact that consumer's home country protection does not apply in certain contracts. On top of this, Rott stresses that the principle of mutual recognition deprives consumers from the more protective member states of their national protection measures in case the creditor is based in a less protective country. Thus, the idea of mutual recognition is in breach of primary EC law, since according to Article 95 EC, the Commission has to consider as a base, a high level of protection, when legislating in

411 The statement which is objectively true, shows again that in the eyes of the Commission same standards (in this case, as regard to due diligence) are applicable to professionals and to consumers.

412 COM (2005) 483 final.

413 F. Alleweldt (Project Director) et al. Broad Economic Analysis...

414 Ibid.

415 See P. Rott, Maximum Harmonisation and Mutual Recognition...

the consumer field. Also, the experts of the Broad Economic Analysis[416] cautioned that introducing mutual recognition would have non desirable effects on cross-border provision of financial services.

As a result of the rather common criticism, mutual recognition as a means of regulation of consumer credit relations alongside maximum harmonisation was removed from the Directive in the Common Position of September 2007.

Full Harmonisation and Pre-emption

McGee and Weatherill[417] distinguish four classes of lawful trade barriers which stand in the way to a full realization of the idea of the single market. Such barriers are: physical, fiscal, technical and, a fourth class of barriers exists which consists of a more general problem which arises as a result of the existence of differing national legal systems. A natural means applied in order to remove these divergent domestic regulations is harmonization of the laws on the EU level. However, even this tool is not capable of ensuring a full uniformity and a complete extraction of all the barriers.

The Community adopts different methods to deal with the barriers. First, the EU legislator may introduce a 'General Regulation' which covers (even though in a very general way), the entire area in question. 'General Regulation' means that, by the same token, member states' legislative activity in the area is excluded. Second, the other lawful way under the Treaty according to which the Community may treat a trade barrier is a 'Partial Regulation'. This refers to cases in which the Community passes legislation which deals with some issues in the area of consideration, and leaves others to domestic regulation. The third method is simply legislative inactivity. This may occur when a certain barrier loses in the priority competition with others or a political agreement on a respective regulation was unfeasible. Finally, the last method is 'No Regulation' that may be a result of a conscious choice to leave this specific field unregulated on the EU level.

The first approach 'General Regulation' evolved from the idea of introducing uniform, mandatory rules for creating 'Europroducts' into the idea of mutual recognition. Thus at present 'General Regulation' signifies that although member states are excluded from the ability to introduce regulation in the area which would be at variance with the Community's premises, the EU legislator does not impose a single inflexible rule on the entire Community. Although 'Partial Regulation' undoubtedly contributes successfully to reaching the goal of the creation of a single market, this tool is not as effective as 'General Regulation'. McGee and Weatherill rightly notice that 'Partial Regulation' is a sign of a certain pragmatic compromise which the authors expect to endure for a considerable amount of time. In turn, the third category - 'No Regulation' - embodies many fields which have not yet been regulated at all

416 F. Alleweldt (Project Director) et al. Broad Economic Analysis...

417 A. McGee, S. Weatherill, "The Evolution of the Single Market – Harmonisation and Liberalisation", The Modern Law Review, Vol. 53, No. 5, "New Perspectives on European Law", Sep., 1990, pp. 578-596.

by the EU legislator. The majority of these areas are those which are traditionally supervised or influenced by member states.

McGee and Weatherill[418] opt for the harmonisation of laws and integration of the EU legal system, nevertheless not at any price. According to the authors, there are areas and cases where the preservation of domestic provisions is justifiable, especially in the situations where a member state has a more generous protective legislation than the Community's regulations, then it seems more beneficial to preserve national legislative competences even at the price of preserving in consequence national divergences.

The discussion on different approaches to the harmonisation problem presupposes Community legislative competence in the potentially harmonised field. The question of the division of competences between the member states and the Community has constantly been a trouble spot creating tensions and ambiguities.[419] The legislation power the Community possesses has been granted to it by member states which thus consented to the loss of some of their sovereign rights.[420] By transferring their sovereign power to the Community via the Treaties, member states thereby deprived themselves of the competence to regulate in the areas agreed by member states. In the sentence Van Gend en Loos the ECJ acknowledged this.[421] The EC lawyers perceive this as a gradual, true transfer, and not a mere delegation of national legislative powers.[422] The Court of Justice made a telling recognition stating that the powers of the Community stem from "a limitation of sovereignty or a transfer of powers from the states to the Community" whereby the member states "have limited their sovereign right" in those fields which they placed within Community competence.[423]

In the Treaty there are in fact no provisions which would provide an explicit list of the spheres in which the Community is exclusively competent; nor are there any provisions which would provide a list of the fields in which member states are exclusively competent. The task of building a list of the areas of Community exclusivity is reserved for the European Court of Justice.[424] The limitation of Community legislative competence is marked by Article 5,[425] which provided a definition of the principle of subsidiarity, according to which, the Community has a title to legislate in the areas which do not fall within its exclusive competence only if and in so far as, the objectives of the proposed action cannot be sufficiently achieved by the member states, whereas the activity of the Community in this respect, by reason of the scale or effects, would better achieve these objectives. The principle of subsid-

---

418 Ibid.

419 N. Foster, "Foster on EU Law", Oxford University Press, 2006, p. 131.

420 D. Obradovic, "Repatriation of Powers in the European Community", Common Market Law Review 34: 59–88, Kluwer Law International, 1997.

421 See: N. Foster, "Foster on EU Law", Oxford University Press, 2006, p. 131.

422 Hartley,The Foundations of EuropeanCommunity Law, 3rd ed. (Oxford, 1994), p. 239.

423 Case 6/64, Costa v. ENEL, [1964] ECR 585, 593.

424 S. Weatherill, "Law and Integration in the European Union", Clarendon Press, Oxford, 1995, p. 135.

425 Article 5 was not amended by the Treaty of Lisbon.

iarity in other words means that the action should be taken at the most efficient level, without any preconception about choices between the national or EU realm.[426] The principle of subsidiarity is tightly linked to the proportionality principle of the EC law which, according to Article 5(3), prohibits the Commission from going beyond what is necessary to achieve the objectives of the Treaty.

Reich[427] also invokes Art. 5(3) and, at the same time, he discusses full harmonisation. The author concludes that - from an EU-constitutional point of view – full harmonisation has its negative effect. By stating this, Reich refers to the pre-emptive effect of European law, that is, the prevention of 'upgrading' consumer law on national levels by transferring to the EU all legislative competences in the sphere of consumer law. Moreover, the author points out that this consequence does not conform to the provision of the Art. 5(1) i.e. the principle of limited Community jurisdiction. Subsequently Reich brings up the unclearness in regard to the judicature, i.e. the boundaries of independence and freedom of the national courts when deciding on cases where the principle of full harmonisation is present.

Micklitz,[428] discussing the proposed full harmonisation approach in the Proposal on Consumer Rights,[429] analyses the constitutional dimension engrained in this approach and asks a crucial (yet provocative) question about the character of the society we want to live in: do we prefer such a society where the European legislator determines the level of protection for the European consumers-citizens or where the legislative power relative to consumer protection belongs to the member states who play an active role in consumer legislation.

In the field reserved for the Community the activity of the member states is precluded not only because the EU rules find their application and prevail in the case of conflict with domestic regulations, but also because even in cases where no EU provisions exist with which national provisions would be in a potential conflict, national action is impermissible.

Apart from a few areas where the Community enjoys exclusive competence and those areas where the member states retain exclusive competence, the majority of matters are object to concurrent ('shared'/'non-exclusive') competence between national and European legislators. According to Article 4,[430] shared competence between the Union and the member states applies inter alia in the areas of internal market, of social policy, for the aspects defined in the Treaty, of economic, social and territorial cohesion, and of consumer protection. Such a situation concerning most areas gives rise to ambiguities as to which actor has the competence for a particular action.

In certain fields (e.g. the internal market) as soon as the European legislator takes an action, he thereby automatically assumes exclusive power to act, and as a result, the member

426 S. Weatherill, "Law and Integration..., p. 169.

427 N. Reich, "Crisis or Future...

428 H.-W. Micklitz, "The Targeted Full Harmonisation..., p. 49.

429 COM (2008) 614 final.

430 After the Treaty of Lisbon, in consolidated versions of the Treaty on European Union and the Treaty on the Functioning of the European Union (2008/C 115/01) Official Journal C 115, 09/05/2008.

states are then deprived of the power to act in conflict with such action i.e. the member states' authorities have thereby lost competence in such fields. In other words, applying the mechanism of pre-emption allows the Community to take over competence in a specific field. In the fields in which the Community has an exclusive competence, the national competence is thus excluded, according to the judgments of the ECJ.[431] In other words, state powers are 'pre-empted' and the Community is exclusively competent i.e. each EU legislative action pre-empts national action in the field.[432] The process of 'pre-emption', whereby the European Community gradually receives titles to legislate in a particular field, can take place through the adoption of internal legislation in the form of common policies, or through the conclusion of internal agreements.[433] However, in the case in which the Community remains passive, the national legislators retain the competence to regulate in a certain area, obviously controlled by primary Community law.

The ECJ expressed this reasoning in the famous Cassis de Dijon judgment[434] stating that only where the EU legislator had not acted, could the national legislators act independently and even then, if concerned with a general area that was otherwise regulated by the EC, the member states could act only within prescribed limits. The Court also added that the consequence of such a power division is a 'genuine grey area' between what is placed within the EU competence and what remains still within the national competence.

According to Waelbroeck,[435] the problem of pre-emption arises in situations where no outright conflict between Community and state law exists, but where a state measure is alleged to be incompatible with the general policy objectives which Community law seeks to achieve. The problem of pre-emption – contrary to that of primacy – consists in determining whether a conflict between a state and a Community measure exists. Waelbroeck[436] classifies the ECJ cases, dealing with the question of pre-emption into two categories based on two distinct approaches: 'the conceptualist-federalist' approach and the 'pragmatic' approach. Whereas the first approach assumes that the essential problem is to define the scope of the Community's competence and then the automatic consequence is the absence of power for national legislators in the area belonging to the Community realm, under the

431 The judgements: Case 190/87, Oberkreisdirektor des Kreises Borken v. Handelsonderneming Moormann, [1988] ECR 4689, Case 16/83 Karl Prantl [1984] ECR 1299, Case C-150/88 Firma Eau de Cologne & Parfümerie-Fabrik Glockengasse v Provide [1984] ECR 1299.

432 S. Weatherill, "Law and Integration in the European Union"..., p. 135.

433 D. Verwey, "The European Community, the European Union and the International Law of Treaties", T.M.C. Asser Press, p. 180.

434 120/78 Rewe-Zentral AG v Bundesmonopolyverwaltung für Branntwein [1978] ECR 649, [1979] 3 CMLR 494.

435 M. Waelbroeck, "The Emergent Doctrine of Community Pre-emption – Consent and Re-delegation", in "Courts and Free Markets. Perspectives from the United States and Europe", T. Sandalow, E. Stein (eds.), Vol. II, Oxford 1982.

436 Ibid.

second approach, the Community's competence is not necessarily exclusive i.e. member states are entitled to regulate in the areas falling within the Community's competence provided that national provisions do not come into conflict with those issued by the Community. The application of these two approaches depends on the field of jurisdiction activity, i.e. the conceptualist-federalist approach finds its application in the areas where the Community's competence is undisputedly exclusive,[437] whereas in the fields where the Community shares its legislative power with domestic legislators, the pragmatic approach prevails.[438] Both approaches are used interchangeably in the areas where the legislative competence is not clearly defined.

According to Weatherill,[439] uniformity in the meaning of the law is part of the constitutional glue that holds the European Community together. However, the present concern, especially after recent enlargement, is whether the idea of pre-emption still poses the optimal solution for the whole European Union.[440] Weatherill[441] assesses that the Community is ill-equipped (it lacks the expertise and the institutional maturity) in order to fulfil the duty to regulate exclusively and totally a certain field imposed on it by the maximum harmonisation approach. Consequently, only minimum harmonisation can ensure that a Community as a multi-functional organism can work properly.

The changes to the original Treaty of Rome inserted by the Single European Act or the Treaty on European Union, envisaging minimum harmonisation served as recognition that Community legal acts can co-exist with those of member states in the same field. In other words, it meant that even if the EU legislator introduced provisions in a certain field, the national legislator is still entitled to add its provisions in that field.[442] Weatherill stresses the significant responsibility, which the Community bears by assuming a burden of harmonisation of the European legal systems, which is inter alia the responsibility for securing the application, for updating the rules etc. By involving the member states' legislator, by the same token, the Community may discharge that responsibility. Additionally, the specifically local problems are then more effectively dealt with i.e. at local levels minimum harmonisation allows for realization of the ideas of innovative techniques of market regulation. In a similar fashion, Reich[443] rightly noticed that the more competence the Community acquires the less exclusive its justification will be.

---

437 For instance the ECJ applied that approach in the Opinion of 11 November 1975, 1/75, [1975] ECR 1355, and later in Donckerwolcke case 41/76, [1976] ECR 1921, the Grosoli case 131/73, [1973] ECR 1555, Indiamex v. Sociaal Fonds voor Dimanatarbeiders joined cases 37 and 38/73, [1973] ECR 1609.

438 The first case representing 'pragmatic' approach is Walt Wilhelm case 14/68, [1969], ECR 1.

439 S. Weatherill, "Law and Integration in the European Union"..., p. 135.

440 Ibid., p. 137.

441 Ibid., p. 153.

442 Ibid.

443 N. Reich, "Competition between Legal Orders: A New Paradigm of EC Law", 29 CMLRev. 851, 1992.

Micklitz[444] analysing the Unfair Commercial Practices Directive and its shift from minimum to maximum harmonisation stresses the great importance of such a move by the EU legislator since such a shift "constitutes in itself a paradigm shift which deserves careful analysis as it requires a re-balancing of the regulatory competences between the European Community and member states." The decision concerning the introduction of a full harmonisation in the place of a minimum one, provokes not only future consequences as to how consumer protection legislation will be shaped,[445] but it also contains a political dimension. In fact, according to the maximum harmonisation approach, it is only the EU legislator who decides about all the provisions in a specific field. Consequently, the result of adopting the new law by the EU legislator is that member states are obliged to accept that law without a title to introduce any amendments. In other words, member states are pre-empted from taking action in that particular field. As a result the decision of what falls within the scope of a legal act and what is excluded becomes of great importance.

Moreover, as Obradovic[446] rightly notices, the views as to what functions are best carried out by member states themselves, or by the member states acting collectively as a European Union, or in a broader international framework, will change over time.

Conclusions

The shift in the EC law from minimum to maximum harmonisation is undoubtedly not only interesting from the academic point of view, but over the last few years it is also a very significant issue in relation to the development of the EU legislation. There are two major dimensions to such a shift: one regarding competence, and the other concerning consumer protection. Again the competence issue is not a one-dimensional problem: on the one hand it means a conflict on the member states versus EC institutions level, which boils down to the issue of the legislative power i.e. the competition between the domestic and EC legislators as to the power to legislate in the specific fields and here pre-emption plays a protagonist role. On the other, a question arises as to whether the societies of all the 27 member states are so homogeneous that there is no needs for them to have a competence to enact a separate, distinct legislation which would take into consideration different national traditions, habits, values etc. The second aspect of the EU policy shift from minimum to maximum harmonisation - next to the competence issue – is the consumer protection dimension. Here a question arises as to what kind of interests are protected as an aim and an intentional result of applying the maximum harmonisation approach to the consumer protection legislation. To discuss this question, one needs to have a brief look at the theoretical background of both contract, and consumer law. Private law as such (a bit simplistic) - and more precise-

444 H.-W. Micklitz, Chapter: "Unfair Commercial Practices...

445 See: chapter 'Full Harmonisation and Confident Consumer'.

446 D. Obradovic, "Repatriation of Powers...

ly the core of contract law - is all about competing interests, whereas consumer law as such is about levelling the chances both parties have on the market in order to preserve in practice the major principles of civil law. These principles are, inter alia, party autonomy, self-determination, and freedom of contract. Thus the question arises as to what exactly consumer law protects. Does it protect the interests of a cross-border consumer-shopper in that this protection means mainly that he is encouraged to become confident enough in order to take advantage of the single European internal market? Or does it protect the interests of a consumer-citizen whose needs go beyond (or whose needs are actually less "sophisticated" than) a favourable bargain in a state other than his own member state (some may argue that these needs are actually less "sophisticated")? Or does it protect the interests of the professional who, as an actor characteristic of the pure contract law principles, wants to extend his geographic scope of activity as much as possible and to keep his outlays being as small as possible?

The EU legislator in the process of designing the shape of the new consumer credit law made a decision very early on, as to the level of harmonisation, and according to this choice, consistently continued to press the maximum harmonisation approach by ignoring the diversity of the individual member states, passing over differences in national traditions habits, and in specific national needs, and furthermore, by downplaying a higher level of protection present hitherto in some of the 27 states, the EU legislator backed market efficiency, thus he opened the EU credit market to all European providers and ensured a better choice for a consumer-shopper.

Information Duties and Right to Withdraw – Agreement on EU Level

In order to impose certain obligations on contracting parties, the legislator, no matter whether domestic or European needs a legitimization which should act as a decent justification. The crucial precondition of a perfect market is that all the players have perfect information about their preferences as well as about the nature and value of the goods and services needed to maximize their utility. In reality, however, markets do not deliver efficient allocation of resources due to market failures,[447] thus there is a need to correct the imbalance in economic power. The provisions containing information disclosure duties are the legislators' response to one of the principle market failures, namely the inequality in bargaining power between consumers and professionals, that is a response to imperfect information (i.e. when a consumer knows less than would be ideal for him to know in order to make conscious market decisions) and to information asymmetry (i.e. when a consumer knows less than a professional). Information disclosure duties are justified as far as they correct market failure and the information asymmetry between parties to a contract since otherwise such, an asymmetry might hamper the natural market mechanism.

Furthermore, the other dimension of imposing the information duties is a 'constitutional' one, as consumers' right to information was mentioned among four other rights[448] in a catalogue of 'consumer rights'. Consumers' right to information was initially expressed by the European Commission in two consumer-political programmes[449] from 1975 and 1981,[450] next, it was recognised as an 'interest to be taken care of' in Article 129a and finally, consumers' right to information was recognised as a 'right' in the Treaty of Amsterdam in Article 153. This right was also confirmed by the ECJ in the decision GB Inno BM v. CCL.[451]

Information failure in consumer markets is a typical rational for governmental intervention in the market place. And although the criterion of 'imperfect information' might almost always legitimize some public action, it has to be kept in mind that not only information disclosure duties bear costs; the information overload can also be detrimental. Hence, the question should be how to accomplish an 'adequate' - and not necessarily a 'perfect' – level of information saturation.[452]

447 P. Cartwright, "Banks, consumers and regulations" Hart Publishing. Oxford and Portland Oregon, 2004, p. 253.

448 The four remaining were: the right to protection of health and safety, the right to protection of economic interests, the right of redress and the right to representation.

449 OJ C 92, 25 April 1975 and OJ C 133, 3 June 1981.

450 N. Reich, Chapter: "Economic Law...

451 7 March 1990, C-362/88, [1990] ECR I-667.

452 I. Ramsay, "Rationales for Intervention in the Consumer Marketplace (1984), pp. 25-35.

A principle objective to provide consumers with a specific set of information is to enable them to make relatively informed decisions with regard to the financial sphere of the potential commitment, as well as to enable them to make relatively informed choices which are an effect of a comparison of the cost of alternative credit options.[453] The main assumption behind information duties in all the consumer protection regulations is that consumers are able to comprehend obligatorily disclosed information and that as a consequence of receiving adequate information on the benefits and dangers of dealing with a professional, they are empowered to make better (rational) choices.[454]

EU consumer protection law i.e. legislation as well as jurisprudence[455] is always in favour of information based protection over interventionist regulations.[456] One major rationale for such a status quo is that at the transnational level, where already many different legal orders have to coexist together, information provisions are easier to accommodate considering the multitude of legal traditions. Moreover, information based protection by nature imposes fewer barriers to free movement than substantive regulations.[457] Indisputably from a political point of view, it is much easier to agree to a compromise when the information duties are the subject of the legislative process, as opposed to other more intervening and thus more contentious matters. Furthermore, on the other hand, as Franken[458] points out, money-lenders resist full disclosure of the price of credit since the financial industry in fact benefits from a lack of transparency (especially limited information provisions in the early stage of the contracting) and high closing fees - thus an imposition of information disclosure duties on the professionals seems to be necessary.

The Commission stresses on many occasions that the harmonisation of pre-contractual and contractual information requirements, and in connection with this, calculation of the APR and right of withdrawal are the key elements and the major aim of the legislation process. The well-informed consumer is the hallmark of the consumer protection legislation, whereas the possibility to withdraw from an only just concluded contract poses a well-established tradition[459] by means of which the consumer has a chance to release himself

---

453 C.W. O'Hare, "Issues in Consumer Credit Law Reform" in "Consumer Protection Law and Theory".

454 C. I. Garcia Porras, W. H. van Boom, "Information disclosure...

455 E.g. Case 178/84, Commission v. Germany [1987] ECR 1227.

456 See more: S. Grundmann, G. Kerber, S. Weatherill (eds.), "Party Autonomy...

457 G. Howells, „The Potential and Limits...

458 S.M. Franken, "The Political Economy...

459 Almost all the MS have something similar. Similar or comparable legislation in the MS - non-exhaustive list: B: right of "renonciation" during a period of seven working days, R: "rétractation" period lasting seven days, IRL: right to "withdraw" for 10 calendar days, L: right "à se départir" but only for credit agreements granted by a supplier and within two days. UK: "cooling-off period" various arrangements, D and A: "Widerrufsrecht" – from Proposal for a Directive of the European Parliament and of the Council on the harmonisation of the laws, regulations and administrative provisions of the Member States concerning credit for consumers, COM/2002/043 final.

from an ill-considered commitment and change a decision taken at a time when the pressure applied by the salesman/creditor outweighed the consumer's free and enlightened will to choose.

Moreover, the legislative activity targeted at combating information asymmetry i.e. the imposition of information disclosure duties on the creditors, is consistent with the Commission's present neoliberal approach towards consumers, since such an activity "pays respect to consumer choice as the cornerstone of proper competition;" the approach which assumes that the consumer is a "rational maximizer of his own utility by making optimal resource allocation decisions when provided with sufficient information".[460]

Adopted quite recently by the European Parliament, the "Report on protecting the consumer: improving consumer education and awareness on credit and finance"[461] stresses the importance of financial information being a significant ingredient of consumer protection regulations, however, states also that financial information should be presented in such a manner that the consumer can process it, since consumers who are burdened with too much information, may not be able to filter it and, consequently, they are prone to make the wrong financial decisions. The authors of the document favour quality over quantity as far as information duties are concerned, i.e. high-quality, and accessible, concrete and easily comprehensible information aimed at enhancing the consumer's ability to make informed and responsible choices.

In order to guarantee an efficiently functioning market, adequate information on prices, terms etc. must be provided. The common assumption that consumers form a group, which lacks proper information, led to the introduction of various protection measures based on information duties. The measures either secure the proper provision of information for consumers or increase consumers' ability to process sets of information.[462] However, one should not forget that first of all not all information is actually advisable for every consumer, and second, not all consumers will in fact take the advantage of the information they are provided with.

The members of the European Financial Services Round Table (EFR),[463] when creating the five principles which were intended to be the guidelines for further integration of retail financial services and for the establishment of common rules for appropriate European consumer protection, mentioned as the first condition the guarantee that the consumer will receive appropriate information in order to enable him to take an informed decision on whether the product suits his own personal needs and circumstances. They stressed that the emphasis should be put more on quality than on quantity, so that the consumer would not

460 C. I. Garcia Porras, W. H. van Boom, "Information disclosure...

461 European Parliament, "Report on protecting the consumer: improving consumer education and awareness on credit and finance", 18 November 2008, (2007/2288(INI).

462 I. Ramsey, "Framework for Regulation...

463 European Financial Services Round Table "Consumer Protection – Consumer Choice. Deepening EFR's Concept on Consumer Protection in Retail Financial Services", January 2006.

be overburdened with information. The EFR distinguishes three types of information: advertising, pre-contractual and finally contractual information; and claims that at least a portion of such information should be fully harmonised on the EC level.

On the one hand, the EFR representatives perceived the risk of uncertainty for a consumer to conclude a contract without having enough knowledge and understanding of the complex technicalities of banking as well as of legal issues, however, on the other hand they warned against a burdensome advice given to the consumer whose minds are focused on the item being financed at the time of the sale of the credit product. They believe that the information contained in the proposed Pan-European Info Box will deliver enough information required at the beginning of the contractual relation.

According to Ramsey,[464] "imperfect consumer information is a fundamental rationale for consumer protection measures." Thus, the legislator in the consumer protection acts primarily builds on information regulations as an effective tool applied in order to redress the information balance between a professional party and a consumer. Consumers who are not informed, at the same time are not capable of making conscious choices especially in the field of financial services. There is a significant probability that consumers' decisions concerning financial services which are however not based on reliable knowledge, would not satisfy their needs, especially considering that the financial services market is constantly changing and evolving, and therefore is very difficult to be comprehended by a layman. Ramsay[465] calls information disclosure in the credit card market a 'Truth in Lending' and praises its advantages as it supports the idea of consumer autonomy through the informed consumer choice, moreover the 'Truth in Lending' has limited costs for governments and finally, it may attract a consensus of support from business and consumer groups.

The disadvantage of this policy tool stems from the main assumption which poses a background of the 'Truth in Lending', i.e. a 'rational consumer' model of decision making, and consequently it entails a risk that disclosures based on this model may be limited as a form of 'debasing intervention'. Ramsay warns, by the same token, of the risk that some 'systematic irrationalities in consumer decision-making' will be deliberately addressed by credit providers. The remedy in such a situation is either greater carefulness in designing effective information policies or, the engaging, by the authorities, in the direct regulation of the activity.

In the same vein, C. I. Garcia Porras and W. H. van Boom[466] claim that the concept of the well-informed (due to information disclosure obligations), average consumer, "alludes to a mythical figure." They stress this especially in the area of financial services because there the

464 I. Ramsey, "Framework for Regulation...

465 I. Ramsay, Chapter 1 "Consumer Credit Society and Consumer Bankruptcy: Reflections on Credit Cards and Bankruptcy in the Informational Economy" in J. Niemi-Kiesiläinen, I. Ramsay, W.C. Whitford (eds.), "Consumer Bankruptcy in Global Perspective", 2003, Hard Publishing, Oxford and Portland, Oregon, p. 33.

466 C. I. Garcia Porras, W. H. van Boom, "Information disclosure...

legislative framework hardly ever takes into account outright irrational consumer behaviour. Moreover, the authors also warn against unfair practices of service providers - who taking advantage of the situations where consumers face difficulties in processing very complex sets of information on credit products - may engage in commercially profitable but at the same time dubious and deceptive practices, thus the process of consumer decision making would certainly differ from the one anticipated in a perfect market scenario, if it is unfairly distorted by deliberate commercial practices of creditors.

Donnelly and White[467] notice that the provision of information and hence a well-informed, confident consumer is the cornerstone of European consumer protection law and policy. The Commission confirms this e.g. in its communication 'Healthier, Safer, more confident citizens – a health and consumer protection strategy,'[468] by highlighting that a confident consumer is a certain sine qua non condition for a proper functioning of the internal market. The authors[469] advocate positive views on engaging information duties as a main consumer protection tool, namely that it involves relatively minimal interference with party autonomy i.e. the legislator requires the professional party to a contract to provide the information and then the whole transaction may proceed without regulatory interference, and at the same time from consumer's perspective, the market remains fully open; in other words consumers can enjoy unrestricted choice.

Micklitz[470] draws attention to a further purpose of the information obligations which is to enhance the position of the consumer prior to concluding the contract by enhancing competition between different service providers. In case in which the legislator demands transparency from the market players, it becomes feasible to compare the offers and choose the most favourable one.

Howells[471] notices, analysing DTI's study,[472] that from the UK's policy perspective, information is the most efficient means of consumer protection, which offers 'a win-win solution', since consumers provided with proper information are at the same time granted with the means to protect themselves and to drive up standards, and on the other hand, since professionals do not suffer from excessive intervention of the regulator, they can flexibly provide the goods and services expected by the consumers without restrictive and potentially anti-competitive substantive regulatory controls.

---

467 M. Donnelly, F. White, "The Effects of Information Based Consumer Protection: Lessons from a Study of the Irish Online Market" in C. Twigg-Flesner, D. Parry, G. Howells, A. Nordhausen (ed.), "The Yearbook of Consumer Law 2008. Markets and the Law", Ashgate 2008.

468 COM(2005) 115 final.

469 M. Donnelly, F. White, "The Effects of Information Based Consumer Protection...".

470 H.-W. Micklitz, "The Relationship between National and European Consumer Policy...

471 G. Howells, "The Potential and Limits...

472 Department of Trade and Industry, "Extending Competitive Markets: Empowered Consumers, Successful Business", 2004.

Next, Howells stresses that the main idea which stands behind the UK government's study "Extending Competitive Markets: Empowered Consumers, Successful Business" can be as follows: the more powerful and assertive the consumer, the healthier economy. Thus, a strong correlation exists between information duties, and consequently consumers' informed choices and more effective competition. The explanation for such correlation is as follows: due to the knowledge consumers gain confidence that flows hence thus they are capable of distinguishing good quality from poor quality goods and services, asserting their rights, and of putting not only firm but most of all effective pressure on the supply side. Furthermore, Howells stresses that an additional argument which offers a justification for consumer protection is that uncontrolled adverse practices of the supply side may undermine confidence in the market. Howells[473] suggests that next to positive information duties, consumers also require negative information about professionals e.g. records of adjudication from public authorities, courts, etc.

Similarly, Schwartz and Wilde[474] suggest that a state can interfere when professionals do not compete to give consumers better terms, but being aware of consumers' ignorance, they exploit that fact to procure for themselves the most favourable terms possible. Furthermore, the authors claim that regulation prevents consumers from making informed decisions between contract terms and prices, since banning harsh terms forces consumers who prefer to accept these terms in order to take advantage of lower prices, to pay higher ones.

Unquestionably, in the traditional understanding of private law dogmas, the information requirements restrict the freedom of a professional in so far as he is required to disclose information he would not otherwise reveal. Howells[475] makes an attempt to 'weigh' on the one hand the damage to a trader's freedom caused by the legislature interference and on the other hand the advantage of the potential growth in autonomy of a consumer who - due to knowledge he has gained - is capable of making an informed market choice. The author comes to a conclusion that that limitation on the professional's autonomy is minimal compared to the simultaneous advantage awarded to the consumer.

Schwartz and Wilde[476] distinguish two sorts of situations where imperfect information may prevent a consumer from making utility-maximizing choices. The first situation is characterized by circumstances in which the consumer may know of available options but lack the information to fully evaluate them. The second group contains those cases in which a consumer is ignorant with respect to some elements of the set of options from which he must choose.

---

473 G. Howells, "The Potential and Limits of Consumer Empowerment...".

474 A. Schwartz, L.L. Wilde, "Intervening in Markets on the Basis of Imperfect Information: a Legal and Economic Analysis", University of Pennsylvania Law Review 1978-1979, Vol. 127: 630.

475 G. Howells, "The Potential and Limits of Consumer Empowerment...".

476 A. Schwartz, L.L. Wilde, "Intervening in Markets on the Basis of Imperfect Information...".

Schwartz and Wilde find two justifications for the state's intervention in consumer markets as far as determination of contract terms is concerned. Assuming that all consumers are identical in terms of their market preference rankings, and that a state (a court or a legislator) is more profoundly able than the interested actors (i.e. consumers), to ascertain which market decisions are consistent with this ranking, then the state's intervention would maximize consumers' utility. The objection to such a state's intervention concerning a better knowledge consumers have as to their personal preferences can be refuted in case the consumers are imperfectly informed. However, since the original assumption as to the identity of consumers' preferences is in general false, then consequently external (i.e. state) determination of contract terms is rarely optimal. From this viewpoint, Schwartz and Wilde reason that the next step which follows after accepting that state should intervene to regulate contract terms in case of uninformed consumers, is that as a result one grants the state the right and at the same time obliges the state to combat the deterrent status quo. According to the authors, since the decreased information acquisition costs will cause the decrease of the number of uninformed consumers, the ideal solution for the issue of imperfect information would be to reduce these costs.

In the older literature[477] one can encounter a view, according to which in order to introduce a fully justified intervention in a market, two conditions have to be fulfilled: the existence of imperfect information, as well as the existence of substantively unfair contract terms. A legal intervention on information grounds can be justified "only if a market is found to be behaving noncompetitively." *A contrario,* in case of a competitive market, which safeguards the utility maximization of all the contractual terms for consumers, any intervention on information grounds would be an abuse. The other problem arises however in the case of perfectly competitive markets and their potentially unfair outcome, and consequently such a possibly imaginable situation provokes a question as to whether the state is entitled or is obliged to interfere on grounds of substantive fairness when no information obstacles exist.

Wilhelmsson and Twigg-Flesner[478] enumerate the general principles of information duties. The first principle is the protection of *the real consent* of the party. However, this is not completely unquestionable in the literature. Such a point is being made by the representatives of the typical traditional contract paradigm approach assuming that the task of contract law is to provide a party with sufficient information so that such party can express his real consent i.e. negotiate in a rational way; in other words information regulations appear as duties close to the rationale of the principle of freedom of contract.[479] However, on the oth-

477 A. Schwartz, L.L. Wilde, "Intervening in Markets on the Basis of Imperfect Information…."

478 T. Wilhelmsson, Ch. Twigg-Flesner, "Pre-contractual information duties in the acquis communitaire", European Review of Consumer Law 4/2006.

479 K. Riesenhuber, „Party Autonomy and Information In the Sales Directive", In S. Grundmann, W. Kerber, S. Weatherill (eds), "Party Autonomy...

er hand, some scholars[480] perceive information duties as the opposite to the freedom of contract. One can also encounter the approach[481] according to which there is no need for state intervention, simply that market forces under certain conditions induce information disclosure.

Secondly, Wilhelmsson and Twigg-Flesner claim that information regulations should as a result provide a party with an *equipment for rational market behaviour* not only during negotiations, but also in a more general sense i.e. a well-informed party becomes a confident actor on the market and thus can make conscious choices (i.e. the second principle). The third objective mentioned by the authors is the use of information duties as a device to uphold informational clarity i.e. information duties ensure that information concerning the contract is preserved for both parties adequately. Fourth, the authors indicate the protective function of information regulations thanks to which the *fair content of the contract* can be achieved, since such duties can pose the incentives especially for professional parties to improve their standards as far as market competition is concerned. Moreover, in case of a lawsuit, the court may use disclosure rules as a hidden control of the substance of the contract.

Finally, according to Wilhelmsson and Twigg-Flesner, the information duties may act as a support of a moral duty of honesty, in other words, the state intervention via imposing on parties' information duties can be justified by moral reasoning. Thus in order to justify the introduction of information regulations (especially the duty to disclose), one does not need to search for any reference to the need or necessity to protect the weaker actor; the fact that such duties are consistent with the common societal perception of honesty and relate to the general consensual contract paradigm is enough. Therefore, information duties find their place not only in consumer protection acts, but they may also refer as well to solely professional and solely non-professional (individual-to-individual) relationships as well. In fact Wilhelmsson and Twigg-Flesner even stress the significance of e.g. pre-contractual duties in the business-to-business realm of large and complex contractual procedures, especially in a potential litigation. Contrary to duties to disclose information, a duty to provide information has almost exclusively consumer law character. Having as its main purpose protective considerations, such a duty is supposed to equip the party for rational market behaviour and guard substantive fairness of the contract.

Unquestionably a decision concerning credit agreement is significant for a consumer's budget. From a consumer's perspective, it represents a serious, long-term commitment for the future, whereas the future income or in general a consumer's future financial situation is only more or less predictable, but never really certain. The decision concerning entering into a credit contract entails a threat to a consumer's financial security especially nowadays

480 E.g. P. Giliker, „Regulating Contractual Behavior: The Duty to Disclose In English and French Law", European Review of Private Law 621-640, 2005.

481 F. Gomez, „The Unfair Commercial Practices Directive: a Law and Economics perspective", European Review of Contract Law 4-34, 2006.

when capital markets are easily accessible for the consumer. While for the creditor there is a wide range of means serving in order to minimize the risk of future unpredictability, the borrower has in fact merely the properly disclosed and sound information regarding contract terms which helps him to select an appropriate product, as well as and the right to withdraw only from the just concluded contract.

It is quite a truism that individuals take advantage of the information they are provided with in very different ways. These differences depend to a large extent on the consumers' level of education as well as their affluence. These differences stand out especially in case of consumer credit where the risk problem differentiates the credit market along socio-economic lines. Moreover, also when it comes to consumer credit issues, Howells[482] suggests that the poor may even rationally give up exploring the information they are provided with, since feeling alienated from mainstream creditors, they doubt any alternatives available for them other than doorstep sellers, predatory lenders etc. Fearing embarrassment due to great probability that they would be turned down, the poor accept every condition they are offered without questioning it. Howells risks a hypothesis that perhaps the wrong sort of information is being provided for low-income consumers.

The Commission in its Green Paper on Retail Financial Services in the Single Market[483] highlights that good information helps consumers to understand the key features of a financial product, not excluding the risks, potential returns and costs. The Green Paper provides the guidelines regarding information which has to be delivered to a consumer. According to the Commission, the information needs to be complete, correct, clear, proportionate, understandable and presented in a timely manner. Moreover, information requirements must also be consistent. From the consumers' perspective, pre-contractual information duties are particularly essential – duties which concern the pre-contractual stage i.e. during the negotiations which may eventually result in a binding contract, or in case a party has indicated his willingness to enter into a contract but the necessary formalities have not yet been completed.[484]

As concerns consumer credit, Reifner[485] distinguishes two types of transparency to be delivered to potential borrowers in order to allow the market to function properly, i.e. competitive transparency which allows consumers to select the cheapest and best offer and is relatively easily guaranteed by the APRC[486] disclosure obligation, and social transparency. The latter – according to the postulates of the European Coalition for Responsible Credit –

482 G. Howells, "The Potential and Limits of Consumer Empowerment...".

483 COM (2007) 226 final.

484 T. Wilhelmsson, Ch. Twigg-Flesner, "Pre-contractual information ...

485 U. Reifner (ed.), "European Coalition for Responsible Credit – Principles of Responsible Credit" in C. Twigg-Flesner, D. Parry, G. Howells, A. Nordhausen (ed.), "The Yearbook of Consumer Law 2008. Markets and the Law", Ashgate 2008.

486 The Annual Percentage Rate of Charge being a standardized mathematically correct form of 'one-price' disclosure.

requires creditors to disclose in a so called 'standardized pre-contractual payment plan' the likely impact of future payments on consumers' household liquidity and future purchasing power including the ability to repay.

There are however several doubts and questions concerning the use of information duties as a consumer protection measure. However, certainly placing information requirements in the act forces the obliged party to comply with these duties and results in providing the consumer with all the required information, but yet it does not ensure that the regulation is effective, and the asymmetry removed. A prudent legislator, in order to introduce a real solution, ought to ensure that the information is useful for consumers, i.e. that consumers actually read and understand the information provided. Donnelly and White[487] as a first argument against information duties, mention that there is a probable risk that the information provided never actually reaches the consumer since it may be too complicated for him in order to be comprehended or the consumer may simply be too bored by the prospect of reading it. The second argument challenges the assumption of a rational consumer's behaviour in response to provided information, and warns that the information may be used by the consumer, for instance, for supporting his own views.

A third concern refers to so called 'information overload' being a result of providing an individual with too much very detailed, specific information which at the end of the day may become counter-productive by decreasing the consumer's ability to make a decision. F. Figueira[488] quotes the studies researching the "information overload" phenomenon,[489] according to which, the increase of the quantity of information available results in the increase of the quality of decisions, but only up to a certain point. As soon as a consumer faces an information overload, the quality of his decision starts decreasing.

Lastly, doubts arise as to whether the 'one size fits all' approach of information provision actually reaches all consumers being yet a much differentiated 'target group'.[490] Many authors[491] stress that such a heterogonous group as consumers, determined by several social and cultural factors, also has a different capacity in respect not only to comprehending the disclosed information, but also to making use of it. This simple observation demonstrates that in an uninformed-based approach to regulation, those consumers - who experience greater difficulty by processing information and who at the same time are poorer, less-educated etc. – finds themselves without adequate protection. However, the other danger concerns those consumers who receive and manage to understand the meaning of certain information, but because of e.g. the complexity of certain transactions, are not able to pro-

487 M. Donnelly, F. White, "The Effects of Information Based Consumer Protection...".

488 F. Figueira, "The European Commission and Financial Capability...

489 M. Handzic, „Does More Information Lead to Belter Informing?", in A. Haringer (ed.), "Proceedings of the 2001 Informing Science Conference, 19-22 June 2001, Kraków, Poland, pp. 251-256.

490 M. Donnelly, F. White, "The Effects of Information Based Consumer Protection...".

491 See e.g.: I. Ramsey, "Framework for Regulation ..., T. Wilhelmsson, Ch. Twigg-Flesner, "Pre-contractual information duties ..., G. Howells, "The Potential and Limits...

cess that information in such a way that would enable them to use it in making a decision concerning entering a certain contract, as they might not be able to comprehend all the implications which follow from this information.[492]

F. Figueira[493] invokes the behavioural economic theory of "bounded rationality" which denies that consumers act in a perfectly rational way which in case of information can be illustrated by the example that consumers may not read all the information that is provided to them before entering the contract, even if thanks to that information they would be able to make a more profitable deal, because they might find the information too complex, too technical, and thus not appealing. In other words, the theory claims that consumers are able to handle only a limited amount of information.[494]

Ramsay[495] alike emphasizes that one should not ignore the issue of high information processing costs, i.e. the cost which a consumer bears in the process of comprehending and later applying information to his situation. The author discusses the social and cultural barriers to information processing among certain, often disadvantaged groups of the society and appeals that these barriers should be considered when designing remedies for information failure. Ramsay remarks that in case of high information processing costs, the better remedy to information failure might be product standard, quality certification or licensing.[496] Also Ramsey brings to mind the idea of "bounded rationality" which explains that individuals have a capacity to receive and process a limited amount of information.

Similarly, Howells[497] dwells on the studies concerning information from which results flow the conclusions that individuals have a limited ability to understand and process information. Furthermore, every person is more likely to believe the information which supports his own views, as well as to ignore statistical evidence in favour of more real-life experiences, and finally studies show that there is a tendency to be too optimistic about one's own ability to avoid a risk, which in the end, leads to the results that consumers will often not give information proper significance, and is strongly linked to a propensity to emphasize immediate benefits and to downplay delayed costs.

Also the Commission[498] cautions against inadequate or too complex information, which paradoxically can make it difficult for a consumer to compare prices, products and providers,

---

492 M.J. Trebilcock, S. Elliot, „The Scope and Limits of Legal paternalism", in P. Benson (ed), "The Theory of Contract Law", Cambridge University Press, 2001, p. 62.

493 F. Figueira, "The European Commission and Financial Capability...".

494 London Economics, "Consumer Detriment under Conditions of Imperfect Information – OFT Research Paper 11 (London: Office for Fair Trading, 1997).

495 I. Ramsey, "Framework for Regulation ....

496 I. Ramsay, "Rationales for Intervention...

497 G. Howells, "The Potential and Limits of Consumer Empowerment...".

498 SEC (2007) 106, 31.1.2007, p. 67 and "Eurobarometer 230: Public Opinion in Europe on Financial Services", August 2005.

and to make an informed financial decision. The Commission bases such caution on practical scrutiny.

The other consequence which follows from information duties imposed on the creditor is the result of an assumption that the information which is supposed to be revealed is known to the service provider. Such assumption may be mistaken in many circumstances, thus, in fact information duty would impose a burden on the professional to gather all the required information, which at the end of the day might turn out to be a costly venture. Wilhelmsson and Twigg-Flesner[499] stress the relevance of the proper balance between consumers' benefits following from additional information and, on the other hand, the increase of the providers' cost. The authors[500] point out another concern, namely they claim that often the timing of disclosure of information is not suitable for a consumer in order to make full use of such information. In other words, the consumer receives the information when he does not yet need it, since it is not immediately relevant. The authors find the fact that a legislator imposes on the professional the duty to disclose all the information on the very initial stage of the commercial relationship to be a manifestation of paternalism. As a remedy it is proposed to reduce the amount of information provided before concluding the contract and make it available after conclusion.[501] However, such a "drip-feeding" clashes with the whole idea of restoring information equilibrium between a professional and non-professional party. Furthermore, it collides with the principles of contract law, and represents a highly paternalistic stance since it allows a legislator to hide certain elements of the contract from the consumer.

As a result, a conclusion can be drawn that a sole disclosure of information by the professional even done in a reliable and law-abiding fashion, does not necessarily mean that the level between a professional and his customer in the scope of information has been evened out; moreover that information-based rules can be a sole response to the need for consumer protection.

Information Duties in the Previous Regulations

The Directive 87/102/EEC of 22 December 1986 contained only minimum provisions concerning information duties, since Article 15 provided the leeway for member states to introduce or retain other tools aiming at a better consumer protection. The general provisions of the Directive contained the guidelines declaring that the borrower should receive adequate information on the conditions and cost of the credit, and on his obligations.

499 T. Wilhelmsson, Ch. Twigg-Flesner, "Pre-contractual information duties...

500 Ibid.

501 See: W.C. Whitford, „The Function of Disclosure Regulation in Consumer Transactions", Wisconsin Law Review, 400-470, 1973, Ch. Twigg-Flesner, "Consumer Product Guarantee", Aldershot: Ashgate, 2003, p. 114-115.

According to Article 3 of the Directive 87/102/EEC any advertisement, or any offer which was displayed at business premises, in which a person offered credit or offered to arrange a credit agreement and in which a rate of interest or any figures relating to the cost of the credit were indicated, had also to include a statement of the annual percentage rate of charge (or at least the total cost of the credit to the consumer in certain specified circumstances), by means of a representative example if no other means were practicable. Furthermore, Article 4 stipulated the minimum content of a credit agreement; the written contract had to contain at least: a statement of the annual percentage rate of charge as well as a statement of the conditions under which the annual percentage rate of charge could be amended. The Directive also provided an exemplary list of the other essential terms of the contract which member states could require to be included in the written agreement. Moreover, Article 6 specified the minimum information duty confirmed in writing in case of the granting of credit in the form of an advance on a current account, other than on credit card accounts. The information duty also applied to the period of the agreement as the creditor was obliged to inform of any change in the annual rate of interest or in the relevant charges at the time it occurred. According to the Directive 87/102/EEC, the financial institution was supposed to inform the borrower of the limit of credit, the annual rate of interest and the charges applicable from the time the agreement was concluded and the conditions under which these charges could be amended and finally, the procedure for terminating the agreement. In the member states where legal order permitted tacitly accepted overdrafts, the creditor had to inform the consumer of the annual rate of interest and the charges applicable, and of any amendment thereof, where the overdraft extended beyond a period of three months.

Contrary to the Directive 87/102/EEC, the Proposal of the directive from September 2002[502] - adopting a maximum harmonisation approach - foresaw a very complex set of information duties as well as regulating the right to withdrawal. Article 4 dealt with the advertising displayed at business premises and which included information on credit agreements, in particular as regards the borrowing rate, total lending rate and annual percentage rate of charge. Such advertising had to be provided in a clear and comprehensible manner, with due regard, in particular, to the principles of good faith in commercial transactions. The commercial purpose of this information had to be made clear. Article 6 stipulated that before the conclusion of the credit agreement the lender had to provide the consumer with enough information about the cost of the credit and his obligations. The pre-contractual information had to cover all aspects of the credit agreement (whether it was a fixed-rate or variable-rate credit agreement, and had to cover: what conditions governed variations in the

---

502 The Proposal of the Directive of the European Parliament and of the Council on the harmonisation of the laws, regulations and administrative provisions of the Member States concerning credit for consumers, COM(2002) 443 final.

rate, the recurrent and non-recurrent charges, drawdown, repayment, the sureties and insurance requirements, the duration of the credit agreement, the amount, number and frequency of payments to be made, the period during which the right of withdrawal could be exercised etc.); and some of that information had to constitute the compulsory information to be included in the credit agreement. The information had to include a reference to the annual percentage rate of charge. The APR placed in the information had to be the same as the final APR shown in the credit agreement. The consumer had to be able to check the components of the APR and of the credit being offered: amounts to be drawn down, amounts to be repaid and the periods. The Proposal also introduced a new indicator which had to be a part of pre-contractual information, i.e. the total lending rate. Any reference to a rate or a cost that did not occur in the indicator was considered to be misleading. Article 10 of the Proposal contained the common provisions for credit agreements and surety agreements concerning the information that had to be included in written credit and surety agreements, copies of which had to be received by all the parties. The Article encompassed a complete and compulsory list of information: the general conditions, in particular those governing the operation of an account or regulating a variable rate of interest, as well as the total amount of credit (the Proposal foresaw no possibility to change that limit without a new agreement and a new solvency check). All the information required by Article 6 and other additional issues had to be covered in the written agreement. That information had to be relevant, legible and accurate as well as consistent with the information that was provided prior to the conclusion of the credit agreement. The credit agreement as well as the surety agreement had to contain an indication of any extrajudiciary procedures that could apply.

The New Directive

Ultimately with the adoption of the new Directive in April 2008, an agreement concerning pre-contractual and contractual information requirements, including the calculation of the APR and the right of withdrawal has been reached on an EU policy level. These provisions have been fully harmonized, so in consequence no departure from the Community provisions in this respect is envisaged, since according to Article 22 point 1, member states are not allowed to maintain or introduce in their national legal orders provisions diverging from those laid down in the Directive which are harmonised. Member states are obliged thereby to place in the transposition acts the regulations provided by the Directive. Moreover, Article 22 point 3 of the Directive states that the duty of member states is to ensure that the provisions adopted by national legal orders as the result of implementation of the Directive cannot be circumvented as a result of the way in which agreements are formulated. However, one can raise a question as to whether the fully harmonised information duties and right to withdraw are the most appropriate means to overcome tension between integrated market and consumer protection?

The newly adopted Directive contains more complex provisions concerning information duties. These duties apply not only to the pre-contractual information and the information which has to be encompassed by the credit agreement, but also the creditor's duties to deliver to the consumer certain information during the contractual relationship. In the 'Deliberations' it is stated that this Directive should contain specific provisions on advertising concerning credit agreements as well as certain items of standard information to be provided to consumers in order to enable them, in particular, to compare different offers. Furthermore it is stressed that such information should be given in a clear, concise and prominent way by means of a representative example. Article 4 stipules the mandatory requirements for advertising of the credit for consumers stressing that any advertising which indicates an interest rate or any figures relating to the cost of the credit to the consumer shall include standard information specified in a clear, concise and prominent way by means of a representative example. However, the Directive gives a certain leeway to member states in this respect exempting from the obligation those cases where national legislation requires the indication of the APR in advertising concerning credit agreements which do not indicate an interest rate or any figures relating to any cost of credit to the consumer. However, Rott rightly notices that in this respect the new Directive contradicts with the Unfair Commercial Practices Directive,[503] which introduced a harmonised EC-wide standard of fairness that would seem to prevent member states from adopting divergent levels of protection.

The Article lists as a standard information requirement inter alia: the specification of the borrowing rate, fixed or variable or both, together with particulars of any charges included in the total cost of the credit to the consumer, the total amount of credit, the APR, and any potential obligation to enter into that contract regarding an ancillary service relating to the credit agreement. The Directive distinguishes the mandatory information which has to be included in advertisement and the pre-contractual information.[504] Article 5 states that the potential client has to be provided with the Standard European Consumer Credit Information (SECCI) form, that is, the information needed to compare different offers in order to make an informed decision on whether to conclude a credit agreement. This form is a recently added innovation introduced by the Council in order to uniform pre-contractual information requirements. The form, exactly the same in all member states, is a mandatory tool used by creditors in order to provide the consumer with a pre-contractual information set. The pre-contractual information has to include inter alia: the borrowing rate, the conditions governing the application of the borrowing rate, as well as the periods, conditions and procedure for changing the borrowing rate, the amount, number and frequency of payments to be

503 2005/29/EC.

504 P. Rott uses a different classification and distinguishes in the new Directive three types of pre-contractual obligations: pre-contractual information (following the model of all modern EC consumer law Directives, the new CC act shifts information obligations to the time prior to the conclusion of the contract), pre-contractual advice and the duty of responsible lending. P. Rott, Chapter 5 'Consumer Credit' in H.-W. Micklitz, N. Reich, P. Rott, "Understanding EU....

made by the consumer, the charges for maintaining one or several accounts (if mandatory) recording both payment transactions and drawdowns, the existence of costs payable by the consumer to a notary on conclusion of the credit agreement (if applicable), the obligation to enter into an ancillary service contract relating to the credit agreement (if applicable), and the consumer's right to be supplied, on request and free of charge, with a copy of the draft credit agreement. Moreover, a novelty in EU credit regulation, as well as in many member states' legal orders is the requirement of providing the consumer with pre-contractual advice - Article 5(6).[505] It is in line with Recital (27)[506] of the Directive. According to Rott,[507] the clear assumption behind these provisions is that the EU legislator was aware that the sole information (that the consumer would be provided with) in many cases might not be enough.

The final set of information duties is provided by Article 10, namely the information which the creditor is obliged to include in credit agreements. In its 'Deliberations', the Directive states a general rule concerning the credit agreement, according to which such an agreement should contain all necessary information in a clear and concise manner. The legislator broadened the requirements specified in the previously mentioned Article 5 with inter alia the information on the procedure to be followed: in exercising the right of termination of the contract; the information on whether or not there is an out-of-court complaint and redress mechanism for the consumer and, if so; the methods for having access to it. The contract must be recorded on paper or on another durable medium, however that provision

505 Article 5(6) Member States shall ensure that creditors and, where applicable, credit intermediaries provide adequate explanations to the consumer, in order to place the consumer in a position enabling him to assess whether the proposed credit agreement is adapted to his needs and to his financial situation, where appropriate by explaining the pre-contractual information to be provided in accordance with paragraph 1, the essential characteristics of the products proposed and the specific effects they may have on the consumer, including the consequences of default in payment by the consumer. Member States may adapt the manner by which and the extent to which such assistance is given, as well as by whom it is given, to the particular circumstances of the situation in which the credit agreement is offered, the person to whom it is offered and the type of credit offered.

506 Recital (27): Despite the pre-contractual information to be provided, the consumer may still need additional assistance in order to decide which credit agreement, within the range of products proposed, is the most appropriate for his needs and financial situation. Therefore, Member States should ensure that creditors provide such assistance in relation to the credit products which they offer to the consumer. Where appropriate, the relevant pre-contractual information, as well as the essential characteristics of the products proposed, should be explained to the consumer in a personalised manner so that the consumer can understand the effects which they may have on his economic situation. Where applicable, this duty to assist the consumer should also apply to credit intermediaries. Member States could determine when and to what extent such explanations are to be given to the consumer, taking into account the particular circumstances in which the credit is offered, the consumer's need for assistance and the nature of individual credit products.

507 P. Rott, Chapter 5 "Consumer Credit"..., p. 113.

shall be without prejudice to any national rules regarding the validity of the conclusion of credit agreements which are in conformity with Community law. In case of some specific types of credit agreements, the European legislator restricted the information requirements of this Directive concerning pre-contractual information and information included in the contract itself.

The Directive gave up the Proposal's emphatic rule concerning unchangeable amount of credit, however it states that a ceiling (indicating the upper limit of credit which can be made available to the consumer) is provided where it is not possible to indicate the total amount of credit as the total sums made available, in particular where a credit agreement gives the consumer freedom of drawdown with a limitation with regard to the amount. The novelty of the adopted version concerning pre-contractual information is that the creditor has to provide the consumer with adequate information on the conditions and cost of the credit and on their obligations, which the consumer may take away and consider, prior to the conclusion of the credit agreement.

The legislator aiming at guaranteeing the consumer the fullest possible transparency and comparability of offers, created a homogeneous way of determining the annual percentage rate of charge applicable to the credit, throughout the Community. As the annual percentage rate of charge - being the main issue in the pre-contractual information set - can be indicated only through an example, such example should be representative, therefore should be based on the average duration and total amount of credit granted for the type of credit agreement under consideration and, if applicable, to the goods purchased. The problematic element of APR, which poses a probable risk that this index will not reflect the real cost of the credit, are the costs of credit insurance. These costs have to be included in the total cost of credit only in cases where insurance has a compulsory character.

The Directive indicates the borrowing rate as the one of the most relevant mandatory parameters which has to be part of the pre-contractual information and which must also be specified in the credit agreement. During the contractual relationship, the consumer should be further informed of changes to the variable borrowing rate and changes to the payments caused thereby, before the change enters into force (Article 11), however the Directive foresees an exception from this obligation.

The Right to Withdraw

However, Sunstein and Thaler[508] stress the inadequateness of the statement that when people lack relevant information the best response is to provide it, since according to the authors, the sole information is not effective without the realization of how people actually think. The authors make the behavioural consequences of otherwise identical pieces of in-

508 C.R. Sunstein, R.H. Thaler, "Libertarian Paternalism Is Not an Oxymoron", The University of Chicago Law Review, Vol. 70, Nr. 4, 2003.

formation conditional on how they are framed, i.e. without paying significant attention to information processing, information disclosure might prove to be not only futile, but under the certain circumstances, even counterproductive.

Sunstein and Thaler propagate the idea of 'libertarian paternalism', being a fairly non-intrusive type of paternalism which assumes that individuals should be "free to choose." The idea is not to block the choices, but to impose trivial costs on those who seek to depart from the legislator's[509] preferred option. However, the fact that the legislator self-consciously attempts to move individuals in the direction that would promote their welfare – according to Sunstein and Thaler - amounts to paternalism. Advocating the concept of libertarian paternalism the authors claim that it is not always true that people who are left free with making their choices, choose perfectly or in other words make choices which are in their best interest. The authors assume that at least in contexts in which people are inexperienced and poorly informed, policy could make them better off by improving their decisions.

According to the supporters of that ideology, the manifestations of the idea of libertarian paternalism in the field of consumer protection are "cooling-off" periods as a measure which allows consumers to free themselves from the binding commitment arisen through ill-considered or improvident decisions. That instrument was not designed to block consumers' choices, but to ensure that consumers get a period for sober reflection before their decision becomes legally binding. The importance of a "cooling-off" period is stressed especially in cases in which consumers are find themselves in situations untypical for them (in that - such choices they make infrequently) and consequently they lack experience in that sphere and secondly in situations in which irrational aspects play a significant role.

The standard example is – granted to consumer-borrowers - right to withdrawal in the field of financial services, especially in consumer credit, since first from a consumers' perspective this is not a routine situation and second, individuals who find themselves in difficult financial circumstances are not very likely to make the credit decisions in a rational, calculated way, especially considering that as a general rule they lack sufficient knowledge in that field.

The right to withdrawal was introduced for the first time to European law by the Doorstep Selling Directive,[510] however "non-European based rights of withdrawal" also existed - long before the Doorstep Selling Directive, (in fact, as early as the end of 19th century, that instrument became familiar to some domestic legal orders).[511] The idea which was behind it was the assumption that clients have a weak psychological position – and the temptation of immediate enjoyment would cause them to underestimate the future obligations. Thus the

509 Sunstein and Thaler use the general notion of "planner" for anyone who faces the job of designing institutional features such as rules, procedures etc.

510 85/577/EEC.

511 See: E. Terryn, "The Right of Withdrawal, the Acquis Principles and the Draft Common Frame of Reference" in R. Schulze (Ed.), "Common Frame of Reference and Existing EC Contract Law", sellier. european law publishers, Munich, 2008.

aim of the instrument is to ensure that the consent to a contract is informed, free of any coercion and well-considered, in other words, that the contract is fair. The right to withdrawal is welcome and advisable in cases where there is a supposition that one party's consent departs from the above characteristics and that the formal freedom of contract fails in providing sufficient guarantees for a fair contract and as a result material freedom of contract is missing.[512] Terryn distinguishes two differing situations where the right of withdrawal should find its application, namely: cases of "psychological deficits" i.e. where a vulnerable consumer is being approached by a mighty professional building on aggressive practices, often taken by surprise and as a result the consumer is put under pressure. The second group is formed by situations where the consumer suffers from "information deficits" as a result of either the substantial complexity of the contract or the mode of concluding the contract.

A more complex problem with reference to the right of withdrawal concerns the legal nature of that right. For the first time, the right of withdrawal was introduced to the legal systems in Austria and in Switzerland (both from the beginning of 1960s), and its legal nature was characterized by different approaches: that is, in Austria, the buyer was allowed to withdraw from a contract that had been concluded, on the contrary, in Switzerland the moment of conclusion of the contract seemed to be postponed.[513] The discussion as to the legal nature of the right of withdrawal is still current after over 40 years. The prevailing view[514] presumes that although a party has a right to withdraw from the contract during a specified period of time, that fact does not affect the conclusion of the contract; the contract is valid, although one cannot deny that the existence of the right to withdrawal creates an unstable situation. In other words, a consumer has a claim for performance during the withdrawal period and accordingly, until the exercise of the right of withdrawal, the contract should be considered valid and enforceable. On the other hand, one can encounter opposite views,[515] according to which, the contract is not "concluded" before the period for withdrawal has expired. However, the second view based on "pending invalidity" (schwebende Unwirksamkeit) as contradictory to Distance Selling Directive cannot be a universal one.[516]

The issue closely related to the effect of the existence of a right of withdrawal on the validity of the contract are the effects of exercising that right on the contract. Again the prevailing opinion states that as a result of exercising the right of withdrawal the performance

512 Ibid.

513 D. Heinrich, „Verbraucherschutz: Vertragsrecht im Wandel", in V. Beuthien (ed.), „Festschrift für Dieter Medicus", Cologne 1999, pp. 206.

514 The view is represented in the Principles of the Existing EC Contract Law, as well as follows from the provision of Art. 6 of the Distance Selling Directive (97/7/EC).

515 Such view is present in some national implementing acts of other directives (e.g. the Doorstep Directive 85/577/EEC).

516 See: E. Terryn, "The Right of Withdrawal, the Acquis Principles and the Draft Common Frame of Reference"...

obligation arising from the contract ceases to exist and consequently the performance of obligations already fulfilled are to be returned or reimbursed.[517] However the question arises as to whether the contract ceases to have effect retrospectively or whether the contract only ceases to have effect for the future from the moment in which the consumer withdraws. According to the Advocate General in Crailsheimer,[518] withdrawal has the effect of making the agreement void from the outset, and therefore it seemed for the Advocate General that the status quo that existed before the conclusion of the contract should be restored. However, the ECJ itself did not give a decisive answer in this respect, since the Court, referring to the restoration of the status quo ante, passed over the problem of the voidness of the contract. In turn, the status quo ante can be achieved by considering that the contract has never existed and is to be regarded as void, and in such an instance, restitution claims can be grounded on the provision of unjustified enrichment. The restoration of the status quo can also be conducted through imposing on the parties specific legal obligations to return what they have received under the contract. Thus, Terryn concludes stating that the directives and case-law grant the leeway to the member states whether the contract the consumer withdraws from is ended retrospectively or only perspectively.

The exercising of the right to withdrawal undoubtedly entails the restoration of the status quo ante, however the EU legislator left considerable leeway to the member states in that respect. The preliminary draft of a Common Frame of Reference acknowledges the fact that the consumer directives presuppose the existence of certain rules in domestic legal orders.[519] Since the national laws generally contain the restitutionary provisions applicable to these legal situations where a contract ceases and the parties are thus obligated to return what they have received from each other as performance of the contract, and these situations resemble greatly in terms of results, those cases where a party withdraws from the contract – Terryn suggests that instead of "duplicating" these rules, one should refer to existing provisions, taking into consideration the amendments where advisable due to the specific nature of that instrument. However, then again the often repeated question arises which concerns the level of harmonisation of law within the European Community, i.e. is there any point to "standardizing" only certain provisions leaving broadly understood enforcement on the side, to the realm of the member states, which obviously means that we will be dealing with 27 different regulations. In national legislation the right of withdrawal existed inter alia in Germany, Belgium, France, Ireland and Luxembourg.

Regarding the right of withdrawal, the members of the European Financial Services Round Table (EFR),[520] when creating the above mentioned five principles (which were in-

517 Ibid. (Terryn).

518 ECJ Case C-229/04, 25 October 2005, Crailsheimer Volksbank eG v Klaus Conrads and Others [2005] ECR I-09273.

519 No. 70 and no. 74 of the introduction to the DCFR.

520 European Financial Services Round Table "Consumer Protection – Consumer Choice. Deepening EFR's Concept on Consumer Protection in Retail Financial Services", January 2006.

tended to be the guidelines for further integration of retail financial services and for establishment of common rules for an appropriate European consumer protection),[521] considered the right of withdrawal as second in order of importance. They state that such right serves as a guarantee that the consumer will have the time and opportunity for reflection after entering the contract. The right of withdrawal means that after concluding the credit contract, the consumer can unilaterally decide within a period of time to step back from that commitment. It is a classical tool which enables the consumer to cancel hastily made commitment.[522]

Kösters, Paul and Stein, the authors of the "Economic analysis…",[523] criticised the whole idea of granting consumers the right to withdrawal. They believed that by offering consumers a withdrawal period, the legislator proves that it does not trust its own idea that the well-informed consumers can best protect themselves. They questioned in general the whole idea of the right to withdrawal as such, which implies that it is the government's responsibility to protect consumers from their own decisions, which contradicts the principle of self-responsible action. Consequently, they criticized such an extended measure of protection as allowing consumers to make hasty and careless decisions. Furthermore, the authors claim that so far thanks to a natural market competition, some banks already adopted such a privilege for their customers, so by introducing a mandatory right, the EU legislator would take away the competitive advantage of the more innovative money lenders. The introduction of that mandatory right would have a negative influence on market efficiency, since on the one hand it would result in further rationing of credit agreements or increasing the prices of same, and on the other, it would result in more careless consumer behaviour.

The Directive 87/102/EEC of 22 December 1986 did not foresee a possibility for a borrower to withdraw from the contract, however Article 15 provided the leeway for member states to introduce or retain other tools aiming at a better consumer protection. So far, under the old Directive there were various durations of that period, starting from seven working days in Belgium, France, and the Netherlands; ten days in Italy and Poland; two weeks in Germany and up to fourteen days in Norway, Spain and the UK.

Yet, the Proposal of the directive from September 2002[524] - offering a maximum harmonisation approach - regulated the right to withdrawal. The Proposal envisaged the right for the consumer to withdraw his acceptance of the credit agreement within a period of fourteen calendar days with no need to give a reason._The creditor could in that instance require such consumer to pay a maximum indemnity that was consistent with the amount

521 See more: p. 128.

522 W. Kösters, S. Paul, S. Stein, "An economic analysis...

523 Ibid.

524 The Proposal of the Directive Of The European Parliament And Of The Council on the harmonisation of the laws, regulations and administrative provisions of the Member States concerning credit for consumers, COM(2002) 443 final.

obtained by applying the annual percentage rate of charge to the amount drawn down with effect from the date of drawdown and up until such time as the APR ceases to apply, following the repayment of the funds or the return of the goods. No other indemnity could be claimed in connection with withdrawal. Moreover, Article 11 stipulated that the consumer would be required to return the goods that he obtained in connection with the credit agreement, to the creditor, whenever the credit agreement stipulated that the goods are to be returned.

Finally, the newly adopted Directive foresees a full harmonisation of the right of withdrawal with a small flexibility for member states. Article 14 guarantees consumers the right of withdrawal during a period of fourteen calendar days from the day of the conclusion of the contract (but not before the consumer receives all the required contractual terms, conditions and information) without penalty and with no obligation to provide justification. Apart from notifying the creditor in a specified manner of his withdrawal from the contract, the consumer has to pay to the creditor the capital and the interest accrued thereon from the date the credit was drawn down until the date the capital is repaid within a specified period of time. The Directive stipulates that the creditor is not entitled to any other compensation from the consumer, except for compensation for any non-returnable charges paid by the creditor to any public administrative body. The EU legislator left a certain leeway for national provisions, namely if in the case of a linked credit agreement, the national order at the time of entry into force of the Directive already provides that funds cannot be made available to the consumer before the expiry of a specific period, member states may exceptionally foresee that the 14-day period may be reduced to this specific period at the explicit request of the consumer. Moreover, according to paragraph 6, member states may provide that the right of withdrawal will not apply to credit agreements which are mandatory notary concluded. Article 15 regulates the situation when the consumer exercises his right to withdraw in case of linked credit agreements.

Remedies

In general in *acquis communautaire* damages for the violation of duties to inform are not expressly provided. However, member states are not precluded from allowing for damages in their legal orders.

Wilhelmsson and Twigg-Flesner[525] take note of the fact that as to remedies for failing to comply with information duties the current *acquis* lack a consistent approach. In other words, generally, most consumer law directives regulate such issue - either very fragmentarily or, in many instances not at all. The regulation of the remedies available in circumstances where the professional has breached information duties is left wholly or partially to member states.

525 T. Wilhelmsson, Ch. Twigg-Flesner, "Pre-contractual information duties...

The provisions in the newly adopted Directive on information duties and the right to withdrawal pose one of many examples present in Community law, where the European legislator affords the individual certain rights, but at the same does not provide the proper tools required in order to enforce these rules. In other words, procedural provisions in Community order are missing. Although Community law through substantive provisions provides European citizens with a wide range of rights, at the same time it does not grant them with any instruments in order to ensure the effective application of these rights derived from Community provisions before the court. The enforcement of these Community rights is feasible merely via national procedural rules. In other words, member states are expected to provide remedies and procedures for the protection of these rights which results from the Community law principle of access to a court, as well as from Art. 6 and 13 ECHR.[526]

As a solution for dealing with damages in case of failure by the professional to fulfil information duties, Mankowski[527] advocates the German application of *culpa in contrahendo,* which naturally refers only to pre-contractual requirements. Furthermore, he states that the legal system can treat the failure in complying with information duties as a misrepresentation which, as a result, would lead to the rescission of the contract.

In the situation of lack of EU law remedies, the case law could take over. In two decisions Courage v. Crehan[528] and Antonio Munoz Cia SA v. Frumar Limited,[529] the European Court of Justice stated that in general damages might be available in case a party acts in contravention of an obligation under EC law based on general principles of effectiveness. Although the above mentioned cases involved directly applicable provisions, according to Wilhelmsson and Twigg-Flesner,[530] it could be possible that the Munoz principle might one day be extended to cover directives, at least in cases where these have been properly implemented into national orders. As a result, national courts might have to accept claims for damages in a situation of a breach of national legislation implementing the directive, and thereby effectively create a new form of action for 'breach of EC statutory duty'. Wilhelmsson and Twigg-Flesner then go further proposing a principle, according to which, "[a] party is liable for damage caused by its breach of information duties, even if no contract has been concluded." Such a principle encompasses the situation where there has been a failure to

526 It was confirmed by ECJ judgment Case 158/80, Rewe-Handelsgesellschaft Nord mbH v. Hauptzollamt Kiel, Case 22/84, Johnston v. Chief Constable RUC.

527 P. Mankowski, "Information Requirements in EC Private Law", European Review of Private Law 6-2005 [779-796].

528 Case 453/99 [2001] ECR I-6297 (ECJ). The ECJ held that a party is entitled to damages where there has been a breach of Article 81 EC.

529 Case 253/00 [2002] ECR I-7289 (ECJ). The ECJ held that - even though the claimant had no specific right under the regulation – still that regulations could be enforced in civil proceeding where another party had breached the rules.

530 T. Wilhelmsson, Ch. Twigg-Flesner, "Pre-contractual information duties...".

comply with a pre-contractual information duty, but in the end no contract has been concluded.

Schwartz and Wilde[531] agree that the responsibility for solving information problems should be assigned to an administrative agency, instead of being assigned to courts, since in case of imperfect information the most effective tool is an action to encourage markets to move towards competitive equilibrium by imposing proper duties on professionals. Such administrative agency provided with adequate resources could investigate market conditions adequately. Furthermore, it could order remedies in order to make markets more competitive and finally, such agency would be more effective in policing disclosure schemes.

The remedy which is however present in many consumers EU acts is a postponement of the starting point of a formal period of withdrawal. In the new Directive on credit agreements for consumers, Art. 14 (right of withdrawal) provides that the 14-day period of withdrawal shall begin (...) from the day in which the consumer receives the contractual terms and conditions and information in accordance with Art. 10, if that day is later than the date of the conclusion of the contract agreement. And since the Directive does not contain any restriction regarding that postponement, the judgment of the European Court of Justice[532] finds application, according to which the start of the withdrawal period is postponed indefinitely - i.e. a consumer may cancel a contract some years after the conclusion of same.

There is a settled case law[533] in this matter, according to which in such a case it is a member states' legislator's task to provide individuals with proper procedural rules in order to ensure the protection of these rights. The initial ECJ rulings – giving only the basic degree of guidance - delegated to national legal systems the task of determining how the interests of individuals adversely affected by an infringement of EC law were to be protected.[534] Member states regulate the enforcement of Community rights under the principle of the procedural autonomy of the member states. However, according to Kakouris,[535] member states or their domestic courts, do not possess national procedural autonomy. Kakouris defines national procedural law as merely an ancillary body of law which is used to ensure the effective application of substantive Community rules. However, in the literature one also finds completely opposing views, e.g. Van Gerven[536] characterizes the issue as one of proce-

531 A. Schwartz, L.L. Wilde, "Intervening in Markets on the Basis of Imperfect Information...".

532 Case 481/99 Heininger v Bayerische Hypotheken- und Wechselbank [2001] ECR I-9945 (ECJ); similarly in case 229/04 Crailshaimer Volksbank v Conrads and others [2006] 1 Common Market Law Review 21 (ECJ).

533 i.g. Case C-78/98 Preston and Others, Joined Cases C-392/04 and C-422/04 i-21 Germany and Arcor, Case C- 168/05 Mostanza Claro v. Movil.

534 P. Craig, G. De Burca, "EU Law. Text, Cases and Materials", Fourth Edition, Oxford University Press 2008, p. 306.

535 C. N. Kakouris, „Do the Member States Posses Judicial Procedural <Autonomy>?", CMLR 6/1997, p. 1389-412, p. 1389f.

536 W. Van Gerven, "Of Rights, Remedies and Procedures", CMLR 37: 501-536, 2000.

dural competences, which he contends resides with the member states. The second principle indicated by ECJ under which the enforcement has to be regulated, is the principle of equivalence or non-discrimination. Here the assumption is that these procedural rules are not less favourable in comparison to those governing similar national situations, in other words, forms of action available to individuals must be the same as for national law rights.

Next, there is the principle of effectiveness, which is being described as an obligation on member states' courts to ensure that they give adequate effect to EU law in cases arising before them;[537] or the principle of practical possibility, efficiency, according to which member states cannot render impossible in practice or excessively difficult the exercise of rights conferred by the EC provisions.[538] In the Mostanza Claro v. Movil Judgment the Court held that in the case where the protection granted to consumers by the Community acts concerns public interest, such protection should be as effective as possible. Consequently, the ECJ encourages setting aside national rules of procedure in order to give effect to European Community provisions on consumer protection. In other words, for the Court, the nature and importance of the public interest underlying the protection which the Directive[539] confers on consumers is a good justification to pass over national procedural rules. Furthermore the ECJ[540] declared that the Treaty had not intended to create new remedies in national courts, nor to require those courts to create new remedies, and that national provisions could be applied as long as they complied with the principles of equivalence and practical possibility. However, not all authors share this opinion.

Van Gerven[541] observing that fact considers the issue of effective judicial protection of these rights as well as the uniform application of Community law in all member states. He stresses that the national remedy provides "adequate" judicial protection, i.e. allows interested party "to obtain redress commensurate with the nature and the degree of interference" with that party's rights, and moreover, the member states safeguard that such a judicial protection is not "virtually impossible", "excessively difficult" nor less favourable than a protection granted in similar national claims.[542] Van Gerven, perceives a tension between the need for uniformity in the enforcement of Community rights, i.e. the demand for an appropriate remedy in the whole European Union, and the responsibility of each member state to provide the appropriate procedural rules. It is entirely natural and logic that such a prerogative of individual member states results in the divergence in content and extent of the remedial relief made available in each national system.

---

537 Case 14/83 Von Colon and Kamann v. Land Nordrhein-Westfalen [1984].

538 Case C- 168/05 Mostanza Claro v. Movil.

539 In that case it was Directive 93/13/EEC of 5 April 1993 on unfair terms on consumer contracts.

540 Case 158/80, Rewe-Handelsgesellschaft Nord mbH v. Hauptzollamt Kiel.

541 W. Van Gerven, "Of Rights, Remedies and Procedures"...

542 It results from the ECJ judgments: Case 33/76, Rewe-Zentralfinanz Eg and Rewe-Zentral AG v. Landwirtschaftskammer für das Saarland, Case 45/76, Comet BV v. Produktschap voor Siergewassen.

According to E. Storskrubb,[543] the consequence of awarding member states with the task of providing rules and remedies for individuals to realize their rights, is a potential conflict with the fundamental Community order principle of uniform application and equality because national procedural rules form a de facto obstacle to the uniform application of substantive EU norms. This might occur in the case when the domestic legal system lacks certain procedural rules or the existing national rules have a limiting effect on the realization of Community rights deriving from substantive Community provisions.

Van Gerven advocates - with regard to the national rules providing remedies intended to enforce the Community rights of individuals - the application of the 'adequate test' instead of the 'minimum effectiveness test', to assess the consistency of national provisions with Community provisions and to define the "executive" conditions of remedies from member states' legal orders, since not minimum but adequate protection must be the standard in relation to which the sufficiency of national rules is assessed.

Conclusions

The consumer protection policy came into existence in the times where professionals were successfully attempting to abuse their power in contractual relations with their customers, for instance, by applying sharp practices or imposing unfair contract terms. At present such adverse to consumers' practices belong to the past, at least in most of the business zones of most of the Community states. This is one of the decisive reasons why information rules seem to be the best tool to apply in consumer protection regulations.

Imposing the information duties on the professionals is the only way for a state/Community to intervene in the market economy without risking accusation of being paternalistic or of limiting market freedoms. I would risk a statement that the information requirements imposed on professionals by policy makers in the frame of consumer protection regulations are the only state/Community intervention which in reality does not interfere in the idea of the free market. Moreover, information duties counteract business failure in that they allow the markets' invisible hand to freely balance demand and supply. Finally, the regulation of information duties is also a manifestation of the respectful attitude the legislator displays towards the consumer's right to make sovereign market decisions. This instrument is absolutely in line with the concept of consumer autonomy, and as such rebuts the potential reproaches of paternalism. Similar to the Community legislature, the European Court of Justice[544] also demonstrates its preferences towards information duties as an effective instrument in consumer protection policy, and which moreover does not threat the in-

543 E. Storskrubb, „Civil Procedure and EU Law. A Policy Area Uncovered.", Oxford University Press, New York 2008, p. 2.

544 ECJ case 178/84, 1987, Commission v. Germany, ECR 1227, ECJ case C-362/88, 1990, Gb-Inno-BM v. Cofederation du Commerce Luxembourgeois, ECR I-667.

tegration. However, at the same time, one should not forget that by creating these specific obligations, the legislator shifts the responsibility from the state or Community to the consumer, since according to the common assumption, the informed consumer or more specifically, the consumer provided with information, makes conscious choices. Whereas in an ideal situation, i.e. a fully aware consumer and an honest business counterparty, such solution seems to be proper, if on the other hand only one of the factors departs from that perfect pattern, then such solution is no longer objectively unquestionable. That is why the legislator who applies information regulation as a main tool in consumer protection can be sometimes reproached with an attempt to place responsibility for any harm on the consumer.

Undoubtedly the idea to use information duties as a main consumer protection measure is for every policy maker a tempting one. It attracts the regulator's attention in the process of designing consumer policy with the prospect of the easiness of shaping consumers' behaviour in a desired way, as well as with the prospect of the avoidance of 'excessive intervention reproaches', however the main purpose – which is the consumer's good – should not disappear from the legislator's intentions. Therefore more focus should be placed on the quality of information and the manner in which it is delivered to the customer, as opposed to multiplying the quantitative requirements.

These provisions of the new Directive (i.e. information duties) met with the approval of many interests groups. Definitely the newly introduced, innovative Standard European Consumer Credit Information (SECCI) wins recognition as a tool which ensures a clear and transparent transmission of the very complex information. On the other hand, the total harmonisation of information duties entails the danger that member states will be restrained from regulating separately certain specificities and peculiarities present in their consumer credit markets and thus, certain problems occurring in the respective member states will not be addressed by the domestic legislators.[545] Notwithstanding, these issues can always be addressed in the future by the national judicature.

The step taken by the EU legislator in respect of information duties, originally, according to the Commission's assumption, is supposed to be a milestone in striving for the realisation of the idea of the internal market. The uniform regulations EU-wide, with in principle no departures, seem to pave the way for standardized 'europroducts' supported by standardized 'euromarketing strategies' of present EU-wide 'europroviders'. Contrary to complaints which were expressed by the industry and which concerned mainly the increase of the costs for the industry due to the introduction of these complex information duties, it seems that at least for the biggest players on the European credit market, the additional costs will be compensated with a significant surplus by the scale of activity. Again, one product, one marketing technique etc. for all the 27 member states, which is after all in line with the initial EU legislator's ideas.

545 C. I. Garcia Porras, W. H. van Boom, "Information disclosure...

Information duties, as emphasised before, are also the only manifestation of a regulator's intervention in the market, which is still 'permitted' by the neoliberal approach, which assumes that the invisible hand in principle should be left free. Imposing information duties very nearly do not violate the pure free market balance of powers. By fully harmonising the information duties, the EU legislator gave the consumer a shield to protect himself, and so armed with information, left him to himself. The lack of traditionally understood protection is compensated though by a greater choice and bigger opportunities. As was remarked also earlier, an efficient internal market needs such confident, empowered consumers seeking best bargains EU-wide.

Nevertheless, one cannot resist the impression that again, the goal of consumer protection plays second fiddle. The EU legislator did not take into consideration either the national diversity, the different traditions or habits which characterize the 27 member states; nor the higher level of legislative consumer protection which has already been reached in some of the countries. And finally, the EU legislator downplayed all the theories of bounded rationality which prove that the mere provision of information does not in fact change the consumer's situation on the market due to many factors (inter alia the problem of rationality of individuals, the problem of information over-load etc.), which were ignored by the legislator.

The mere information duties - as one of the tools of consumer protection - are absolutely advisable and desirable, and here the consensus exists. The main problem, however, is that in case of the new consumer credit Directive, information duties are actually the only instrument of consumer protection, as the main assumption of the EU legislator is that the market regulates everything in the most proper way, and a more firm intervention in the market could possibly disturb its natural processes, and thus, weaken its effectiveness. The other crucial problem seems to be, as mentioned above, the shifting of responsibility, as an informed (at least originally) consumer does not need any handicap on the market, thus can be treated on a par with the business party. Such an approach not only releases the legislator from taking any additional protective measures, but it also excludes any potential responsibility of the money-lender for the consumer's possible failure.

Responsible Credit, Principles for Responsible Lending

"Unfortunately, not everyone could borrow money from the banks. Those individuals who lived on the margin of society and were not able to give sufficient guarantees had only one option: to resort to usurers. Faced with such poverty and with people that had to cede all their material possessions to pay usury interests, the Franciscans promoted the charitable initiative of the 'Monti di Pietŕ' pawnshops which issued no-interest loans or loans at the 'right price'."[546] This is an excerpt from "Primitive forms of agrarian credit: 'Monti Frumentari' in the Kingdom of Naples", by P. Avallone. Although this problem is described as concerning the population of the second half of the XVth century, nowadays such a problem still occurs among the poorest European citizens.

"Lasting peace cannot be achieved unless large population groups find ways in which to break out of poverty": these words are very recent and aptly applied to present circumstances. They come from Ole Danbolt Mjoes's speech, who is the chairman of the Norwegian Nobel Committee and who rewarded Muhammad Yunus and the Grameen Bank with the Nobel Prize. The Prize was rewarded for developing the concept of "microcredit." In fact, such credit gives entrepreneurs who are too poor to qualify for traditional bank loans, very small sums to start up their own enterprises and consequently such credit helps "low-income families to break the vicious circle of poverty".[547]

In order to fully understand the premises of the concept of "responsible credit", one ought to acquaint oneself with the circumstances under which consumers, those peculiarly vulnerable borrowers, enter into the loan contract. The process of globalisation, visible in almost all commercial and in some non-commercial human activities as well, also characterises the credit market. Creditors seeking a solution for lowering costs enter into horizontal co-operation (also familiar to other branches of entrepreneurship), and as a consequence, it leads into the development of a large number of separate contracts: different tasks (the provision of money, the acquisition of clients, the securing of debts and their recovery etc.) are thus executed by different units. These units are legally and financially responsible only for their particular section of lending activity, and as a result, there is no single entity that is liable and concerned about the whole contract and the entire performance of the consumer, from the moment in which the contract is signed until the debt is paid off.

In the economy there are few factors which have an immeasurable value, which are impossible to grasp by means of numbers, indexes etc. Notwithstanding, nobody can deny substantial influence on the entire economy of such factors, since at the end of the day, they do

546 P. Avallone, "Primitive forms of agrarian credit: 'Monti Frumentari' in the Kingdom of Naples", Naples, ISEM-CNR, Working Paper, 2001.

547 UN Secretary General Kofi Annan.

have an economic dimension, although they keep clear of the basic economic notions and measurable constructions. One of these difficult to define factors is 'trust'. Indisputably, trust plays a crucial role in the relationships between legal entities dealing with themselves. It is also of great importance between natural persons in their trade relationships, as well as in the business-to-consumer transactions. Trust is a result of two main coexisting factors: time and experience. In a way, trust can be defined as a common good in the sense that it builds up 'social capital'; it is an element of the common mentality of the members of the respective societies. K. Arrow notices that trust as such increases efficiency of the system and thus it has a "real, practical, economic value".[548] On the other hand, in general terms, the lack of trust is corrosive for society because of its powerful destructive influence.

Needless to say, trust plays a very different role in different fields of trade interactions. Nevertheless, credit relationships are such that the feeling of trust is of enormous importance: no matter how complex and sophisticated credit instruments become, still these relationships are to a great extent based on trust. This is the reason why the notion of trust is the starting point of the new "responsible credit" philosophy.

For consumer protectionists, the goal for the present time is to introduce "responsible credit" on a mass scale - credit which creates trust, so that only this type of service would be available in the European arena. Speaking more generally, the idea has arisen to reorganize our present "society of mistrust, of constant control", since mistrust only generates costs, destroying productivity, and the goal is to create new relations, based on trust, which will enable the economy to grow. The advocates of "responsible lending" also seek the balance between providing the poor with access to credit while preventing the exploitation of the weakness, need or naivety of the consumers. Responsible lending is an example of the Amatya Sen's capability approach,[549] since it represents a model in which credit providers can integrate social values.[550] The whole concept of responsible lending is a further, more advanced and sophisticated step in the consumer protection evolution: changing the rules of contracts – making a shift in the responsibility burden.

"Credit was blamed for promoting extravagance and encouraging recklessness. It was alleged to cause individuals to lose a sense of who they were and what they could and could not afford, and to lead them to replace thrift and careful saving with the immediate gratification of trivial or even improper desires."[551] Such an understanding of credit relations unquestionably belongs to the very remote past, notwithstanding, still nowadays in many societies credit relations carry a certain stigma, and the idea of "responsible lending" attempts to change this. The first and most important assumption of "responsible credit" is the state-

548 K. Arrow, "Social choice and individual values", New Haven: Yale University Press, 1963.

549 Amatya Sen's Capability approach introduces the integration of social goals with market functioning.

550 U. Reifner, "The Lost Penny...

551 P. Haagen, "Imprisonment for Debt in England and Wales" (PhD, Princeton, 1986) at 108-109 in I. Ramsay, Chapter 1 "Consumer Credit Society and Consumer Bankruptcy..., p. 38.

ment - which in fact is a truism, but still not familiar to banking institutions - that consumers lend their own future income, making potential future income available for current spending on consumption or investments. In other words, consumers-borrowers do not use other people's money. It follows logically that the bank institution is actually a trustee of the consumer.

"Responsible credit" is an entirely new concept, not inherent in the market mechanism, and applicable at the junction between capital and consumption in real life. In order to be put into effect, the conception requires a round table discussion between these parties: consumer advisers, money advisers and bank-customer advisers.[552] The advocates of "responsible lending" claim that even though the legislators focus their attention on the period before and during the conclusion of a credit contract, in reality the most crucial period of the transaction, i.e. - the most unpredictable and the most uncertain period comes only afterwards. Although they do not discourage legislators from enacting protection provisions concerning the transparency of the contract, and the right to withdrawal etc., their attention is focused on the guarantees granted to the consumer in order to protect and support him if he should already be in need after entering into the contract, but before paying off the whole debt. Thus, consumer protectionists talk about "responsibility before lending," as well as "during the loan," whereby a creditor shares with the customer the responsibility for the successful repayment of the credit, also after concluding the credit contract. In other words, a creditor is obliged to concern himself with the situation of his customer who has already started to pay off the debt (e.g. the lender should consider how he can secure the liquidity of his customer instead of accelerating the instalments, as well as protection against termination, by not automatically cancelling the loan and insisting on the repayment of the balance of the loan, when the customer experiences merely temporal financial difficulties). This idea is in line with the concept of 'legitimate consumer expectations'[553] - i.e. the legitimate expectations of consumers which pose a basis for obligations of the professionals. This idea, by some authors considered to be a general principle of European private law, having a clear social dimension, refers to the stage of performance of a contract, and therefore neither the previous nor the new Directive contains these provisions. The application of the concept of 'legitimate consumer expectations' to consumer credit relationships would be a realisation of the postulate of the advocates of "responsible lending."

The creditor is expected to assume responsibility for misrepresentation, false advice or missing information, but also in cases when the creditor, already at the moment of selling the service, is aware that the product is unsuitable for the borrower - excluding cases of deliberate and malicious intent on the part of the consumer to defraud.

---

552 U. Reifner, „New Year Newsletter 2006", Institute für Finanzdienstleistungen e.V.

553 See: Wilhelmsson, "The principle of legitimate expectations as a basic principle of Community private law", in Paasivirta and Rissanen (Eds.), "Principles of Justice and the Law of the European Union", Helsinki, 1995), p. 325 et seq.

Both consumer protection organizations - The European Coalition for Responsible Credit and Debt on our Doorstep[554] give the recommendations for the shape of the future European consumer credit. They claim that credit providers should be required to seek information in order to be able to determine the purpose of the loan and the reason for borrowing. Moreover, consumer advocates recommend that lenders, by taking this information into consideration, should explain to consumers the suitability of their credit product for the latter. In other words, they emphasise that a credit provider should be responsible for judging the potential impact of the credit on a consumer's economic situation, hence such a creditor should examine affordability and make assumptions about future trends in order to avoid granting credit which may potentially cause overindebtedness.

One should not forget though that the issue of using personal information in credit granting decisions raises many ethically complex discussions. Whereas in some countries it would seem perfectly acceptable to base a credit decision on race, gender, or religion of a potential customer, in others such features as marital status or the age of an individual as the bases for decision making, are considered unethical. According to the human rights theory, an individual has a right not to have decisions made about him using information over which he has no control.[555] However this brings up the question of how much personal freedom can be limited for the sake of the welfare of an individual. Furthermore, it raises the problem of all the prejudices against certain categories of people and that of discrimination coming to life. On the other hand, if life experience supported by statistical scrutinises confirms certain interdependencies, can the creditors be expected not to take them into account while making a credit decisions?

Responsible lending is not about shifting the responsibility from debtors onto creditors, and here too consumer advocates agree that it is the consumer alone who must make the decision as to whether or not to enter the loan contract, and who must also bear the consequences of such decision. This is what concerns the advocates of responsible lending, that is, the legal regulations should provide consumers with appropriate tools (information duties and education) so that they are aware of their own share of responsibility at an earlier stage. Furthermore, in this regard the creditor is responsible for providing products and services and for 'guiding', 'guarding' and monitoring the process of repaying the loan by the debtor, as well as for predicting the impact of the obligation on the second party of the contract. The stage "responsible lending" is mainly focused on is the repayment period, because this is the moment in which the major problems occur.

554 D. Gibbons, The European Coalition for Responsible Credit and Debt on our Doorstep, the response to UK Government's consultation on the implementation of the Consumer Credit Directive. Available at: http://www.responsible-credit.net/index.php?id=1980&viewid=43056.

555 S. Finlay, "Consumer Credit Fundamentals. Second Edition", Palgrave Macmillan, 2009, p. 61.

Similarly, Rahman[556] proposes calling more attention to responsibility in lending; however he goes beyond the civil law construction. He proposes a legal recognition of criminal responsibility for creditors who act irresponsibly, i.e. – those creditors who lend money to borrowers who cannot afford such loans. Furthermore, Rahman offers a rather transgressing statement, according to which, responsibility is not shared; hence an insolvent consumer-borrower – taken to court by a creditor - could have a counter-claim against such a money-lender due to the violation by the latter of the responsible lending principle, while granting the loan. Rahman suggests the criminal responsibility of creditors in place of interest rate cap regulation - as presumably the most effective legislative reply to the problem of usury in predatory lending practices.

The concept of lending on interest (accompanied by the phenomenon of usury) is unquestionably the most controversial subject - from a moral point of view - in the debate concerning credit. The Bible, the Torah, the Koran - three holy tomes which are the foundations of the Europeans' identity - prohibits the idea of lending on interest. And even if the concept of charging interest in order to compensate for the fact that the sum of money was not invested elsewhere in the end gained the common acceptance; yet the issue of usurious interest rates remained.[557] One cannot help mentioning the problem of usury while discussing consumer credit issues. Although the EU legislator neither in the previous nor in the present Directive deals with usury – an issue which was in passing one of the crucial reproaches from consumers' circles - such regulations exist in many member states, and there are no provisions in the new Directive which would abolish national regulations in this respect. Hence, the debate about the interest rate cap will have (or already had) an exclusively national character. Still few problems shall be indicated in this work.

It is in generally believed that usury as such is a negative phenomenon which should be eliminated from the market by means of legal (preferably legislative) solutions. This is also quite commonly accepted, starting from Caplovitz's[558] "the poor pay more" statement, meaning that those members of society who are worse off, are more vulnerable to being trapped by all kinds of predatory lenders who lurk with payday loans of extortionate interests. It has been observed that the poorest pay the highest price for credit to pay for essentials whilst the richest have access to large sums of capital at low cost which they can use to make profitable investments. The problem of financial inequality in society is thus magnified, as "the cost of credit charged to the poor prevents them from using credit in productive

556 F. Rahman is director of financial inclusion social enterprise Fair Finance. "Capping interest rates is not the way to stop irresponsible lending to people who can't afford the loan" by Faisel Rahman, The Guardian, Wednesday 23 September 2009.

557 S. Finlay, "Consumer Credit Fundamentals...

558 D. Caplovitz, The poor pay more : consumer practices of low income families New York : Free Press, 1967.

ways, since the level of debt repayment is so high, that there is no way they can achieve a profitable level of return".[559]

This is the reason why many domestic legislators decided to prohibit usury. As always, however, this is just one side of the coin. The authorities can certainly prohibit and punish charging excessive interests by creditors, nevertheless, at the same time, and one should be aware of this, the problem of the poor consumers who experience rejection from the mainstream providers has not been resolved. In other words, a simple introduction of the interest rate cap regulations does not secure credit from other, more 'responsible' sources for the poor. One can consider actually few imaginable consequences of the introduction of such restrictions: either the hitherto predatory lenders would hide the real price of the credit in all kinds of additional, yet mandatory options in the contract, or they would go with their credit activity underground. The third reply to the usury regulation would be refusing credit to a certain category of consumers, i.e. excluding them from the circle of potential customers. And whereas both first scenarios could be completely eliminated or at least reduced to a large extent - thanks to the conceivable efficient state's enforcement - the third option should be translated into financial exclusion of the poor. Again, I do not intend to support usury nor to object to the idea of abolishing extortionate interest contracts. Such a intervention in the market should however entail other measures which could prevent the serious side effects (like inter alia financial exclusion of the poor) from happening.

Nevertheless, one can also encounter a criticism of the anti-usury regulations. For instance, according to F. Rahman,[560] an interest rate cap is no way to cope with doorstep lenders, payday lenders and pawnshops. In a way, the author justifies predatory lenders for charging extortionate amounts of interest rates for short-term loans, claiming that first: collecting the data on people with thin credit files is expensive and laborious; second, managing defaults can be expensive; and finally, there is not enough competition to bring the price down. Moreover, the customers of the predatory lenders use these services because they find them accessible and flexible, due to small, affordable repayment, and the amount collected fitting the income patterns of the worse off consumers. For Rahman it is not the rate or price of the loan which constitutes the problem, but the amount and number of debts a consumer can end up with. Thus, this is a problem of over-borrowing by some, which is matched, by over-lending, and not a problem of one payday loan taken for a short period of time, even with excessive interests. Of course, setting an interest rate cap could, at the end of the day, put the still legal doorstep lenders and payday lenders out of business and would consequently reduce the amount of credit available, while doing nothing to actually address the way in which loans are made. Furthermore, taking into account the scale of demand, one can easily conclude that consumers need this kind of lending, and moreover, Rahman doubts that banks would step in to fill the gap with lower interest rates.

---

559 The Scottish Lib Dems Spring Conference held in Perth on 6.03.2010.

560 F. Rahman. "Capping interest rates...

The reply[561] to these concerns could be a middle-of-the-road solution, i.e. putting caps on the level of interest rates which would on the one hand still guarantee lenders "normal" (i.e. not excessive) profits and on the other, would reduce the prices of credit. Since one of the reasons why so far predatory lenders can afford to fix such high levels of credit prices is that the markets are uncompetitive and these uncompetitive markets allow lenders to mark up prices over and above where they would be under normal market conditions, the credit providers can make excess profits. Then, however, following this path of reasoning, one cannot resist the counter argument: i.e. why is there no competition on such a lucrative market? Why do the mainstream providers refuse certain consumers when granting credit? Perhaps the answer to these questions is that the profits which predatory lenders make are actually not excessive, otherwise there would be other lenders willing to compete on this market. And again, I do not want to deny that the problem of usury exists. The authorities, who intend to declare war on usury, cannot settle for the simple solution of imposing interest rate caps on creditors. The solutions to this problem should be much more complex.

Although a discussion about 'responsible credit' and about 'responsibility' in general is typical of civil law culture, in the common law system it is more acceptable to speak about 'fair finance' and 'fairness', which are in fact very similar notions characterised by similar goals, but offering different meanings: 'responsibility' refers more to the state and the law; while 'fairness', to moral persuasion and ethics - which entails voluntary agreements and codes of conduct.[562]

Nowadays, although much has been done in regard to consumer credit regulations, many contracts are still far from transparent and involve confusing or even misleading terms and conditions. The advocates of the "responsible lending" idea believe that in order to introduce responsible credit into the market, two types of transparency should be guaranteed to consumers: 1) competitive transparency, and 2) social transparency. While competitive transparency gives consumers a chance to choose the product that is the most appropriate for them and requires a standardized mathematically correct form of "one price" disclosure (the Annual Percentage Rate of Charge), social transparency requires a standardised pre-contractual payment plan which would indicate the potential impacts of entering into the

561 Comments of the post by Debt on our Doorstep (23 Sept 2009) a comment from ECRC founding UK member Debt on Our Doorstep - questioning its analysis. Available at: http://www.responsible-credit.net.

562 However, certain changes can be observed e.g. in the US. US President Obama has set out proposals to levy $90 billion over the next 10 years from the banking sector through the implementation of a 'financial crisis responsibility fee'. He justified such a initiative citing increasing bank profit levels and excessive bonuses. The fee (the punishment?) particularly targets investment banks and is expected to be paid by around 50 financial institutions. The Times has estimated that Barclays, HSBC, and RBS may have to pay as much as $10 billion to the US Government if the proposal goes ahead as currently structured. Source: http://www.responsible-credit.net.

contract on future household liquidity and future purchasing power; such an impact can be predicted by a statistical analysis of past experience with similar contracts.

The advocates of "responsible credit" claim that credit, since it is essential for a full participation in the society, is a basic element of participation in economic life and should be provided for all members of society with no discrimination.[563] Consumer advocates stress the necessity of a social guarantee to prevent the creditor from abusing the kind of situation that occurs when a consumer's financial position worsens through no fault of their own, by inter alia seeking higher charges on default.

The Green Paper on Retail Financial Services in the Single Market[564] contains a section entitled 'Advising consumers', in which the Commission draws a distinction between the service provider's duty to provide information and the duty to provide advice. Namely, whereas the aim of providing information is to describe service, providing advice means *recommending* to a *given* consumer to opt for a *specific* product. Furthermore, such a recommendation should be objective, based on the profile of the consumer, and commensurate with the complexity of the products and the risk involved.

The industry of financial service providers represented by the European Financial Services Round Table (EFR)[565] in their five principles which were intended to form a peculiar constitution of consumer protection in the field, placed in the third position (after the guarantee of appropriate information and the right of withdrawal) the opportunity for a consumer to receive advice. The consumer would be provided with such a generic information or information tailored to his individual preferences only upon specific request of same. The EFR also stresses that the creditors should not be burdened with the excessive advice duties since their main duty is to provide money and to take the risk of the customer's ability to pay his instalments, and considering the other aspect, namely the diverse size of different creditors' fields of activity – the advice offered by a big bank having a variety of lending products would differ significantly from that given by a mono-line provider.

However, the financial services providers recognize that in exceptional circumstances, for example, in the case of financial difficulties of the consumer (in case the borrower's circumstances change and he experiences troubles with paying off his debt) in the middle of the duration of the credit agreement, it would be appropriate that money lenders advise the consumer how to overcome such crisis. Such a mandatory (e.g. in the UK's Banking Code) or non-mandatory solution is already the case for most of creditors, since they have a common interest in a quick and effective financial recovery of their contractual partner.

563 See more: Subchapter 'Financial Exclusion'.

564 COM (2007) 226 final.

565 European Financial Services Round Table "Consumer Protection – Consumer Choice. Deepening EFR's Concept on Consumer Protection in Retail Financial Services", January 2006.

Reifner,[566] one of the fathers of this concept, warns that if private sector lending firms are "not tempered by moral institutions, public awareness, protective law and administrative supervision", then they might irresponsibly grant credit "in the sole interest of gaining maximum profit." Furthermore, the author draws a picture of exploitation of vulnerable individuals by greed, usury, and predatory lending. However that statement does not seem to take into consideration that lending firms, in order to reach maximum profit, are interested in keeping their clients in good financial condition, i.e. an insolvent or bankrupt consumer would mean primarily a financial loss for the lender. Consequently, one could argue that it is in the lenders' interest to take care of the solvency of their clients.

In the circumstances regarding recovery from the world financial crisis, one can identify more and more advocates inclined towards the idea of responsible lending. One such examples is John Monks, General Secretary of the European Trade Union Confederation (ETUC), who addressed the World Economic Forum in Davos (February 2010), and warned against a return to risky financial practices. Arguing against short-termism and 'amnesia' about the causes of the crisis, Monk called for the creation of a 'more socially responsible model' of banking and for policymakers to focus on that, rather than on just getting back the repayment of the costs of the bail-outs.

The Idea in Legislative Acts

The concept of responsible lending – often described as being rather philosophical - is based on the requirement that financial institutions act as 'good creditors' who grant further credit only to those consumers capable of repaying new debts. This principle was included in Art. 9 of the first Proposal for a 'Directive on the harmonization of laws, regulations and administrative provisions concerning credit for consumers' presented in the autumn of 2002. According to its provision, creditors had a duty not only to consult centralized credit data bases, but also to examine responses provided by the consumer and guarantors and supplied by intermediaries. Moreover, creditors were obliged to offer the best possible form of credit to consumers. The responsible concept, present in the first proposal,[567] is known only to very few national legal orders inter alia in Belgium, Switzerland[568] and France (in the last case it was actually developed by the judicature).[569]

566 U. Reifner (ed.), "European Coalition for Responsible Credit ...

567 Article 9 provided for a duty of the creditor to previously assess, by any means at his disposal, whether the consumer can reasonably be expected to pay off the debt, whereas according to Article 6(3) the creditor was obliged to advise the consumer accordingly.

568 See: P. Rott, „Mitverantwortung des Kreditgebers bei den Kreditaufnahme – Warum eigentlich nicht?", BKR 2003, 851-859.

569 P. Rott, Chapter 5 "Consumer Credit".

The authors of the "Economic analysis..."[570] criticized the three articles - Art. 6 (exchange of information and duty to provide advice), Art. 8 (central database) and Art. 9 (assessment of creditworthiness) - placed in the first CCD proposal gathered under a common title - "Responsible lending." First, they claimed that in fact the Proposal's provisions would be superfluous as banks currently already use a credit rating system before concluding a contract with the customer – yet it is in the interest of creditors to prevent credit default due to overindebtedness. That tendency is reflected by the New Basel Capital Accord which is forcing the lenders to implement risk-sensitive ratings that give a realistic assessment of an individual borrower's risk.

Moreover, the "responsible lending" idea was in general reproached for its vagueness. Kösters, Paul and Stein doubted the possibility of accurately assessing the risk of overindebtedness of private borrowers due to findings on the causes of debt overload. They raised the problem of unfeasibility of predictability of most events which in practice are responsible for consumer overindebtedness like illness, divorce, death, and thus consequently they claimed that many disputes might be triggered off. The authors of the analysis did not question the already established good banking practice, i.e. refusing a loan to anyone who will not be able to repay it etc. They accepted that a creditor should offer a customer the most suitable products, but at the same time they criticized the unclearness of such duty. Since the Proposal did not specify whether to fulfil the duty was it enough to check credit databases or did the creditor also have to perform his own research concerning a potential borrower's private life, his health conditions etc. Such vagueness of responsible lending provisions would give much leeway for the courts at the national level, which as a result – considering the legal and cultural diversity of member states – would lead to different interpretations of that principle, conflicting with the goal of fostering the development of a single European Market.

Kösters, Paul and Stein also noticed a certain gap – the Proposal regulating the exchange of information about outstanding debts, did not deal with the significant national differences in creating databases, which caused that such a provision in fact to be pointless. An idea of the "best advice obligation", present already in the first CCD Proposal, assumed that the bank should extensively inform a consumer as to the terms and costs of a loan as well as point out the most "suitable" loan for a consumer. Such a duty raised several doubts concerning the way of implementing that provision. Kösters, Paul and Stein, the authors of the "Economic analysis..."[571] asked about consequences of an easily imaginable situation when the consumer ignores the creditor's advice and decides to get a different loan than that which is most "suitable." The Proposal did not envisage the borrower's responsibility in such a case. As a result of lack of legal regulations, in case the consumer becomes insolvent, the content of a court sentence would be unpredictable. In turn, that meant additional risk

570 W. Kösters, S. Paul, S. Stein, "An economic analysis...

571 Ibid.

for credit providers, thus at the end of the day the consumer would pay the price of the regulation that was supposed to award him additional protection. The other consequence might be also the exclusion by credit institutions of certain consumers (those in weaker social positions) from their circle of their customers.

Referring to the "best advice obligation", the authors of the "Economic analysis..." made a statement that such a provision present in the future directive would limit consumer independence, since the consumer would be deprived of making a free decision. Remaining in the hands of the "considerate" lender, the consumer would follow his guidance. Kösters, Paul and Stein also noticed in the Proposal duties a sort of information asymmetry: on the one hand the creditor is obliged to provide the consumer with all the relevant information, however, on the other, the Proposal did not envisage the responsibilities of borrowers to provide accurate information – the information concerning the borrower which might affect loan repayment.

By the same token, the concept of responsible lending included in the first version of the Proposal, also met strong criticism from A. San José Riestra.[572] First, the proposal of 2002 was reproached with lacking any concrete provisions on the consumers' responsibility regarding the application for, and management of, credit in the case of by the latter breach of his responsibility to provide truthful information. The predictable conflicts at the junction between national reporting agencies or credit bureaux from positive and negative reporting countries (with regard to exchange information) were also stressed. Also, the requirement of offering the best credit possibility for consumers raised at least two doubts: what if the consumer has his own preferences which are definitely not 'the best' for him, and, second, – what if (where the consumer conforms to the bank's advice) the default occurs anyway. Moreover, a contradiction was indicated: on the one hand, creditors were obliged to destroy any records obtained from the credit registry after concluding the contract (in other words they were obliged to rid themselves of any relevant documentation), and, on the other hand, the onus of proof in a litigation rested on them.[573]

Already in the amendment proposal, however, in response to a request from the banking sector, it was clarified that the consumer is always responsible for his final decision to conclude a credit agreement, although the Proposal maintained the concept that a creditor should not merely fulfil the pre-contractual information requirements, but should also provide additional explanations in order to enable the consumer to make a well-informed decision. It was specified as a duty for the creditor to put the consumer in a position whereby he could assess the advantages and drawbacks of the loan.

The amended Proposal no longer contained Art. 9, stating a definition of responsible lending. Art. 5 declared that the creditor (the credit intermediary) should 'adhere to the

572 A. San José Riestra, "Consumer credit directive: a feasible attempt to harmonization?", http://www.ecri.be.

573 Ibid.

principle of responsible lending'. In the second sentence, there was an explanation of this notion: the creditor (the credit intermediary) had to comply with its obligations concerning the provision of pre-contractual information and the requirement for the creditor to assess the consumer's creditworthiness on the basis of accurate information provided by the latter, and, where appropriate, on the basis of a consultation of the relevant database.

In response to the amendments, consumer advocates claimed that, the existing concept of a consumer as a human being has irreparably disappeared, since the amended CCD Proposal reduced consumers to mere "users" of the money systems - to irresponsible borrowers. As a result of such reasoning, it was the creditor (the saviour of society) whose task was to exclude those who wanted to irresponsibly improve their present existence. At the same time, it had been forgotten that, in fact, bank institutions are lending consumers their own money, their own future income.

However, on the other side, the representatives of the banking industry – the European Financial Services Round Table (EBF),[574] were also disappointed with the amendments. The EBF expressed many reservations about the provisions on responsible lending from the amended CCD Proposal, more specific on the creditor's obligation to adhere to the principle of responsible lending when providing pre-contractual information to his client, assessing the consumers' creditworthiness. Without offering an explicit definition of the notion of "responsible lending" and without determining the limit of its interpretations, such regulation – according to the banking industry - would seriously undermine the legal certainty of credit contracts and would discourage creditors from offering credit in order to avoid such a risk.

The second reservation, raised by the EBF, referred to the fact that - although in the daily banking reality the principle of behaving responsibly (e.g. "Know Your Customer" principle for anti-money laundering purposes, public law obligation to assess the level of risk of the customers etc.) is already one of the guidelines and a benchmark for the development of a bank-customer relationship - still identifying it as a legal obligation implies a private law liability regime. Consequently, a new additional private law regime of liability would arise and potentially overlap with the existing EU rules as well as those of member states. In other words, instead of confirming a due diligence duty, the introduced regime would give the consumer the possibility to claim for damages from the creditor against the violation of such a further obligation whenever the consumer would experience difficulties with paying back his credit. The EBF claimed that the consumer would be able to easily free himself from the obligation of paying back the loan by arguing that his failure is the result of the creditor's culpable failure in assessing the consumer's creditworthiness adequately. Thus, the responsibility would be transferred away from consumer, and the liability burden would be put on the creditor. And again, similar to the banks' opinion in response to the Proposal from 2002, according to the EBF, the concept of "responsible borrowing" was missing then. Alongside

574 European Financial Services Round Table "Consumer Protection – Consumer Choice...

the creditor's responsible lending obligation, the EU legislator should require the reciprocal obligations of borrowers.

Regarding duty to advise – which is related to responsible lending - the EBF claimed that any provision of advice constituted a service per se and could not be made mandatory. On the contrary, the regulation of same should be left to the market. Moreover, the banking industry argued that only the consumer himself, based on his own perception and his individual preferences and situation, could assess which product suits him best. Additionally, the EBF perceived the introduction of the duty to advise, as a serious obstacle in contracting via electronic media in case of cross-border distance selling of credit products.

According to the representatives of the European Banking Industry Committee,[575] advice is the "recommendation of a specific product to an individual consumer taking into account the specific circumstances of the latter. It is a subjective, non-standardized, separate and personalized service (i.e. a 'tailor made' service) available at the explicit request of, and paid for by, the Consumer".[576] EBIC specifies a meaning of the notion "advice" which differs significantly from the meaning adopted by consumer advocates. From a bankers' perspective, the provision of "advice" is an additional service provided solely on demand of the consumer, and assuming that, in consequence, if the legislator put on creditors the obligation to advise consumers, the consumers would have to pay for an additional service, regardless of whether or not they wanted and needed such advice. The other argument against the mandatory duty to advice with a liability risk for the creditors is that such a solution would automatically lead to an increase in litigation. On the contrary, only discretionary advice i.e. delivered on the consumer's specific request, would fulfil its goal since only then would it be well-tailored to a certain consumer's needs in specific circumstances.

The authors of the Analysis[577] identify the need to clarify what precisely is the aim of the principle of responsible lending and the "duty to assist" to be introduced, namely a better choice for consumers or reduction in defaulted contracts.

The Idea in the New Directive

The newly adopted Directive contains provisions which, only in a very limited scope, reflect the complex idea of responsible lending. In fact, the EU legislator gave up almost utterly the idea of legally recognizing the issue of responsible lending in the EU-wide act. Only in the Recitals is it stated that regulating responsible lending is the duty of member states to take appropriate measures to promote responsible practices during all phases of the credit relationship, taking into account the specific features of their credit market. Also in the Recital

---

575 EBIC Response to the Greek Paper on Retail Financial Services in the Single Market, 19 July 2007.

576 EBIC Response on Information & Advice Mortgage Industry & Consumer Dialogue Group, 16th August 2006.

577 F. Alleweldt (Project Director) et al. Broad Economic Analysis...

the Directive merely provides suggestions through enumerating what those measures may include. The catalogue of examples contains the provision of information as well as the education of consumers, including warnings about the risks attached to default on payment and to overindebtedness.

The Directive also encourages member states to enact the necessary supervision to avoid creditors' engagement in irresponsible lending and giving out credits without prior assessment of creditworthiness, as well as to determine the necessary means to sanction creditors who act otherwise. In the recital (26) the Directive offers recommendations regarding creditors, who should not engage in irresponsible lending or give out credit without prior assessment of creditworthiness. Furthermore, in respect of the member states' duties, the latter should carry out the necessary supervision to avoid such behaviour and should determine the necessary means to sanction creditors in the event of their doing so. The recital (26) also states that creditors should bear the responsibility of checking individually the creditworthiness of the consumer. However, to sum up, the new Directive itself does not introduce legal consequences as a result of the consumer's lack of creditworthiness.[578]

As to the creditors' duties concerning examination of consumers' creditworthiness, the Directive states that without prejudice to the credit risk provisions of Directive 2006/48/EC,[579] creditors should bear the responsibility of checking individually the creditworthiness of the consumer, taking advantage of information provided by the consumer not only during the preparation of the credit agreement in question, but also during a long-standing commercial relationship. The Directive further specifies its superficial messages, according to which again the member states' authorities could give appropriate instructions and guidelines to creditors, and consumers should also act with prudence and respect their contractual obligations.

The Directive also mentions a duty to assist the consumer, however again leaves it to the member states' realm: in order to help the consumer to choose which credit agreement, within the range of products proposed by a certain creditor, is the most appropriate for a particular consumer's needs and financial situation, member states should ensure that creditors provide such an assistance. The Directive also offers the guidelines – which can be determined further by member states concerning the duty to assist, namely the pre-contractual information as well as description of the product proposed, "should be explained to the consumer in a personalized manner so that the consumer can understand the effects they may have on his economic situation".

The element of the concept of responsible lending, which was indeed placed in the Directive, is the creditor's duty to consult relevant database in order to assess the creditwor-

578 P. Rott, Chapter 5 "Consumer Credit"...

579 Directive 2006/48/EC of the European Parliament and of the Council of 14 June 2006 relating to the taking up and pursuit of the business of credit institutions, OJ L 177, 30.6.2006, p. 1. Directive as amended by Commission Directive 2007/18/EC (OJ L 87, 28.3.2007, p. 9).

thiness of the consumer before the conclusion of the credit agreement. Also in this case, in Art. 8 the Directive determines that it is the duty of the member states to ensure that the money lender follows this imprecise obligation. However, the Directive also guarantees that creditors have access to all databases concerning consumers in a member state where they are not established under non-discriminatory conditions, in comparison with creditors in that member state. In the case in which after such a consultation the creditor decides to reject an application for credit, his duty is to inform the consumer immediately and without charge, of this fact and of the particulars of the database consulted. However, the EU legislator foresaw several exceptions in relation to this duty.

Although Article 9 calls upon the member states to ensure access for creditors from other member states to use databases in that particular member state for assessing the creditworthiness of consumers, in the end the Commission failed in introducing centralized databases at the national levels, so the advantage of that provision in case of cross-border credit will depend on the kind of databases already existing in the individual state, and the quality of same (e.g. a database showing all the credit obligations of a consumer or a database providing only information about those who have defaulted ones).[580] The assessment of the consumer's creditworthiness is also mandatory before any significant increase in the total amount of credit after the conclusion of the credit agreement. The influence of the responsible lending concept can be perceived also in Art. 5 concerning pre-contractual information, according to which, the creditor while delivering the information to the consumer in good time before the consumer is bound by the contract, should base such set of pre-contractual information, inter alia, on the preferences expressed and information supplied by the consumer.

Although strongly criticised by consumer advocates, one has to stress that this assessment of creditworthiness is new to the Consumer Credit Directive and to many national legal systems. The Consumer Credit Directive 87/102 also did not contain any provision encompassing the duty to assist which is now provided in the new Act. This is new to many national legal systems too (an exception is, for example, represented by Belgian law).[581] According to the Directive, member states shall ensure that creditors provide adequate explanations to the consumer, in order to put the latter in a position to assess whether the proposed credit agreement is adapted to his needs and financial situation where appropriate, by explaining the pre-contractual information. Member states are expected to determine in detail this general provision, so they may adapt the manner by and to the extent in which this assistance is given, as well as by whom it is given, to the particular circumstances of the situation in which the credit agreement is offered.

Like in the case of every single consumer protection provision, also here one should pose a question about the effects of these regulations on consumer protection. Indisputably

580 P. Rott, Chapter 5 "Consumer Credit"...

581 F. Alleweldt (Project Director) et al. Broad Economic Analysis...

responsible lending and the "duty to assist" could potentially lead creditors to provide consumers with more personalised information on a specific credit product which would mean - from the consumers' perspective - a better-informed choice. However, on the other hand, this provision entails the particular risk, that is, while creditors will be obliged to assist their clients and to advise them, in consequence it is likely that in more cases (than it is under current law) creditors will refuse granting credit. At the end of the day, it will lead to the exclusion of some consumers from the possibility of obtaining credit.

From the creditors' perspective, undeniably there exists a significant interest to assess the ability of a customer to repay a credit. Even without any specific legal requirements according to hitherto law, the creditors exchange information among themselves making use of private credit bureaux and public credit registers. The data gathered by the authors of Broad Economic Analysis of the Impact of the Proposed Directive on Consumer Credit[582] show that according to nearly all national banking associations pre-contractual analysis of creditworthiness is an already established good banking practice in their respective country. On the other hand, which is quite puzzling, a legal obligation in this respect is not welcomed by creditors. The reason for this seemingly paradox situation is that such an additional duty for lenders would entail additional expenses and complications. The second factor discouraging the banking industry in this respect is that a civil law requirement would result in liability risks. The creditors would have to document the type, content and extent of the information and advice supplied to every borrower before concluding a contract in order to have the evidence. The evidence would be necessary in case the borrower subsequently claims damages on the grounds that he was not adequately advised. Moreover, the money-lenders would have to make a higher effort to explain to customers the new information required and the credit decision in line with the Directive. All these efforts would not be compensated by any significant change of the risk premium for the expected loss (standardised risk cost) through the more differentiated and individualised analysis. In other words, better assistance would - according to their view - not lead to less risk of default and related savings.

The Study,[583] which was still based on the version from 2005 of the CCD amended Proposal, shows that a major concern for creditors is the obligation introduced in the Proposal to explain the advantages and disadvantages of a specific product proposed. The main line of argument is that only the consumer can have an overall perception of his own financial situation and can assess what is advantageous or disadvantageous for himself. It has been stressed also that a clear line has to be drawn between the provision of information (including explanations in face-to-face situations) and the provision of any other service: be it consultation, assistance or advice. In the first case, the lender is only supposed to provide the facts necessary to describe a product (something which can be fulfilled in online transac-

582 Ibid.

583 Ibid.

tions), whereas giving advice does imply some form of recommendation (something which cannot be easily fulfilled in online transactions), and increases liability.

However, one could challenge such an undoubtedly pro-creditor estimation. Assuming that creditors are definitely more experienced in the field of credit relations, thanks to this they are able to make a better evaluation of a potential borrower's situation on the basis of obviously true data provided by the client. This assistance should definitely be based on objective criteria. Also now, after the adoption of the new Directive, these remarks remain current, however, since the Directive gave a leeway to member states in this respect, the whole battle will be fought on the national field.

The protagonist of consumer advocates, U. Reifner,[584] sarcastically translates this new provision (contained in the amended Proposal from 2005, but also present in the adopted version in Articles 5 and 8) as a duty for a creditor to "obey the law and act as a banker." Indeed, the new Articles 5 and 8 are an obvious unsophisticated repetition of the obligation which anyhow burdens a creditor as a party of a loan contract. A stated obligation already exists for a creditor to provide pre-contractual information, and furthermore, the checking of creditworthiness is a standard procedure in all banking institutions: bankers follow this procedure on a regular basis not only in the customer's interest but also, first and foremost, in their own interest, as well as that of their shareholders. Not to mention in passing the fact that surely for the banking institutions, the threat of an insolvent customer is much more terrifying and, consequently, more stimulating, than any pompous legal orders or prohibitions.

Moreover, with regard to the "responsible lending" provision in the 2005 Proposal (however still current under the new regime), consumer protectionists perceived a 'second bottom' to that provision. In fact, instead of improving the consumers' position as a party to a credit contract, Art. 5 provided dishonest creditors with a pretext either: to exploit the poor, by stipulating excessive interest rates and explaining that entering into a contract with such consumers entails substantial risk; or a priori, to deprive the poorer members of the society of the possibility of receiving a loan in the framework of the legal system. Both effects will be without any doubt damaging for a section of society, and in no case will the new provision protect consumers or prevent overindebtedness; especially when one also considers the evasive and very ambiguous language applied in such regulation. All these dilemmas are still current under the newly adopted Directive; however, again, they have been shifted to the national field.

So far in member states there are very different approaches to the issue of assessing the creditworthiness of the consumer. The Directive provides for minimum harmonisation in this field. Although Article 8 implies that the creditor is obliged to assess the consumer's creditworthiness on the bases of sufficient information that is provided by the consumer

584 U. Reifner, 'Credit in Europe. Responsible Lending?', Responsible Credit, Brussels 2006, 6th International Conference on Financial Service, conference materials.

(where appropriate), and on the bases of consultation of the relevant database (where necessary), it is still the duty of the member states to oblige the creditor to do so. And moreover, the Article foresees that in the case where in the member states' legal order such a requirement already existed, then this provision can be retained. This is a total switch in comparison to what the Proposal of 2005 envisaged, since the latter provided the total harmonisation in that respect and consequently it ruled out any national provisions existing to date in member states. In fact, in this respect, the Directive will not introduce any change in relation to the present situation.

Article 8 does not contain an obligation for the member states' legislator to specify the requirements for the assessment of creditworthiness of the potential borrowers. However, according to the recital (26), as to the responsibility of checking individually the creditworthiness of the consumer, the member states' authorities could also give appropriate instructions and guidelines to creditors.[585]

Conclusions

Applying the responsible lending idea to the new Directive had the potential to be a solution which could defend consumer protection in the competition with the market efficiency goal. Nevertheless, the EU legislator decided to leave the issues of responsible lending either completely outside the scope of the new Directive, or to the discretion of the domestic legislators. For instance, the problem of irresponsible over-lending, the problem of usury, and the problem of shared responsibility of lenders - are not addressed at all by the new Act, whereas, inter alia the duty to advise and the duty to assess consumers' creditworthiness are entrusted to the competence of member states. Such an approach by the EU legislator may raise some questions. For example: is it not a paradox that the act which concerns the protection of consumers does not actually regulate the 'flagship' of consumer protection principles, i.e. responsible lending? If one comes back to the issue of the two major goals of the EU and the tension between them, i.e. an efficient internal market and consumer protection, one can clearly see that the EU legislator gives precedence to the first goal over the second when dealing with the issue of responsible credit. The efficient internal market definitely does not need paternalistic (or quasi-paternalistic) regulations. The European confident, active consumer-shopper, can do perfectly without such a legislative umbrella, and his preference is understandably not to pay for additional advice nor for other protectionist tools. And finally, the credit providers industry functions and grows much better in a legal environment which is free from any protectionist restrictions. In other words, the introduction of even only a few of the responsible lending ideas could only disturb the realization of the internal market project. The only problem is again represented by a vulnerable consumer-citizen, who is subject to usurious practices, and who is provided with a set of complex

585 P. Rott, Chapter 5 "Consumer Credit"...

information which does not convey much to him: a consumer who has experienced a refusal from a mainstream credit provider and hence ends up in the spiral of payday loans offered by predatory lenders. And the statistics show that currently, such a consumer does not belong to an unnoticeable, insignificant fraction of the European society; on the contrary more and more consumers face financial hardships and financial exclusion. Thus, one can conclude that this is one of the social problems of the citizens of modern day Europe. Therefore, the fact that the responsible lending principle was not regulated in the new *consumer protection* Directive can, and indeed does, arouse justified criticism.

The other questions which arise are, for instance: how consistent is the approach of the EU legislator towards leaving the principle of responsible lending outside the scope of the new Directive with the Commission's declarations with regard to the intensions of regulating this field of activity exhaustively? Furthermore, how consistent is this approach with, again, the Commission's assumption according to which, any national differences in the field of consumer credit would distort competition and would interfere with the realisation of the idea of the European internal credit market? Yet, if the domestic legislators are entitled to design their own provisions on duty to advise, usury, and shared responsibility, the landscape of the consumer credit EU-wide may vary as much as the geographical one.

'Will Europe Ever Get a Fresh Start?' Consumer Overindebtedness – Seeking Legal Solutions

Although credit remains a driving force for economic growth and the well-being of consumers, nevertheless it represents a risk for credit providers and, for a growing number of consumers; there is also the threat of being surcharged and becoming insolvent.

In closing, there is a need to mention the successive and pressing problem of consumer credit relations, namely consumer over–indebtedness, because the phenomenon of over–indebtedness is closely related to the complex issue of consumer credit legislation. For centuries credit was a tool enabling people to obtain commodities which they otherwise in existing circumstances would not have been able to afford. However only recently i.e. in the 20th century, has credit become a protagonist in the economy: it is freely available in large amounts and for long-term periods leading to a certain socially harmful phenomenon: i.e. the enlargement of the disparity of wealth distribution, and overindebtedness.[586] Since access to credit has been popularized in most European countries and, furthermore, a variety of loans are available nowadays to debtors originating from most of the income levels, the rates of indebtedness among families in the European arena are constantly growing.[587] J. Niemi-Kiesiläinen, I. Ramsay, and W.C. Whitford[588] call this phenomenon the 'democratisation of consumer credit' – due to several factors e.g. the deregulation of credit markets, securitization, the technological progress which enabled predictive credit scores and risk-based pricing, and the popularity of all kinds of credit cards.[589] In fact, nowadays credit has become available to basically all groups of society, including those who in the past were considered not creditworthy and hence 'financially excluded'.[590]

Overindebtedness of a consumer as an economic and social phenomenon has two dimensions: one is the detrimental (material and emotional) effect it bears for the overindebted himself and for his family (the private, individual dimension); the second dimension is of a public nature. Overindebtedness means a cost for the whole society. First, from the perspective of the society (not from that of the overindebted), overindebtedness translates into a

---

586 C.W. O'Hare, "Issues in Consumer Credit Law Reform" in "Consumer Protection Law and Theory".

587 M.E. Leitao Marques, C. Frade, "Searching for an Over-indebtedness ...", p. 121.

588 J. Niemi-Kiesiläinen, I. Ramsay, W.C. Whitford (eds.), "Consumer Bankruptcy in Global Perspective", 2003, Hard Publishing, Oxford and Portland, Oregon, p. 2-4.

589 I. Ramsay, "Consumer Law and Policy..., p. 515.

590 Social class divisions in credit and debtor relationships is not a new issue. Quite on the contrary, the nonexistence of an anyhow regulated by the state financial services infrastructure caused naturally big differences in the credit supply as regard to the sources and the cost of credit depending on the social class of a potential borrower. However at the same time, the poorest members of the society were not subject to overindebtedness since they were a priori excluded from accessing credit. See: D. Burton, "Credit and Consumer Society", Routledge, p. 11.

relatively short-term expense, i.e. other members of the society have to cover the loss and naturally the indebted and his family become the beneficiaries of the social help. Second, it translates into a long-term loss - i.e. overindebtedness of individuals has a detrimental effect for the healthy functioning of the economy.

The need for a legal solution to this 'by-product of the greater availability of credit' in order to solve the problem common to a growing number of consumers, is increasingly emphasised in the literature as well as in the discussion panels.[591] Credit allows consumers to flexibly choose to access the market place and to manage their finances, enabling resources to be put to their most efficient use. However, there is always a threat of overindebtedness and consequently, of insolvency. J. Niemi[592] constructs a subjective definition of overindebtedness, i.e. such condition applies when the debtor or debtor's household feels that they are not able to cope with their debt burden. Clearly it is not the credit contract itself which is responsible for the financial difficulties of insolvent consumers, contrary to what some authors are trying to attribute such contract. The causes of this phenomenon are mainly two: unexpected, unfavourable life events, and excessive indebtedness. Overindebtedness is linked to poverty, financial and consequently social exclusion, and has a real impact on the health (mental as well as physical) and hence on the well-being of the insolvent individuals. Overindebtedness also has a serious impact on the social relationships of an indebted individual and his family, creating feelings of shame, of being stigmatised, of failure, and at the end of the day, it is a factor which excludes such a debtor from participating in social activities.[593] Furthermore, the cost of over–indebtedness does not fall only on an individual borrower. Grossly simplifying, it can be contended that the cost of an individual's overindebtedness also affects the financial institution that granted the credit to the consumer; other debtors who are forced to pay higher interest rates; and higher insurance premiums etc., in order to at least partially compensate a creditor his loss. Such costs are born by the state, as it is a public task to rescue the individual who experiences hardships which he is not able to overcome by himself. In general, society as a whole bears the cost of its insolvent members. Unemployment, losses in income, illnesses etc. are only some examples of the typical social and economic risks which endanger a consumer's welfare, his social relations and his ability

591 For example: in US total number of personal bankrupted stands at almost 1 600 000, whereas only in Poland we may talk about one million households in arrears and experiencing financial difficulties.

592 J.Niemi, "Overindebted Households and Law: Prevention and Rehabilitation in Europe" in J. Niemi, I. Ramsay, W.C. Whitford (eds.), "Consumer Credit, Debt and Bankruptcy. Comparative and International Perspectives.", 2009, Hard Publishing, Oxford and Portland, Oregon, p. 91-104.

593 See N. Cooper, 'Does Consumer Credit Threaten Family Ties?', Responsible Credit, Brussels 2006, 6th International Conference on Financial Service, conference materials.

to act in society. Moreover, the fact that an individual, due to his insolvency, is excluded from the society itself endangers also the security of the society.[594]

In the discussion on the harmful consequences of consumer overindebtedness one issue is often missing: that is, consumer overindebtedness is not only a social and micro-economic problem, rather it is also a long-term macro-economic issue. McKenzie Skene and Walters[595] call it the 'ticking time bomb' problem which refers to consumer overindebtedness which, affecting consumption automatically over a longer period of time adversely affects economic growth, again with the price to be paid by the whole society.

The already above mentioned Broad Economic Analysis[596] reports that it is estimated that close to every tenth household in Germany is overindebted, i.e. more than 3 million households, while figures from the UK suggest that over one million adults are falling behind with payments for bills and credit commitments and additional two million are constantly struggling. The data from 2008 are even more striking as the numbers regarding consumer bankruptcy filings are recently rapidly soaring.[597] In the U.S. the number of consumer bankruptcy filings surpassed 1 million in 2008 - an increase of 31% compared to 2007 – due to the subprime crisis initially, and in general, due to the global credit crisis. This number is expected to reach 1.4 million or more in 2009.[598] In Europe, charge-offs at banks increased as well, according to the ECB reports - the level of write-offs in the euro area in the year 2008 amounted to €4.5 billion (in comparison to 2003 when the level of write-offs was €2.7 billion), which represents 0.6% (in the year 2003) and 0.7% (in 2008) of all outstanding loans in the respective years. These numbers clearly demonstrate that the problem of consumer overindebtedness is not a marginal one and as such cannot be ignored by the authorities. And finally, according to the European Consumer Debt Network (data from 31st of October 2009), at least 20 million people are over-indebted in the EU. Moreover it is expected that with the increasing unemployment rates the number of people with debt problems could grow substantially in the near future.[599]

The problem of overindebtedness resembles a domino puzzle: even if only one domino dice falls over, the whole meticulous arrangement is destroyed. If a debtor experiences even

---

594 J. Niemi-Kiesiläinen, "Collective or Individual? Constructions of Debtors and Creditors in Consumer Bankruptcy" in J. Niemi-Kiesiläinen, I. Ramsay, W.C. Whitford (eds.), "Consumer Bankruptcy in Global Perspective", 2003, Hard Publishing, Oxford and Portland, Oregon.

595 D. McKenzie Skene, A. Walters, "Consuming Passions: Benchmarking Consumer Bankruptcy Law Systems" in P.J. Omar (eds.), "International Insolvency Law. Themes and Perspectives.", Sussex Institute, Ashgate.

596 F. Alleweldt (Project Director) et al. Broad Economic Analysis...

597 M. Gerhardt, "Consumer Bankruptcy Regimes and Credit Default in the US and Europe", CEPS Working Documents 27 July 2009 available at: http://shop.ceps.eu/BookDetail.php?item_id=1887.

598 The data comes from the American Bankruptcy Institute (http://www.abiworld.org), the US Federal Reserve (http://www.federalreserve.gov) and the ECB's website (http://www.ecb.eu).

599 Press Release available at: http://www.responsible-credit.net.

only minor financial problems, and falls into insignificant arrears with one or two instalments due to some mishaps, a creditor - afraid of the possible threat of an insolvent customer - automatically accelerates the payment of the remaining instalments insisting that they be paid back in a single lump sum. At this point the debtor is entirely alone, and the whole burden falls on him.[600] It also has to be kept in mind that all kinds of predatory lending such as: the revolving credit and the chain system loans etc. - granted to people who are already experiencing financial difficulty are under no circumstances an effective means of solving the problem. On the contrary, they lead to a helpless insolvency and hence long-term poverty.

As has been mentioned above the two major causes of financial difficulties of consumers—borrowers are: mishaps and excessive indebtedness. According to the Broad Economic Analysis,[601] from the creditors' perspective, the reasons for the loan defaults lie outside the loan relationship and are not foreseeable (e.g. divorce, unemployment etc.). One of the banks interviewed stated that defaults on average occurred at around 15 to 18 months after the signature of the contract, and it is therefore difficult to assess relevant problems early on. According to Reifner,[602] the most common causes of overindebtedness are unemployment, illness, material breakdown or death of a partner and the birth of a child. Debt overload in more than 80 % of the cases is brought about not by the carelessness of consumers, but by the events which were impossible or very difficult to predict in the moment of concluding a credit contract, namely: unemployment, working fewer hours, loss of income when changing jobs, divorce and accidents.

Whitford[603] distinguishes three kinds of social problems associated with overindebtedness. First, he talks about "perverse incentives", namely, an over-indebted person perceives less incentive to carry out additional work or to undertake entrepreneurial risks, since he is aware that any profits will land in the creditors' account. The second social problem that Whitford distinguishes combines overindebtedness with hardship in the sense of a dramatic decline in the quality of life of the borrower: since part of his income covers the repayment of the credit, less is left to satisfy daily needs. In addition, to these two indicated problems, there is also the matter of the psychologically harassing interaction between the two parties of the contract, which cannot be taken lightly. The third kind of social problem which can be identified refers to economic insecurity: this means that everyone can experience unforeseen events, and in such cases, credit is a remedy. However, in the case of over-indebted consumers, such a solution is unavailable due to their lack of creditworthiness.

600 U. Reifner, 'Credit in Europe. Responsible Lending?'...

601 F. Alleweldt (Project Director) et al. Broad Economic Analysis...

602 U. Reifner, „Zur gesellschaftlichen Funktionen der Schuldnerberatung – Schuldnerberatung zwischen Ghettowirtschaft und Reintergration. Lecture in Mainz on 14. November 2002, Fachtagung des Ministeriums für Arbeit, Soziales, Familie und Gesundheit.

603 W. Whitford, in "Will Europe Ever Get a Fresh Start? Debt Settlement Plans as a Substitute for Quick and Easy Bankruptcy?", Responsible Credit, Brussels 2006, 6th International Conference on Financial Service, conference materials.

A society that has reached a certain level of self-development and culture, a society that also perceives some higher values other than just satisfying its basic instincts (and I assume that our European society belongs to this category), should pay more attention to people who, due to various circumstances (very often not being at fault), are in facing the onset of financial troubles. To put it into other, more down-to-earth terms society cannot. exclude, treat as non-existent, or simply forget its members who, due to death, illnesses, divorces, etc., experience serious problems with paying off their loans. If one assumes that only the strongest, and the most resistant can survive, and that others should be "eliminated" from economic life, then one should answer the question, as to why, in general, we need an organised society in the form of a state, the European Community etc.

Consumer protectionists are not isolated with their respective views; on the contrary, there seems to be a common agreement at least in the theoretical stage of certain considerations: in fact, they emphasize that overindebtedness should be a public concern and consequently a public responsibility. The goal of an effective legislation in this matter should be to rehabilitate and reintegrate over-indebted consumers into the economic life of a society. Where credit no longer reflects a productive investment into the economic life of consumers, they should have the possibility to access the public procedure of discharge through which their duties to repay debts are adapted to the remaining productivity of the borrowed funds.[604] K. Gross defines bankruptcy as "a form of social security net for failures that manifest themselves in economic terms."[605] A state or the Community should secure such a net for its citizens.

The recommendations in this respect stemming from consumer organizations dealing with the problems of overindebtedness, financial exclusion etc. are rather similar and embrace such issues as: introducing legal debt settlement legislation and regulations for responsible lending within the whole Community; improving money and debt advice services; developing the universal (common for the whole Community) data collection procedures for the estimation of the scale of overindebtedness; ensuring access to basic financial services (including social credits); setting guidelines for financial service providers to present their products in a standardized, transparent and understandable way; and improving financial educational programmes.[606]

604 From 'Round Table on Credit Directives an EU Action Plan', Responsible Credit, Brussels 2006, 6th International Conference on Financial Service, conference materials.

605 K. Gross, "Establishing Financial Literacy Programmes for Consumer Debtors: Complex Issues on the Platter" in J. Niemi-Kiesiläinen, I. Ramsay, W.C. Whitford (eds.), "Consumer Bankruptcy in Global Perspective", 2003, Hard Publishing, Oxford and Portland, Oregon, p. 342.

606 European Consumer Debt Network, October 2009, Press Release available at: http://www.responsible-credit.net.

In the same vein the Report on "Living on Tick: The 21st Century Debtor"[607] contends that "(i)nsolvency should not be an encouragement to default, nor should it reduce a debtor to permanent penury." However, one should not forget about the crucial rule insolvency law should represent: i.e. a balance between the interests of two opposing parties – debtors and creditors - should always be struck.

One can distinguish a few ways of approaching the issue of overindebtedness. The state or the Community can take steps in order to prevent this problem from arising at all. The means for such prevention would be: the educational programmes, debt counselling, and putting the concepts of responsible lending and insolvency insurance into practice. However, when a consumer-borrower is already facing the problem of overindebtedness, the various legal systems at the national level know, in general, two measures to solve the problem of the insolvent individuals who find themselves in a financially difficult situation i.e. when their burden of debt significantly exceeds their capacity to pay the credits back.[608] The first option consists in the restrictions on the enforcement of the remedies of an individual creditor, sometimes described as a protection against excessive enforcement. Thanks to this solution, certain items essential from debtor's point of view are exempted from the seizure (e.g. a debtor's basic household goods, his tools of trade, etc.), as well as the debtor's salary up to a certain percentage level. However, in the individual member states, there are some important differences between legal provisions concerning the minimum level of a debtor's income that cannot be garnished.

The issue of exempting certain parts of a debtor's assets and a certain percentage of his income is not unquestionable in the literature. According to Jackson,[609] the garnishment of future salary threatens the productivity of an individual because the productivity may be reduced in the end, as a consequence of such garnishment. The argument supporting the idea of exemptions is that after the bankruptcy procedure, the debtor should still remain a productive member of society. However, Schwartz[610] disagrees with this statement since according to this author, the exemption of assets is clearly in conflict with the goal of bankruptcy law, which is to liquidate debtors' assets and in this way, to satisfy at least partially the creditors' claims. The author stresses the necessity to keep the balance between debtors' and creditors' rights. Schwartz considers the issue of the balance between costs of bankruptcy and the availability of credit, and predicts that if it becomes too easy to default on loans, creditors will undoubtedly limit the availability of credit. To the first alternative option (i.e. the restrictions on the enforcement of the remedies of an individual creditor) one can

607 Report on "Living on Tick: The 21st Century Debtor", PricewaterhouseCoopers, (2006), available at: www.pwc.com/uk/eng/about/svcs/brs/PwC-IVAReport.pdf.

608 J.S. Ziegel, "Comparative Consumer Insolvency Regimes – A Canadian Perspective", Oxford-Portland Oregon, 2003, p. 3.

609 T. Jackson, "The Fresh-Start Policy in Bankruptcy Law", (1985) 98 Harvard Law Review 1393-448.

610 P. Schwartz, "Personal Bankruptcy..., p. 61.

also rate the imposition of moratoria on the enforcement of the creditor remedies within the certain time periods.

However, all these above sketched solutions can be applied exclusively in cases of the temporary financial hardship of an individual debtor. That is why, another alternative - a collective solution to debtor's insolvency – is of interest to the modern insolvency systems, which offer such a debtor a possibility to petition for the bankruptcy and to obtain a discharge under certain conditions. There are many differences between national regulations concerning consumer bankruptcy. Among the various regulations is the so called "fresh start" solution providing the indebted consumer with an immediate discharge of the unpaid debt.

The discharge of a pre-bankruptcy debt has always been an inherent element of the U.S. bankruptcy law, as the concept of the 'fresh start' in the U.S. has a deeper moral essence.[611] In liberal thinking, the market is the central sphere of the economic action, thus the consumer bankruptcy law is defined as a market function since the bankruptcy itself is an exit from the credit market and a complement of the open access to the same market and thus serves the efficiency of the market, reduces risk, and encourages individuals to borrow and to be economically active. Hence, the idea of debt discharge and consequently 'fresh start' serves moral values and market efficiency.

The major disadvantage of this treatment is that it may cause moral hazard problems, namely, it might encourage the consumers "to take inappropriate risk with respect to debt, causing an avoidable increase in overindebtedness," or it may induce the consumers "to develop or fail to correct bad habits with respect to the management of debt, to the inevitable long-term decline in their quality of life." Ramsay[612] states – as Bankruptcy law solutions are concerned – that there are generally no doubts as to providing individuals who have suffered a change of circumstances with relief, though it is not so unquestionable anymore what the exact scope is of the concept of the 'honest but unfortunate' debtor. Hence, one should consider – by introducing the "fresh start" solution - whether all the consumers-debtors should have the availability of having their debts discharged, keeping in mind that although the majority of over-indebted consumers are those who found themselves in such an unfortunate situation due to misfortune (accidents, other unpredictable circumstances), still there are always individuals who either became over-indebted due to their highly glaring irresponsibility or these who planned to abuse the advantageous provisions in order to reap profits.

Moreover, the next disadvantage of the "fresh-start" solution is that the affected creditor is very likely to terminate the contract relationship with the consumer, depriving the

611 See e.g.: C. Tabb, „The Historical Evolution of the Bankruptcy Discharge" (1991) 65 American Bankruptcy Law Journal 325, J. Niemi-Kiesiläinen, "Collective or Individual...

612 I. Ramsay, Chapter 1 "Consumer Credit Society and Consumer Bankruptcy..., p. 35.

consumer of this relationship "that has in the past provided a degree of financial security".[613] Also, the negative consequence of a "fresh start" treatment is the problem of costs. Keeping in mind the old economic rule of 'no free lunch' according to which, someone always has to bear the costs of the benefits enjoyed by others, it appears logical that the other customers of this creditor would have to 'compensate' the creditor for the majority of costs incurred due to the over-indebted consumer, through increased interest rates or other additional charges.

The other approach is the debt-settlement plan, which is not characterised by the above disadvantages. The idea is not to discharge the whole debt, but to require the indebted consumer to pay off the sum which is reasonable in his circumstances, at the same time - discharging the rest of the debt. The benefits of this solution are in favour of the creditors - (who bear less cost or more correctly, whose loss is smaller), as well as – maybe paradoxically - the consumer, as this arrangement may have educational effects and dissuade the consumer from behaving imprudently in the future, not to mention the preventive effect it may have on the other potential consumers-borrowers.

During the last twenty years in almost fifteen countries, consumer bankruptcy law has been enacted: the consumer insolvency law in continental Europe can for the most part be traced back to the period between 1984 and 1998. During the last years of the previous century the majority of 'old' Western European countries adopted the legislation on debt adjustment procedures for consumers, which assumes in general that after execution of the plan the consumer is discharged from payment of the outstanding part of the debts. J. Niemi[614] classifies European rehabilitation systems into three categories. The 'Nordic' pattern emphasizes the good faith test in their regulation of access to debt adjustment in the sense that not all consumers – debtors are granted such an opportunity, for instance, those debtors who have incurred the debts in an irresponsible manner etc. can be deprived from the possibility of accessing the debt adjustment procedure. The 'Nordic' regulations also encourage the idea of voluntary settlements between debtors and creditors. On the other hand, there is a German-Austrian model which emphasizes the payment plan i.e. discharge appears as a result of fulfilling though not exclusively the main payment obligations included in the payment plan. The third model of debt adjustment is represented by the Benelux countries and France where the prevention of debt problem is especially emphasized. With difficult conditions for a discharge and long payment plans, this model, similar to the 'Nordic' model, it encourages voluntary agreements between debtors and creditors.

The European insolvency systems reveal many disparities; however, they also have a few features in common. Niemi-Kiesiläinen,[615] scrutinizing several of the European insolven-

613 W. Whitford, "Will Europe Ever Get a Fresh Start? ...

614 J. Niemi, "Overindebted Households and Law...

615 J. Niemi-Kiesiläinen, „Consumer Bankruptcy in Comparison: Do we Cure a Market Failure or a Social Problem? (1999) 37 Osgoode Hall Law Journal 473, p. 475.

cy systems, enumerates certain common denominators as follows: "(a) access is restricted to debtors deemed deserving of assistance"; "(b) all of the scrutinized systems require a mandatory payment plan for five to seven years and there are no facilities for an automatic discharge"; in most of the cases, consumer debt adjustment requires a five-year payment plan before the discharge becomes final; "(c) all of them place special emphasis on debt counselling services provided by a variety of state-sponsored or state-funded social agencies, which not only help the consumer draw up a debt adjustment plan and to mediate its acceptance by creditors", but also aim at prevention, encouraging consumers to keep their finances balanced in the future.[616] Very similarly, N. Huls[617] in his juxtaposition distinguishes three features which describe the European consumer bankruptcy model: 1) first, the access to consumer bankruptcy still cannot be characterized as an open one, 2) second, the presence of the mandatory payment plan as a condition for a discharge and finally, 3) the incorporation of debt counselling and preliminary negotiations with creditors into the judicial procedure.

In the literature, several models of consumer bankruptcy law are distinguished according to the prevailing functions that the legal provisions are expected to fulfil.[618] Whereas I. Ramsay[619] makes a differentiation among models distinguishing: 1) those which firstly emphasize consumer protection; 2) those which attach the most attention to the control of a debtor's deviant behaviour and finally; 3) those models which focus on social welfare. Furthermore, regarding to consumer bankruptcy law, U. Reifner[620] distinguishes fresh start models, educational models and social protection models. Niemi-Kiesiläinen[621] adopts as a primary distinguishing feature, the aims of different models, that is: rehabilitation, repayment, prevention and efficiency.

In the Reifner's juxtaposition of different consumer bankruptcy laws, the models are connected with their ideological underpinnings. Thus the fresh start model is backed by the liberal ideas familiar to the U.S. leading way of thinking where the economic value of debt discharge is emphasized and the social and educational aspects with regard to consumers are neglected, and simultaneously, the position of a consumer debtor and a professional creditor is very similar.

616 See: J. Niemi-Kiesiläinen, A.-S. Henrikson, 'Over-Indebted Households: Prevention and Rehabilitation In Europe', Responsible Credit, Brussels 2006, 6th International Conference on Financial Service, conference materials.

617 N. Huls et al, „Overindebtedness of Consumers in the EC Member States: Facts and Search for Solutions" (European Communities, Kluwer, 1994) and N. Huls, "Overindebtedness and Overlegalization: Consumer Bankruptcy as a Field for Alternative Dispute Resolution" (1997) 20 Journal of Consumer Policy 143.

618 J. Niemi-Kiesiläinen, "Collective or Individual...

619 I. Ramsey, "Models of Consumer Bankruptcy: Implications for Research and Policy" (1997) 20 Journal of Consumer Policy 269.

620 U. Reifner in N. Huls et al., "Overindebtedness of Consumers..., p. 17.

621 J. Niemi-Kiesiläinen, "Consumer Bankruptcy in Comparison..., p. 499.

In comparison with that, the educational model – in force for instance in Germany - is however, poles apart, as it assumes that one's insolvency is due to his own personal and moral failure, and consequently an insolvent individual is obliged to pay debt at least partially, and moreover the debtor's 'good behaviour' is required during the period of execution of the payment plan.

The third social protection model present in the European debt counselling schemes emphasizes the fact that the other social problems faced by the consumer debtor - apart from the overindebtedness issue - also have to be addressed, since the consumer - debtor needs widely understood social support.

In a different approach, the term 'social *force majeure*'[622] describes a situation where a debtor is unable to pay a debt because of the unforeseen circumstances in his life which took place beyond his control. This is the concept behind the consumer bankruptcy law in Scandinavia where "the explicit aim of the consumer debt adjustment law is to alleviate the burden of a debtor who, for reasons beyond his own control, has ended up with insurmountable debt".[623]

However, the most conspicuous differences between national consumer bankruptcy law systems are being traced between the European and American systems. Yet whereas the fact that these differences are very substantial and concern the crucial aspects of the bankruptcy system is an objective and unquestionable observation, the assessments of such systems seems to differ significantly. Gerhardt,[624] in her report which scrutinizes both systems, observes that the differences between such systems relate inter alia to the purpose and the aim of the laws, however her explanation seems to be rather contentious as she claims that the American system focuses on providing a fresh start and a 'clean slate' for consumers, whereas the European insolvency legislation mostly aims at the satisfaction of creditors' claims. At the same time, adopting a position which might seem a bit paradoxical, she notices that "even though creditors' rights to recuperate outstanding loans are severely limited in the US, it is remarkable that this did not prevent lenders from giving out easy credit in the past", with a remark that due to the subprime loan crisis the American lenders became more hesitant in granting new credits to the consumers. What Gerhardt calls 'consumer-friendly' does not necessary reflect how other authors understand or interpret this notion. According to Gerhardt, in Europe, it is the UK consumer bankruptcy legislation which is considered to be the most 'consumer-friendly', although in comparison with the U.S. system, the British consumers' property is much less protected, and consequently, in the UK creditors are granted with more possibilities to enforce their claims.

622 The concept was developer by T. Wilhelmsson in "Critical Studies in Private Law. A Treaties on Need-Rational Principles in Modern Law", Dordrecht, Kluwer, 1992.

623 J. Niemi-Kiesiläinen, "Collective or Individual...

624 M. Gerhardt, "Consumer Bankruptcy Regimes...

Gerhardt's criticism of the European bankruptcy system also concerns the fact that consumers-debtors not only have to give up most of their property – including their homes – in order to serve creditors' claims, but they also have to undergo a period of good conduct with a settlement plan. According to the author of the report, the especially 'consumer-unfriendly' or in other words 'creditor-friendly' is that before the debts are discharged by the court, the consumer has a greater incentive to strictly follow the rules of the repayment plan as, in the end, his behaviour will be evaluated. The other tool familiar to European borrowers (e.g. compulsory in Germany, and widespread in Ireland) and not very common in the American system, is the procedure of renegotiating the loan between creditors and debtors in order to agree on a new settlement plan with new conditions.

The conclusions which stem from Gerhardt's scrutiny of the two differing bankruptcy systems is that the European and especially the Continental systems are designed in a way which is much more in favour of money lenders as opposed to consumers-borrowers. In fact, the latter category often fall into the trap of insolvency and at the end of the day, these are the European consumers who have to fulfil more conditions in order to obtain debt relief, and on the top of this, they still have to make some kind of payment in order to receive debt relief; hence, European consumers are granted discharge only with certain costs and efforts.

The other authors do not remain silent either, when the American bankruptcy system is at stake which is viewed from a European perspective, as controversial. Under the European continental model of bankruptcy law a "debtor is granted a court-imposed quasi-contract in which debts are reduced, adjusted to income and limited in time",[625] hence contrary again to the American 'fresh-start' system, the debtor's situation before and after the bankruptcy procedure is not clearly distinct. Reifner in turn, judges this as a disadvantageous solution; however he does not extol the American system either.

Niemi-Kiesiläinen[626] explains a crucial difference between the U.S. market orientation and the Scandinavian welfare state approach, namely in the American system the main concern of the consumer bankruptcy law is the market itself, whereas in the Scandinavian approach, the object of interest of the consumer bankruptcy rules is not the market, or market regulation, but the protection against social risks. Consequently, the American legislator is not bothered by scrutinizing the reasons for the consumer's inability to pay off the debts, whereas in Scandinavia the reasons of the consumers' insolvency themselves attract a lot of attention. According to Niemi-Kiesiläinen, this demonstrates that in Scandinavia, in contrast with the U.S., the role of the debtor-consumer is not reduced to a market actor. Furthermore, whereas in Scandinavia the ethical dimension of repaying one's debt is strongly emphasized (this includes the mandatory payment plan which poses again, not an economic,

625 U. Reifner, "'Thou shalt pay thy debts' Personal Bankruptcy Law and Inclusive Contract Law" in J. Niemi-Kiesiläinen, I. Ramsay, W.C. Whitford (eds.), "Consumer Bankruptcy in Global Perspective", 2003, Hard Publishing, Oxford and Portland, Oregon.

626 J. Niemi-Kiesiläinen, "Collective or Individual…

but a moral issue, as the factual economic value of the plan is generally low), in the U.S. the complete discharge of the whole debt is common. In the U.S. (but also in Canada) the right to discharge regarding most debts, in most circumstances is a central element of bankruptcy law, and borrowers cannot agree - at the time of concluding the credit contract - to waive that right.[627] In Scandinavia it is very difficult in general to get into whole debt adjustment procedure, contrary again to the American practice. From the perspective of a more fundamental paradigmatic orientation, one can conclude that the Scandinavian legislators are oriented towards: social security and the protection against economic risks and welfare, taking into consideration the debtor's social needs as a starting point, whereas the American legislator focuses on the regulation of market functioning and treats debtors and creditors as market actors allowing for bargaining between a debtor and individual creditors. In the continental legislation, indebtedness is seen not so much in its social context as is the case in Scandinavia, but more in an individual context.

The variety of existing solutions to consumer bankruptcy does not prevent lawyers to sketch different models. In the literature one can find many examples of alternative approaches to the problem of consumer bankruptcy legislation. One cannot help noticing U. Reifner's[628] input here. Reifner criticizes the direction of the development of the traditional consumer bankruptcy law, the so called 'straight bankruptcy' approach, since this tool due to its mass application in 1990s has in fact replaced consumer protection law. The author reproaches such bankruptcy law with focusing only on the discharge from debts and at the same time neglecting the terms of the contract in question. Moreover, the concept of the 'fresh start' assumes that a consumer is an economic entity that invests capital, thus - applying the logic of businesses, bankruptcy instead of liquidating a person, a debt is abolished. Hence, an individual freed from his debts can 'legitimately' live on. However, Reifner claims that the assumptions standing behind the 'fresh start' philosophy are deeply wrong, since in reality it is not overindebtedness which is the cause of the financial failure of consumers, but circumstances which are unpredictable and which are not originally linked to incurring debt (like unemployment, illness etc.); thus the mere discharge of debts does not remedy the initial causes and moreover it does not address the future debts either.

As an alternative for the traditional consumer bankruptcy law, Reifner presents a completely different approach towards consumer bankruptcy and states that this section of law should be reintegrated into the 'socially inclusive contract law' - the law which would incorporate social needs throughout the life of a credit contract and which would provide for adaptation to changes in an individual's situation caused by any unforeseen events. In consumer bankruptcy unlike in business bankruptcy, a bankrupt person (a natural person in this case) survives bankruptcy not only as a person, but also as a functional capital in the market. Even with respect to the capital, unlike in business bankruptcy, a consumer's significant as-

---

627 P. Schwartz, "Personal Bankruptcy Law..., p. 61.

628 U. Reifner, "'Thou shalt pay thy debts...

set is exempted from liquidation; in fact, the capital which is usually the object of bankruptcy procedure is the individual's earning capacity.

A dogma which stems from the sharp rise of consumer credit in the 1980s is that the economy itself should solve the problems caused by the credit society. Reifner explains it as the integration of the welfare state functions into the economy through a new approach to contract law, and calls it after François Mitterrand 'responsabilisation de l'economie' i.e. the courts receive a power to interfere with contract terms that may contribute to over-indebtedness. The 'rehabilitation' doctrine differs from the 'fresh start' one: the over-indebted consumers may recover under state tutelage ("in the shadow of the welfare state") and are entitled to continue their regular market activity only after a certain period of time. The idea of 'rehabilitation' combines the concept of consumer bankruptcy with that of social consumer protection in the field of contract law. However still, according to Reifner, due to the introduction of consumer bankruptcy procedures, the authorities felt exempted from interfering in the contract law terms and gave up on protection within contracts themselves.

Reifner claims that since overindebtedness arises from contract law, contract law should provide for remedies for this problem. Thus he proposes 'a fair concept of contract law' that would take the social inequalities into account at every stage of the contractual relationship, i.e.: consumers would be provided with adequate information; the content of contracts would take into consideration their needs; and contracts would be characterized by equal access. The 'fair, inclusive contract' would also assume a more even distribution of the cost of inequality to all contracting parties within society, which is close to Caplovitz's concept of the general compulsory insurance against overindebtedness. The credit providers have two choices i.e.: they can either exclude certain groups of customers or they can distribute costs equally among all customers, thus an inclusive contract law has in the end the same effect as a proposed general compulsory insurance against overindebtedness. All this is in line with an idea of a continuous relationship between creditors and debtors after bankruptcy, as both parties of the credit contract are still responsible for the outcome of the credit relationship.

Although the phenomenon of overindebtedness is acknowledged to have assumed an increasing importance at the national level in the various member states, thus warranting the adoption of specific laws and administrative measures in most of these countries, no policy measures whatsoever have been taken yet at the Community level.[629] The only piece of EU legislation that addresses legal and natural persons bankruptcy collectively is the Council Regulation on insolvency proceedings.[630] The Regulation established a solution for the recognition of the bankruptcy judgments between member states. Initially intended ex-

---

629 Opinion of the Section for the Single Market, Production and Consumption on Household Over-indebtedness (own-initiative opinion), Rapporteur: Ataíde Ferreira, available at http://www.toad.esc.eu.int/EESCViewDoc.aspx.

630 Council Regulation (EC) No 1346/2000 of 29 May 2000 on insolvency proceedings.

clusively for professional actors (international trade), recently the Regulation became a tool for non-professional debtors who, evading more severe discharge conditions in their countries, relocate their residences to the UK and after 12 months (the period of good conduct in the UK) go back to their countries 'debt-free'.[631] However, this piece of legislation does not change the overall picture regarding the EC platform, characterized by the lack of a comprehensive legal solution for over-indebted consumers.

During the internal market, Consumer Affairs and Tourism Council meeting on 26 November 2001, it was stated that 'divergences as regards both the preventive and the social, legal and economic treatment of overindebtedness in the member states could therefore give rise to considerable disparities both between European consumers and between credit-providers' and as a consequence, 'taking into account both the European Community's desire to develop cross-frontier activities relating to financial services and the growing scale of the phenomenon of indebtedness and overindebtedness, consideration could be given at the Community level to complementing the measures to promote the development of cross-frontier credit with measures to prevent overindebtedness throughout the one credit cycle'.

Furthermore, in respect of the subsidiary principle and the new wording of Articles 3t) and 153 of the Treaty of Rome and of Articles 2 and 34 of the Treaty of Amsterdam, a Community–wide approach to the regulations of over–indebtedness is advisable for the single market's effective operation.[632] And even though for the majority of the payments of default cases, there is a remedy in consumer credit laws, there is a whole series of measures for dealing with over–indebtedness which fall more within the policy areas of justice and the single market, so it appears to be absolutely vital to regulate consumer over–indebtedness on the EU level, especially since so far not all member states have passed laws which deal with this issue. It is stressed[633] that as the credit market becomes more and more international, protection from overindebtedness should be placed on the European level also because the development of such provisions should give considerable benefits to all the countries in the long run.

Another point to be taken into consideration is that unless over–indebtedness is framed in a Community policy ensuring the harmonization of national initiatives in this field, unjustifiable discrimination occurs against either the seller or the consumers, and serious distortions of business competitiveness are generated. It is also argued that, although the European market may be described as 'single' in cross–frontier contract matters, when it comes to the problems generated by this market – in this case, over–indebtedness – it becomes very localized, and is divided between various domestic legal systems.

631 M. Gerhardt, "Consumer Bankruptcy Regimes...

632 Opinion of the Section for the Single Market.

633 J. Niemi-Kiesiläinen, A.-S. Henrikson, 'Over-Indebted Households: Prevention and Rehabilitation in Europe'...

However, this justifiable idea of harmonising over–indebtedness regulations on the EC level always raises a wide range of questions as to how to regulate consumer over–indebtedness: the choice between hard and soft law; who should be in charge of passing the laws: member states or the Commission (if the latter, then the consumer overindebtedness regulation should be considered as a necessary measure for the smooth running of the internal market), and, finally, should consumer overindebtedness be regarded as a social problem or as an economic one (in the latter case the Commission has wider powers).

Although all these questions remain unanswered, some actions can be indicated: for instance, that of the Economic and Social Committee (ESC) initiated by Community institutions and heading in the right direction, which in 2002 issued a report containing certain recommendations on the regulation of over–indebtedness.[634] Even though the ESC does not insist on introducing identical regulations or similar procedures in every member state, it does aim to 'implement' the common goal of providing consumers with counter – measures in the case of over–indebtedness. More recently, in 2005, the Ministers of Justice of member states of the Council of Europe invited the European Committee on Legal Co-operation (CDCJ) to launch an analysis of the problem of overindebtedness (analysing existing legislation and good practices, and identifying the difficulties encountered) and to prepare the appropriate measures within the Council of Europe to address the problem.[635] The Recommendation (2007)8E of the Council of Europe, Committee of Ministers on legal solutions to debt problems from 2007, is the first international document recognizing the need for international co-operation in alleviating the problems of overindebtedness. However there was no binding EC initiative in the field.

The INSOL - International Consumer Debt Report – Report of Findings and Recommendations from May 2001[636] focuses on the social and economical impact of consumer over-indebtedness on an international scale. The aim of the authors[637] of the Report is to provide the resources for the countries dealing with the insolvency laws. The Report includes the principles and recommendations on which the consumer insolvency laws might be based, as well as the recommendations with regard to the reduction of the consumer debtor insolvencies. The Committee proposes as a first principle a 'fair and equitable allocation of consumer credit risks' within the domestic consumer bankruptcy systems, and in order to follow this principle, legislators should primarily "enact laws which provide for a fair and equitable, efficient and cost-effective, accessible and transparent settlement and discharge of debts."

634 Opinion of the Section for the Single Market, Production and Consumption on Household over-indebtedness (own-initiative opinion), Rapporteur: Ataíde Ferreira, available at http://www.toad.esc.eu.int/EESCViewDoc.aspx.

635 The 26th Conference of the European Ministers of Justice (Helsinki, 7-8 April 2005) resulted in a Resolution No 1 on Seeking Legal Solutions to Debt Problems in a Credit Society.

636 INSOL International Consumer Debt Report – Report of Findings and Recommendations (May 2001), available at: www.insol.org/pdp/consdebt.pdf.

637 INSOL Consumer Debt Committee established in 1999.

Moreover, the legislator may consider providing for separate proceedings, as well as should ensure that consumer insolvency laws are mutually recognized in other jurisdictions. The second principle refers to the provision of some form of discharge of indebtedness, rehabilitation or 'fresh start' for the debtor. Third, the Report's proposition is to encourage extra-judicial or out-of-court proceedings for solving the debt problems. The last principle focuses on prevention, i.e. educational and advice programmes.

Undoubtedly, access to debt relief – for the sake of the difficult situation the over-indebted consumers find themselves in - should not be restricted, thus should be maximally facilitated and cheap. The Report[638] proposes to ensure the consumers a choice between a 'bankruptcy' and 'rehabilitation' procedure, as one can distinguish those debtors who have no redemption capacity and no immediate prospects in changing this status quo, from those debtors, on the other hand, whose bad financial situation has only a transitory character. The Report[639] also makes a recommendation regarding debt counselling: governments or quasi-governmental or private organizations should ensure the availability of sufficient competent and independent debt counselling. The above presented recommendation could serve as a good starting point and a very general guideline for a legislative initiative on the European Community level in case such initiative comes into being.

An Act – the new Consumer Credit Directive - whose initial goal was to comprehensively harmonise consumer credit relations, only harmonises the normal, that is, desirable stages of the credit contract (i.e. the conclusion of such contract, and the paying off a loan, and does not devote any attention to the most complicated stage - having innumerable consequences - i.e. consumer insolvency. Thus as far as the new Directive is concerned, one cannot talk about a complete harmonisation nor about a complete legislative product. Despite hopes put into the new consumer credit legislation and despite an objective need for regulating the issue on the European level, and despite, perhaps first and foremost, an inseparable connection between consumer credit as such and consumer insolvency, ultimately the newly adopted Directive remains silent when it comes to the question of regulating over-indebtedness. The Act contains only an insignificant, entirely superficial mention of over-indebtedness: namely, in the Deliberations, in point 26 referring to responsible lending, the Directive recommends member states – while taking "appropriate measures to promote responsible practices" – to include in these measures inter alia warnings about the risks attached to default on payment and to overindebtedness. It has to be emphasized that this provision has a specific character, since as a recommendation it does not bind member states. In other words, the Directive creates no obligation at all in this respect.

638 INSOL International Consumer Debt Report – Report of Findings and Recommendations (May 2001), available at: www.insol.org/pdp/consdebt.pdf at 25.

639 Ibid., at 27.

Thus as could be easily predictable, the Directive, and first and foremost, the lack of the overindebtedness provisions in it, met with sharp criticism. Reifner[640] states that the basic question of the market economy i.e. whether the market economy should respond to the needs of individuals or whether individuals should rather adapt to the needs of the market - trusting its invisible hand, is reflected when it comes to the means for preventing over-indebtedness i.e. either refinancing; discharge and rescheduling mechanisms to adapt the credit to the factual needs and abilities of the debtor, or debt enforcement practices to adapt the debtor to the repayment needs of the creditors. The new consumer credit regulation adopted the latter.

According to Reifner,[641] the result of consumer credit law is a complete shift of responsibility for the social outcomes of the credit system to the consumer side, since the legal regulation assumes that markets offer all the necessary opportunities to prevent over-indebtedness through a consumer's rational choice. This is very much 'in line' with the European Commission views according to which, in the European credit market three tools – education, information and reflection – are needed to overcome consumers' weaknesses.[642]

Such an approach or more correctly, ignoring this urgent problem by the Directive gives the impression – not only to consumer advocates – that this newly adopted Act is simply unfinished and incomplete. The Directive deals very much in detail with all the range of procedures for concluding a credit agreement as well as for early discharge of the consumer's obligation, but it does not deal with the peculiar, but also in a way natural consequences of these legal relationships, namely, with the risk following from incurring a debt. Obviously one can understand the very pragmatic approach of the EC legislator of not getting involved at all in drafting common European consumer bankruptcy standards, since such issues as consumer insolvency and consumer bankruptcy are very contentious in the hugely diverse EU arena.

Financial Education

Unquestionably, society in one way or another has to pay the cost of overindebtedness of an individual anyway. The cost of the public social aid, the increase of the cost of consumer credit, the additional mandatory collaterals required by banks, the higher insurance premiums etc. are only some elements of the price paid by all the citizens. Keeping this in mind, one can easily draw the conclusion that it is not only cheaper, but also from an ethical point of view more favourable, to invest in prevention, than to bear all the negative consequences

640 U. Reifner, " 'A call to Arms' – For Regulation of Consumer Lending" in J. Niemi, I. Ramsay, W.C. Whitford (eds.), "Consumer Credit, Debt and bankruptcy. Comparative and International Perspectives.", 2009, Hard Publishing, Oxford and Portland, Oregon, p. 105-128.

641 Ibid.

642 EU Commission, Consumer Policy Strategy 2007-2013 COM (2007) 99 final.

of an unpaid debt. One cannot help talking about successfully improving the position of consumers on the credit market without taking into consideration the issue of financial education.

The other reason for investing in financial education, besides alleviating the threat of overindebtedness, is the relationship between the consumers' understanding of the financial services market, and their profiting from the single market. Moreover, without an in-depth understanding of the market mechanisms, consumers would not be able to choose the right products, i.e. the products that suit their needs on a market which is constantly becoming more and more complex. The financial capability of consumers can significantly increase not only through training, informing and explaining to consumers about the financial products available to them, but also through instructing consumers on how to manage their budgets. Financial education - alongside the legally binding information and advice duties imposed on creditors by a legislator - is a very effective tool for improving the level of understanding of financial services and in general in fostering consumers' confidence.

The Lisbon European Councils stressed the "social goals" of the internal market agenda.[643] The meeting held in March 2000 concerned inter alia social cohesion. According to the 'new' strategic goal, the European Union was supposed to become "the most competitive and dynamic knowledge-based economy in the world, capable of sustainable economic growth with more and better jobs and greater social cohesion".[644] The steps leading to the realization of this goal were the completion of the internal market and the modernisation of the European social model through the building of an active welfare state. It was stressed that "the emergence of this new economy does not compound the existing social problems of unemployment, social exclusion, and poverty".[645] One finds a similar declaration made at the Feira[646] as well as at the Nice European Council.[647] The latter considered "New Impetus for an Economic and Social Europe" and approved the European Social Agenda, being characterised by the 'indissoluble link between economic performance and social progress'. Economic growth and social cohesion were seen as mutually reinforcing. The Stockholm European Council emphasised this even more forcibly, declaring that a 'dynamic Union should consist of active welfare states'.[648] The following documents: 2000 Review of the Internal Market Strategy and Economic Reform: Report on the Functioning of Community Capital and Product Markets[649] were in the vein of stressing interconnections between the economic

643 P. Craig, G. De Burca, "EU Law. Text, Cases and Materials", Fourth Edition, Oxford University Press 2008, p. 632.

644 Lisbon European Council, 23-24 March 2000, para. 5.

645 Ibid., para. 24.

646 Feira European Council, 19-20 June 2000, paras. 19-39, 44-49.

647 Nice European Council, 7-9 December.

648 Stockholm European Council, 23-24 March 2001, para. 2.

649 2000 Review of the Internal Market Strategy [COM (2000) 257 final.], Economic Reform: Report on the Functioning of Community Capital and Product Markets [COM (2000) 881 final.

and social aspects of the internal market. In economic terms, the prosperity of Community citizens was the result of a properly functioning internal market.[650] Moreover, it was stressed that high levels of consumer protection were needed for a well-functioning internal market.

OECD[651] in its document concerning the need for proper financial education for consumers-borrowers claims that financial literacy is a necessary condition for financial market efficiency. However, at the same time it is stated that financial literacy cannot be treated as a substitute for financial consumer protection and regulatory frameworks, since it exemplifies only one part of an effective policy response to empowering consumers.

The concept of financial capability consists of three basic elements: 1) financial knowledge and understanding; 2) financial skills and competence and finally; 3) financial responsibility. The authors of the "Report on protecting the consumer: improving consumer education and awareness on credit and finance"[652] recommend that a basic level of financial capability should be established, i.e. consumers should be able to understand basic financial terminology, and the technical, legal and mathematical procedures involved. Being equipped with that knowledge consumers should develop the ability to use it to their benefit, i.e. via gathering financial information, proper evaluation of the gathered information, comparison between the different offers etc. And finally, the last ingredient assumes that consumers should be ready and willing to use their acquired knowledge and skills properly, i.e. to make financial decisions which are responsible in macroeconomic terms. In addressing the matter of financial literacy, the authors of the Report[653] pay special attention to the issue of raising consumers' awareness of the consequences of their actions on the financial market and contractual agreements in which they enter into i.e. what the consequences would be if they did not pay their instalments or in case of early repayment.

Many analyses of financial markets demonstrate that in general, consumers have a very low level of understanding of these markets.[654] Continuously more and more new products are being introduced, and banks are hiring more and more professional specialists, whereas

650 P. Craig, G. De Burca, "EU Law. Text, Cases and Materials"..., p. 633.

651 OECD recommendation on good practices on financial education and awareness relating to credit, "Financial Literacy and Consumer Protection: Overlooked Aspects of the Crisis", June 2009. Available at: http://www.oecd.org/dataoecd/32/3/43138294.pdf.

652 2007/2288(INI).

653 Ibid.

654 The surveys show that in general financial literacy in consumers is very bad. According to the results from the U.S. report of E. Renuart and D. E. Thompson, most credit contracts require literacy at 15th grade level (three years of college). Consumers do not live up to that standard. Above two thirds of US consumers cannot extract and compute credit cost information from contract and disclosure documents. A third of consumers surveyed could not find the default rate in a credit card contract - E. Renuart, & D. E. Thompson, "The Truth, The Whole Truth, and Nothing but the Truth: Fulfilling the Promise of Truth in Lending", Yale Journal on Regulation, 25, 2008, 181-244.

on the consumer side, the level of knowledge is not necessarily increasing. The whole situation creates a starting point where a consumer is typically very confused and helpless, which at the end of the day adversely affects his confidence on the market.

The study on financial exclusion[655] demonstrates that the one of the essential causes of this phenomenon lies on the demand side, i.e. the poorer consumers strongly believe that financial services are reserved only for those who are well-off. Having such a mistaken conviction in addition to a low self-esteem, they do not even try to apply for a bank account or bank credit. Here the authors of the analysis perceive a role for financial education as a potential solution which could help to financially include those individuals by simply clarifying facts from belief.

The Green Paper on Retail Financial Services in the Single Market[656] in the subchapter 'Empowering consumers,' stresses the necessity for the financial literacy of consumers. It is not surprising that consumers with poor financial literacy have problems with understanding and making use of the information they receive when entering into a contract. According to the Commission, consumers are able to make the most of the single market: if they have the financial literacy to make decisions for themselves; if they are well-informed, provided with independent high-quality advice; and if they can move freely between providers. There is a strong correlation between financial literacy and the growth of the EU-wide financial service markets, namely a well-informed, advised consumer is confident enough to seek out the best deals to meet his needs regardless of the location of the service provider, which at the end of the day, may successfully stimulate competition and make financial service markets work better.

The European Parliament – preoccupied with the situation regarding the vulnerability of consumers on the market of financial services being confronted with financial services of increasing complexity and, second, with the fact that consumer information cannot keep up with the level of complexity - on 18 November 2008 adopted the "Report on protecting the consumer: improving consumer education and awareness on credit and finance".[657] This Report stresses the existence of the problem of the lack of financial knowledge and the necessary skills among consumers to evaluate products and services. Such circumstances automatically lead to poor decisions.

According to the Report,[658] raising the level of financial literacy of consumers should be a priority for policy-makers both at the member state and European levels, and the rational

655 L. Anderloni, B. Bayot, P. Błędowski, M. Iwanicz-Drozdowska and E. Kempson, "Financial Services Provision and Prevention of Financial Exclusion", European Commission Directorate-General for Employment, Social Affairs and Equal Opportunities Inclusion, Social Policy Aspects of Migration, Streamlining of Social Policies, March 2008.

656 COM (2007) 226 final.

657 European Parliament, "Report on protecting the consumer: improving consumer education and awareness on credit and finance", 18 November 2008, (2007/2288(INI).

658 Ibid.

for that should be not only the benefits for individuals but also the benefits for society and the economy, such as: reducing the level of problem debt, increasing the level of savings, increasing competition, making appropriate use of insurance products and making adequate provision for retirement. Moreover, if the gap in information and financial expertise between financial intermediaries and consumers is reduced, this would decrease the risk of overindebtedness, as well as that of default or bankruptcy. The other positive effect of the reduction of the gap would be increased competition between lenders and thus the increase of the overall efficiency of the market because better informed consumers can distinguish between different financing proposals and select the one closest to their needs.

The document outlines a differentiated approach of financial education and financial information in order to tackle the problem. First, according to the authors, financial education should be practical and take into account the needs of the consumers, i.e. it should be tailored to the needs of specific target groups and, where appropriate, it should be personalised. And second, the authors recommend to introduce educational schemes which would focus on important life-planning aspects (such as basic saving, debt, insurance etc.), as has already been done by the European Commission, developed at the European level with the support of national stakeholders. The Report[659] perceives the need for an ongoing two-way educational process for both sides, namely for financial advisors and for consumers, in order to ensure the provision of accurate information in step with the most recent developments in the financial services sector.

Also Reifner[660] sees a need for education of creditors. He criticizes however the financial education programmes which try to convey a message 'avoid credit by saving first'. He stresses the great significance of credit as an integral part of the economic life of consumers and thus he expresses the beliefs that preventing individuals from using credit deprives them from the possibility of increasing their productivity. The author comes to the conclusion that the goal of financial education should be to teach consumers how to use credit contracts by making good choices and by taking advantage of consumer protection law etc.

The European Banking Industry Committee stresses the cardinal role of financial education.[661] The industry representatives claim that the main assumption - when it comes to deliberating the extent of consumer protection – should be the supposition of the informed, reasonable consumer who makes his market decisions confidently, while also bearing the financial consequences of his choices. Hence, EBIC states that, in order to make an appropriate decision, a consumer must be given via a proper financial education the necessary skills and knowledge.

Education of consumers in the field of financial services can be explained by two in fact overlapping theories: the 'empowerment theory,' and the 'social control' theory. In the 'em-

---

659 Ibid.

660 U. Reifner, "'Thou shalt pay...

661 EBIC response to the Green Paper on Retail Financial Services in the Single Market, 19 July 2007.

powerment theory' the role of financial education is to empower debtors by teaching them how to manage and plan their budgets, whereas the 'social control' theory assumes that financial education serves to encourage debtors to: pay more attention to provided information, resist manipulations of service providers, and to exercise more self-control etc. According to K. Gross,[662] one of the major goals of financial education is to shift the consumer - borrower's economic locus of control from external to internal. It is premised on a belief, familiar to the empowerment theory that debtors who feel more in control of their economic futures, behave more responsibly.

On the other hand, J. Braucher[663] criticizes the empowerment theory since he claims that lack of financial management skills does not necessarily result in financial problems. The features that characterize consumers who file for bankruptcy are: lower income and more debt. J. Braucher introduces the third perspective 'interest analysis,' which deals with the ways in which financial education serves the needs of bankruptcy administrators and policymakers to defend a flawed bankruptcy system, while also serving the interests of creditors and, to some extent, debtors. His main assumption is that it has never been fully and reliably proved that financial education indeed improves the financial security of consumers-borrowers in the long-term. He claims that in the case of the permissive and incoherent U.S. bankruptcy system creating "growing caseloads of persons experiencing complex problems from ambiguous causes", the American authorities found a safe way out and turned to education. Furthermore, it is suggested that financial education poses a non-controversial way in which bankruptcy administrators can easily expand their domain and gain legitimacy. In turn, for credit providers, according to J. Braucher, financial education has the major advantage of making bankruptcy more burdensome and expensive to access, hence it prevents some consumers from filing for bankruptcy at all. Moreover, the concept of financial education implies (and emphasizes) immediately the debtor's exclusive individual responsibility for overindebtedness (i.e. - the consumer needs to be instructed not to make mistakes in the future and to manage his budget in a prudent way). However, what may seem quite surprising taking into consideration what was said above, is J. Braucher's position. In fact, this author states that debtors-consumers also find the concept of financial education beneficial for their own personal improvement, i.e. they "appreciate being treated with respect and being given a sense of positive purpose about reordering their financial lives"; education helps them to construct reputable self-images. According to J. Braucher, the only gain consumers obtain is limited however, merely to the emotional sphere.

J. Braucher breaks ranks as far as common enthusiasm for the idea of financial education is concerned. He transgresses a generally prevailing belief that financial education is a

---

662 K. Gross, "Establishing Financial Literacy..., p. 342.

663 J. Braucher, "Debtor Education in Bankruptcy: The Perspective of Interest Analysis" in J. Niemi-Kiesiläinen, I. Ramsay, W.C. Whitford (eds.), "Consumer Bankruptcy in Global Perspective", 2003, Hard Publishing, Oxford and Portland, Oregon, p. 319-342.

perfect tool in the struggle against overindebtedness and as such, does not reveal any shortcomings. The author emphasizes that firstly education costs and secondly financial education imposed as a mandatory tool in the process of bankruptcy filing would cause, as a consequence the reduced access to bankruptcy, as the cost in money and time would increase.

In the same vein, K. Gross[664] joined in on the criticism of the tool and agrees with J. Braucher that mandatory financial education for consumers who want to fail in bankruptcy at their expense, limits borrowers' access to bankruptcy. Moving from the theoretical consideration upon the concept of financial education, K. Gross[665] presents the difficulties which are faced in the stage of implementation, as the politics of the bankruptcy system and its administration, the sociological profile of consumers – debtors, the psychological dimension of money and overindebtedness, should all be taken into consideration.

Financial education is primarily a matter which belongs to the member states' competence. However, the Commission itself has already launched also some financial literacy initiatives. The Commission's role as far as financial education is concerned has to be limited though merely to offering guidelines, new innovative approaches, and collecting and promoting best practises. The issue of financial education raises the question as to whether that activity should take place on the Community level. One can cite the arguments from advocates and opponents of such idea. On the one hand financial services and the single market are almost entirely EU domain, so consequently, the Community should deal with the overall problem in a comprehensive way. On the other, the education as such, is safeguarded as a member states' realm.

F. Figueira[666] argues that from the consumers' perspective it would be more efficient to coordinate financial education on the national levels, since then consumers would be provided with information well-tailored to their specific needs, and training within frames of already existing infrastructures for welfare and education, whereas the Commission could be a common ground for exchanging experiences and hence could provide "comparative information."

Similarly, the banking industry claims that measures to improve consumer education and financial literacy should remain the responsibility of the relevant entities at the national level.[667] At present, the Commission currently carries the idea of overindebtedness prevention into effect within the framework of "Dolceta" (Development of On-Line Consumer Education Tools for Adults, www.dolceta.eu) and "Europa Diary." At the same time however, similar initiatives have been launched in several member states. A good example is provided by the actions of the Financial Services Authority in the UK which targets groups of consumers who find themselves at different stages of life. Apart from offering training and infor-

---

664 K. Gross, "Establishing Financial Literacy..., p. 342.

665 Ibid.

666 F. Figueira, "The European Commission and Financial Capability...

667 EBIC response to the Green Paper on Retail Financial Services in the Single Market, 19 July 2007.

mation directed to specific groups, on the FSA's website[668] one also finds a comparison of financial products available for the British consumers. The "Centiq" in the Netherlands is an organization established by the Dutch Ministry of Finances which gathers all the national initiatives focused on consumer financial education. A similar idea has been set by the OECD in the frames of "Financial Education Project".

Unquestionably there are many very strong arguments for using financial education as a suitable measure directed at preventing and combating financial difficulties (including over-indebtedness) experienced by the unprofessional borrowers in connection with consumer credit contracts.[669] In general, education as such, no matter what kind of adjective is attached to it, does not arouse major controversies. The idea of improving citizens' knowledge, capacities, skills etc. is one of the very few ideas in relation to which almost all politicians from the right to the left declare to deeply care about and as such, this idea is considered to be noble and admirable. Financial education is a tool which can be applied not only by the public authorities, but also by all the conceivable NGOs and finally by both interested parties: credit providers and consumers organizations themselves. The additional advantage of financial education is its extremely universal and specifically neutral character, namely neither the representatives of liberal views nor socialist thinkers could possibly reproach financial education initiatives, since first such a tool is not a manifestation of the paternalistic tendencies nor a real intervention into the free market and, second financial education is considered to be a significant element of consumer protection policy, and as such embodies ideas of distribution and solidarity always welcomed by the socialists.

Thus, taking into account everything that has been said above, it seems to be difficult to express criticism for the idea of financial education. The common delight of the advantages of financial education almost does not allow the questions to fight their way through; however one can bring up several doubts concerning this tool.

First, treating financial education as a major element of consumer protection policy together with information duties and the other 'soft' tools so forcibly highlighted in the new Directive, seems to be very welcome by all the groups of interest on the European consumer credit arena, and thus, bears a risk of 'putting vigilance to sleep': an uncritical enthusiasm for financial education may make it difficult to perceive the real result i.e. incompleteness of consumer protection measures. In other words - to sketch a variegated example - an 'average' consumer, no matter how well educated, will never be able to match a professional in

668 http://www.moneymadeclear.fsa.gov.uk.

669 Inter alia: T.-A.Autio, M., Wilska, R. Kaartinen, J. Lähteenmaa, "The use of small instant loans among young adults - a gateway to a consumer insolvency?" Int. J. of Consumer Studies, 33, (2009), 407-415; Office of Fair Trade. "Consumer Education: a Strategy and Framework." London: OFT (2004); P. S. Norum,. "The role of time preference and credit card usage in compulsive buying behaviour", Int. J. of Consumer Studies, 32, (2008), 269-275; L. Willis, "Against Financial Literacy Education. Iowa Law Review", Vol. 94, 2008; U of Penn Law School, Public Law Research Paper No. 08-10; Loyola-LA Legal Studies Paper No. 2008-13, 57pp.

his comprehension of the financial mechanisms which govern the consumer credit market, hence with education or without it, a consumer remains a vulnerable actor on the credit market scene. It is especially crucial to stress that, as far as finances are concerned, education as such will not change the picture much. The reason for this is that either the education programmes match the level of comprehension of an 'average' consumer by conveying a very incomplete and limited set of information; or they offer a presentation of the whole complexity of the consumer credit market, which makes it likely that the average consumer might not be able to fully understand all the complexities involved. The latter is reflected by the other 'soft' tool of protection policy namely information duties. As a result we can end up with an even more confused and unaware consumer: and consequently such consumer would still need other measures of protection i.e. consumer education alone does not solve the problem of an unequal distribution of powers between professional service providers and their unprofessional customers. The other counter-productive effect is linked to a danger that due to financial education consumers' confidence can be boosted, without improving the real ability to act prudently on the market.[670]

I am not suggesting therefore that education as such is useless and that the whole idea should be dropped. I simply foresee a potentially dangerous situation caused by the fact that, by introducing the entire range of financial education programmes on a large scale, the authorities of states and the European Community might feel totally excused from taking other steps in order to equal the chances both parties have on the credit market. The popularity and therefore the general availability of the financial education programmes could deprive consumers of a certain leniency that they used to enjoy i.e. "educated", "perfectly informed" consumers would be treated as equal partners who would be expected to bear the whole responsibility also in case of their insolvency.

The second issue concerns a rarely questioned supposition according to which, one of the advantages of the financial education programmes is the fact that they do not entail cost, or the cost is so marginal or paid by 'the others' (e.g. credit providers), that it does not enter into the equation. Obviously such wishful thinking is deeply mistaken. No matter who is in charge of educating consumers, consumers themselves in one way or another bear the cost either through the increased costs of credit or via the general tax system. I am not suggesting hereby that financial education is not worth all the costs it entails. I simply oppose such a selective perception of the reality which does not allow certain truths to become unearthed. Therefore, I believe that with every step undertaken, there should be less blind applause and more sober calculation.

And finally, in the tangle of extolling of the advantages of financial education very often something is missing, namely the answer to a question, that is: "what kind of message should the lessons of financial household management convey?" Should a consumer be encouraged to limit his borrowing and hence his consumption? As such a commandment

670 L. Willis, "Against Financial Literacy Education", Iowa Law Review, Vol. 94, 2008.

would undoubtedly guarantee an 'over-indebtedness–free' society, however, the well-being of the respective individuals would definitely decrease, and the overall economic growth would significantly slow down. Should a consumer be discouraged from dealing with a certain category of credit providers and from being tempted by a certain category of products? That would entail perhaps making illegal some forms of business offered nowadays to consumers. It seems that every group of interest has a different message in the back of their minds that they wish to convey, so the final outcome will depend again on where the money comes from.

Financial Exclusion

The present European society cannot go without broadly understood financial services. This general statement applies also to the citizens of the "new" member states, whereas still in the 1980s in Central and Eastern Europe the consumer financial services market had no *raison d'ětre*, as the most simple, unsophisticated financial instruments like current accounts, credit cards, and credit in general, were almost unknown to the cash society of the former Soviet bloc. However, since the beginning of the 1990s, even in these countries the situation has changed rapidly and for good. The fact that nowadays consumers use financial services on a regular everyday basis in order to purchase goods, transfer money, and to receive their salaries, pensions etc. is undoubtedly very welcome and perceived as a factor which actually facilitates everyday life. Financial services make life more convenient and easier, until a certain point where it becomes unimaginable to be a rightful member of the European society and at the same time, to be deprived of the possibility of utilizing such financial services. This is particularly true since presently financial services have been real universal necessities, in that they are the essential 'goods', which are perceived as a standard element of the contemporary world. However, does such reasoning imply that the possibility to use financial services has become a citizens' right? Furthermore, in the same vein, does it mean that a consumer has a legal, justified claim to a bank for instance, to be granted credit? Does such a specific claim consistently bring about a reciprocal obligation to be imposed on the bank? Furthermore, what is the role of the state, and of the European Community in this jigsaw puzzle? Does such a consumers' right deserve to be granted state protection, and to be provided with a state guarantee?

The first of the several Principles of Responsible Credit launched by the European Coalition for Responsible Credit[671] states that credit is an essential element necessary to enable full participation in an industrialized society. One of the postulates of this pro-consumer organization is to raise public awareness by an active state/communities' attitude leading the lenders to accept the poor and disfavoured consumers. ECRC also proposes to create legal

671 U. Reifner (ed.), "European Coalition for Responsible Credit ...

obligations for inclusion, e.g. to impose on bank services providers an obligation to provide basic bank accounts.[672]

The term 'financial exclusion' dates back to the beginning of the 1990s and at that time it referred to a problem of limited access to banking services, however only in a physical respect, since it arose as a result of the closure bank branches. Leyson and Thrift[673] claimed that financial exclusion involves "those processes that serve to prevent certain social groups and individuals from gaining access to the financial system." The grounds for those processes – according to the authors – followed from the fact that those individuals who have a low income or, who are at a disadvantage in general, represent too high a risk for financial institutions, and consequently financial services providers avoid poorer geographical areas when locating their seats and branches. Later on the notion 'financial exclusion' received a broader sense: it concerned the situation where certain society groups were experiencing a constrained access to: modern payment instruments, consumer credit, and insurance, as well as the situation of individuals lacking savings of any kind.[674] However, only in 1999 was the term 'financial exclusion' used to describe the conditions of people who had limited access to the mainstream financial services.[675] The authors of the study on "Financial Services Provision and Prevention of Financial Exclusion,"[676] basing their argument on the several observations conducted by both academics and policy makers, claim that the term 'financial exclusions' nowadays "refers to a process whereby people encounter difficulties accessing and/or using financial services and products in the mainstream market that are appropriate to their needs and enable them to lead a normal social life in the society in which they belong." That definition is completed by a recognition according to which, 'financial exclusion' is merely an element of the major whole, namely this major whole is social exclusion described as a constrained access to quality essential services such as jobs, housing, education and health care. In other words, there is a deep interrelation between financial and social exclusion: financial exclusion leads almost automatically to social exclusion, thereby as such reinforces the risk to face social exclusion. In turn, perfect financial inclusion is defined by the capacity to access and use the appropriate financial services offered by the providers defined as mainstream or as alternative – on the condition that they comply with law and do not exploit low-income consumers.

The authors of the HM Treasury document titled "Promoting financial exclusion,"[677] consider different definitions of 'financial exclusion'. According to a broad concept, the term

672 Ibid.

673 A. Leyson, N. Thrift, „Geographies of financial exclusion: financial abandonment In Britain and the United States", Transactions of the Institute of British Geographers, New Series, 20, pp.312-341, 1995.

674 L. Anderloni, B. Bayot, P. Błędowski, M. Iwanicz-Drozdowska and E. Kempson, "Financial Services...

675 E. Kempson and C. Whyley, „Kept Out or Opted Out? Understanding and Combating Financial Exclusion.", Bristol: Policy Press, 1999.

676 L. Anderloni, B. Bayot, P. Błędowski, M. Iwanicz-Drozdowska and E. Kempson, "Financial Services...

677 HM Treasury, "Promoting financial exclusion", December 2004, available at:

'financial exclusion' means a lack of access to a range of financial services. However, a narrower concept reflects particular circumstances, for instance, geographical exclusion. Self-exclusion – is also mentioned – and describes a situation in which a person decides not to apply for a certain financial product, since he assumes a priori that his application will definitely be declined.

There are a great deal of serious consequences brought about by the phenomenon of financial exclusion – apart from that already mentioned above, namely social exclusion. The HM Treasury document enumerates several costs associated with financial exclusion for an individual deprived of access to a bank account, credit etc. A few such costs are: inter alia higher charges for the basic financial transactions (as for instance electronic banking is excluded); no access to certain products or services (e.g. to internet booking with credit cards); barriers to employment (among other things – the credibility of a potential employee without any bank history can be called into question). In general, financial exclusion leads to an enormity of negative consequences such as: changing patterns of consumption, changing the ways of participating in the economic activity of the society; changing the ways of accessing social welfare and of participating in distribution of incomes and wealth – to mention only a few. However, next to the economic consequences which affect the financially excluded individuals – one can identify several social consequences which essentially affect the situation that an individual used to have in the society.[678] Furthermore, the financial exclusion of an individual imposes significant costs not only on the excluded individual, but as a result, the costs are also borne by the entire society to which the excluded person belongs. The different types of financial exclusion are characterized by different repercussions concerning an individual's economic and social activity.

The banking transaction exclusion is a specific litmus test for the general financial exclusion, and moreover it causes a domino effect, since the lack of access to the basic banking service i.e. a bank account, stigmatizes such an individual and, as such, makes it difficult or even impossible for him to access the other financial services e.g. credit, and as a consequence, it may increase his risk of poverty. Individuals who are deprived of the possibility of: receiving the regular payments of funds, storing money safely, paying for goods with the non-cash means, making remittances, converting the securities into cash, etc., are referred to in the literature[679] as 'unbanked', and are followed by the next category termed 'margin-

---

http://www.hm-treasury.gov.uk/d/pbr04_profininc_complete_394.pdf, p. 522.

678 B. Bayot, "Social, economical and financial consequences of financial exclusion", Working Paper in L. Anderloni et al., "Financial Services Provision...

679 See among other: L. Anderloni, E. Carluccio, "Access to Bank Accounts and Payment Services" in L. Anderloni, E. Carluccio & M. Braga, "New Frontiers in Banking Services: Emerging Needs and Tailored Products for Untapped Markets.", Berlin: Springer Verlag, 2006 and BMRB, "Access to Financial Services by those on the Margins of Banking: Final Report for the Financial Inclusion Taskforce.", London: BMRB, 2006.

ally banked' (i.e. - those with a deposit account, however without payment cards, cheque books or electronic payment facilities), and the 'fully banked' category.

Strongly linked to the banking transaction exclusion is the credit exclusion which has, in turn a significant impact on social exclusion in general. A person who faces credit exclusion – is unable to obtain credit from any mainstream financial provider – and consequently often ends up with the sub-prime lenders'[680] or intermediaries' realms who offer much higher rates and inferior terms and conditions of the credit contracts, and who demand extra fees for extending loans, and issue penalties for defaulting, and most importantly, such alternative lenders in major cases do not carry out credit ratings, and thus, unaware of the consumer's creditworthiness, put that consumer in fact at an enormous risk of defaulting.[681] From that point onwards consumer overindebtedness, and therefore insolvency, is simply a matter of time.[682] Concluding a credit contract with an illegal money provider may have serious social consequences in case a borrower falls into arrears, namely there is a risk that such a lender himself uses violence and intimidation in order to execute paying off the debt, or that the lender passes on the information to an outsourcing company, which then in turn applies harsh methods to recover the debt.

Moreover, an individual who has no capacity to be granted a loan of any type experiences a certain stigmatization; not only the level of his standard of living is reduced but also his self-esteem is lowered as well. The authors of the above mentioned study[683] distinguish several possible levels of credit exclusion. The groups of customers which find themselves in the two extreme categories are the "credit excluded" who totally lack access to credit and those "appropriately served by mainstream lenders." The consumers who belong to the first category are forced to deal with illegal creditors or money providers with a particularly high interest rate etc. Therefore, they often experience exploitation and often are served in an inappropriate way i.e. they are offered credit which is inappropriate with respect to their needs or their capacity to pay it back. The remaining categories are: individuals inappropri-

680 "Sub-prime lending" is defined - by C. Corr "Alternative commercial credit providers", Working Paper in L. Anderloni et al., "Financial Services Provision... - as high interest loans offered to low-income consumers and credit impaired; being often extortionate such loans may entail high cost, unclear terms and conditions of agreements, unfair sales practices, dishonest brokers and/or illegal debt recovery.

681 A new report commissioned by Circle Anglia and written by the Financial Inclusion Centre estimates that between 650,000 and 850,000 UK's households have lost access to legal credit options as a result of the credit crisis. The authors of the report estimate that this would expand the market for illegal loans and that up to 200,000 people could now be using illegal lenders in the UK, assuming that supply expands to meet demand. It is concluded that the withdrawal of legal door step lenders has left a gap, and that gap has been filled by illegal doorstep lenders. "The Real Cost of Christmas Assessing the impact of illegal money lending on consumers", January 2009.
Available at: http://inclusioncentre.org.uk/doc/The_Real_Cost_of_Christmas_FINAL_VERSION.pdf.

682 C. Corr, "Alternative commercial credit providers"...

683 L. Anderloni, B. Bayot, P. Błędowski, M. Iwanicz-Drozdowska and E. Kempson, "Financial Services...

ately served by the alternative or mainstream creditors or those appropriately served however by the alternative providers.

Similar to the problem of poverty, the phenomenon of financial exclusion can also be subject to gradation as it too is a rather relative concept. The authors of the above mentioned study adopted the term "financially excluded" - next to the term "marginally included" for those individuals who have a limited access to financial services. There are data coming from the Eurobarometer Survey 60.2 and 2003.5 undertaken at the end of 2003, according to which every tenth adult from the 'old' EU member states and as much as almost half of the adult population of the "new" member states belonged to the category of 'unbanked'. Whereas, further 8 % and 6 % respectively were defined as 'marginally banked' i.e. with only a deposit account, but without a payment card or cheque book etc. facilities. These data are strongly linked to credit exclusion which caused a situation in which 40 % of the 'old' EU adults and almost three adults out of four in the 'new' EU had no access to credit cards or overdraft (i.e. to revolving credit). The Eurobarometer Survey shows that the problem of financial exclusion at the end of 2003 affected 7 % of the adult population from the 'old' EU member states and 1/3 of those in the 'new' member states, and as such, definitely cannot be classified as a marginal phenomenon; on the contrary – it poses a significant social issue which requires further scrutiny on the EC level.

Additionally, a striking observation was the geographic distribution between members of the same organism i.e. the European Community with the huge differences in percentage of the population e.g. Benelux citizens (where the financially excluded made up 1 % or less) and Latvia (respectively 48 %). Consequently, it is not surprising that hand in hand with the high level of financial exclusion is a low level of affluence combined with a high level of income inequality. However, an extremely high level of financial exclusion in the Central-Eastern European member states[684] is not necessarily strongly correlated with the low standard of living and the general low level of affluence the citizens experience - as it may superfluously appear - in these post-communistic countries. In other words, the factors which result in the above mentioned indexes and consequently, which are applied to distinguish within a society the individuals who are 'financially excluded', are very relative, and since they are very subjective, they also depend a lot on the culture of the inhabitants of a respective country. The societies of the 'old' and of the 'new' member states attribute a different value to e.g. the fact that they may or may not have a transaction bank account. Whereas in the most affluent, well-developed countries of Western Europe an individual with no banking history finds himself on the margin of society and most probably (or at least

684 Besides Latvia's extreme index – 48 %, the data from other Central Eastern European Member States show a similar tendency: Lithuania – 41 %, Poland – 40 %, Hungary – 34 %.

there would be such a common assumption) such a person also lacks basic goods, in the Eastern societies however, such a distinction is not that clear anymore.[685]

Undoubtedly, the factor of a common past plays a significant role here. The imposed system of economy, diversely defined, however unquestionably far from the capitalistic one which was growing in the other parts of Europe, resulted in – what I perceive as - a lack of "banking culture" in those countries. In my understanding the term 'banking culture' is very complex, consisting of causes, factors and their consequences. For half of the century individuals from the Soviet bloc were facing on one hand a chronic shortage of any sort of consumption goods, including flats, and on the other hand, a lack of any banking infrastructure whatsoever, with literally one state bank which was fulfilling the sort of evidential functions for the *units of socialized economy* and for which a consumer as such was totally outside the bank's scope of interest. In addition, keeping in mind that in the centrally planned system it was the State - and not financial means i.e. money – who was in charge of the distribution of all the goods, then it should not be surprising that the banking culture of the individual customers then was simply non-existing. If in the year 1989 one had ventured to undertake a survey similar to the one mention above, applying the present standards to the existing situation at that time, in any of the upcoming countries, then the results would have revealed that almost the entire society was, in fact, financially excluded.

During the next thirteen years the development which took place in those countries also in financial services was unquestionably grand, however one cannot ignore the other element which is involved in the widely grasped 'banking culture', namely the mentality of the people - in other words the 'social capital'. The new branches of the international banks that entered the Eastern European markets as quickly as possible in the beginning of 1990s, did not manage to attract a certain portion of the society. Those two generations who were brought up without the physical possibility or a feeling of need (there was no supply which would have created such a need, and there were almost no goods which would have been potentially available) for the opening of a current account, purchasing with a payment card, or for incurring a loan - at present experience difficulties in comprehending the premises of the new system. Moreover, these individuals lack a feeling of trust: those citizens whose comparative stability of a very basic existence was ensured by the omnipotent state, now feel insecure in a system which is based on capitalistic premises, whereas on the other hand, banking belongs to this sphere of economic activity where trust, as such, plays a crucial role. Furthermore, if one also adds to this, the problem of *electronic exclusion* (access to the internet is in these countries still not a common good), then the data coming from the Eurobarometer should not arouse too much astonishment.

---

685 The most vivid, telling and credible at the same time example is Jarosław Kaczyński – a Polish politician who was not hiding the fact that he had no banking history at all (no current account), still won the free, democratic parliamentarian elections in 2005 and became a prime minister of the government of an almost 40 million nation.

The issue of credit exclusion appears to be more difficult to grasp, since the surveys fain to take into consideration two crucial factors which influence the data, namely on the one hand there are consumers who are opposed to borrowing in principle, and on the other certain parts of society simply do not need to incur loans as they are guided by the rule 'first save, then spend'. Moreover, those two variables play a different role in the statistics of each respective state. Consequently, one should make allowances for a certain overestimation of the level of the exclusion. The Eurobarometer makes a distinction between two variables applied in order to measure the magnitude of the unsecured credit exclusion, i.e. the percentage of people with no credit in the form of an overdraft, credit cards or loan; and the percentage of people lacking access to revolving credit facilities, namely those with no access to overdraft and credit cards.[686] And here, similar to the financial exclusion data, the geographic discrepancy is significant: whereas in the 'old' EU member states 40 % of adults did not have any revolving credit facilities in 2003, the same applies to almost ¾ of the 'new' EU adult population. When observing the data for specific countries, the difference is even more noticeable: in France only 14 % of adults did not borrow money at all, whereas in Lithuania the same proportion of adult population indeed used a revolving credit facility.

Telling, and at the same time very alarming observations, come from another survey,[687] which examined credit behaviours of the French, Spanish and Italian inhabitants on low income. According to this research, a large amount of those interviewed had indeed access to credit, notwithstanding, the service provider in most of the cases was not a bank. About 50 % of the respondents had never applied for credit at a bank or at a credit institution. Those customers paid no attention though to the difference in cost and terms between the different money lenders, and moreover the borrowers had no capacity to estimate the amount of the costs they accepted to pay.

The results coming from the Eurobarometer statistics[688] concerning financial exclusion lead to the conclusion that in all the EU countries this problem touches on certain groups of a society, and here the geographic location no longer plays a significant role. The most vulnerable individuals are: those living on low income or who are unemployed; those who are single parents; and the sick or the disabled. The "new" member states had a certain shameful input too: they have brought a new category to the statistics, namely the retired.

Several analyses[689] attempted to group the factors leading up to financial exclusion into 2 categories: those motivating the supply side, and those motivating the demand side. The

---

686 L. Anderloni, B. Bayot, P. Błędowski, M. Iwanicz-Drozdowska and E. Kempson, "Financial Services...

687 L. Nieri, „Access to Credit: the Difficulties of Households", in in L. Anderloni, E. Carluccio & M. Braga, "New Frontiers in Banking Services: Emerging Needs and Tailored Products for Untapped Markets.", Berlin: Springer Verlag, 2006.

688 Eurobarometer Survey 60.2 and 2003.5.

689 L. Anderloni, E. Carluccio & M. Braga, "New Frontiers in Banking Services..., E. Kempson and C. Whyley, „Kept Out or Opted Out..., E. Kempson, "Policy Level Response to Financial Exclusion in Developing

financial services providers – as to the reasons for their refusal to open transaction bank accounts to certain groups of consumers – indicate the following: a poor credit history of the consumers who were turned-down; their unstable patterns of employment; failing the credit scoring system by the appliers, their history in the negative register for payment failure; and their inability to satisfy certain identity requirements (e.g. the fact that they are migrants). Besides the above mentioned factors, there are several other causes of financial exclusion, for instance the general tendency concerning a greater "flexibility" on the job market causes in turn job insecurity and increases the risk of unemployment, as well as the tightening of money laundering rules. Also on the consumers' side there are factors which cause aversion of this group to deal with the financial institutions. The growing complexity of the financial services for a range of consumers creates confusion and, consequently an obstacle to dealing with banks. The analysis distinguishes the three categories of the consumers who deny entering into contracts with banks. The first group are the elderly people described as a "cash only generation"; second, is the category of migrants and, finally, the low income persons perceiving banking as a sort of "luxury" service, hence presumably not available for them.

When it comes to credit exclusion, the main reason for this phenomenon, however also a consequence of several other factors, is the refusal by financial institutions. It touches on 16% of adult inhabitants of France, Italy and Spain. The money lenders refuse to grant credit when a consumer lacks stable employment, or has a low income etc. and as a consequence such consumer fails the score card operated by the creditors. A consumer who has an adverse credit history or in relation to which there is no information at all about him at the credit reference bureaux, can also expect to be turned down. The surveys[690] demonstrate that there is also a category of individuals who – anticipating a priori that their application will be refused – simply do not apply for a loan. Apparently such a behavioural pattern concerns 6 % of the Italian, French and Spanish adult population. The problem linked to credit exclusion among the people with low incomes is explained by Caplovitz's famous truth: "poor pay more." These individuals are deterred by the high costs and the financially unfavourable terms of credit agreements, particularly often offered to them (and to be precise - actually designed for their sake) through the intermediaries or on the sub-prime market.[691] It has also been observed that an offer from the mainstream lenders does not always correspond with the consumers' needs, that is, whereas many of the poorer consumers apply for a fairly small loan for a short period of time and with fixed terms, most mainstream lenders are not willing to satisfy such demand. The other cause for credit exclusion – however this

---

Economies: Lessons for Developing Countries", Paper for "Access to Finance: Building Inclusive Financial Systems", World Bank, Washington DC, May 30-31 2006.

690 L. Nieri, „Access to Credit..., E. Kempson, C. Whyley, "Kept Out or Opted Out....

691 L. Nieri, „Access to Credit..., S. Collard, E. Kempson, "Affordable Credit: The Way Forward", York: Joseph Rowntree Foundation, 2005.

time not depending directly on banks – is a fear of borrowing among this category of consumers, especially with regard to the fear of losing control over spending in case of using overdrafts or credit cards.

Unquestionably, the "societal" factors illustrated above also play a significant role in credit exclusion. The authors of the study[692] mention here the liberalization of the markets which, through the levelling of the different financial institutions' regulations, resulted in the disappearance of those types of institutions which traditionally used to serve the poorer consumers. Moreover, the changes which took place on the labour market caused more flexibility which, consequently, for the potential borrowers means less stable employment and less creditworthiness. Although the fiscal policy can bring borrowers certain advantages (e.g. reducing costs, granting fiscal advantages etc.), for the consumers on low income, duties and taxes may represent a heavy burden. In singling out the societal factors that play a role in credit exclusion, one cannot ignore the issue of demographic changes – the ageing population lacks the confidence in all these new credit facilities and in addition, lacks access to the internet.

Unsurprisingly, there is a strong correlation between the two phenomena concerning consumers' financial existence: financial exclusion and overindebtedness.[693] The scarce data (available only for the Unite Kingdom and Belgium) demonstrate that in general the group of financially excluded individuals and that of over-indebted individuals overlap, i.e. the unemployed, single parents, and the disabled are disproportionately likely to face over-indebtedness as well as financial exclusion, although those who are over-indebted are more likely to have a higher socio-economic status. The conclusions which can be drawn from Gloukoviezoff's research boil down to an observation that the link between financial exclusion and overindebtedness resembles a vicious circle. On the one hand, overindebtedness leads to financial exclusion – the study shows that in some of the EU countries an over-indebted consumer is prevented from e.g. opening a bank account; in other words he is deprived of any access to the financial services. On the other hand, it is also true that over-indebtedness may be a consequence of financial exclusion, more specifically; over-indebtedness may be a result of the access and use difficulties. A vivid example could be an easily imaginable situation of that in which a consumer whose previous credit application has been refused by a mainstream bank, incurs a loan with an alternative financial institution, which in turn, does not attend the consumer properly granting him an excessive loan or applying exploiting terms to the contract. As a result, such a situation leads to the over-indebtedness of the consumer.

The problem of financial exclusion, although it concerns only a small percentage of at least the Western European inhabitants, does pose, in fact, an economic and social problem

692 L. Anderloni, B. Bayot, P. Błędowski, M. Iwanicz-Drozdowska and E. Kempson, "Financial Services...

693 G. Gloukoviezoff, „The link between financial exclusion and over-indebtedness", Working Paper in L. Anderloni et al., "Financial Services Provision...

for the whole society. The percentage changes as one takes into consideration the European Community as a whole, also taking into account its "new" members in relation to which financial exclusion appears to be a more common and hence more severe problem. Therefore, there should be no doubts as to the moral duty on the one hand, and understandable pragmatic motives of the respective governments, but also of the whole European Union on the other, to take the appropriate steps in order to combat this phenomenon.

The national legal systems differ significantly with regard to combating financial exclusion and in general, approaching the problem of overindebtedness. It should be stressed that behind law regulations stand very diverse premises with regard to the role of consumer credit in human lives, i.e. whereas the English and American legislators as well as the EU Commission DG Social Policy always emphasize that exclusion from access to credit is equal to poverty and deprivation; in Belgium, the French speaking community celebrates "days without credit" claiming that the use of credit increases the number of defaults and therefore overindebtedness, and that this is in itself a source of poverty. On the other hand consumer advocates argue that credit as such is like money or machinery which can serve many purposes as it allows to "bridge the time where income is earned and when it has to be spent for consumption, education and labour," thus they conclude that credit which is a well-adopted to specific conditions and productive as such, is necessary. [694]

Also private actors (the NGOs and financial services providers) – having however different aims in mind - take steps to join or launch themselves in such actions. In practice, the responses to that imperative differ from one state to another.[695] The most active financial exclusion debate within the European Community takes place in France and in the United Kingdom. Whereas the French activity encompasses the establishment of the Comité Consultatif du Secteur Financier - responsible for the negotiations and the dialogue between the key stakeholders, the Postal Office network, and mutual and agricultural banks focusing on facilitating financial inclusion; in the United Kingdom, the crowning achievement of the very active role of its government is the creation of the Financial Inclusion Taskforce gathering all the key stakeholders alongside the Financial Inclusion Fund designed to promote financial inclusion. In the other member states the fight against financial exclusion is perhaps not that active, but also in a number of situations in some member states it encompasses governmental activity. A few examples of such activity are as follows: the introduction of the new legislation in Ireland, the initiatives launched to promote access to an affordable credit in Belgium; the cooperation between the state agencies and the private actors (commercial and non-profit entities) like for instance agreements with banks in Germany or the working groups in the Netherlands, the activity of consumer organizations (in Germany – the debate on responsible credit; and finally, in Austria, Germany, Italy – the debate on financial education).

694 http://www.responsible-credit.net/index.php?id=1980&viewid=44823.

695 L. Anderloni, B. Bayot, P. Błędowski, M. Iwanicz-Drozdowska and E. Kempson, "Financial Services...

The European Commission made a first step initiating the complex process of combating the problem of financial exclusion. This action was undertaken in response to the data drawn from "Eurobarometer 260 'Consumers' opinions on services of general interest' 2007" – which revealed that in a number of countries, people find it difficult or even impossible to access the banking system through a current account, and then usually, citizens are subsequently prevented from consuming financial services such as credit or bank payment transactions which are related to the current account. The Commission launched public consultation on "Financial Inclusion: Ensuring access to a basic bank account." By launching this project, the Commission seeks to gather the general comments and expert advice "on the possibilities to ensure that by a certain date nobody will be denied access to a basic bank account." There are also initiatives where the EC institution acts only as a co-commission.[696]

The authors of the study[697] classified in general all the anti-exclusion actions into three categories: in the first position they placed market responses by commercial providers, co-operative and savings banks, and non-profit organizations; in the second position - self-regulation through voluntary charters and codes of practice, and finally - governmental intervention. The first category is comprised of the initiatives launched not only by the "social-oriented" services providers such as the co-operatives, savings or postal banks, micro-finance institutions;[698] but also by the ordinary mainstream i.e. non stigmatizing (regarding the national context) commercial "profit-oriented" providers. Guided by the idea of *corporate social responsibility* the financial services providers develop a new offer which is more appropriate for the financially excluded individuals. In order to reduce costs and barriers to access for the worse-offs, the financial institutions establish financial partnerships together with the non-profit entities or the governmental organizations. Moreover, they take part in promoting financial education. And even if some sceptics claim that financial institutions do so in order to promote a positive self-image as an element of the commercial PR, still such activity fulfils its task, i.e. at the end of the day it increases financial inclusion. In particular, such initiatives bring favourable results in the field of consumer credit, since particularly here creditors are very reluctant to deal with the not necessarily well-off, not rarely high risk

696 E.g. with support from the European Commission was conducted throughout the last two years the Mutual Learning in Financial Inclusion ('MULFI') project, which has now published its final report. The project supported the organisation of a learning network of practitioners involved in financial inclusion activities from across 11 core partner EU Member States and more broadly. As a consequence of the work of the MULFI project a new European Financial Inclusion Network ('EFIN') has now been formed. The report available at: http://www.fininc.eu/index,en.html.

697 L. Anderloni, B. Bayot, P. Błędowski, M. Iwanicz-Drozdowska and E. Kempson, "Financial Services...

698 The good example of such activities are credit unions in the UK. These are financial co-operatives which are owned and controlled by its members and are run for the benefit of their members and the community. Credit unions operate on low-income market like a local 'community bank', however, with profits put back into the business and given to savers. Credit unions are safguarded by FSCS and FSA. Sources: http://www.abcul.org/credit-unions, http://www.ukcu.co.uk.

borrowers, whose creditworthiness is not unquestionable. Ziegel[699] extols the idea of the non-profit low cost credit facilities for the low-income consumers as an effective remedy against financial problems of the poor. Among the advantages of such a solution is the fact that it allows certain groups of consumers to combat financial exclusion. There are also many other potential benefits created by this approach, such as: inter alia "giving the consumers hands-on experience in the handling of credit under the watchful eyes of friendly lenders not driven by profit motives." As a result, enriched in a new experience, which (for a change) is a positive one, and thus more confident and aware of the complexity of the market, previously excluded consumers are given, thanks to such a solution, an opportunity to enter the financial market provided with the most efficient tool of financial education, namely their own experience.

The second category distinguished in the whole group of anti-exclusion actions includes voluntary charters and codes of practices. Here the initiative comes from the banks' trade associations, although often it is prompted and encouraged by the public authorities.[700] The most spectacular example is provided by France, again with the activity of Fédération Bancaire Française and its commitment to opening affordable accounts under the banner of the 'right to an account'. Such initiative seriously improved the statistics concerning financial exclusion by increasing significantly the number of "banked" individuals in the country. Similar scenarios can be found in the Netherlands, where the "basic bank account convenant" was established as a result of cooperation between the banking association, the Ministry of Finance and the Salvation Army, and in the United Kingdom (with its Banking Code). However, other similar initiatives - for instance, in Germany: "Everyman" current account launched by Zentraler Kreditausschuss; and in Belgium a "call deposit account" by the Belgian Bankers' Association – met with strong criticism from the consumer circles as lacking the effective necessary enforcement, i.e. such initiatives were criticized, since providers did not apply them in practice and arguably they did not really improve the situation of the financially excluded. One can therefore come to the conclusion that the mere declarations in the form of the voluntary codes or charters, without however a strong commitment from the financial services providers, are not sufficient to ensure the increase of financial inclusion.

In the previous two categories of the pro-financial-inclusion activities, the state's interference was either very minor or non-existent. The last category however, embraces the pure governmental interventions.[701] The public authorities have the widest scope for the activity focused on combating financial exclusion. They can offer a direct help to their citi-

---

699 J.S. Ziegel, "Comparative Consumer Insolvency Regimes – A Canadian Perspective", Oxford-Portland Oregon, 2003. p. 152.

700 Ibid.

701 E. Kempson, B. Bayot, „Regulation In Europe promoting financial inclusion", B. Bayot, "The Role of Corporate Social Responsibility to promote financial inclusion" Working Papers in L. Anderloni et al., "Financial Services Provision...

zens,[702] they can facilitate the financial inclusion or introduce legislation which, in a direct or indirect way, influences the financial landscape; and the only element which constrains them is that of the fundamental legal limits which constitute the freedoms of all actors, i.e. individuals, private commercial and non-profit entities. The term "scope" refers not only to a substantial range of the means which can be involved, but also to the different levels on which the government can exercise its interventionist actions; that is, the authorities can influence the general public, or confine themselves only to exert an influence on the demand or the supply side. Such a state intervention in the financial services market in order to combat financial exclusion can be allowed on the grounds of market failure as a result of information asymmetry (both on the part of providers and on the part of the financially excluded) and on the grounds of equity, as more and more significant parts of society have their financial needs unmet, or - due to being excluded from the mainstream business - pay more than necessary for financial products and services. [703]

It is in fact impossible or at least ineffective to launch any anti-exclusion actions without a previous full understanding of the issue and without grasping the full extent of this phenomenon. Thus, before the public authorities (those of the respective member states or the of the EC) take any positive steps, appropriate research should be undertaken in order to first collect data, and next, to investigate the causes of financial exclusion, to better understand the whole complexity of the problem, and then to assess the policy measures applied to date, and finally, to recommend the adequate measures to combat the financial exclusion.

The governments acting as "facilitators" have at their disposal all the measures to promote and support market initiatives, i.e. they can apply a "soft" intervention on the supply side by (inter alia): encouraging banks to offer to the low-income individuals basic bank accounts, by stimulating business to introduce low-cost products designed for the poor; and furthermore, by encouraging industry to adopt voluntary charters etc. The state-"facilitator's" activity can consist of a specific mediation between the supply and demand sides. Through creating a positive environment, raising awareness and improving the image of financial providers also in the eyes of worse-off consumers, as well as through initiating

702 The Social Fund in the UK is a good example of the activity of the state itself as regards credit for the poor. A Budgeting Loan is an interest-free loan intended to help spread the cost of certain one-off expenses over a longer period. Such loan can help towards the cost of various items for example, things needed for or to improve the home, certain debts, etc. These loans have to be repaid. A Crisis Loan may be available to everyone, who needs help to meet expenses in an emergency or because of a disaster. Such loan must be the only way of preventing serious damage or risk to the health or safety of the person or to their family. Crisis loans are interest free but have to be repaid. Source: http://www.dwp.gov.uk.

703 HM Treasury, "Promoting financial exclusion", December 2004, available at: http://www.hm-treasury.gov.uk/d/pbr04_profininc_complete_394.pdf, p. 522.

dialogue between the stakeholders, the authorities can successfully prepare the field for future healthy contractual relations.

On the other hand, by offering educational programmes and proper advice the authorities influence the demand side, reinforce consumers' confidence, and encourage the financially excluded to use financial services. Such an educational activity is especially effective when it is aimed exclusively at the specific groups of the society, such as the elderly or the migrants, since every category has different motives for self-exclusion. Finally, the governments contribute directly to the provision of the financial services to the low-income people via establishing special funds or even by directly providing the poor with the basic financial services.

The most recognized role the authorities play in order to increase financial inclusion is their activity as legislators. The legislative activity concerns organizing, regulating, monitoring and controlling the financial services industry, as well as imposing certain obligations on providers and prohibiting them from exercising certain activities. In some of the European countries (France, Belgium and Norway), a requirement exists in their legal orders, according to which, every inhabitant should have access to banking transaction and payment services. The fulfilment of that obligation (from the providers' point of view) is controlled by the independent supervisory bodies. Next to such an obligation, a compensation system is established in order to guarantee that service provision is evenly shared among all the providers.

There are also propositions of an anti-exclusion activity on the European Community level, namely the introduction of the Community Reinvestment Act (CRA) in order to promote the *corporate social responsibility* idea in the financial sector. The idea of the CRA with its transparency objective put into life in the United States at the end of 1970s, was aimed at encouraging the financial industry to "fulfil their continuing and affirmative obligation to meet the credit needs of their communities." The Act addressed the phenomenon reflecting financial exclusion i.e. the fact that providers of financial services draw a red line around certain areas, and the refuse to provide their services within this area. Via developing knowledge of these areas, the mainstream creditors would be encouraged to enter the subprime lending markets. Bayot[704] for instance proposes that the EU legal order adopts the principle of information disclosure from the U.S. CRA, in the form of a "Disclosure Directive", i.e. the regular evaluation of the lending performance.

There are several other initiatives on the EU level which aim at eliminating financial exclusion. The European Social Fund (ESF),[705] an EU Structural Fund was established to reduce difference in prosperity and living standards across European member states and regions, and therefore promoting economic and social cohesion. Its Funding is spread across the member states and regions, in particular those where economic development is less ad-

704 B. Bayot, "The Role of Corporate Social Responsibility to promote financial inclusion...

705 Source: http://ec.europa.eu/employment_social/esf/index_en.htm.

vanced. The traditional ESF areas are: employment, social exclusion and workforce skills, as well as addressing challenges in education and training.

The European Commission launched also the new European Progress Microfinance Facility.[706] It aims at easing access to finance for people who want to start up or further develop their own business but have difficulties in accessing banking loans. The European Progress Microfinance Facility does not directly provide financing to entrepreneurs, but enables microfinance institutions in the EU countries to increase lending to them. To this end, the European Progress Microfinance Facility uses two instruments: it issues guarantees to providers of microfinance thereby it shares their risk of loss, and it increases their micro-credit volume through funded instruments.

Perhaps a so far inconspicuous discussion on the right to a bank account, and the right to credit, present only in consumer advocates' circles, should become more public and more audible. Among a substantial number of different definitions of the notion of social exclusion, one can find a very broad definition, which encompasses not only poverty (low material means), but also "the inability to participate effectively in economic, social, political and cultural life; and in some characterisations alienation and distance from the mainstream society".[707] One can encounter a similar definition in the document of the Financial Services Authority, "In or Out? Financial Exclusion: A Literature and Research Review" 2000,[708] i.e. the author agrees that social exclusion is a broader concept than poverty, it "is a shorthand term for what can happen when people or areas suffer from a combination of interrelated problems such as unemployment, poor skills, low incomes, poor housing, high crime environments, bad health, poverty and family breakdown." Thus, one could argue that the issue of financial exclusion also has a constitutional dimension: those deprived of credit, are also deprived of other basic rights which are commonly protected in the European legislation, like: dignity, a decent standard of living, housing etc. The fact that some individuals are deprived of credit, at the end of the day curtails their freedom of choice.[709]

In the theoretical discussions we very often treat all the consumers as a relatively homogenous group of individuals who more or less are expected to act rationally in the market place and moreover, roughly speaking, they are all measured by the same standards, whereas we tend to forget that people actually differ from each other also in the way they act in the short- and long-terms. These differences are to a great extent determined by the social backgrounds from which various consumer groups originate. As Johnson[710]observed, the point of reference of the well-off is different than that of the poor. The insecurity of a work-

706 See more: http://ec.europa.eu/social/main.jsp?langId=en&catId=836.

707 K. Duffy, „Social Exclusion and Human Dignity in Europe. Background report for the proposed initiative by the Council of Europe." Strasbourg: Council of Europe. (1995), p. 92.

708 Financial Services Authority, "In or Out? Financial Exclusion: A Literature and Research Review" 2000, p. 7-8, available at: http://www.cabinet-office.gov.uk/seu/index/faqs.html.

709 I. Ramsay, "Rationales for Intervention pp 15-24, I. Ramsay, "Consumer Law and Policy...

710 P. Johnson 1985: 218-219.

ing class income determines a different approach towards money, towards long-term savings plans, towards credit etc. Hence the behaviours which from the perspective of the well-off might seem very irrational, conversely from the perspective of the poor, can be not only understandable, but even justifiable.

Unquestionably in modern society nowadays consumer rights are a part of commonly accepted social rights. Some authors even contend that consumer rights should be treated as human rights. As Deutch[711] claims: "In a consumer society, protection of the individual consumer is part of maintaining human dignity. If not given the right to free trade, the right to a fair contract, and the right of access to courts, a person's dignity is disregarded. At the end of the day, these rights are no less important than other human rights." Reifner[712] mentions some basic fundamental principles like: access to service, equal treatment, and transparency - which have to be respected by the creditors in order to ensure minimum consumer protection.

The issue of the right to credit, as another to be included in the catalogue of an individual's rights, is for the time being only the popular topic of various theoretical discussions, since there is no country that recognizes such a right in the sense that the opposite party – the lender would be obliged to lend money to an individual.[713] To answer the question of whether or not such a right should be a part of the legal order, one should first answer another question, i.e.: "is access to credit a crucial device for accessing goods and services which are commonly perceived as necessary for an individual's rights to be fully exercised?"[714] The discussion about the right to a bank account, the right to a credit etc. could find its vent in the other solution regarding the problem of financial exclusion, namely in the idea of including the basic financial services in the category of the "services of general economic interest." Such an approach would ensure access to those services at affordable prices for every individual.

In the EU legal order the services of general interest have their well-established place (Art. 16 and 86 of the EC Treaty, Art. 36 of the Charter of Fundamental Rights of the EU), however, European legislation does not provide a definition of this term. According to a broad agreement, services of general economic interest are these services which are first, of economic interest, and second, "which the member states or the Community subject to specific public service obligations by virtue of a general interest criterion".[715]

However contentious the issues concerning services of general economic interest, there are no doubts as to the fact that they should be affordable to all the citizens in the EU. This

---

711 S. Deutch, "Are Consumer Rights, Human Rights?", 1994 Osgood Hall LJ 537 at 551-553, p. 576.

712 U. Reifner, "The Lost Penny...

713 S. Finlay, "Consumer Credit Fundamentals..., p. 61.

714 S. Finlay (ibid.) gives the examples of credit cards required by Heath care system or a satisfactory credit history in employment relationships.

715 Commission of the European Communities Green Paper on services of general economic interest COM (2003) 270.

argument was also confirmed by the Commission's White Paper on Services of General Economic Interest COM (2004) 374. The idea of an effective accessibility to essential services involves establishing the right of every citizen to access them. Universal service as a Community concept establishes the right of every citizen to access certain services considered as essential and at the same time, it imposes obligations on service providers to offer these services according to set conditions, including complete territorial coverage. This concept turned out to be effective for those individuals who could not otherwise obtain access to essential services. Furthermore, the White Paper[716] stresses the significance of access to cross-border services and the ensured access for all groups of the population which also embodies affordability of services provided. Such access includes (inter alia): special schemes for persons with low income, continuity, and access to information from providers etc. Thus, the recognition of the basic financial services as services of general interest would mean that they would no longer be provided on the basis of market mechanisms alone, thus at the same time certain providers would be entitled to receive compensation from the authorities.

The idea of a right to credit, and a right to a bank account realized either through putting these basic financial services into the category of the "services of general economic interest" or via placing them into the category of citizens' rights – however, with a corresponding necessity to recognize such rights at the constitutional level, does not appear to be convincing nowadays, at least for the time being. Broadening the catalogue of the "services of general interest", itself always poses a certain risk of an excessive intervention in the market in the area of banking, an area which, at least in theory, is at any rate rather tightly supervised by the public authorities. The idea of binding the financial services providers with additional obligations (as one cannot ignore the fact that granting any right to citizens entails certain obligations - which reflect the content of the right - imposed on the other party) should first be very carefully scrutinized from the point of view of the real necessity of such action, as such interventions are never free from a range of negative side effects. One should also ask the question regarding the limits of redistribution imposed by the authorities as far as this idea is concerned. As a result of recognizing basic financial services as "services of general interest" and consequently, imposing the obligations on bank institutions to open a bank account and to grant credit to every applier, the cost of banking would undisputedly increase (as banks would deal then also with customers who otherwise would have been rejected as inter alia non-reliable or without sufficient creditworthiness). Consequently, such cost would be covered by those who were the banks' customers also prior to such an intervention. Moreover, the whole idea is attainable only by applying the administrative law measures which, as such, should in general be avoided, if at all possible, in the sphere of private law. Finally, taking into account a very fast development of the consumption society market in terms of an increasingly growing amount of modern technologies, newer kinds of products and services, and also taking into account demand, which immediately adjust to

716 COM (2004) 374.

this wide and constantly broadening market offer, it does not seem inconceivable that still more and more services will compete for their place in the catalogue of the "services of general interest." However, certain services are located in this catalogue primarily because they are *essential* and *indispensable* for individuals in order to ensure their basic existence, whereas bank accounts or credit are solely a means for the improvement of the standard of life of consumers.

As far as the second solution is concerned i.e. rating a right to credit, and a right to a bank account among those rights guaranteed by the state catalogue of 'citizens' rights', apart from the arguments claimed above (here similarly there is a question as to the negative consequences of cost to be paid by other consumers, excessive interfering in the market, and in the sphere of private law, and finally of these services not actually being essential and indispensable), one can come up with the observation that, as a result, the importance of the other crucial citizens' rights would radically decrease and such a depreciation of their importance at the end of the day might lead to a negative or disrespectful stance towards the idea of the essential citizens' rights. This having been said, I do not intend to dispute consumers' rights to a dignified existence and I definitely and firmly defend the opinion that the urgent problem of financial exclusion should be resolved as soon as possible, since as a serious illness, it not only harms those who struggle with it at the moment, but it can also be transmitted to the future generations, and hence it is only a matter of time before it possibly involves a growing number of individuals.

The statement that the authorities have a duty to tackle the problem of financial exclusion does not generally raise any objection. However, the means with which the authorities should combat this problem remain questionable and contentious. In my opinion, the legislator should take steps to solve the problem through the appropriate regulations which would promote the idea of responsible lending as well as would direct the mainstream providers' attention to design their offer also with respect to the low-income individuals, so that their services would be affordable to the poor. However, in return the creditors should receive some compensation. Besides a probable promise of gaining potential new customers, providers should be entitled to expect the state/public guarantees. In addition, some social funding should also be involved. Simultaneously, the authorities' task to detect and enforce appropriate measures against the illegal financial providers should be executed efficaciously. Finally, the state activity should be completed with the financial education programmes offered not only to those who are already financially excluded, but also those who experience minor financial difficulties.

Nevertheless, perhaps it would be worth considering another solution to the problem of financial exclusion, namely a specific form of the public-private partnership. In general public non-commercial units – although existing within the frames of the market economy (whose goal is to satisfy demand, and not the real needs of its actors) - they do satisfy the specific needs of the citizens. Otherwise some of the needs would never be satisfied; and others would be satisfied to a lower degree than expected. These needs are usually education, health, culture, and environmental protection, however, perhaps basic bank services should also be rated among them. According to M. Cuomo,[717] it is not the government's duty to provide the services, but the government is to make sure that the services are indeed being provided. A public-private partnership is a means to provide society with certain services which are crucial for its citizens. It is a form of a long-term cooperation between the public and private sectors. The PPP means entrusting a private actor with execution of a public task, instead of imposing on that actor the execution of these tasks. In other words, in a contract a private actor commits himself for a fixed financial equivalent to provide certain services for a benefit of the society using public infrastructures. One of the main features of this venture are its social as well as commercial goals, which enable such practice to involve public as well as private financial resources. The second characteristic is the active participation of public sector in the venture, since it is the public actor who bears responsibility for providing the society with these services. Whatever the reason for the partnership, the common theme in all the PPP is that they bring together the strengths of both sectors: public and private, using the innovative capacities of the private enterprises (organizational and financial innovations and technologies, etc., and the broadly defined know-how) to create efficiencies that allow the government to free public funds for more core economic and social programmes. The solution of the PPP allows for combining both public and private resources. A private actor as a player more oriented toward the customer and more flexibly managed, can react faster and with greater ease to the changing needs of the customers and to the changing environment, and can better adjust its offer to the expectations of the members of society.

The way the PPP could be introduced in the area of banking would have to be adjusted to the specific character of these services. The financial resources would be provided by the private bank institutions, however, the state would have to necessarily guarantee such a venture, thus the risk would be to a large extent taken by the state. Furthermore, proportions of the risk sharing between private and public actors would have to relate to the category of the served consumers divided according to their reliability and creditworthiness.

This solution does not show the major disadvantages of the two above analysed options, i.e. the basic financial services defined as the "services of general economic interest" or brought down to the category of citizens' rights. The cooperation between public and private entities as well as the relationship between bank institutions and consumers would be based on the pure private law rules. No compulsion via administrative legal means would be in question. Secondly, the intervention in the market would be very slight since in the end it would not change the picture of the distribution of powers on the market place: otherwise, i.e. without introducing that specific PPP, the needs of the poor would not be satisfied at all – which is actually the case nowadays - according to the market rule of satisfying only demand. Thirdly, such an activity initiated by the public authorities would be clearly a kind of

717 Governor of New York State from 1982 to 1994.

social assistance granted to the poorest, disadvantaged citizens, however, the superiority of this kind of social help would result from the fact that the basic bank services would be available via the PPP in a way that neither discredits the beneficiary nor would it be humiliating to him, as the poor would be served within the bank structures and hence would feel that they are being treated as 'regular' customers. Moreover, the fact that the poor would be served - although under special conditions, but still - by the mainstream providers would possibly smooth their future passage to the regular mainstream bank market, also thanks to the positive experience presumably gained under the state's umbrella. And although the suggested solution is, in the end, one that comes close to pure social help, it still resembles more providing the fishing rod rather than the fish, and as such should be seriously considered.

The idea of the specific PPP seems to be a beneficial one for the poor themselves, as they would be given a chance to return to a "rightful" society by escaping from the realm of predatory lenders. It could be beneficial from the point of view of the public authorities whose task is to rescue their citizens from drowning by preferably giving them a fishing rod: showing them the positive examples, fostering their self-esteem, self-confidence and at the same time giving them a feeling that their life is in their own hands. And finally, the mainstream bank institutions could gain profits by broadening their future 'target group' with a substantial group of the potential financially included customers, and the additional incentives for them would be naturally the improvement of their public image which is also not irrelevant nowadays due to the financial crisis in which the role of banks was – to put it mildly - ambiguous.

Undoubtedly, such a solution entails significant public financial means, however one should answer the question of whether it is not actually more expensive financially, and on top of this morally, to allow the existence of a situation in which a certain percentage of the society lives, in fact, outside this society. The existence of the complex system of public help granted to those who find themselves already standing on the edge of a precipice is undoubtedly necessary. In other words the principle that the state should guarantee the minimum level of subsistence is largely unchallenged in modern societies even though there is considerable disagreement about which type of welfare state is preferable. However, one should consider first, whether this is really and absolutely all that a state, and the Community can do in this respect, and second, whether the intervention in the earlier stages would not prevent many of the potentially insolvent consumers from getting into real financial troubles and automatically becoming a significant financial and moral burden for the society. And in the end, in considering the problem from a very pragmatic perspective the question arises as to whether it would not be cheaper to intervene before a citizen is already financially 'excluded' from the society and as a consequence finds it very difficult or even impossible to come back as a 'healthy', 'productive' member of such society. That is, perhaps, easier and cheaper to provide an individual with a life jacket and to give him a few swimming lessons, similarly, maybe it is easier and cheaper to check the sailing capacity of the crew and to service a ship than to rescue a drowning person from the troubled waters and then attempt to revive him.

Conclusions

The new consumer credit Directive does not regulate consumer bankruptcy; furthermore, it does not deal with consumer insolvency nor with financial exclusion. Regulating in the pettiest detail the process of concluding a credit contract, simultaneously the EU legislator decided to ignore the problems which are the unfortunate, but at the same time natural side effects of consumer credit, like consumer insolvency and financial exclusion. Such issues, which are objective social facts, nevertheless, are not conceived on the level of academic discussion dilemmas. The Community respects the national autonomy in this field, which in a way is even favourable for consumers living/dealing in the member states where the bankruptcy law exists and where the domestic authorities take steps to combat the problem of financial exclusion. As the recent example of maximum harmonisation demonstrates, this seems to be especially favourable when one takes into account recent trend with the EU to harmonise consumer law to the detriment of consumers from hitherto more protective member states. However, from a perspective of the consumers-borrowers from member states which have not yet reached a required and satisfying level of legislation on consumer bankruptcy and financial exclusion (or do not deal with these problems at all), this solution is unfavourable. As a result, consumers from such less protective member states are left to themselves.

The incompleteness of the new Act with respect to consumer bankruptcy and financial exclusion is very much in line with the already described neo-liberal approach which prevails in the legislative activities of the Commission. In order to foster an integrated internal market, and to reach the optimum level of economic efficiency, the EU legislator focused on a well-informed, confident consumer-shopper, and at the same time a certain fiction was adopted, according to which, both consumer insolvency and financial exclusion are eventually foreign to the consumer credit contract. The fiction boils down to an assumption that consumer credit contract law encompasses all the aspects of concluding such a contract and successfully paying off a debt, and that the potential failure lies outside the scope of the Directive; thus it lies outside the scope of the credit contract. Such reasoning seems to be quite short-sighted, and this is not even about moral concerns like the issues of equality, of social justice etc. as these problems are left to the realm of competence of the member states. This specific move emphasises that the tension between European pro-market consumer law and member states' pro-social consumer law exists, and will not be resolved in the near future. The unsolved problem afflicts the citizens of those member states which due to various reasons did not introduce pro-social consumer law. However, it seems to be entirely outside the scope of the Commission's interest. The problem with the short-sightedness of the above sketched fiction is the assumption that the Community of 27 countries can share common economic successes without sharing the failures, which are yet the natural, potential side effects of the economic activity. In other words, unquestionably pro-market EU law contributes to building an efficient EU internal market which is competitive worldwide. Nevertheless, one should not forget that the economy as such is a much more complex phenomenon, i.e. the story of success of the internal market can be devalued by the failures which are side effects of exclusively pro-market measures. The problem of consumer insolvency and of financial and soon social exclusion will ricochet off the well-being of the whole economy. Insolvent, financially/socially excluded therefore 'unhealthy' consumers will represent a cost in the short-run as well as in the long-range, with the price to be paid by all the participants of the 'story of success'. The increase of credit interest rates, the increase of credit insurance premiums, and the increase of charge-offs in the budgets of creditors are only short-term, immediately noticeable consequences. Moreover, such short-term consequences are followed by long-term negative outcomes for the entire society due to the fact that our common European ethical consciousness does not allow us to ignore those fellow citizens who are in need. Thus, the long-term side effect of a policy which neglects issues like insolvency and exclusion is the increase of the social help expenses from the public funds, and as a result, the increase of taxes or the increase of public budget deficits, and finally, the slowing down of the economy. Finally, it must not be forgotten that in the long-range perspective the uncured problem of financial exclusion can turn out to be 'hereditary' consequently, perpetuating a problem that will afflict more and more of the European citizens.

As has been roughly demonstrated above within Europe itself it is not only the bankruptcy procedures which differ enormously from one country to the next. What I find even much more striking are the very diverse premises, sometimes even mutually conflicting principal goals, which stand behind the respective national regulations. The EU legislator making an effort to design common EC consumer bankruptcy provisions would have to address certain greatly questionable concerns. First and foremost it would be the issue of the goals of such a regulation. Hence, should the EC law aim at real consumer protection - i.e. protection according to the European (or even more precisely Scandinavian) meaning of this notion? This approach assumes the moral aspects of overindebtedness of an individual, and it attempts to solve the entire problematic situation of a borrower not by an immediate simple discharging of same, but by adopting a peculiar "parole" solution which means inter alia keeping consumers safely clear from their market activity via above all costly repayment plans etc. On the other hand, should the Community legislator adopt the American approach, i.e. allowing over-indebted individuals to return to the marketplace as soon as it is possible, and encouraging them to start their market activity from scratch (i.e. 'with a fresh start')? And here again, the repeatedly above mentioned tension resumes, i.e. the tension between two, often conflicting ideas - namely consumer protection and internal market: from the purely internal market, economic perspective, the 'fresh-start' solution makes the most of it as it 'rescues' over-indebted consumers from vanishing from the marketplace. According to this solution, consumers can continue or are actually encouraged to exercise their activity as market players. Whereas the European approach assumes a temporary exclusion of the over-indebted consumer from the marketplace. However, the question remains as to whether such a short-term activity, at the end of the day can turn out to be beneficial also in the long run. Solving an individual debt problem does not solve the permanent financial difficulties such a borrower struggles with. Furthermore, solving an individual debt problem does not mean that in the very immediate future the same consumer will not experience identical financial disaster. And finally, what seems to be often forgotten is the reality that 'healthy' consumers are the condition 'sine qua non' of a 'healthy' market.

I agree with the criticism formulated towards the EU legislator who, on the one hand, made an attempt to totally harmonise on the EC level the provisions on credit for consumers, but on the other hand entirely ignored one very complex and at the same time, very crucial aspect of consumer credit, namely consumer bankruptcy. The only justification in this respect for the designer of the new Directive is the fact that – as was cursorily shown earlier in this chapter – there are huge differences between the consumer bankruptcy systems in the various member states. These differences are very nationally determined, and one cannot deny that national traditions, and dominant values etc. play a significant role here. Hence, the question arises as to why the undeniable fact of the existence of huge differences in the 27 member states with respect to consumer credit relations in general, did not prevent the EU legislator from desisting from introducing identical rules for all the 27 member states.

Final Remarks

Unquestionably financial services represent a special segment of the market where, due to several reasons, a need for consumer protection is particularly high.[718] First, although one deals here only with consumer contracts, the sums of money which are the object of such agreements are often relatively (from the point of view of an individual) significant. Second, a great majority of these agreements, especially credit and insurance contracts, are concluded for a long period of time. And finally, in the field of financial services the information asymmetry between the provider of a service and a consumer particularly stands out, since contrary to other kinds of services, financial services are "intangible legal instruments that are only determined by the contract itself,"[719] where even the sole understanding of the contractual provisions is often very difficult from a perspective of an inexperienced consumer. This is especially true considering that in many cases the effects of the contract only come to light much later (after the conclusion of such contract).

Consumer credit legislation is an especially complex and particular issue, since it involves the overlap of several trouble areas. This situation is illustrated by the vulnerability of consumers who require protection and by the peculiarity of the credit services being rendered. First of all, the peculiarity is characterized by the fact that such a service could be classified as a service of general economic interest, because of its crucial meaning for consumers in the present society; second, such a service involves very specific obligations which are often even life-long; third, such service refers to the future, thus to an unpredictable situation of the borrower, which entails a permanent risk; and finally, credit contract entails a certain amount of technical complexity, incomprehensible to a layman.

Consumer credit poses a peculiar paradox: on the one hand it helps people to obtain goods and services which they otherwise would not be able to get at a particular given moment in their lives, however on the other hand, credit can also be a cause for huge disasters which afflict consumers-borrowers and their whole families all over the world. The word 'credit' itself comes from the Latin word 'credo' 'to trust', and as such, has very positive associations. Moreover, consumers are often encouraged to, and praised for, using credit as a tool which undeniably is a driving force of the economy. However, in some societies (and here inter alia the factor of nationality is of great relevance) individuals receive the message: 'first save, then spend' and in this sense credit is often associated with indebtedness, thus from a certain point onwards, it often becomes a very short road to overindebtedness, followed by insolvency, bankruptcy, and financial or even social exclusion.

This paradox of credit (or its ambivalent, in a sense 'schizophrenic' facets) provokes discussion about the location of consumer credit law: does it belong to the sphere of economic or social law? It also brings up the question about the dimensions of consumer credit: is it

718 P. Rott in H.-W. Micklitz, N. Reich, P. Rott, "Understanding EU...

719 Ibid.

only of an economic nature or perhaps also a social one? The technicalities of credit contracts, and more broadly of credit relationships, alongside the impact of credit on the overall economy, as well as the impact of the economy on credit itself, suggests that consumer credit is very deeply ingrained in the economic sphere of activity and thus, indisputably belongs to economic law. On the other hand, there are several issues which comprise credit relationships - like the issues of: protection of a vulnerable consumer, sharing responsibility, trust, the problem of social exclusion, the question of a right to credit etc. - and which do not allow consumer credit regulations to be classified so unambiguously into the category of economic law. Therefore, any debate on consumer credit cannot be one-dimensional. Consequently, the fact that consumer credit has an economic as well as a social dimension cannot be ignored.

Before the autumn of 2008, the arguments concerning access to consumer credit were practically unanimous and tended to emphasize the need to facilitate its widespread availability. The example of the U.S. economy was repeatedly invoked as a system based to a great extent on credit. American credit for consumers was supposed to be one of the dominant factors which was supporting the economic development of that financial power. The lesson being taught by the U.S. seemed to be very simple: if the European Community in line with the Lisbon Strategy wanted to reach American standards, it would have to make credit more accessible to its consumers, since that would result in an increased competitiveness of its internal market. The encouragement and, in fact, the glorification of credit expansion turned out to be a very damaging trap not only for the American society.

At present however, the whole concept of a credit driven market economy has been called into question. At the same time it is inconceivable in contemporary society to reject entirely, or even to a large degree, the existence or relevance of consumer credit, since depriving consumers of credit would in many cases automatically lead to their social exclusion. This would undoubtedly provoke dramatic consequences not only for those directly afflicted, but would also cause negative repercussions for society as a whole.

Furthermore, one should not ignore the fact that credit as such is a powerful economic tool which fosters economic development. Generally, in the economy of a respective state, or of a respective unit, everything is associated, interfaced, and strongly correlated. Credit accessibility causes an increase in demand. Consequently, the market reacts to the increased demand with a bigger supply, which in turn automatically causes higher employment rates, technological progress and as an ultimate result, the development of the economy. The question then arises as to how legislators should deal with that sore point, i.e. should consumer credit be more accessible, or on the contrary should the legislator make it more difficult for consumers to obtain such credit? What would be an appropriate compromise? All in all, how accessible should consumer credit be?

We could certainly limit ourselves to considering only a concept of 'healthy credit', i.e. credit accessible only for absolutely solvent borrowers, in an adequate amount. Such credit would be secure and therefore would eventually lead to decreasing credit costs, as creditors, to simplify, would not have to add the risk of potentially unpaid debts to the interest rates (or at any rate, they would have to add significantly less). Certainly such a concept of credit would influence the condition of the economy in a very positive way. At the same time, however, this would mean the exclusion of a certain fraction of society, and at the end of the day – as what usually occurs when the society is seriously stratified – those who are better-off would also have to pay the price.

This leads us to the thesis according to which - from a purely economical perspective, thus putting moral aspects aside - it pays off for society to protect and support the poor, i.e. it pays not to exclude them from the possibility of being granted credit; on the contrary, they should be given a chance to fully participate in this sphere of activity. One of the main issues which arises in the process of scrutinizing European consumer credit legislation boils down to the question of what the European society can afford, taking into consideration the various costs that all the solutions obviously would cause. In other words, one should find an answer to the problem of profitability in the very general meaning of the notion, i.e. which steps taken by the legislator will pay off in the long-term from a perspective of the whole society? Next to the question of profitability, is the problem of the scope and deepness of public (i.e. legal: state's or Community's) intervention in private relationships (based on the principle of private autonomy). As has been pointed out above, every intervention into the market coming from public authorities requires a proper justification, since every intervention causes costs to be borne by the whole society. The justification for public intervention in the market should be the common good. Nevertheless, next to the costs of intervention, one should not forget about the costs of a lack of intervention.

Certainly, considering only the economic dimension, problems which stem from consumer credit relationships should be solved by the economy itself. The neoliberal approach requires an almost complete rejection of public intervention and opts for market mechanism solutions trusting its invisible hand, with consumers adjusting to the needs of the market. When it comes to consumer credit policies, however, limitation to pure economic considerations alongside a pure neoliberal approach can work efficiently only in the short-term: mainstream providers deal exclusively with solvent, fully creditworthy consumers, and since the consumer credit market is wide open, there is also room for predatory lenders who serve the poor, charging them extortionate interests over and above the need to cover the potential, unavoidable losses. In this line of argument, credit propels the economy, and the affluence of the majority of the market participants gradually increases. Such a (simplistically presented) 'jigsaw' tends to ignore the side effects of the system, i.e. a certain fraction of the society becomes insolvent, and finally a certain group of consumers is excluded from the market. While from the perspective of the market itself the equilibrium is not disturbed, society as a whole experiences a severe financial burden due to a significant impoverishment of some of its members. After all, modern societies have reached a consensus to guarantee a minimum subsistence for all its members.

Actually, it is this very pragmatic reason (all moral considerations cast aside) which speaks in favour of taking a social dimension into account. This leads us to a social market approach where the market economy responds to the needs of consumers and public authorities prevent individuals from disastrous financial failures via accurate protection and more generally, intervention in the market. Introducing responsible lending principles, constructing a right to credit, passing anti-usury law, regulating credit markets, and as a result changing the major dogmas of private law, and finally accepting redistribution and some elements of social justice, should be considered as the measures which, in the long-term prevent the whole society from incurring more significant costs, that is, the measures which, from purely economic perspective actually pay off. Thus, such measures should be considered as a preparation for future productivity and economic well-being. Otherwise, the overall economy is likely to experience problems in the long-run.

The famous slogans of the U.S. President Obama "Change" and "Yes we can", so popular in his election campaign, were echoed in the New Year Newsletter 2009 issued by iff,[720] entitled "Financial Crisis and Fresh Start." Iff reads "We can" as an appeal for moving closer together, taking responsibility for each other, learning to act collectively, and thereby making changes. According to this institute, Obama – by adopting these slogans as a leitmotiv of his presidential campaign – "has announced the end of a neo-liberal illusion that the blind egoist or the invisible hand is the best guide towards the common good" - thereby expressing the people's longing.

In the same vein, explaining in a very vivid way the complexity of one of the several items of his strategy on combating the financial crisis Obama[721] said:

> "(m)ost of the stuff that got us into trouble was perfectly legal. And that is a sign of how much we've got to change our laws (...) When you buy a toaster, if it explodes in your face there's a law that says your toasters need to be safe. But when you get a credit card, or you get a mortgage, there's no law on the books that says if that explodes in your face financially, somehow you're going to be protected."

As a remedy to the financial crisis, Obama stressed that there is the need for getting back to some common sense regulations. Not rejecting, but on the contrary, supporting innovation in the financial markets, as well as expressing acceptance for a society of success with its citizens who are able to make profits, Obama mentioned the critical role of the banks in the economy, and the desirability of credit flowing again. However, at the same time he stipulated that there must be enough regulatory common sense in place that ordinary Americans and taxpayers are not taken advantage of.

And in all likelihood, this is what the world needs today, namely a new, revised approach to the economy. For some that appeal would sound like a propaganda manifesto, but

720 Institute for financial services in Hamburg, registered association.

721 B. Obama – from a transcript of President Obama's interview on NBC's "The Tonight Show with Jay Leno," as provided by the White House. Available at: http://www.nytimes.com.

perhaps indeed in order to save the overall economy, there is a need to dust off the surface and dig into the ideas of social justice, of solidarity; perhaps there is a need to unite, since so far all the other remedies have resulted in failure. In a time of global crisis and of an unsure financial situation cooperation both, between the market actors and between the individual states should find its place, and furthermore should start playing a crucial, protagonistic role. On the European level such a platform for a constructive, positive cooperation is presented precisely by the European Union.

In a similar vein, in the summary of the Lisbon Strategy,[722] it has been stated that the European economies are interdependent, in the sense that prosperity in one member state creates prosperity in others. At the same time, sluggishness in one member state holds others back. The conclusion which flows from that observation is that the Europeans need to work together to achieve economic reform, sharing policies that work. It seems that the EU legislator took into account only the first part of the above message, as the outcome of the new consumer credit Directive is to share the success of the internal market fostered by the pan-European consumer credit. However, at the same time it ignores certain issues (like consumer insolvency or financial exclusion) and decided that the 'sluggishness' and actually the failure should be dealt with exclusively in national arenas.

Since Europeans wished to establish (or access the already existing) European Community, they should also remain consistent with following the once adopted trail and consequently, with keeping to the EU premises. Unquestionably one of the crucial ideas of the EU is the idea of a united activity. The motto of the European Union reads: 'United in diversity'. This means that "via the EU, Europeans are united in working together for peace and prosperity, and that the many different cultures, traditions and languages in Europe are a positive asset for the continent."[723] Furthermore, in the preamble of the Treaty on European Union,[724] one finds the following declaration of the signatories: "...desiring to deepen the solidarity between their peoples while respecting their history, their culture and their traditions." The Article 3 point 3. (ex Article 2 TEU)[725] provides that the European Union should establish an internal market and it should work for the sustainable development of Europe based on balanced economic growth and price stability, and a highly competitive social market economy, aiming at full employment and social progress. The same Article obliges the Community to combat social exclusion, and imposes thereon the promotion of social justice. According to the Treaty, the ideas of the EU could be realized via promotion of economic, social and territorial cohesion, and solidarity among member states.

722 European Commission, available at: http://ec.europa.eu/growthandjobs/faqs/background/index_en.htm.

723 http://www.delidn.ec.europa.eu/en/eu_guide/eu_guide_4.htm.

724 From the consolidated versions of the Treaty on European Union and the Treaty on the functioning of the European Union, as they will result from the amendments introduced by the Treaty of Lisbon. Available at: http://www.consilium.europa.eu/uedocs/cmsUpload/st06655-re01.en08.doc.

725 The Treaty on European Union.

The issue of a united Europe is reflected by the dilemmas concerning regulating consumer credit problems with a maximum or minimum harmonisation approach, or adopting the mutual recognition principle, which is tightly linked to a wider debate. Namely, it would be advisable to pose the question of the status of European consumer credit law, or going even further, into constitutional aspects – what should the relation be between the individual member states of the European Community? What should the European Union be like? Because if we agree that the strength, and at the same time the appeal of the European Community is based on diversities that can exist together, if we accept that we can learn from each other and take the best solutions from one another, i.e. – those solutions which have already proved to be effective and correct in practice, then the EU, as an organism which is still not unified and heterogenic, formed as a conforming coexisting unit of sovereign states with mutual respect for and acceptance of each other, shows us that consumer credit law should also not become a unified, harmonised regulation that has been torn apart or separated from any national roots, but on the other hand, "a law which takes advantage of continuous experimentation at the national level".[726] Such a flow of ideas is obviously not feasible and possible in a perfectly unified environment.

The issue of the choice which the Community legislator faces on the occasion of designing the EU law, namely minimum or maximum harmonisation is very complex. As has been shown in above, both of these legislative approaches have their pros and cons, and consequently they are negated also by many adversaries and backed by many supporters. The debate between the advocates of the minimum harmonisation and the advocates of the maximum one is in fact the continuation of the discussion about the legal character of the European Community, of its legal power and the role left to the member states, and finally considered from a more general perspective, such debate could possibly be viewed as the one reflecting the dispute between euro-enthusiasts and euro-sceptics.

726 G. Howells, T. Wilhelmsson, 'EC Consumer Law...

Conclusions

The main reason why I decided to focus my research on consumer credit is its fascinatingly paradoxical nature combined with the undisputedly ambiguous character of its legal regulation. It provokes a debate about a range of issues which alternate with each other and which I address in my book. Finally, consumer credit legislation is a perfect field for analysing most of the aspects of the EU consumer protection law.

Credit as such is a condition for the well-being of consumers and for the development of the overall economy. At the same time, it poses a huge risk to consumers. So it is, in a sense, a 'blessing' as it helps people to obtain goods and services which they otherwise would not be able to get at a particular moment in their lives. However, at the same time, credit can also be a cause for huge disasters which seriously afflict its beneficiaries. Consumer credit legislation is an especially complex and particular issue, since it involves the overlap of several problematic areas.

The paradox of consumer protection regulation in general is that, on the one hand, it refers to economic relationships ruled by the market and determined to a great extent by pure civil law principles with their freedom of contract and with the at least theoretically equal bargaining position of the parties. Such consumer protection law is described as a quasi-branch within the private law sector. One should however not ignore the fact that these essential civil law rules have been disregarded by introducing a vulnerable party who has a much weaker bargaining power, and whose market decisions are not necessarily always rational, and who simply seeks to satisfy personal needs.

Hence, we face here a problem of classification. On the one hand, consumer credit is an important economic activity and as such could be assigned exclusively to the sphere of economic law. Nevertheless, on the other hand, consumer credit entails a significant number of social problems, which implies that consumer credit legislation belongs also to the area of social private law. Thus, the question arises as to whether one can consider only an economic dimension of such legislation or, in addition to this, a social dimension as well.

This in turn entails certain considerations concerning the remedies to the problems caused by consumer credit, namely whether the economy itself should/is capable of solving these problems or whether certain doses of public intervention are advisable or even necessary (and if so, how big), and finally, what are the potential side effects of such interference in the market.

On the European level, the issue of the character of law which regulates consumer credit translates into the question of the legislative competences shared by the EU and member states legislators; in other words, whether the entire consumer protection legislation should stem from the EU legislative institutions or whether it should be left in part to the national ones. This, in turn, is inseparable from the choice between the minimum or maximum harmonisation approach.

My core argument was that all issues mentioned in the book converge into a common focal point. Therefore, first and foremost, I wanted to demonstrate the tension between two fundamental goals of the European Community, namely, on the one hand economic efficiency (understood as a competitive market society), that is, the realization of the idea of the internal market, and on the other hand, consumer protection (and broadly speaking a social justice society with its distributive role).

This tension cannot easily be reconciled (if at all), and my study aimed at reconstructing this tension as it is reflected within scholarly debate using the example of consumer credit. I argue that this is an almost ideal case study to exemplify these inherent contradictions. In the field of consumer credit regulation, this tension can be identified in almost all crucial facets of this policy area. Hence, the general question of my book was as follows: At the end of the day, which of these two goals of the European Union prevail?

At last, this tension translates into two opposing concepts: the neoliberal and the social market approach. Adopting one of these approaches determines the way in which one defines the meaning of the notion 'consumer' and consequently, the way one perceives the consumer-oriented intervention in the market which comes from public authorities. This applies to both, the scope and the intensity of such intervention.

The neoliberal approach maintains that the realisation of the idea of a perfectly functioning internal market is the key goal that should be achieved by the EC. Furthermore, it persuades us that by the same token the consumer welfare can be reached, in the sense that the internal market is the best tool to ensure an adequate consumer protection for a confident consumer. Thus, the neoliberal approach assumes that the public authority's intervention in the consumer credit market should be marginal, as anything above the mere minimum could upset the market mechanisms and, in the long-term could even decrease the efficiency of the market. The confident consumer and the internal market are mutually connected with each other: they are complementary elements and at the same time sine qua non conditions of the heyday of the European economy. This neoliberal approach is strongly backed by the EU legislator, which is clearly illustrated by the last decision made in the field of consumer credit, namely by the premises of the new consumer credit Directive.

On the other hand, however, there is the social market approach, which arguably is more concerned with non-economic problems and social values of the European market reality than with market efficiency as such. Thus, the social market approach focuses on the consumer protection goal of the EU, i.e. the protection in the 'old' traditional meaning of the term. This approach is in favour of state intervention in the market, as well as of a certain amount of paternalism exercised by legislators in order to prevent a consumer from failure. Such a way of thinking is represented to a large extent by the consumer advocates.

In order to conduct this analysis i.e. to prove that on the EU level the neoliberal approach prevails and by the same token that the EU legislator has chosen economic efficiency as the predominant goal, I took into consideration four aspects of consumer credit law which represent a suitable case study to illustrate my main argument, that is the choice between the minimum and maximum harmonisation approach, the issue of information duties and the right to withdrawal, the principles of responsible lending and the problem of consumer bankruptcy and financial exclusion.

On the outset, however, I discussed the question of the addressees of consumer credit legislation. The specific approach adopted by a legislator, and hence the methods of protection applied, depend on the types of addressees of a legal act. The EU legislator amending consumer law had to answer the following question: at the end of the day, who will benefit from the consumer protection credit regulations? The legislator should indicate his 'target group', since consumers are an enormously big and heterogeneous category encompassing conscious, well-informed, well-organized individuals as well as the poor financial "illiterates" and it seems to be impossible to find a common denominator between these two categories.

The tension between the internal market and consumer protection is reflected by the two different meanings of the notion 'consumer', namely: a vulnerable 'consumer-citizen' - a 'consumer-political actor' and 'consumer-shopper' – a rational 'consumer-economic actor'. The consumer-citizen requires protection in the 'old' meaning of the word, he is characterised by the wide range of specific, also nationally determined needs, and his market choices are often far from a rational behaviour. The consumer-shopper tries to maximise his profits on a par with all the commercial market players, he confidently searches for the best bargains and hence, he needs 'empowerment', the 'arms' given to him mainly in the form of disclosed information, and apart from such 'empowerment', the confident consumer needs an open, universal (i.e. 'nationally unrestricted') European market.

The social market approach assumes the existence of a vulnerable consumer-citizen. Such a consumer expects public authorities to intervene in the market; otherwise he may very likely suffer defeat. On the other hand, the neoliberal approach assumes that a consumer is a rational economic actor whose choices are led by the same premises as is in the case of commercial entities. A European consumer-shopper has an aim to reap all the possible profits from the internal market i.e. he requires an unrestricted choice while shopping around Europe, and a more favourable price. He hardly needs any public intervention in the market. The latter pattern of behaviour corresponds to the reasoning of the EU legislator mainly because there is a strong conviction that only a 'confident consumer' can possibly realise the idea of the efficient internal market. It actually seems as if only a confident consumer is of interest to the EU legislator. A confident consumer propels the growth of the economy; he propels innovations through a higher demand and through higher expectations. Furthermore, the EU legislator faces (even to a greater extent than the national ones) the problem of representation, i.e. the gap between European lawmakers and the members of the societies of their respective 27 member states - a gap which does not allow them to fully understand the widely different social realities across the EU member states and, again, between them and the very specific universe of Brussels. The EU legislator seems to ignore the major fact that fostering the internal market is good only for some consumers, that is, for a special stratum of confident, aware individuals who consider themselves to be European citizens.

However, this description does not exhaust the broad notion of 'consumers'. On the contrary, this category also encompasses (and I would even risk to state that they form the majority) individuals who are not aware of existing laws, nor are they willing to shop outside their own countries. The neoliberal approach does not respond to their needs, nor does it take into account their existence. All the recent official documents issued by the Commission, as well as the provisions of the new consumer credit Directive confirm that the EU legislator takes into consideration the European consumer-shopper, however, at the same time, he ignores or denies the existence of the consumer-citizen. While a "pure" vulnerable consumer-citizen may be an exaggeration, it is equally clear that the consumer-shopper is a fiction which flows from the abstractions of economic theory.

As has been stressed on many occasions in my work, the alternative between a minimum and maximum harmonisation approach reflects the tension between the realisation of a perfectly functioning internal market and of protecting consumers. The minimum harmonisation approach, as has been shown, safeguards protective legal provisions present in the national legal systems and, at the same time, guarantees consumers from the respective member States a certain high level of protection that they are used to having. The minimum harmonisation approach respects national diversities, national values, traditions, habits etc., even at the price of preserving some obstacles for the development of the internal market. Maximum harmonisation, on the other hand, is an apt reply to the market efficiency goal, as it provides professionals with all the required conditions to extend their activity EU-wide without bearing additional costs which would result from national differences. The maximum harmonisation approach downplays national diversities for the sake of a pan-European product, pan-European regulation and a pan-European market.

Whereas the minimum harmonisation approach means consumer protection, i.e. protection of the interests of individual consumers who have specific features and needs, reflecting national specific features, maximum harmonisation means market efficiency (as for services providers the whole European market is open, and consumer-shoppers – on a par with commercial entities - have an unlimited choice). Hence, actually everything boils down to a tension between the national pro-social consumer law, and the European pro-market consumer law. By completely harmonising all the provisions on the European level, this tension gradually disappears. National diversities can be preserved merely in the fields not regulated by the EU legislator. This is the exit clause for the domestic legislators.

At present, it is clear that the neoliberal approach prevails on the EU level. This conclusion stems, first and foremost, from the way the new consumer credit Directive is designed: that is, consumer protection has lost in the competition with the internal market idea, and with that of market efficiency. The EU legislator directed the new Act to the consumer-shopper. Consistently, the maximum harmonisation approach has been chosen, as the one which removes the national obstacles from the internal market. The opening of the consumer credit market to all the providers from all the member states is in line with the neo-liberal approach. The information disclosure duties and the right to withdrawal have been harmonised totally in order to give consumers a shield to protect themselves. 'Armed' in this way, consumers are left to themselves, and at the same time creditors can decrease their costs by introducing pan European products supported by the pan-European selling strategies.

There had been attempts in the 2002 proposal for the new directive to introduce the responsible lending principle to the new EU regulation. The attempts included in the proposal for the new directive to introduce a responsible lending principle to the new EU regulation, which potentially meant a manifestation of paternalism, but also a manifestation of some social considerations in the new act, were (almost) entirely given up. Adopting a responsible lending principle would have meant that a consumer's well-being would in a way have been sheltered i.e. his financial decisions would have been guarded by the public authority. However, according to the EU legislator, the modern European consumer-shopper does not need this additional protection and, most importantly, does not want to bear the costs of it.

Finally, my argument that the Commission adopted the neoliberal approach is corroborated by the fact that the EU lawmaker did not take into account the issues of consumer overindebtedness and financial exclusion in the new Directive. In the neoliberal approach there is no place for the regulation of these issues. The EU legislator adopted a certain fiction, according to which, consumer overindebtedness and financial exclusion lie outside the scope of the consumer credit contracts. It resembles – to sketch a vivid picture – the behaviour of a doctor who prescribes a patient a certain medicine and at the same time refuses to cure the side effects caused by applying this drug. It could be concluded that the EU legislator backs only a 'healthy', confident consumer, as only such a consumer can be successfully used as a tool in reaching market efficiency.

What should be stressed is that the mere fact that the EU legislator puts certain issues of (broadly understood) consumer credit regulations aside and by the same token entrusted national legislators with regulating these matters, is not necessarily negative. Both responsible lending as well as consumer bankruptcy are deeply ingrained in the national legal systems, and in the national economies. Any potential pan-European legislation in this area would have found it very difficult to perfectly embrace the entire spectrum, and on the other hand national legislators have all the leeway to deal with these issues in a much more tailored and apt way in that they can take into account the national specificities and reply adequately to national needs. Yet, the EU legislator did not give national lawmakers any definitive indications and he did not even oblige them to introduce domestic regulations in this sphere. Hence, given the undeniable diversity between the EU member states, consumers from individual member states can be left with no regulations in this respect. In other words, the maximally harmonised EU regulations with respect to, inter alia, concluding credit contracts etc. are valid for all the consumer credits throughout the EU, whereas when it comes to the negative consequences of such contracts, there is an easily predictable risk that in some member states the protection of the consumers in this respect will not exist.

The EU legislator adopted the neoliberal approach in the 2008 Directive on credit agreements. He consistently subordinated the major aspects of consumer credit in an instrumental way, to the execution of the overriding goal of the EU, that is, the realization of the idea of the European internal market. Thus consumer protection not only lost in the competition with the market efficiency idea, it actually became a tool for the realization of the prevailing goal. The EU legislator – by downplaying national diversities, and passing over the crucial problems like consumer insolvency or responsible lending - only took into account the economic dimension of the consumer credit issue, leaving the social one untouched.

The reasoning adopted by the Commission in respect of the tension between two major goals of the European Community, i.e. the internal market and consumer protection, would be correct and proper, if it were a commercial, profit-oriented entity, and not a public, non-profit institution. That is to say that, assuming that the context were strictly commercial and no other non-market considerations could possibly 'upset' it, then the Commission's decisions should be absolutely praised. Under the conditions concerning competition between the European economy and the rest of the world, as defined by the Lisbon Agenda 2000, the Commission has chosen the right direction which consists of empowering consumers and transforming them into strong market players.

In other words, I would not like to question the thesis that a 'confident consumer-shopper' is a positive contribution to the overall European economy. Such a consumer is certainly more active on the European market, and this automatically causes the market itself to start functioning more efficiently, in that it evolves into a more pan-European one where confident consumers expand demand, and at the same time, express higher expectations. Furthermore, such increased levels of market activity invigorate the economy which, after all, means (on average) a higher level of affluence of the European society.

This is all true and as long as we believe in the basic market mechanisms, such a statement is difficult to refute. However, as has been argued above, the purpose of a state, or of any public authority, is to mitigate these market mechanisms; the aim is to change certain paradigms of the pure market economy, and finally, to introduce a certain element of social values, of non-market considerations to this self-regulating and self-sufficient sphere of the market. And this is something that is largely missing in the recent activity of the EU legislator. It actually results from the above scrutiny of the evolution of the EU consumer credit legislation that the EU legislator is much more concerned with the progress of the European economy, thus with economic efficiency and with the realisation of the idea of an internal market, than with consumer protection.

However, economic efficiency cannot be accomplished under conditions ignoring the well-being of the majority of consumers. In other words, considering the entire issue from a purely economic perspective, ignoring the well-being of the majority of citizens may undermine the viability of the neoliberal approach in the long run. After all, modern societies have reached a consensus that those substantially worse off than the majority should receive some public assistance.

Arguably, such an approach may be counter-productive in the long-run. The general welfare of a society cannot be accomplished through a legal order that caters to the needs of some members of society while ignoring those of others. Hence, any regulatory strategy which ignores socially unacceptable side effects creates economic costs which will have to be borne by society as a whole. Following this line of reasoning, it can be argued that ex ante intervention by public authorities will always bring better results than ex post repairs intervention because preventing problems (here: overindebtedness, financial exclusion etc.) from arising is, in the long-run, economically more efficient than curing them afterwards. This is why the consumer credit law, first and foremost, should provide a comprehensive legal framework which will prevent the exclusion of the poor from the mainstream (official) credit system. After all, it is a reasonable assumption that the costs necessary for this are lower than those which otherwise need to be incurred to rescue over-indebted individuals.

This means, in a nutshell, that there is a fundamental contradiction between the dominant neoliberal approach of the EU and the dominant philosophies in the EU member states. All of them adhere, to a greater or lesser extent, to the principles of the modern welfare state, which means that citizens enjoy a minimum standard of subsistence. Basically the EU, by following the maximum harmonisation approach, externalises costs to the member states, and more precisely to the citizens. In other words, the costs for a perfectly harmonised consumer credit market, the costs of rejecting the social market approach in the new Directive, will have to be borne by national tax payers.

No matter which premises stand behind the legislation, whether these are the moral or social values or, on the contrary, purely economic, pragmatic considerations, the conclusions are paradoxically similar. At the end of the day, both kinds of reasoning lead us to the same outcome, that is: an 'unhealthy' consumer who is insolvent and excluded from the market in the long-term results in an 'unhealthy' economy and a declining affluence of all market participants.

Having said this, it should be emphasized again that EU consumer protection regulation is not exclusively guided by a philosophy of "pure" free market economy even though this strife for market efficiency has conspicuously won the upper hand. Rather, it is also inspired to a certain degree by the ideas of welfare capitalism which maintains that the market needs to be constrained (or tamed) by regulation. Exactly how much and what kind of regulation is needed however, is inevitably subject to political debate and compromise – hence the tensions in both scholarly debate, and EU law-making.

Sources

Bibliography

Alleweldt F. (Project Director) et al., Broad Economic Analysis of the Impact of the Proposed Directive (IP/A/IMCO/FWC/2005-058/LOT 4/SC1), Policy Department Economic and Scientific Policy.

Anderloni L., Bayot B., Błędowski P., Iwanicz-Drozdowska M. and Kempson E., "Financial Services Provision and Prevention of Financial Exclusion", European Commission Directorate-General for Employment, Social Affairs and Equal Opportunities Inclusion, Social Policy Aspects of Migration, Streamlining of Social Policies, March 2008.

Anderloni L., Carluccio E. & Braga M., "New Frontiers in Banking Services: Emerging Needs and Tailored Products for Untapped Markets", Berlin: Springer Verlag, 2006.

Arrow K., "Social choice and individual values", New Haven: Yale University Press, 1963.

Atiyah P.S., "Essays on Contract", Clarendon Press, Oxford, 1986.

Atiyah P.S., "The Rise and Fall of the Freedom of Contract", Oxford, 1979.

Autio T.-A., Wilska M., Kaartinen R., Lähteenmaa J., "The use of small instant loans among young adults - a gateway to a consumer insolvency?" Int. J. of Consumer Studies, 33, (2009), 407-415.

Avallone P., "Primitive forms of agrarian credit: 'Monti Frumentari' in the Kingdom of Naples", Naples, ISEM-CNR, Working Paper, 2001.

Balate, E., et Dejemeppe, P., "Conséquences de l'inexécution des contrats de crédit à la consommation." Etude AO-2600/95/000270 Commission européenne, rapport final.

Bayot B., "Social, economical and financial consequences of financial exclusion", B. Bayot, "The Role of Corporate Social Responsibility to promote financial inclusion" Working Papers in L. Anderloni et al., "Financial Services Provision and Prevention of Financial Exclusion", European Commission Directorate-General for Employment, Social Affairs and Equal Opportunities Inclusion, Social Policy Aspects of Migration, Streamlining of Social Policies, March 2008.

Bourgoignie T., "Elements pour une theorie du droit de la consommation" (Universite Catholique de Louvain, E. Story-Scientia, Centre de droit de la Consommation, No. 16, 1988) after J. Stuyck, "European Consumer Law after the Treaty of Amsterdam": Consumer Policy in or beyond the Internal Market?", CMLR 37 : 367-400, 2000.

Bourgoignie T., Trubek D., "Consumer Law, Common Market and Federalism", Berlin 1987, De Gruyter.

Braucher J., "Debtor Education in Bankruptcy: The Perspective of Interest Analysis" in J. Niemi-Kiesiläinen, I. Ramsay, W.C. Whitford (eds.), "Consumer Bankruptcy in Global Perspective", 2003, Hard Publishing, Oxford and Portland, Oregon, p. 319-342.

Brownsword Ed. R., Howells G., Wilhelmsson T., "Welfarism in Contract Law", Dartmouth Publishing Company Limited, 1994.

Burton D., "Credit and Consumer Society", Routledge, 2007.

Caplovitz D., "The poor pay more: consumer practices of low income families", New York: Free Press, 1967.

Cartwright P. in "Consumer Protection in Financial Services", P. Cartwright (Ed.), Kluwer Law International, 1999.

Cartwright P, "Banks, consumers and regulations" Hart Publishing, Oxford and Portland Oregon, 2004.

Cayne D., Trebilcock M.J., Market Considerations in the formulation of consumer protection policy. University of Toronto Journal, 23, 396-430, 1973.

Churchill W.S., "Liberalism and the Social Problem", Hodder and Stoughton, London, 1909.

Cockfield F.A., "The European Union. Creating the Single Market", Wiley Chancery Law, 1994.

Collard S., Kempson E., "Affordable Credit: The Way Forward", York: Joseph Rowntree Foundation, 2005.

Collins H., "Disclosure of Information and Welfarism" in Ed. R. Brownsword, G. Howells, T. Wilhelmsson, "Welfarism in Contract Law", Dartmouth Publishing Company Limited, 1994.

Collins H., "La giustizia contrattuale in Europa", Rivista critica del diritto private, 2003.

Cooper N., "Does Consumer Credit Threaten Family Ties?", Responsible Credit, Brussels 2006, 6th International Conference on Financial Service, conference materials.

Corr C., "Alternative commercial credit providers", Working Paper in L. Anderloni, B. et al., "Financial Services Provision and Prevention of Financial Exclusion", European Commission Directorate-General for Employment, Social Affairs and Equal Opportunities Inclusion, Social Policy Aspects of Migration, Streamlining of Social Policies, March 2008.

Cosgrove Twitchett C., "Introduction", in C. Cosgrove Twitchett (ed.), "Harmonization in the EEC, St Martins Press, New York, 1981.

Craig P., De Burca G., "EU Law. Text, Cases and Materials", Fourth Edition, Oxford University Press, 2008.

Davies G., "European Union. Internal Market Law", Cavendish Publishing Limited, London 2003.

Daswood D., "The Harmonization Process", in C. Cosgrove Twitchett (ed.), "Harmonization in the EEC, St Martins Press, New York, 1981.

Deutch S., "Are Consumer Rights, Human Rights?", 1994 Osgood Hall LJ 537 at 551-553.

Diez Guardia N., European Credit Research Institute Research Report No. 1, available at: http://www.ecri.be/media/research_report/ECR1en.pdf.

Domont-Naert, F., et Lacoste, A.-C., Etude sur le problème de l'usure dans certains états membres de l'espace économique européen, Louvain-la-Neuve 1997, Contrat n° AO-2600/96/000260.

Domont-Naert, F., et Dejemeppe, P, 'Etude sur le rôle et les activités des intermédiaires de crédit aux consommateurs', contrat n° AO-2600/95/000254, 1996.

Donnelly M., White F., "The Effects of Information Based Consumer Protection: Lessons from a Study of the Irish Online Market" in C. Twigg-Flesner, D. Parry, G. Howells, A. Nordhausen (ed.), "The Yearbook of Consumer Law 2008. Markets and the Law", Ashgate 2008.

Dougan M., "Minimum Harmonization and the Internal Market", Common Market Law Review 37, 2000 Kluwer Law International.

Drexl J., "Die wirtschaftliche Selbstbestimmung des Verbrauchers", Jus Privatum, Beiträge zum Privatrecht", Band 31, Mohr Siebeck, Tübingen, 1998.

Drexl J., Habilitationschrift, published with the title „Die wirtschaftliche Selbstbestimmung des Verbrauchers", Tuebingen, J.C.B. Mohr, 1998.

Dudek M.A., „Zagłaskać na śmierć", Gazeta Bankowa, available at: http://www.gb.pl.

Duffy K., "Social Exclusion and Human Dignity in Europe. Background report for the proposed initiative by the Council of Europe", Strasbourg: Council of Europe. (1995).

Dworkin R., "Paternalism', in R. Wasserstrom (ed.), 'Morality and the Law", Wadsworth, 1971.

Eeckhout P., "The European Internal Market and International Trade. A legal Analysis", Oxford, Clarendon Press, 1994.

Egan M.P., "Constructing a European Market. Standards, Regulation, and Governance", Oxford University Press, New York, 2001.

Eucken W., "What Kind of Economic and Social System" in "Germany's Social Market Economy: Origins and Evolution", Ed. Alan Peacock and Hans Willgerodt, Palgrave Macmillan, 1989.

Everson M., Joerges C., "Consumer Citizenship in Postnational Constellations", EU Working Papers Law No. 2006/47.

Ferreira A., Opinion of the Section for the Single Market, Production and Consumption on Household overindebtedness (own-initiative opinion), available at: http://www.toad.esc.eu.int/EESCViewDoc.aspx.

Figueira F., "The European Commission and Financial Capability: Simplifying Financial Services", ECRI Policy Brief No. 2/July 2007.

Figueira F., "The Consumer Credit Directive: Lost in the labyrinth of EU policy-making?", ECRI Commentary No. 3, 25 January 2008.

Finlay S., "Consumer Credit Fundamentals. Second Edition", Palgrave Macmillan, 2009.

Foster N., "Foster on EU Law", Oxford University Press, 2006.

Freidman M., "Capitalism and Freedom", University of Chicago Press, 1962.

Franken S.M., "The Political Economy of the EC Consumer Credit Directive" in J. Niemi, I. Ramsay, W.C. Whitford (eds.), "Consumer Credit, Debt and Bankruptcy. Comparative and International Perspectives", 2009, Hard Publishing, Oxford and Portland, Oregon.

Gelpi R.M., Julien-Labruyère F., "The History of Consumer Credit: Doctrines and Practices", Macmillan Press LTD, La Fondation Cetelem, 2000.

Gerhardt M., "Consumer Bankruptcy Regimes and Credit Default in the US and Europe", CEPS Working Documents 27 July 2009 available at: http://shop.ceps.eu/BookDetail.php?item_id=1887.

Gibbons D., The European Coalition for Responsible Credit and Debt on our Doorstep, the response to UK Government's consultation on the implementation of the Consumer Credit Directive. Available at: http://www.responsible-credit.net/index.php?id=1980&viewid=43056.

Giliker P., "Regulating Contractual Behaviour: The Duty to Disclose In English and French Law", European Review of Private Law 621-640, 2005.

Gloukoviezoff G., "The link between financial exclusion and over-indebtedness", Working Paper in L. Anderloni at al., "Financial Services Provision and Prevention of Financial Exclusion", European Commission Directorate-General for Employment, Social Affairs and Equal Opportunities Inclusion, Social Policy Aspects of Migration, Streamlining of Social Policies, March 2008.

Gomez F., "The Unfair Commercial Practices Directive: a Law and Economics perspective", European Review of Contract Law 4-34, 2006.

Goodin R. E., "Protecting the Vulnerable. A Reanalysing of Our Social Responsibilies", The University of Chicago Press, Chicago, 1985.

Goyens M. (Ed.), "EC Competition Policy and the Consumer Interest", Cabay Louvain-la-Neuve, 1985.

Gross K., "Establishing Financial Literacy Programmes for Consumer Debtors: Complex Issues on the Platter" in J. Niemi-Kiesiläinen, I. Ramsay, W.C. Whitford (eds.), "Consumer Bankruptcy in Global Perspective", Hard Publishing, Oxford and Portland, Oregon, 2003.

Grundmann S., Kerber G., Weatherill S. (eds.), "Party Autonomy and the Role of Information in the Internal Market", Walter de Gruyter, 2001.

Grundmann S., Stuyck J., "An academic green paper on European contract law", Kluwer Law International, The Hague, 2002.

Haagen P., "Imprisonment for Debt in England and Wales" (PhD, Princeton, 1986) at 108-109 in I. Ramsay, Chapter 1 "Consumer Credit Society and Consumer Bankruptcy: Reflections on Credit Cards and Bankruptcy in the Informational Economy" in J. Niemi-Kiesiläinen, I. Ramsay, W.C. Whitford (eds.), "Consumer Bankruptcy in Global Perspective", Hard Publishing, Oxford and Portland, Oregon, 2003.

Hadfield G., Howee R., Trebilcock M., "Information-Based Principles for Rethinking Consumer Protection Policy", 22 JCP 131, 1998.

Handzic M., "Does More Information Lead to Better Informing?", in A. Haringer (ed.), Proceedings of the 2001 Informing Science Conference, 19-22 June 2001, Kraków, Poland.

Hartley T., "The Foundations of European Community Law", 3rd ed., Oxford, 1994.

Hartlief T., "Freedom and Protection in Contemporary Contract Law", Journal of Consumer Policy 27: 253 – 267, 2004.

Heinemann F., Jopp M., "The Benefits of a Working European Retail Market for Financial Services", Report to European Financial Services Round Table, Institut für Europäische Politik (IEP), Berlin, 2002.

Heinrich D., „Verbraucherschutz: Vertragsrecht im Wandel", in V. Beuthien (ed.), „Festschrift für Dieter Medicus", Cologne 1999.

Hondius E., "Consumer Law and Private Law: the Case for Integration" in 'Neues Europäisches Vertragsrecht und Verbraucherschutz: Regelungskonzepte der Europaeichen Union und ihre Auswirkungen auf die nationalen Zivilrechtsordnungen', edited by W. HeuselBundesanzeiger Verlagsges, Köln, 1999.

Howarth D., "What is Social Liberalism?" in D. Brack, R. S. Grayson, D. Howarth eds, "Reinventing the State: Social Liberalism for the 21st Century", Politico's Publishing, 2007.

Howells G. (Ed.), "European Business Law", Aldershot, Dartmouth, 1996.

Howells G., "The Potential and Limits of Consumer Empowerment by Information", Journal of Law and Society, Vol. 32, Nr. 3, Sept 2005.

Howells G., "The Rise of European Consumer Law – Whither National Consumer Law?" 28 Sydney Law Review 63 (2006).

Howells G., Wilhelmsson T., "EC Consumer Law", Ashgate Dartmouth, 1997.

Howells G., Wilhelmsson T., "EC Consumer Law: Has It Come of Age", E. L. Rev. 2003, 28(3).

Huls N. et al, "Overindebtedness of Consumers in the EC Member States: Facts and Search for Solutions", European Communities, Kluwer, 1994.

Huls N., "Overindebtedness and Overlegalization: Consumer Bankruptcy as a Field for Alternative Dispute Resolution", 20 Journal of Consumer Policy 143, 1997.

Isaak R.A., "European Politics. Political Economy and Policy Making in Western Democracies", St. Martin's Press, NY, 1980.

Jackson T., "The Fresh-Start Policy in Bankruptcy Law", 98 Harvard Law Review 1393-448, 1985.

Jentzsch N., Lannoo K., "Much Ado about Little? Agreement on the Consumer Credit Directive Reached", ECRI Commentary No. 2, 23. May 2007.

Joerges Ch., Rödl F., '"Social Market Economy" as Europe's Social Model?', EUI Working Paper LAW No. 2004/08.

Kakouris C. N., "Do the Member States Posses Judicial Procedural <Autonomy>?", CMLR 6/1997.

Kempson E., "Policy Level Response to Financial Exclusion in Developing Economies: Lessons for Developing Countries", Paper for "Access to Finance: Building Inclusive Financial Systems", World Bank, Washington DC, May 30-31 2006.

Kempson E., Bayot B., "Regulation In Europe promoting financial inclusion" Working Paper in L. Anderloni et al., "Financial Services Provision and Prevention of Financial Exclusion", European Commission Directorate-General for Employment, Social Affairs and Equal Opportunities Inclusion, Social Policy Aspects of Migration, Streamlining of Social Policies, March 2008.

Kempson E., Whyley C., „Kept Out or Opted Out? Understanding and Combating Financial Exclusion", Bristol: Policy Press, 1999.

Kösters W., Paul S., Stein S., "An economic analysis of the EU Commission's proposal for a new Consumer Credit Directive. Offering consumers more protection or restricting their options?", RWI: Materialien, Heft 9, Essen, 2004.

Krämer L., "The European Union. Consumption and Consumer Law", in Thévenoz L. and Reich N. (eds.), Droit de la consummation – Konsumentenrecht – Consumer Law. Liber amicorum Bernd Stauder, Baden-Baden, 2006.

Kuneva M., the speech, available at:
http://ec.europa.eu/consumers/strategy/docs/ip_crossbordershopping.pdf.

Kuneva M., "Stakeholders' Conference on the „Review of the Consumer Acquis"", Brussels, 14 November 2007, the speech - text available at:
http://ec.europa.eu/commission_barroso/kuneva/speeches/speech_14112007-2_en.pdf.

Lannoo K., de la Mata Muňoz A., "Integration of the EU Consumer Credit Market. Proposal for a More Efficient Regulatory Model.", CEPS Working Document No. 213/November 2004, http://www.ecri.be.

Lea M.J., Welter R., Dübel A., Study on the mortgage credit in the European Economic Area. Structure of the sector and application of the rules in the directives 87/102 and 90/88. Final report on tender n° XXIV/96/U6/21.

Leyson A., Thrift N., "Geographies of financial exclusion: financial abandonment in Britain and the United States", Transactions of the Institute of British Geographers, New Series, 20, 1995.

Leitão Marques M.E., Frade C., "Searching for an Over-indebtedness Regulatory System for Portugal and the European Union" in J. Niemi-Kiesiläinen, I. Ramsay and W. C. Whitford (eds), "Consumer Bankruptcy in Global Perspective", Hard Publishing, Oxford and Portland, Oregon, 2003.

Majone G., "Regulating Europe: Problems and Perspectives" in Jahrbuch zur Staats- und Verwaltungwisselschaft 3, 1989.

Mak V., "Review of the Consumer Acquis: Towards Maximum Harmonization?", ERPL 1-2009[55-73].

Mankowski P., "Information Requirements in EC Private Law", European Review of Private Law 6-2005 [779-796].

Markesinis B., Unberath H., Johnston A., "The German Law of Contract. A Comparative Treatise", Oxford and Portland, Oregon, 2006.

Mau St., "The Moral Economy of Welfare States. Britain and Germany Compared", EUI, Florence, 2002.

McGee A., Weatherill S., "The Evolution of the Single Market – Harmonisation and Liberalisation", The Modern Law Review, Vol. 53, No. 5, "New Perspectives on European Law", Sep., 1990.

McKenzie Skene D., Walters A., "Consuming Passions: Benchmarking Consumer Bankruptcy Law Systems" in P.J. Omar (eds.), "International Insolvency Law. Themes and Perspectives.", Sussex Institute, Ashgate, 2008.

Micklitz H.-W., "The Relationship between National and European Consumer Policy – Challenges and Perspectives" in C. Twigg-Flesner, D. Parry, G. Howells, A. Nordhausen (ed.), "The Yearbook of Consumer Law 2008. Markets and the Law", Ashgate 2008.

Micklitz H.-W., „Zur Notwendigkeit eines neuen Konzepts für die Fortentwicklung des Verbraucherrechts in der EU. Verbraucher und Recht", No. 18, 2-12 (2003).

Micklitz H.-W., "The Targeted Full Harmonisation Approach: Looking Behind the Curtain" in G. Howells, R. Schulze (eds.) "Modernising and Harmonising Consumer Contract Law", sellier european law publishers, Munich, 2009.

Micklitz H.-W., Chapter: "Unfair Commercial Practices and Misleading Advertisement" in H.-W. Micklitz, N. Reich, P. Rott, "Understanding EU Consumer Law", Antwerp-Oxford-Portland, intersentia, 2009.

Micklitz H.-W., Reich N., "Cronica de una muerte anunciada. The Commission Proposal for a <Directive on consumer rights>", Common Market Law Review Vol. 46, Nr. 2, April 2009.

Micklitz H.-W., Weatherill S., "European Economic Law", Ashgate Dartmouth, 1997.

Micklitz H.-W., Weatherill S., "Consumer Policy in the European Community: Before and after Maastricht" in "European Consumer Policy after Maastricht", N. Reich and G. Woodroffe (Ed.), Kluwer Academic Publishers, 1994.

Mill J.S., "On Liberty", Library of Liberal Arts, 1956.

Mortelmans K., "Minimum Harmonization and Consumer Law", 1988 ECLJ 2.

de la Mata Muňoz A., Commentary The EU Commission amends its Proposed Consumer Credit Directive. European Voice, December 2004 – January 2005, http://www.ecri.be.

Müller-Armack A., "Soziale Marktwirtschaft" in v. Beckerath et al., Handwörterbuch der Sozialwissenschaften, Vol. 9, 1956.

Nieri L., "Access to Credit: the Difficulties of Households", in L. Anderloni, E. Carluccio & M. Braga, "New Frontiers in Banking Services: Emerging Needs and Tailored Products for Untapped Markets", Berlin: Springer Verlag, 2006.

Niemi J., "Overindebted Households and Law: Prevention and Rehabilitation in Europe" in J. Niemi, I. Ramsay, W.C. Whitford (eds.), "Consumer Credit, Debt and Bankruptcy. Comparative and International Perspectives.", Hard Publishing, Oxford and Portland, Oregon, 2009.

Niemi-Kiesiläinen J., „Consumer Bankruptcy in Comparison: Do we Cure a Market Failure or a Social Problem? (1999) 37 Osgoode Hall Law Journal 473.

Niemi-Kiesiläinen J., Henrikson A.-S., "Over-Indebted Households: Prevention and Rehabilitation In Europe", Responsible Credit, Brussels 2006, 6th International Conference on Financial Service, conference materials.

Niemi-Kiesiläinen J., "Collective or Individual? Constructions of Debtors and Creditors in Consumer Bankruptcy" in J. Niemi-Kiesiläinen, I. Ramsay, W.C. Whitford (eds.), "Consumer Bankruptcy in Global Perspective", Hard Publishing, Oxford and Portland, Oregon, 2003.

Niemi-Kiesiläinen J., Ramsay I., Whitford W.C. (eds.), "Consumer Bankruptcy in Global Perspective", Hard Publishing, Oxford and Portland, Oregon, 2003.

Norum P. S.,. "The role of time preference and credit card usage in compulsive buying behaviour", Int. J. of Consumer Studies, 32, (2008), 269-275.

Obradovic D., "Repatriation of Powers in the European Community", Common Market Law Review 34: 59–88, Kluwer Law International, 1997.

Ogus A., "Regulation: Legal Form and Economic Theory", Clarendon Press, 1994.

O'Hare C.W., "Issues in Consumer Credit Law Reform" in A.J. Duggan and L.W. Darvall (eds.), "Consumer Protection Law and Theory" (Sydney, The Law Book Company, 1980.

Van Oudenaren J., "Uniting Europe. An Introduction to the European Union", Rowman & Littlefield Publishers, Inc., Lanham, 2005.

Parish R., "Consumer Protection and the Ideology of Consumer Protectionists" in A.J. Duggan and L.W. Darvall (eds.), "Consumer Protection Law and Theory" (Sydney, The Law Book Company, 1980.

Peacock A., Willgerodt H. (Ed.), "Germany's Social Market Economy: Origins and Evolution", Palmgrave MacMillan, London, 1989.

Pelkmans J., "Consumer Interest in the EC Competition Regime. An Economic Perspective", in Goyens (Ed.), 'EC Competition Policy and the Consumer Interest', Cabay Louvain-la-Neuve, 1985.

Porras C. I. Garcia, van Boom W.H., "Information disclosure in the EU Consumer Credit Directive: Opportunities and limitations", electronic copy available at:

http://ssrn.com/abstract=1538111.

Posner E., "Contract Law in the Welfare State: a Defence of the Unconscionability Doctrine, Usury Laws, and Related Limitations on the Freedom to Contract", Journal of Legal Studies, vol. XXIV, June 1995.

Prechal S., "Directives in EC Law", Oxford University Press, New York, 2005.

Rahman F., "Capping interest rates is not the way to stop irresponsible lending to people who can't afford the loan", The Guardian, Wednesday 23 September 2009.

Ramsey I., "Framework for Regulation of the Consumer Marketplace", Journal of Consumer Policy, 353-372, 1985.

Ramsay I., "Rationales for Intervention in the Consumer Marketplace", Office of Fair Trading, London, 1984.

Ramsay I., Chapter 1 "Consumer Credit Society and Consumer Bankruptcy: Reflections on Credit Cards and Bankruptcy in the Informational Economy" in J. Niemi-Kiesilainem, I. Ramsay, W.C. Whitford (eds.), "Consumer Bankruptcy in Global Perspective", Hard Publishing, Oxford and Portland, Oregon, 2003.

Ramsay I., "Consumer Law and Policy: Text and Materials on Regulating Consumer Markets", Hart Publishing, 2007.

Ramsey I., "Models of Consumer Bankruptcy: Implications for Research and Policy", 20 Journal of Consumer Policy 269, 1997.

Reich N., "A European Contract Law, or an EU Contract Law Regulation for Consumers?", Journal of Consumer Policy, 28:383-407, 2005.

Reich N., "Competition between Legal Orders: A New Paradigm of EC Law", 29 Common Market Law Review 851, 1992.

Reich N., „Europäisches Verbraucherrecht", Baden-Baden: Nomos, 1996.

Reich N., "Protection of Consumers' Economic Interests by EC Contract Law - Some Follow-up Remarks", 28 Sydney L. Rev. 37, March, 2006.

Reich N., "Crisis or Future of European Consumer Law?" in "The Yearbook of Consumer Law 2009", D. Parry, D. Parry, A. Nordhausen, G. Howells, Ch. Twigg-Flesner (eds.), Ashgate, 2008.

Reich N., Chapter: "Economic Law, Consumer Interests and EU Integration" in H.-W. Micklitz, N. Reich, P. Rott, "Understanding EU Consumer Law", Antwerp-Oxford-Portland, Intersentia, 2009.

Reifner U., "Credit in Europe. Responsible Lending?", Responsible Credit, Brussels 2006, 6th International Conference on Financial Service, conference materials.

Reifner U., "'A call to Arms' – For Regulation of Consumer Lending" in J. Niemi, I. Ramsay, W.C. Whitford (eds.), "Consumer Credit, Debt and bankruptcy. Comparative and International Perspectives.", Hard Publishing, Oxford and Portland, Oregon, 2009.

Reifner U. (ed.), "European Coalition for Responsible Credit – Principles of Responsible Credit" in C. Twigg-Flesner, D. Parry, G. Howells, A. Nordhausen (ed.), "The Yearbook of Consumer Law 2008. Markets and the Law", Ashgate, 2008.

Reifner U., "'Thou shalt pay thy debts' Personal Bankruptcy Law and Inclusive Contract Law" in J. Niemi-Kiesilainem, I. Ramsay, W.C. Whitford (eds.), "Consumer Bankruptcy in Global Perspective, Hard Publishing, Oxford and Portland, Oregon", 2003.

Reifner U., in Round Table on Credit Directives and EU Action Regulation, Responsible Credit, Brussels 2006, 6th International Conference on Financial Service, conference materials

Reifner U., "Proposal for a Directive of the European Parliament and of the Council on the harmonisation of the laws, regulations and administrative provisions of the Member States concerning credit for consumers", Expertise and Alternatives developed for the Verbraucherzentrale Bundesverband e. V. (vzbv), the Federation of German Consumer Organisations, available at: www.ecri.be/media/documents/ Reifner-consumer_credit_directive.pdf.

Reifner U., "New Year Newsletter 2006", Institute für Finanzdienstleistungen e.V.

Reifner U., "The Lost Penny, Social Contract Law and Market Economy, p. 164 in T. Wilhelmsson, S. Hurri (eds) From Dissonance to Sense, Ashgate, 1998.

Reifner U., „Zur gesellschaftlichen Funktionen der Schuldnerberatung – Schuldnerberatung zwischen Ghettowirtschaft und Reintergration", Lecture in Mainz on 14. November 2002, Fachtagung des Ministeriums für Arbeit, Soziales, Familie und Gesundheit.

Reifner U., ECRC Newsletter 12.0, May 2008, available at: http://www.responsible-credit.net/index.php?id=1980&viewid=41182.

Reifner U., "Harmonisation of cost elements of the annual percentage rate of charge, APR", Hamburg 1998, Project n° AO-2600/97/000169.

Renuart E., & Thompson D. E. (2008). The Truth, The Whole Truth, and Nothing but the Truth: Fulfilling the Promise of Truth in Lending. Yale Journal on Regulation, 25, 181-244.

Riesenhuber K., "Party Autonomy and Information In the Sales Directive", In S. Grundmann, W. Kerber, S. Weatherill (eds), "Party Autonomy and the Role of Information in the Internal Market", Berlin, de Gruyter, 2001.

Riestra A. San José, "Consumer credit directive: a feasible attempt to harmonization?", available at: http://www.ecri.be.

Rott P., "Minimum Harmonization for the Completion of the Internal Market? The Example of Consumer Sales Law", Common Market Law Review 40: 1107-1135, 2003.

Rott P., "Consumer Guarantees in the Future Consumer Credit Directive: Mandatory Ban on Consumer Protection?", European Review of Private Law 3-2005, Kluwer Law International.

Rott P., Maximum Harmonisation and Mutual Recognition versus Consumer Protection: The Example of Linked Credit Agreements in EC Consumer Credit Law, EuLF 2006, I-61-I-68.

Rott P., Chapter 5 'Consumer Credit' in H.-W. Micklitz, N. Reich, P. Rott, "Understanding EU Consumer Law",Intersentia, 2009.

Rott P., "Mitverantwortung des Kreditgebers bei den Kreditaufnahme – Warum eigentlich nicht?", BKR, 2003.

Scharpf F., "Economic Integration, democracy and the weather state", Journal of European Public Policy 4 (1997), p. 18-36.

Scheiber H.N. (Ed.), "The State and Freedom of Contract", Stanford, California, 1998.

Schwartz A., Wilde L.L., "Intervening in Markets on the Basis of Imperfect Information: a Legal and Economic Analysis", University of Pennsylvania Law Review 1978-1979, Vol. 127: 630.

Schwartz P., "Personal Bankruptcy Law: A Behavioural Perspective" in J. Niemi-Kiesilainem, I. Ramsay, W.C. Whitford (eds.), "Consumer Bankruptcy in Global Perspective", Hard Publishing, Oxford and Portland, Oregon, 2003.

Seckelmann R., Methods of calculation, in the European Economic Area, of the annual percentage rate of charge, Final Report 31 October 1995, Contract n° AO 2600/94/00101.

Smith J., "Towards a multi-layered contract law for Europe", in S. Grundmann and J. Stuyck "An academic green paper on European contract law", The Hague, 2002.

Somma A., "Social Justice and the Market in European Contract Law", European Review of Contract Law 2/2006 pp. 181–198.

Sunstein C.R., Thaler R.H., "Libertarian Paternalism is not an Oxymoron", The University of Chicago Law Review, Vol. 70, Nr. 4, 2003.

Storskrubb E., "Civil Procedure and EU Law. A Policy Area Uncovered.", Oxford University Press, New York, 2008.

Stuyck J., "European Consumer Law after the Treaty of Amsterdam: Consumer Policy in or beyond the Internal Market?", Common Market Law Review 37 : 367-400, 2000.

Stuyck J., van Dyck T., Consumer Credit Directive, Briefing Note, requested by the European Parliament's Committee on Internal Market and Consumer Protection, IP/A/IMCO/NT/2006-16, PE 373.567.

Tabb C., "The Historical Evolution of the Bankruptcy Discharge" (1991) 65 American Bankruptcy Law Journal 325.

Terryn E., "The Right of Withdrawal, the Acquis Principles and the Draft Common Frame of Reference" in R. Schulze (Ed.), "Common Frame of Reference and Existing EC Contract Law", sellier. european law publishers, Munich, 2008.

Tesón F. R., Klick J., "Global Justice and Trade: A Surprising Omission" available at:
http://works.bepress.com/cgi/viewcontent.cgi?article=1000&context=jonathan_klick

Trebilcock M.J., "The Limits of Freedom of Contract", Harvard University Press, 1993.

Trebilcock M.J., Elliot S., "The Scope and Limits of Legal paternalism", in P. Benson (ed), "The Theory of Contract Law", Cambridge University Press, 2001.

Trumbull G., "Consumer Capitalism: Politics, Product Markets, and Firm Strategy in France and Germany", Cornell University Press, 2006.

Twigg-Flesner Ch., "Consumer Product Guarantee", Aldershot: Ashgate, 2003.

Unberath H., Johnson A., „The Double-Headed Approach of the ECJ Concerning Consumer Protection", Common Market Law Review 44 (2007): 1237.

Van Gerven W., "Of Rights, Remedies and Procedures", Common Market Law Review 37: 501-536, 2000.

VerLoren van Themaat P., "The Contributions to the Establishment of the Internal Market by the Case-Law of the Court of Justice of the European Communities" in R. Bieber, R. Dehousse, J.

Pinder, J.H.H. Weiler (eds.), "1992: One European Market?", Baden-Baden, Nomos Verlagsgesellschaft, 1988.

Verwey D., "The European Community, the European Union and the International Law of Treaties", T.M.C. Asser Press, 2005.

Waelbroeck M., "The Emergent Doctrine of Community Pre-emption – Consent and Re-delegation", in "Courts and Free Markets. Perspectives from the United States and Europe", T. Sandalow, E. Stein (eds.), Vol. II, Oxford, 1982.

Wasserstrom R. (ed.), 'Morality and the Law', Wadsworth, 1971.

Weatherill S., "EU Consumer Law and Policy", Cheltenham, UK/Northampton, MA, USA, Edward Elgar, 2005.

Weatherill S., "Cases and Materials on EU Law", Oxford University Press, New York, 2006.

Weatherill S., "Law and Integration in the European Union", Oxford, Clarendon Press, 1995.

Weatherill S., "Pre-emption, Harmonisation and the Distribution of Competence", in "The Law of the Single European Market. Unpacking the Premises.", C. Barnard, J. Scott (eds.), Hart Publishing, 2002.

Weatherill S., "European Private Law and the Constitutional Dimension" in Cafaggi (ed.), "The Institutional Framework of European Private Law", Oxford University Press, 2006.

Whitford W., "Will Europe Ever Get a Fresh Start? Debt Settlement Plans as a Substitute for Quick and Easy Bankruptcy?", Responsible Credit, Brussels 2006, 6th International Conference on Financial Service, conference materials.

Whitford W., "The Function of Disclosure Regulation in Consumer Transactions", Wisconsin Law Review, 400-470, 1973.

Whitman J. Q., "Consumerism versus Producerism: On the Global Threat/Menace of <Consumerism> and the Mission of Comparative Law." Yale Law School, Yale Law School Faculty Scholarship Series, Year 2006 Paper 6.

Wilhelmsson T., "The Abuse of "Confident Consumer" as a Justification for EC Consumer Law', Journal of Consumer Policy 27 (2004).

Wilhelmsson T., "The Philosophy of Welfarism and its Emergence in the Modern Scandinavian Contract Law" in Ed. R. Brownsword, G. Howells, T. Wilhelmsson, "Welfarism in Contract Law", Dartmouth Publishing Company Limited, 1994.

Wilhelmsson T., "The principle of legitimate expectations as a basic principle of Community private law", in Paasivirta and Rissanen (Eds.), "Principles of Justice and the Law of the European Union", Helsinki, 1995.

Wilhelmsson T. in "Critical Studies in Private Law. A Treaties on Need-Rational Principles in Modern Law", Dordrecht, Kluwer, 1992.

Wilhelmsson T., Twigg-Flesner Ch., "Pre-contractual information duties in the *acquis communitaire*", European Review of Consumer Law 4/2006.

Willis L., "Against Financial Literacy Education. Iowa Law Review", Vol. 94, 2008.

Ziegel J.S., "Comparative Consumer Insolvency Regimes – A Canadian Perspective", Oxford-Portland Oregon, 2003.

Zweigert K., Koetz H., "Introduction to Comparative Law", Clarendon Press, Oxford, 1998.

Documents

"Adoption of the Consumer Credit Directive: A First Step but Reservations remain", Brussels, 16 January 2008, available at: http://www.ebf-fbe.eu/DocShareNoFrame/Docs/3/KOJBHCNADJPFEGMDAMKFCNEI1DB3GT9CKTHN6CYDYDBN/EBF/docs/DLS/D0074C-_Press_release__final__on_CCD_vote_16_Jan-2008-00063-01-E.pdf.

BMRB, "Access to Financial Services by those on the Margins of Banking: Final Report for the Financial Inclusion Taskforce.", London: BMRB, 2006.

Business attitudes towards cross-border sales and consumer protection. Fieldwork: February 2008. Publication: August 2008. Available at: http://ec.europa.eu/consumers/strategy/docs/fl224%20_eurobar_cbs_summary.pdf.

Consumer protection in the internal market. Fieldwork February – March 2008. Publication October 2008. Available at: http://ec.europa.eu/consumers/strategy/docs/eurobar_298_summary_en.pdf.

Department of Trade and Industry, UK, document "Extending Competitive Markets: Empowered Consumers, Successful Business", 2004.

Department of Trade and Industry, UK, document "A Fair Deal For All: Extending Competitive Markets: Empowered Consumers. Successful Business" 2005.

EBIC Response on Information & Advice Mortgage Industry & Consumer Dialogue Group, 16th August 2006.

EBIC response to the Green Paper on Retail Financial Services in the Single Market, 19 July 2007.

ECRI Statistical Package (2004).

Eurobarometer 56.0, December 2001.

Eurobarometer 230: Public Opinion in Europe on Financial Services, August 2005.

Eurobarometer Survey 60.2 and 2003.5.

European Banking Federation Observations on the Modified Proposal for a Directive on Credit to Consumers, 31.08.2006.

"European Banks hopeful of Solution for Consumer Credit Directive", Brussels, 30.04.07, available at: http://www.ebf-fbe.eu/DocShareNoFrame/Docs/5/KOJBHCNADJPFEGMDAMKFCNEI5T16BDG3PDB39DBWT19D/EBF/docs/DLS/CCD3004-2007-00875-01-E.pdf.

European Commission, FSAP Evaluation - Part I: Process and implementation, available at: http://ec.europa.eu/internal_market/finances/docs/actionplan/index/070124_part1_en.pdf, 2007.

European Financial Services Round Table "Consumer Protection – Consumer Choice. Deepening EFR's Concept on Consumer Protection in Retail Financial Services", January 2006.

European Parliament, "Report on protecting the consumer: improving consumer education and awareness on credit and finance", 18 November 2008, (2007/2288(INI).

European Parliament, "MEPs adopt consumer credit directive, cross-border credit easier and simpler", available at: http://www.europarl.europa.eu/news/expert/infopress_page/063-18342-014-01-03-911-20080111IPR18242-14-01-2008-2008-true/default_en.htm.

European Parliament, "Report on protecting the consumer: improving consumer education and awareness on credit and finance", 18 November 2008, (2007/2288(INI).

Financial Inclusion Centre "The Real Cost of Christmas Assessing the impact of illegal money lending on consumers", Report, January 2009, Available at: http://inclusioncentre.org.uk/doc/The_Real_Cost_of_Christmas_FINAL_VERSION.pdf.

Financial Services Authority, "In or Out? Financial Exclusion: A Literature and Research Review" 2000, p. 7-8, available at: http://www.cabinet-office.gov.uk/seu/index/faqs.html.

Final Report of the Committee on Consumer Protection, 1962.

HM Treasury, "Promoting financial exclusion", December 2004, available at: http://www.hm-treasury.gov.uk/d/pbr04_profininc_complete_394.pdf.

Institute for financial services (iff) (Hamburg), Draft Consumer Credit Directive 2005 Critical Introduction and Selected Reading from the Modified proposal for a Directive of the European Parliament and of the Council on credit agreements for consumers amending Council Directive 93/13/EC Brussels, 7.10.2005 COM(2005) 483 final 2002/0222(COD).

INSOL International Consumer Debt Report – Report of Findings and Recommendations (May 2001), available at: www.insol.org/pdp/consdebt.pdf.

Lending to Households in Europe (1995-2008), ECRI Statistical Package 2009, ECRI, Brussels. http://www.ecri.be/new/system/files/2009StatisticalPackage_KeyFindings.pdf.

"Living on Tick: The 21st Century Debtor", Report, PricewaterhouseCoopers, (2006), available at: www.pwc.com/uk/eng/about/svcs/brs/PwC-IVAReport.pdf.

London Economics, "Consumer Detriment under Conditions of Imperfect Information – OFT Research Paper 11 (London: Office for Fair Trading, 1997).

OECD recommendation on good practices on financial education and awareness relating to credit, "Financial Literacy and Consumer Protection: Overlooked Aspects of the Crisis", June 2009. Available at: http://www.oecd.org/dataoecd/32/3/43138294.pdf.

Office of Fair Trade. "Consumer Education: a Strategy and Framework." London: OFT 2004.

President B. Obama's interview on NBC's "The Tonight Show with Jay Leno," as provided by the White House. Available at: http://www.nytimes.com.

Press Release "Banks welcome the release of the new consumer credit proposals", available at: http://www.ebf-fbe.eu/DocShareNoFrame/Docs/7/KOJBHCNADJPFEGMDAMKFCNEISHAP87QLBOQHUYBD2YBY/EBF/docs/DLS/communication20051010-2005-02210-01-E.pdf.

Resolution No. 1 on Seeking Legal Solutions to Debt Problems in a Credit Society The 26th Conference of the European Ministers of Justice (Helsinki, 7-8 April 2005).

Responsible Credit, Brussels 2006, 6th International Conference on Financial Service, conference materials.

'Round Table on Credit Directives an EU Action Plan', Responsible Credit, Brussels 2006, 6th International Conference on Financial Service, conference materials.

Schufa's Schuldenkompass 2003 and 2004, available at: http://www.schuldenkompass.de/downloads/index.php.

Synthesis report on consumer and business attitudes to cross-border sales and consumer protection in the internal market. Publication: October 2008. Available at: http://ec.europa.eu/consumers/strategy/docs/eurobar_298_synthrep_oct2008_en.pdf.

The Scottish Lib Dems Spring Conference held in Perth on 6.03.2010.

University of Pennsylvania Law School, Public Law Research Paper No. 08-10; Loyola-LA Legal Studies Paper No. 2008-13.

Cases

Case C-238/89, Pall Corp. v P. J. Dahlhausen & Co, [1990] ECR I-4827.

Case C-315/92, Verband Sozialer Wettbewerb eV v Clinique Laboratories SNC, [1994] ECR I-317.

Case C-470/93, Verein gegen Unwesen In Handel und Gewerbe Köln V v Mars GmbH, [1995] ECR I-1923.

Case C-373/90, Procureur de la République v X, [1992] ECR I-131.

Case C-210/96, Gut Springenheide and Tusky, [1998], ECR I-4657.

Case C-208/98 Berliner Kindl Brauerei AG v Andreas Siepert [2000] ECR I-1741.

Case C-264/02 Cofinoga Meringnan SA judgment [2004].

Case C-437/05 ITF & FSU v Viking at al. [2007] ECR 1-(11.12.2007).

Case C-376/98 Federal Republic of Germany v European Parliament and Council of the European Union (2000) ECR I-8419.

Case C-55/94 Gebhard v Consilio dell'Ordine degli Avvocati e Procuratori di Milano [1995] ECR I-4165.

Case 6/64, Costa v ENEL, [1964] ECR 585, 593.

Case 190/87, Oberkreisdirektor des Kreises Borken v Handelsonderneming Moormann, [1988] ECR 4689.

Case 16/83 Karl Prantl [1984] ECR 1299.

Case C-150/88 Firma Eau de Cologne & Parfümerie-Fabrik Glockengasse v Provide [1984] ECR 1299.

Case 120/78 Rewe-Zentral AG v Bundesmonopolverwaltung für Branntwein [1978] ECR 649, [1979] 3 CMLR 494.

Opinion of 11 November 1975, 1/75, [1975] ECR 1355.

Case 41/76, Suzanne Criel, née Donckerwolcke and Henri Schou v Procureur de la République au tribunal de grande instance de Lille and Director General of Customs. [1976] ECR 1921.

Case 131/73, (Grosoli) [1973] ECR 1555, Indiamex v Sociaal Fonds voor Dimanatarbeiders joined cases 37 and 38/73, [1973] ECR 1609.

Case 14/68, Walt Wilhelm and Others v Bundeskartellamt, [1969], ECR 1.

Case C-154/89, Commission v France [1991] ECR I-659.

Case C-362/88, GB-INNO-BM v Confédération du commerce luxembourgeois [1990] ECR I-667.

Case 376/98 Germany v Parliament and Council (Tobacco Advertising) [2000], ECJ 5 Oct. 2000, ECR I-8419.

Case C-229/04, Crailsheimer Volksbank eG v Klaus Conrads and Others, [2005] ECR I-09273.

Case 158/80, Rewe-Handelsgesellschaft Nord mbH v Hauptzollamt Kiel.

Case 22/84, Johnston v Chief Constable RUC.

Case 453/99 Courage Ltd v Bernard Crehan and Bernard Crehan v Courage Ltd and Others [2001] ECR I-6297 (ECJ).

Case C-253/00 Antonio Muñoz y Cia SA and Superior Fruiticola SA v Frumar Ltd and Redbridge Produce Marketing Ltd. [2002] ECR I-7289.

Case 481/99 Heininger v Bayerische Hypotheken- und Wechselbank [2001] ECR I-9945.

Case 229/04 Crailshaimer Volksbank v Conrads and others [2006] 1 Common Market Law Review 21.

Case C-78/98 Shirley Preston and Othes v Wolverhampton Healthcare NHS Trust and Others and Dorothy Fletcher and Others v Midland Bank plc. [2000].

Joined Cases C-392/04 and C-422/04 i-21 Germany GmbH, Arcor AG & Co. KG, before ISIS Multimedia Net GmbH & Co. KG v. Bundesrepublik Deutschland [2006].

Case C- 168/05 E.M. Mostanza Claro v Centro Movil Milenium SL [2006].

Case 14/83 Von Colon and Kamann v Land Nordrhein-Westfalen [1984].

German Constitutional Court Judgment of 30 June 2009

– 2 BvE 2/08, 2 BvE 5/08, 2 BvR 1010/08, 2 BvR 1022/08, 2 BvR 1259/08 and 2 BvR 182/09. Press release available at: http://www.bundesverfassungsgericht.de/en/press/bvg09-072en.html.

Judgment of the Polish Constitutional Tribunal on bio-components in gasoline and diesel (K 33/03) from April 21st, 2004. Available at: http://www.trybunal.gov.pl.

Official documents

Treaty on European Union (1992) Official Journal C 191 of 29 July 1992.

Treaty establishing the European Community (consolidated text) Official Journal C 325 of 24 December 2002.

Treaty on European Union (consolidated text) Official Journal C 325 of 24 December 2002.

Treaty establishing the European Community (Consolidated version 1992) Official Journal C 224 of 31 August 1992.

Treaty of Lisbon amending the Treaty on European Union and the Treaty establishing the European Community, signed at Lisbon, 13 December 2007 Official Journal C 306 of 17 December 2007.

Treaty of Nice Official Journal C 80 of 10 March 2001.

Treaty of Amsterdam Official Journal C 340 of 10 November 1997.

Single European Act (1986) Official Journal L 169 of 29 June 1987.

Communication from the Commission to the European Council a Citizens' Agenda Delivering Results for Europe, Brussels, 10.5.2006 com(2006) 211 final.

Communication from the Commission to the Council, the European Parliament and the European Economic and Social Committee, "EU Consumer Policy strategy 2007 – 2013, Empowering consumers, enhancing their welfare, effectively protecting them", COM (2007) 99 final.

Communication from the Commission to the European Parliament, the Council, the Economic and Social Committee and the Committee of the Regions Consumer policy strategy 2002-2006 (COM(2002) 208 final) (2002/C 137/02).

'Completing the Internal Market' White Paper from the Commission to the European Council COM (85) 310 final, June 1985.

Consumer Policy Strategy for 2002-2006, COM (02) 208, OJ 2002 C137/2.

Consumer Policy Strategy 2007-2013 COM (2007) 99 final.

Council Regulation (EC) No 1346/2000 of 29 May 2000 on insolvency proceedings.

Directive 2006/48/EC of the European Parliament and of the Council of 14 June 2006 relating to the taking up and pursuit of the business of credit institutions, OJ L 177, 30.6.2006 and OJ L 87, 28.3.2007.

Explanatory Memorandum of Amended proposal for a Directive of the European Parliament and the Council on Credit Agreements for Consumers amending Council Directive 93/13/EC COM (2005) 483 final 2002/0222 (COD).

Green Paper on the "Review of the Consumer Acquis", (COM (2006) 744 final from 8th February 2007).

Programme of the Commission for 1985.

Regulation (EC) 593/2008 on 17 June 2008 (Rome I).

O.J. C 133, 3.06.1981.

O.J. 1987 L 169/1.

O.J. 1987 L42/48.

O.J. 1990 L61/14.

O.J. C 92, 25.4.1975.

O.J. 1993 L 141/27.

O.J. 1997 L 43/25.

O.J. 1997 L 162/1.

O.J. 1998 L101/17.

O.J. 2001 L 344/13.

O.J. 2002 L 271/16.

OJ 2002 C137/2.

O.J. 2004 L 145/1.

O.J. 2005 L 148, 22.

O.J. 2007 L 319/1.

COM (90) 98.

COM (93) 378.

COM (96)209.

COM (97) 309 final version 26.6.1997.

COM (97) 465 final of 24.09.97.

COM (1998) 625 final version 28.10.1998.

COM (2001) 531 final.

COM (2002) 443 final.
COM (2005) 115 final.
COM (2005) 483 final/2.
COM (2006) 744 final.
COM(2006) 483 final.
COM(2007) 99 final.
COM (2007) 226 final.
COM (2008) 614 final.
SEC (2007) 106, 31.1.2007.

Fiona Cox / Hans-Walter Schmidt-Hannisa (eds.)

Money and Culture

Frankfurt am Main, Berlin, Bern, Bruxelles, New York, Oxford, Wien, 2007.
373 pp., num. fig.
ISBN 978-3-631-56790-6 · pb. € 64,60*

This interdisciplinary collection of twenty-five essays examines the construction of national, social and individual identities in response to money, or the lack of it, and the ways in which such identities are reflected in media as disparate as coins and films, literary texts and museums, autobiographies and architecture. It takes the reader from Roman Britain to the consumer society of twenty-first century Ireland, from the coins of the German Middle Ages to the virtual economies of postmodern America. *Money and Culture* focuses not only on economic aspects of cultures but also on specific cultural forms to deal with money, and reminds us of the symbiotic relationship between money and culture.

Contents: Money and Culture · The Cult of Money · Money in Film · Virtual Economies · Tiger Economies · Romantic Economies · Money and Post-modernism · Money and Religion · Prostitution · Gambling · Medieval Money · Money and the Gothic · Love and Money · Money and Art · Money and Literature · Museums and Commerce · Poverty and Identity

*The e-price includes German tax rate. Prices are subject to change without notice